FOREWORD

by Des Kelly

Mirror Sports Editor & Sports Columnist of the Year 1999

THERE is one boast the Carling Premiership can justifiably lay claim to without fear of contradiction: It is the most thrilling league in the world.

The best? Well, that is another matter. Some purists point to Italy and hail the technical sophistication of their matches, but not many of us can be bothered to admire the clever tactics of a goalless draw if we're sitting in the cold, clutching an increasingly expensive season ticket.

These escalating costs are the biggest cause for concern as the game heads into the new millennium, carelessly leaving grassroots fans in its wake. Families simply find it more and more difficult to justify the cost of going to top-flight football matches.

Grounds have improved from the ramshackle pits of the late 1980s and there are now more stars in the Premiership than on Broadway. But if the boom is to continue, football must ensure it takes its audience along for the ride. This is something one or two greedy chairmen would do well to remember.

The saving grace for the followers of 19 envious clubs in the season ahead is that it cannot get any better for treble-winners Manchester United. The question is, how much worse will it be? On the face of it, not much.

United's challengers for the Carling Premiership crown look ominously familiar as Arsenal and Chelsea are the only clubs with the resources to stay within striking distance of the Old Trafford empire.

Beyond the capital, only Leeds have a realistic chance of taking advantage of this trio's participation in the Champions' League.

Liverpool are in the midst of yet another huge transition under Gerard Houllier and may have to wait another painful year before they find the consistency required for a title challenge. Newcastle, Aston Villa, West Ham and Tottenham remain among the second tier of clubs seeking cup silverware and a passage into Europe, but nothing more. Maybe promoted Sunderland can gatecrash that group too.

Graham Taylor's Watford are already being written off as relegation fodder and, following the heady but brief flirtations of Barnsley and Charlton in the top flight, it is hard to see them defying that gloomy forecast. The same applies to Bradford.

English football being what it is, perhaps someone will buck the trend and surprise us all. Let us hope so. We could do with a new fairytale or two. But, right now, the Premiership script looks a little predictable.

Introduction

IT WAS A SEASON of inconsistency. Not, not from referees but from a number of managers who exposed the two-face nature of football. When a blatant penalty award is not given against them it is described as a "magnificent decision", when a penalty decision goes against them then it cost them the match or even the trophy concerned and the referee is lambasted with just about every adjective you can think of. Then there have been other occasions when the referee has been given the full-frontal attack because of a decision, when the real verbal assault should have been made on the multi-million pound player who missed the chances that would have won the game and pacified the manager. How often have you heard a manager roast a referee after his team has won?

Professional referees have to happen and not just so they can be sacked as another manager commented during last season. They also need help but not from new technology – it is the first step to a game that will then someday be played out in a virtual world. The man-in-the-middle is often more than twice the age of those around him. No matter how fit he may be tiredness will set in, maybe not physically but certainly mentally, and it can be no coincidence that most debatable decisions come in the later stages of games. A referee in each half, an assistant for each line and goal line judges would all help – it is not new and works perfectly well in virtually all other team sports you can think of.

And what of video replays? Well they come back into American Football this year, but are limited to two a team per game, but they were originally dispensed with not just because they were time consuming but also because the efficiency of the referees went down as they tended to turn even basic decisions to the replay judge. Equally, remember that sometimes even the 21 cameras Sky Sports have at a game cannot resolve a situation with total certainty, and even with then the wrong decision can be made – as the Cricket World Cup showed. And as Sky Sports' coverage of SuperLeague shows week-in and week-out, even with the aid of a Video Judge the decision is not often that clear-cut.

The introduction of Professionalism within the ranks of referees may not improve the stand immediately but it will have a long-term benefit. Regular weekly meetings can be used to review games and important decisions, helping referees to cope in future situations. The new breed of referee will have time to go out into the clubs – professional, amateur and schools – to discuss the rules and to hear the player and manager side of incidents. And perhaps as importantly, the professional route might encourage players to consider it as a career when their playing days are finished.

Wouldn't it also be a positive move if every professional player in this country was made to take and pass a referees exam and then contribute something back to their club locality by taking charge of school games. It would be a real eye-opener – then the boot would truly be on the other foot!

Congratulations are more than due to Manchester United on their 'Treble' performance. But given the over-board euphoria that surrounded their win in Barcelona you would have thought that no other English club had won the competition before. True it was the first English club triumph in the competition since the dark days of Heysel, but have we forgotten that Liverpool won the trophy *four* times, Nottingham Forest twice and Aston Villa also chipped in with one win. While United's victory in the Camp Nou was brilliant for our national game it was achieved with the general good fortune that surrounded many of the key moments in United's season. The rub of the green was something that they had in abundance. It will never be repeated again because the green will have been all rubbed out.

With three UEFA Cup places open to English teams it is ludicrous that only one went to a team on the merit of their league position. Newcastle ousted the place West Ham deserved because they lost in the FA Cup Final, while the devalued League Cup (Tottenham fans will disagree but the top clubs now and will increasingly use it as a competition for their reserve teams) pinches the other. Hopefully UEFA will adjust the rules in the first case and then convince the EU of the injustice of the other.

The Bosman Ruling was going to be the death of the game. You may recall that it was also going to herald the end of the transfer market. Yet, since its implementation some three years ago, the transfer record has been broken no less than nine times and shows no sign of stopping there.

Should Manchester United play in the FA Cup? Should they get a bye? Heavens forbid – don't make this change to the world's oldest cup competition. What! No more than one replay. Penalty kicks to decide games. No more semi-final or final replays. Penalty kicks to decide these games. The changes started years ago. Manchester United should receive a bye as should all clubs competing in the Champions' League at the very least.The problem is that the 3rd Round has been brought forward to December, so any byes would need to be to the 5th Round, which is plainly ludicrous. The tampering here has backfired.

Finally, can someone explain to me how a Manchester United player did not win at least one of the *Footballer of the Year* awards and how not one member of the Arsenal defence (who set a new Premiership record by a mile by conceding just 17 goals in the Premiership all season) was voted into the PFA Premiership Team of the Year Award?

Where's the consistency there?

The Mirror

THE FORECASTS

Harry Harris

Chief Football Writer

THE big three will take some catching, perhaps only Leeds and maybe George Graham's newly motivated Spurs might break into the elite. Manchester United, Arsenal and Chelsea will be at the top, but the only doubt is in which order. If Mark Bosnich can be as influential as Peter Schmeichel then there will be no change. Arsenal's hopes are bound to have been disrupted by the constant bickering in the Nicolas Anelka camp and will fall short again, while Chelsea's acquisition of Didier Dechamps will be influential but they still need something more in attack.

Champions: Manchester United
Runners-up: Arsenal
Third Place: Chelsea
Relegated: Southampton, Bradford City, Wimbledon
FA Cup: Leeds United
Worthington Cup: Newcastle United

John Dillon

JUST one point separated champions Manchester United from Arsenal in the thrilling title climax last season. This time around Bergkamp, Overmars, Petit, Vieira and Co will be fresh from a summer's rest rather than jaded after a long World Cup campaign, and that, coupled with any fresh impetus from new signings, will be what hands the Gunners the initiative as they attempt to usurp Fergie's Treble winners.

Champions: Arsenal
Runners-up: Manchester United
Third Place: Liverpool
Relegated: Southampton, Bradford City, Wimbledon
FA Cup: Leeds United
Worthington Cup: Chelsea

David Maddock

UNITED and Arsenal to slug it out for the Premiership and FA Cup, Chelsea to sign foreigners who come close and then bottle it. Sounds familiar? Well get used to it because financial might means the cartel at the top is unlikely to be disturbed much in the next few years. Only, perhaps, George Graham's native cunning will make any difference on last season.

Champions:	Arsenal
Runners-up:	Manchester United
Third Place:	Chelsea
Relegated:	Watford, Bradford City, Sunderland
FA Cup:	Manchester United
Worthington Cup:	Tottenham Hotspur

Mike Walters

CERTIFIABLE as it may sound, not least to the bookies, here's one for the men in white coats: Watford to stay up. And a gong for Graham Taylor in the New Year's Honours List.

Champions:	Arsenal
Runners-up:	Tottenham Hotspur
Third Place:	Manchester United
Relegated:	Southampton, Sheffield Wednesday, Middlesbrough
FA Cup:	Leeds United
Worthington Cup:	Ipswich Town

Steve Millar

YOU don't have to look any further than Manchester United for the new millennium champions. They will be on the biggest high of all time after clinching the historic treble and with David Beckham a year older and wiser, in him, they will have the player of the year.

Champions:	Manchester United
Runners-up:	Leeds United
Third Place:	Chelsea
Relegated:	Sunderland, Everton, Watford
FA Cup:	Arsenal
Worthington Cup:	Leeds United

Kevin Garside

THE millennium season could mark the end of Merseyside as a major force in the domestic game. Liverpool, who last won the title 10 years ago, look set to follow Everton into terminal decline unless Gerard Houllier can end a decade of underachievement.

Champions: Manchester United
Runners-up: Arsenal
Third Place: Chelsea
Relegated: Middlesbrough, Watford, Bradford City
FA Cup: Liverpool
Worthington Cup: Sunderland

David Moore

MONEY, money, money will continue to drive everything that happens in the Premiership. That means the usual suspects will be there at the top of the table – Manchester United, Arsenal, Chelsea plus probably Liverpool and Leeds. Old Trafford skipper Roy Keane will confirm his reputation as the country's most influential player, superb at the heart of Alex Ferguson's side as the European champions attempt to emulate last season's fabulous treble.

Champions: Manchester United
Runners-up: Arsenal
Third Place: Leeds United
Relegated: Watford, Wimbledon, Southampton
FA Cup: Liverpool
Worthington Cup: Chelsea

Tony Stenson

PETER SCHMEICHEL'S absence will have a great effect on Manchester United. They have not only lost a world-class goalkeeper, but a player with immense presence. Mark Bosnich, good as he is, cannot be expected to fill those gloves. The Great Dane's disappearing act will cost United the title.

Champions: Arsenal
Runners-up: Leeds United
Third Place: Manchester United
Relegated: Southampton, Bradford City, Watford
FA Cup: Chelsea
Worthington Cup: Leeds United

John Cross

NO ONE will come close to breaking the big three's domination of the Premiership – although there will be a major shift in power. Arsenal, with major squad re-inforcements and a desire for revenge, will knock Manchester United off the Premier League summit.

Champions: Arsenal
Runners-up: Manchester United
Third Place: Chelsea
Relegated: Watford, Southampton, Bradford City
FA Cup: Chelsea
Worthington Cup: Leeds United

Martin Howey

MANCHESTER United's dominance will continue. However, if anyone other than Arsenal is going to pose a serious threat, then expect it to be Leeds. They're poised to become one lean, mean machine.

Champions: Manchester United
Runners-up: Leeds United
Third Place: Arsenal
Relegated: Southampton, Watford, Bradford City
FA Cup: Arsenal
Worthington Cup: Sunderland

And Finally…

Bruce Smith

FA Carling Premiership Pocket Annual

MANCHESTER United – with a World Club Championship in Brazil and a Champions League trophy to defend – will find it difficult to retain the title from an Arsenal side out to prove a point and pushed by Chelsea. The Reds are not interested in the FA Cup and the League Cup will be the lowest of their other priorities. A red year but with white from London.

Champions: Arsenal
Runners-up: Chelsea
Third Place: Manchester United
Relegated: Middlesbrough, Sunderland, Bradford City
FA Cup: Leeds United
Worthington Cup: Southampton

The Carling OPTA stats are designed to assess the overall contribution of each player. Points are awarded, depending on position, for goals, saves, clean sheets, tackles, goal assists, and long and short passes. Players are penalised for giving away possession, missing tackles and conceding goals. OPTA stands for Optimum Performance Through Analysis. Apart from the 1997-98 Team of the Season, all statistics refer to the 1998-99 season.

1997-98 Team of the Season

Player	*Team*	*Pts*
Peter Schmeichel	Manchester United	617
Gary Neville	Manchester United	850
Steve Staunton	Aston Villa	1015
Tony Adams	Arsenal	1025
Frank Leboeuf	Chelsea	1099
Steve McManaman	Liverpool	1274
Jamie Redknapp	Liverpool	1108
Paul Ince	Liverpool	1075
David Ginola	Tottenham Hotspur	1315
Dennis Bergkamp	Arsenal	942
Dwight Yorke	Aston Villa	820

1998-99 Team of the Season

Mark Bosnich	Aston Villa	1038
Roland Nilsson	Coventry City	944
Nigel Winterburn	Arsenal	983
Sol Campbell	Tottenham Hotspur	1103
Frank Leboeuf	Chelsea	1102
David Beckham	Manchester United	986
Dietmar Hamann	Newcastle United	1119
Emmanuel Petit	Arsenal	1084
Gustavo Poyet	Chelsea	1103
Dennis Bergkamp	Arsenal	1079
Dwight Yorke	Manchester United	1017

Top Ten Goalkeepers

Mark Bosnich	Aston Villa	1038
Shaka Hislop	West Ham United	990
Mart Poom	Derby County	915
Nigel Martyn	Leeds United	902
Neil Sullivan	Wimbledon	896

Pavel Srnicek	Sheffield Wed	797
Mark Schwarzer	Middlesbrough	784
David Seaman	Arsenal	763
Kasey Keller	Leicester City	700
Ed de Goey	Chelsea	699

Top Ten Defenders

Sol Campbell	Tottenham Hotspur	1103
Frank Leboeuf	Chelsea	1102
Jaap Stam	Manchester United	1079
Tony Adams	Arsenal	1063
Lucas Radebe	Leeds United	1033
Nikos Dabizas	Newcastle United	1031
Paul Williams	Coventry United	1001
Nigel Winterburn	Arsenal	983
Matt Elliott	Leicester City	969
Emerson Thome	Sheffield Wed	961

Top Ten Midfielders

Dietmar Hamann	Newcastle United	1119
Emmanuel Petit	Arsenal	1084
Roy Keane	Manchester United	1035
Patrick Vieira	Arsenal	1029
Mark Kinsella	Charlton Athletic	1023
Paul Ince	Liverpool	1018
Jamie Redknapp	Liverpool	1001
Nicky Butt	Manchester United	985
Neil Lennon	Leicester City	980
Olivier Dacourt	Everton	979

Top Ten Attacking Midfielders

Gustavo Poyet	Chelsea	1103
Patrik Berger	Liverpool	1061
David Ginola	Tottenham Hotspur	994
David Beckham	Manchester United	986
Hassan Kachloul	Southampton	953
Steve McManaman	Liverpool	951
Paul Scholes	Manchester United	926
Mark Overmars	Arsenal	921
Ray Parlour	Arsenal	907
Darren Anderton	Tottenham Hotspur	906

Top Ten Strikers

Dennis Bergkamp	Arsenal	1079
Dwight Yorke	Manchester United	1017
Gianfranco Zola	Chelsea	1013
Michael Owen	Liverpool	1002
Andy Cole	Manchester United	978
Nic Anelka	Arsenal	964
Duncan Ferguson	Newcastle United	948
Robbie Fowler	Liverpool	939
Tore Andre Flo	Chelsea	910
Jimmy F Hasselbaink	Leeds United	902

Most Shots

Dion Dublin	Aston Villa	112
Jimmy F Hasselbaink	Leeds United	106
Nic Anelka	Arsenal	95

Most Shots on Target

Jimmy F Hasselbaink	Leeds United	56
Nic Anelka	Arsenal	51
Andy Cole	Manchester United	50

Most Off Target

Dion Dublin	Aston Villa	67
Jimmy F Hasselbaink	Leeds United	50
Neil Redfearn	Charlton Athletic	46

Most Passes

Jamie Redknapp	Liverpool	2,212
Neil Lennon	Leicester City	2,094
Roy Keane	Manchester United	2,072

Most Successful Passes

Roy Keane	Manchester United	1,830
Neil Lennon	Leicester City	1,786
Jamie Redknapp	Liverpool	1,733

Most Tackles

Olivier Dacourt	Everton	216
Patrick Vieira	Arsenal	209
Neil Lennon	Leicester City	193

Most Dribbles

David Ginola	Tottenham Hotspur	409
Harry Kewell	Leeds United	285
Steve McManaman	Liverpool	251

Most Crosses

Steve Guppy	Leicester City	415
David Beckham	Manchester United	414
David Ginola	Tottenham Hotspur	240
Mark Kinsella	Charlton Athletic	240

Most Offsides

Darren Huckerby	Coventry City	98
Benito Carbone	Sheffield Wed	87
Egil Ostenstad	Southampton	61

Most Saves

Neil Sullivan	Wimbledon	203
Shaka Hislop	West Ham United	194
Mark Schwarzer	Middlesbrough	147

Most Fouls

John Hartson	Wimbledon	106
Patrick Vieira	Arsenal	85
Paulo Wanchope	Derby County	84

Most Fouled Players

David Ginola	Tottenham Hotspur	96
Emile Heskey	Leicester City	89
Don Hutchison	Everton	86

Team With Most Fouls

Leeds United	590
Everton	587
Southampton	576

Team With Most Passes

Newcastle United	16,717
Manchester United	16,217
Liverpool	16,208

Team With Most Shots

Arsenal	524
Liverpool	505
Chelsea	481

Team With Most Tackles

Everton	1,395
Leicester City	1,334
Arsenal	1,333

Top Ten Goals Assists

David Beckham	Manchester United	14
Dwight Yorke	Manchester United	13
Dennis Bergkamp	Arsenal	12
Jimmy F Hasselbaink	Leeds United	12
Steve Guppy	Leicester City	11
Eyal Berkovic	West Ham United	10
David Ginola	Tottenham Hotspur	10
Harry Kewell	Leeds United	10
Darren Anderton	Tottenham Hotspur	9
Paul Scholes	Manchester United	9

Most Prolific Strikers – Minutes Between Goals

		Goals	*MPG*
Ole Solskjaer	Manchester United	12	71.08
Kevin Campbell	Everton	9	76.89
Nwankwo Kanu	Arsenal	6	90.33
John Aloisi	Coventry City	5	138.60
Andy Cole	Manchester United	17	138.71
Michael Owen	Liverpool	18	140.44
Robbie Fowler	Liverpool	14	143.57
Deon Burton	Derby County	8	153.50
Dwight Yorke	Manchester United	18	159.94
Francis Jeffers	Everton	6	161.50

Team Discipline

	Fouls	*Yellow*	*Red*	*Pts*
Everton	587	91	5	1092
Chelsea	548	85	4	1013
Blackburn	530	80	8	1010
Nottingham Forest	510	84	6	990
Southampton	576	76	3	986
Leeds United	590	77	1	985
Derby County	540	84	2	980
West Ham United	480	81	5	935
Charlton Athletic	574	63	4	929
Middlesbrough	488	81	2	913
Tottenham Hotspur	539	66	4	909
Coventry City	497	76	1	887
Arsenal	470	62	7	850
Aston Villa	485	63	2	820

Liverpool	460	65	3	815
Manchester United	481	59	3	806
Newcastle United	504	51	4	799
Wimbledon	480	59	1	785
Leicester City	494	51	1	759
Sheffield Wed	456	47	5	741

Players With Most Bookings

Mark Hughes	Southampton	14
Olivier Dacourt	Everton	13
Paul Gascoigne	Middlesbrough	12
Paul Telfer	Coventry City	11
Alf Inge Haaland	Leeds United	10
Andy Townsend	Middlesbrough	10
George Boateng	Coventry City	10
Danny Mills	Charlton Athletic	10
Matt Le Tissier	Southampton	9
Gianluca Festa	Middlesbrough	9

Players With Most Red Cards

Richard Rufus	Charlton Athletic	2
Emmanuel Petit	Arsenal	2
Nikos Dabizas	Newcastle United	2
Tim Sherwood	Tottenham Hotspur	2
Martin Keown	Arsenal	2

Average Time To Concede A Goal (Mins)

Arsenal	201
Aston Villa	74
Blackburn Rovers	66
Charlton Athletic	61
Chelsea	114
Coventry City	67
Derby County	76
Everton	73
Leeds United	101
Leicester City	74
Liverpool	70
Manchester United	92
Middlesbrough	63
Newcastle United	63
Nottingham Forest	50
Sheffield Wednesday	81
Southampton	53
Tottenham Hotspur	68
West Ham United	65
Wimbledon	54

Team Attacking

	Goals a Game	*Shots on Target*	*Goals to Shot*	*Shooting Accuracy Ratio*
Manchester United	2.11	233	16%	49%
Liverpool	1.79	229	13%	45%
Leeds United	1.63	216	14%	49%
Arsenal	1.55	247	11%	47%
Chelsea	1.50	205	11%	43%
Aston Villa	1.34	167	13%	43%
Newcastle United	1.26	190	11%	43%
Middlesbrough	1.26	178	12%	47%
Tottenham	1.24	202	10%	45%
West Ham United	1.21	167	12%	45%
Everton	1.11	168	11%	45%
Charlton Athletic	1.08	195	9%	47%
Sheffield Wed	1.08	158	11%	41%
Leicester City	1.05	175	10%	47%
Wimbledon	1.05	158	12%	46%
Derby County	1.05	156	11%	45%
Coventry City	1.03	164	10%	42%
Blackburn Rovers	1.00	171	10%	45%
Southampton	0.97	175	9%	44%
Nottingham Forest	0.92	173	9%	47%

Team Defending

	Conceded per Game	*Tackles*	*Tackle Success Rate*
Arsenal	0.45	1,333	62%
Chelsea	0.79	1,238	63%
Leeds United	0.89	1,186	62%
Manchester United	0.97	1,293	61%
Sheffield Wed	1.11	1,115	62%
Derby County	1.18	1,135	62%
Leicester City	1.21	1,334	58%
Aston Villa	1.21	1,056	59%
Everton	1.24	1,395	63%
Liverpool	1.29	1,167	61%
Tottenham Hotspur	1.32	1,190	58%
Coventry City	1.34	1,151	62%
Blackburn Rovers	1.37	1,132	60%
West Ham United	1.39	1,092	60%

Middlesbrough	1.42	1,251	59%
Newcastle United	1.42	1,155	60%
Charlton Athletic	1.47	1,106	64%
Wimbledon	1.66	1,070	64%
Southampton	1.68	1,108	61%
Nottingham Forest	1.82	1,150	57%

Strikers With Highest % Of Team Goals

Hamilton Ricard	Middlesbrough	31%
Alan Shearer	Newcastle United	31%
Jimmy F Hasselbaink	Leeds United	29%
Nic Anelka	Arsenal	29%
Julian Joachim	Aston Villa	28%
Michael Owen	Liverpool	25%
Noel Whelan	Coventry City	25%
Tony Cottee	Leicester City	25%
Dougie Freedman	Nottingham F	25%
Marcus Gayle	Wimbledon	25%
Gianfranco Zola	Chelsea	22%
Paulo Wanchope	Derby County	22%
Dwight Yorke	Manchester United	23%
Ian Wright	West Ham United	21%
Kevin Campbell	Everton	21%
Robbie Fowler	Liverpool	20%

Team Top Scorers

Arsenal	Nic Anelka	17	29 %
Aston Villa	Julian Joachim	14	28 %
Blackburn Rovers	Ashley Ward	5	13 %
Charlton Athletic	Clive Mendonca	8	19 %
Chelsea	Gianfranco Zola	13	22 %
Coventry City	Noel Whelan	10	25 %
Derby County	Paulo Wanchope	9	22 %
Everton	Kevin Campbell	9	21 %
Leeds United	Jimmy F Hasselbaink	18	29 %
Leicester City	Tony Cottee	10	25 %
Liverpool	Michael Owen	17	25 %
Manchester United	Dwight Yorke	18	23 %
Middlesbrough	Hamilton Ricard	15	31 %
Newcastle United	Alan Shearer	14	31 %

Nottingham F	Dougie Freedman	9	25 %
Sheffield Wed	Benito Carbone	8	9 %
Southampton	Egil Ostenstad	7	18 %
Tottenham Hotspur	Steffen Iversen	9	19 %
West Ham United	Ian Wright	10	21 %
Wimbledon	Marcus Gayle	10	25 %

Premiership Stats

Matches played	380
Goals scored	959
Average goals/match	2.52
Average goals/week	25.2
Most goals/week	36
Least goals/week	15
Home wins	169 (44%)
Draws	115 (30%)
Away wins	96 (25 %)
Total crowds	11,557,640
Average crowd/match	30,414

Goals Per Position

	Defence	*Midfield*	*Attack*
Arsenal	3 %	36 %	60 %
Aston Villa	9 %	26 %	63 %
Blackburn Rovers	8 %	28 %	62 %
Charlton Athletic	10 %	28 %	61 %
Chelsea	12 %	29 %	57 %
Coventry City	10 %	29 %	59 %
Derby County	12 %	26 %	60 %
Everton	12 %	29 %	58 %
Leeds United	13 %	30 %	56 %
Leicester City	13 %	30 %	56 %
Liverpool	12 %	32 %	55 %
Manchester United	11 %	30 %	57 %
Middlesbrough	12 %	29 %	58 %
Newcastle United	12 %	29 %	57 %
Nottingham F	13 %	29 %	57 %
Sheffield Wed	13 %	30 %	56 %
Southampton	13 %	30 %	56 %
Tottenham Hotspur	13 %	30 %	56 %
West Ham United	13 %	31 %	55 %
Wimbledon	12 %	32 %	54 %

Periods With Most Goals

Mins	Goals
76-90	206
61-75	175
46-60	162
31-45	160
16-30	138
0-15	118

Most Frequent Scores

	Times	%
0 - 0	49	12 %
1 - 1	42	11 %
1 - 0	39	10 %
2 - 1	37	9 %
2 - 0	29	7 %
0 - 1	29	7 %
1 - 2	23	6 %
2 - 2	20	5 %
3 - 0	17	4 %

Highest Scores

Nottingham F	1	Manchester United	8
Liverpool	7	Southampton	1
Everton	6	West Ham	0

Percentage of Goals From Penalties

	Pens Scored	%
Charlton Athletic	5	12
Newcastle United	6	12
Derby County	4	10
Liverpool	7	10
Everton	3	7
Arsenal	4	7
Blackburn Rovers	2	5
Chelsea	3	5
Coventry City	2	5

FINAL TABLES 1998-99

FA Carling Premiership

		HOME					AWAY					
	P	*W*	*D*	*L*	*F*	*A*	*W*	*D*	*L*	*F*	*A*	*Pts*
Manchester United ...	38	14	4	1	45	18	8	9	2	35	19	79
Arsenal	38	14	5	0	34	5	8	7	4	25	12	78
Chelsea	38	12	6	1	29	13	8	9	2	28	17	75
Leeds United	38	12	5	2	32	9	6	8	5	30	25	67
West Ham United ...	38	11	3	5	32	26	5	6	8	14	27	57
Aston Villa	38	10	3	6	33	28	5	7	7	18	18	55
Liverpool	38	10	5	4	44	24	5	4	10	24	25	54
Derby County	38	8	7	4	22	19	5	6	8	18	26	52
Middlesbrough	38	7	9	3	25	18	5	6	8	23	36	51
Leicester City	38	7	6	6	25	25	5	7	7	15	21	49
Tottenham Hotspur ...	38	7	7	5	28	26	4	7	8	19	24	47
Sheffield Wednesday	38	7	5	7	20	15	6	2	11	21	27	46
Newcastle United ...	38	7	6	6	26	25	4	7	8	22	29	46
Everton	38	6	8	5	22	12	5	2	12	20	35	43
Coventry City	38	8	6	5	26	21	3	3	13	13	30	42
Wimbledon	38	7	7	5	22	21	3	5	11	18	42	42
Southampton	38	9	4	6	29	26	2	4	13	8	38	41
Charlton Athletic	38	4	7	8	20	20	4	5	10	21	36	36
Blackburn Rovers ...	38	6	5	8	21	24	1	9	9	17	28	35
Nottingham Forest ...	38	3	7	9	18	31	4	2	13	17	38	30

Composite Table

Psn		*P*	*W*	*D*	*L*	*F*	*A*	*Pts*
1	Manchester United ...	38	22	13	3	80	37	79
2	Arsenal	38	22	12	4	59	17	78
3	Chelsea	38	20	15	3	57	30	75
4	Leeds United	38	18	13	7	62	34	67
5	West Ham United ...	38	16	9	13	46	53	57
6	Aston Villa...	38	15	10	13	51	46	55
7	Liverpool	38	15	9	14	68	49	54
8	Derby County	38	13	13	12	40	45	52
9	Middlesbrough	38	12	15	11	48	54	51
10	Leicester City	38	12	13	13	40	46	49

11	Tottenham Hotspur	38	11	14	13	47	50	47	
12	Sheffield Wed	38	13	7	18	41	42	46	
13	Newcastle United	38	11	13	14	48	54	46	
14	Everton	38	11	10	17	42	47	43	
15	Coventry City	38	11	9	18	39	51	42	
16	Wimbledon	38	10	12	16	40	63	42	
17	Southampton	38	11	8	19	37	64	41	
18	Charlton Athletic	38	8	12	18	41	56	36	R
19	Blackburn Rovers	38	7	14	17	38	52	35	R
20	Nottingham Forest	38	7	9	22	35	69	30	R

Nationwide League Division 1

Psn		*P*	*W*	*D*	*L*	*F*	*A*	*Pts*	
1	Sunderland	46	31	12	3	91	28	105	P
2	Bradford City	46	26	9	11	82	47	87	P
3	Ipswich Town	46	26	8	12	69	32	86	
4	Birmingham City	46	23	12	11	66	37	81	
5	Watford	46	21	14	11	65	56	77	P
6	Bolton Wanderers	46	20	16	10	78	59	76	
7	Wolverhampton W.	46	19	16	11	64	43	73	
8	Sheffield United	46	18	13	15	71	66	67	
9	Norwich City	46	15	17	14	62	61	62	
10	Huddersfield Town	46	15	16	15	62	71	61	
11	Grimsby Town	46	17	10	19	40	52	61	
12	WBA	46	16	11	19	69	76	59	
13	Barnsley	46	14	17	15	59	56	59	
14	Crystal Palace	46	14	16	16	58	71	58	
15	Tranmere	46	12	20	14	63	61	56	
16	Stockport County	46	12	17	17	49	60	53	
17	Swindon Town	46	13	11	22	59	81	50	
18	Crewe Alexandra	46	12	12	22	54	78	48	
19	Portsmouth	46	11	14	21	57	73	47	
20	QPR	46	12	11	23	52	61	47	
21	Port Vale	46	13	8	25	45	75	47	
22	Bury	46	10	17	19	35	60	47	R
23	Oxford United	46	10	14	22	48	71	44	R
24	Bristol City	46	9	15	22	57	80	42	R

ALL-TIME TABLES 1992/93-98/99

Positions Based on Points

Psn		*P*	*W*	*D*	*L*	*F*	*A*	*Pts*	*Yrs*	*H*	*L*
1	Manchester United	278	168	73	37	526	239	577	7	1	2
2	Arsenal	278	127	84	67	383	229	465	7	1	12
3	Liverpool	278	126	73	79	454	309	451	7	3	8
4	Blackburn Rovers	278	122	74	82	409	315	440	7	1	19
5	Aston Villa	278	114	73	91	353	309	415	7	2	18
6	Leeds United	278	108	85	85	368	314	409	7	4	17
7	Chelsea	278	108	84	86	382	334	408	7	3	14
8	Newcastle United	236	108	61	67	371	263	385	6	2	13
9	Tottenham Hotspur	278	94	82	102	365	378	364	7	7	15
10	Sheffield Wednesday	278	93	82	103	371	383	361	7	7	16
11	Wimbledon	278	92	82	104	338	398	358	7	6	16
12	Everton	278	85	78	115	330	373	333	7	6	17
13	Coventry City	278	79	94	105	304	373	331	7	11	17
14	Southampton	278	81	72	125	335	417	315	7	10	18
15	West Ham United	236	82	62	92	275	316	308	6	5	14
16	Nottingham Forest	198	60	59	79	229	287	239	5	3	22
17	QPR	164	59	39	66	224	232	216	4	5	19
18	Manchester City	164	45	54	65	180	222	189	4	9	18
19	Leicester City	156	43	49	64	182	221	178	4	9	21
20	Middlesbrough *	156	44	48	64	188	239	177	4	9	21
21	Norwich City	126	43	39	44	163	180	168	3	3	20
22	Derby County	114	40	33	41	137	152	153	3	8	12
23	Crystal Palace	122	30	37	55	119	181	127	3	19	20
24	Ipswich Town	126	28	38	60	121	206	122	3	16	22
25	Sheffield United	84	22	28	34	96	113	94	2	14	20
26	Oldham Athletic	84	22	23	39	105	142	89	2	19	21
27	Bolton Wanderers	76	17	18	41	80	132	69	2	18	20
28	Sunderland	38	10	10	18	35	53	40	1	18	18
29	Charlton Athletic	38	8	12	18	41	56	36	1	18	18
30	Barnsley	38	10	5	23	37	82	35	1	19	19
31	Swindon Town	42	5	15	22	47	100	30	1	22	22

Positions Based on Points Percentage

Psn		P	W	D	L	F	A	Pts	Yrs	%
1	Manchester United	278	168	73	37	526	239	577	7	69.18
2	Arsenal	278	127	84	67	383	229	465	7	55.76
3	Liverpool	278	126	73	79	454	309	451	7	54.08
4	Blackburn Rovers	278	122	74	82	409	315	440	7	52.76
5	Aston Villa	278	114	73	91	353	309	415	7	49.76
6	Leeds United	278	108	85	85	368	314	409	7	49.04
7	Chelsea	278	108	84	86	382	334	408	7	48.92
8	Newcastle United	236	108	61	67	371	263	385	6	54.38
9	Tottenham Hotspur	278	94	82	102	365	378	364	7	43.65
10	Sheffield Wednesday	278	93	82	103	371	383	361	7	43.29
11	Wimbledon	278	92	82	104	338	398	358	7	42.93
12	Everton	278	85	78	115	330	373	333	7	39.93
13	Coventry City	278	79	94	105	304	373	331	7	39.69
14	Southampton	278	81	72	125	335	417	315	7	37.77
15	West Ham United	236	82	62	92	275	316	308	6	43.50
16	Nottingham Forest	198	60	59	79	229	287	239	5	40.24
17	QPR	164	59	39	66	224	232	216	4	43.90
18	Manchester City	164	45	54	65	180	222	189	4	38.41
19	Leicester City	156	43	49	64	182	221	178	4	38.03
20	Middlesbrough *	156	44	48	64	188	239	177	4	37.82
21	Norwich City	126	43	39	44	163	180	168	3	44.44
22	Derby County	114	40	33	41	137	152	153	3	44.74
23	Crystal Palace	122	30	37	55	119	181	127	3	34.70
24	Ipswich Town	126	28	38	60	121	206	122	3	32.28
25	Sheffield United	84	22	28	34	96	113	94	2	37.30
26	Oldham Athletic	84	22	23	39	105	142	89	2	35.32
27	Bolton Wanderers	76	17	18	41	80	132	69	2	30.26
28	Sunderland	38	10	10	18	35	53	40	1	35.09
29	Charlton Athletic	38	8	12	18	41	56	36	1	31.58
30	Barnsley	38	10	5	23	37	82	35	1	30.70
31	Swindon Town	42	5	15	22	47	100	30	1	23.81

** Middlesbrough 3 points deducted 1996/97 season.*
Yrs=Number of Years (seasons) competed in Premiership.
H=Highest Premiership Position.
L=Lowest Premiership Position.
%=Points won divided by total possible points x 100

PROMOTIONS and RELEGATIONS

1998-99
Promoted: Sunderland (1st), Bradford City (2nd), Watford (5th)
Relegated: Charlton A. (18th), Blackburn R. (19th), N. Forest (20th)

1997-98
Promoted: N. Forest (1st), Middlesbrough (2nd), Charlton A. (4th)
Relegated: Bolton W. (20th), Barnsley (21st), C. Palace (22nd)

1996-97
Promoted: Bolton W. (1st), Barnsley (2nd), C .Palace (6th)
Relegated: Sunderland (20th), Middlesbrough (21st), N. Forest (22nd)

1995-96
Promoted: Sunderland (1st), Derby Co. (2nd), Leicester C. (5th)
Relegated: Manchester C. (20th), QPR (21st), Bolton W. (22nd)

1994-95*
Promoted: Middlesbrough (1st), Bolton W. (3rd)
Relegated: C.Palace (19th), Norwich C. (20th), Leicester C. (21st), Ipswich T. (22nd)

** FA Premier League reduced to 20 clubs.*

1993-94
Promoted: C. Palace (1st), N. Forest (2nd), Leicester C. (4th)
Relegated: Sheffield U. (20th), Oldham A. (21st), Swindon T. (22nd)

1992-93
Promoted: Newcastle U. (1st), West Ham U. (2nd), Swindon T. (5th)
Relegated: C. Palace (20th), Middlesbrough (21st), N. Forest (22nd)

1991-92†
Promoted: Ipswich T. (1st), Middlesbrough (2nd), Blackburn R. (6th)

† *Promoted from Division 2 to newly formed FA Premier League.*

FA PREMIER LEAGUE

	Arsenal	Aston Villa	Blackburn R.	Charlton A.	Chelsea	Coventry C.	Derby Co.	Everton	Leeds U.	Leicester C.
Arsenal	–	1-0	1-0	0-0	1-0	2-0	1-0	1-0	3-1	5-0
Aston Villa	3-2	–	1-3	3-4	0-3	1-4	1-0	3-0	1-2	1-1
Blackburn R.	1-2	2-1	–	1-0	3-4	1-2	0-0	1-2	1-0	1-0
Charlton A.	0-1	0-1	0-0	–	0-1	1-1	1-2	1-2	1-1	0-0
Chelsea	0-0	2-1	1-1	2-1	–	2-1	2-1	3-1	1-0	2-2
Coventry C.	0-1	1-2	1-1	2-1	2-1	–	1-1	3-0	2-2	1-1
Derby Co.	0-0	2-1	1-0	0-2	2-2	0-0	–	2-1	2-2	2-0
Everton	0-2	0-0	0-0	4-1	0-0	2-0	0-0	–	0-0	0-0
Leeds U.	1-0	0-0	1-0	4-1	0-0	2-0	4-1	1-0	–	0-1
Leicester C.	1-1	2-2	1-1	1-1	2-4	1-0	1-2	2-0	1-2	–
Liverpool	0-0	0-1	2-0	3-3	1-1	2-0	1-2	3-2	1-3	0-1
Manchester U.	1-1	2-1	3-2	4-1	1-1	2-0	1-0	3-1	3-2	2-2
Middlesbrough	1-6	0-0	2-1	2-0	0-0	2-0	1-1	2-2	0-0	0-0
Newcastle U.	1-1	2-1	1-1	0-0	0-1	4-1	2-1	1-3	0-3	1-0
N. Forest	0-1	2-2	2-2	0-1	1-3	1-0	2-2	0-2	1-1	1-0
Sheffield W.	1-0	0-1	3-0	3-0	0-0	1-2	0-1	0-0	0-2	0-1
Southampton	0-0	1-4	3-3	3-1	0-2	2-1	0-1	2-0	3-0	2-1
Tottenham H.	1-3	1-0	2-1	2-2	2-2	0-0	1-1	4-1	3-3	0-2
West Ham U.	0-4	0-0	2-0	0-1	1-1	2-0	5-1	2-1	1-5	3-2
Wimbledon	1-0	0-0	1-1	2-1	1-2	2-1	2-1	1-2	1-1	0-1

RESULTS 1998-99

	Liverpool	Manchester U.	Middlesbro'	Newcastle Utd	N .Forest	Sheffield W.	Southampton	Tottenham H.	West Ham U.	Wimbledon
Arsenal	0-0	3-0	1-1	3-0	2-1	3-0	1-1	0-0	1-0	5-1
Aston Villa	2-4	1-1	3-1	1-0	2-0	2-1	3-0	3-2	0-0	2-0
Blackburn R.	1-3	0-0	0-0	0-0	1-2	1-4	0-2	1-1	3-0	3-1
Charlton A.	1-0	0-1	1-1	2-2	0-0	0-1	5-0	1-4	4-2	2-0
Chelsea	2-1	0-0	2-0	1-1	2-1	1-1	1-0	2-0	0-1	3-0
Coventry C.	2-1	0-1	1-2	1-5	4-0	1-0	1-0	1-1	0-0	2-1
Derby Co.	3-2	1-1	2-1	3-4	1-0	1-0	0-0	0-1	0-2	0-0
Everton	0-0	1-4	5-0	1-0	0-1	1-2	1-0	0-1	6-0	1-1
Leeds U.	0-0	1-1	2-0	0-1	3-1	2-1	3-0	2-0	4-0	2-2
Leicester C.	1-0	2-6	0-1	2-0	3-1	0-2	2-0	2-1	0-0	1-1
Liverpool	–	2-2	3-1	4-2	5-1	2-0	7-1	3-2	2-2	3-0
Manchester U.	2-0	–	2-3	0-0	3-0	3-0	2-1	2-1	4-1	5-1
Middlesbrough	1-3	0-1	–	2-2	1-1	4-0	3-0	0-0	1-0	3-1
Newcastle U.	1-4	1-2	1-1	–	2-0	1-1	4-0	1-1	0-3	3-1
N. Forest	2-2	1-8	1-2	1-2	–	2-0	1-1	0-1	0-0	0-1
Sheffield W.	1-0	3-1	3-1	1-1	3-2	–	0-0	0-0	0-1	1-2
Southampton	1-2	0-3	3-3	2-1	1-2	1-0	–	1-1	1-0	3-1
Tottenham H.	2-1	2-2	0-3	2-0	2-0	0-3	3-0	–	1-2	0-0
West Ham U.	2-1	0-0	4-0	2-0	2-1	0-4	1-0	2-1	–	3-4
Wimbledon	1-0	1-1	2-2	1-1	1-3	2-1	0-2	3-1	0-0	–

FA PREMIER LEAGUE

	Arsenal	Aston Villa	Blackburn R.	Charlton A.	Chelsea	Coventry C.	Derby Co.	Everton	Leeds U.	Leicester C.
Arsenal	–	38,308	37,762	38,014	38,121	38,073	37,323	38,088	38,025	38,069
Aston Villa	39,217	–	37,404	37,705	39,217	38,799	38,007	32,488	37,510	39,241
Blackburn R.	30,867	27,536	–	22,568	23,113	23,779	24,007	27,219	27,620	22,544
Charlton A.	20,043	20,043	20,041	–	20,046	20,043	19,516	20,043	20,043	20,021
Chelsea	34,644	34,765	34,382	34,639	–	34,869	35,016	34,909	34,762	34,535
Coventry C.	23,040	22,654	19,701	20,259	23,042	–	16,627	19,290	23,049	19,894
Derby Co.	29,018	26,836	27,386	27,853	29,056	32,450	–	27,603	27,034	26,738
Everton	38,049	40,112	36,404	40,089	36,430	32,341	39,206	–	36,687	32,792
Leeds U.	40,142	33,446	30,652	32,487	36,292	31,802	38,971	36,344	–	32,606
Leicester C.	21,628	20,652	21,083	20,220	21,401	20,224	20,535	21,037	18,101	–
Liverpool	44,429	44,306	41,753	44,526	44,404	41,771	44,020	44,852	44,305	36,019
Manchester U.	55,171	55,189	55,198	55,147	55,159	55,193	55,174	55,182	55,172	55,052
Middlesbrough	34,630	34,643	34,413	34,529	34,406	34,293	34,121	34,563	34,162	34,631
Newcastle U.	36,708	36,766	36,623	36,719	36,711	36,352	36,750	36,775	36,783	36,718
N. Forest	26,021	25,753	22,013	22,661	26,351	22,546	24,014	25,610	23,911	25,353
Sheffield W.	27,949	25,989	20,846	26,010	21,652	28,136	24,440	26,952	28,142	33,513
Southampton	15,255	15,242	15,209	15,222	15,253	15,152	14,762	15,254	15,236	15,228
Tottenham H.	36,019	35,963	28,338	32,202	36,878	34,376	35,392	36,053	35,535	35,415
West Ham U.	26,042	26,002	25,529	26,041	26,023	25,662	25,485	25,998	25,997	25,642
Wimbledon	26,003	15,582	12,526	19,106	21,577	11,717	12,732	16,054	16,437	11,801

ATTENDANCES 1998-99

	Liverpool	Manchester U.	Middlesbro'	Newcastle Utd	N .Forest	Sheffield W.	Southampton	Tottenham H.	West Ham U.	Wimbledon
Arsenal	38,107	38,142	38,075	38,102	38,064	37,792	38,027	38,278	38,098	37,982
Aston Villa	39,241	39,241	29,559	39,241	34,492	39,217	32,203	39,241	36,813	32,959
Blackburn R. ...	29,944	30,463	27,482	27,569	24,565	24,643	22,812	29,643	25,213	21,754
Charlton A.	20,043	20,043	20,043	20,043	20,007	20,043	16,488	20,043	20,043	20,002
Chelsea	34,822	34,741	34,811	34,795	34,809	34,451	34,920	34,881	34,765	34,757
Coventry C.	23,056	22,596	19,231	22,656	17,172	16,006	21,402	23,098	20,818	21,200
Derby Co.	32,913	30,867	32,726	32,039	32,217	26,209	26,557	30,083	31,666	25,747
Everton	40,185	40,079	31,606	30,357	34,175	35,270	32,073	39,378	40,049	32,574
Leeds U.	39,451	40,255	37,473	40,202	39,645	30,012	30,637	34,521	36,320	39,816
Leicester C.	21,837	22,091	20,635	21,125	20,891	20,113	18,423	20,787	20,402	17,725
Liverpool	–	44,702	44,384	44,605	44,595	40,003	44,011	44,007	44,511	41,902
Manchester U. ...	55,181	–	55,152	55,174	55,216	55,270	55,316	55,189	55,180	55,265
Middlesbrough ...	34,626	34,665	–	34,629	34,223	34,163	33,387	34,687	34,623	33,999
Newcastle U. ...	36,740	36,500	36,552	–	36,760	36,698	36,454	36,655	36,744	36,623
N. Forest	28,374	30,025	21,468	22,852	–	20,480	23,456	25,181	28,463	21,362
Sheffield W.	27,383	39,475	24,534	21,545	19,321	–	30,078	28,204	30,236	24,116
Southampton ...	15,202	15,251	15,202	15,244	14,942	15,201	–	15,204	15,240	14,354
Tottenham H. ...	36,521	36,070	30,437	36,047	35,832	32,129	28,580	–	36,089	32,422
West Ham U. ...	26,029	26,039	25,902	25,997	25,458	25,642	23,153	26,044	–	25,311
Wimbledon	26,080	26,121	14,114	21,172	12,149	13,163	24,068	23,031	23,035	–

FA PREMIER LEAGUE RECORDS 1998-99

SCORERS

Top Scorers – All Competitions

Player	*Club*	*P*	*F*	*W*	*E*	*Tot*
Dwight YORKE	Manchester United	18	3	0	8	29
Michael OWEN	Liverpool	18	2	1	2	23
Andy COLE	Manchester United	16	2	0	5	23
J-Floyd HASSELBAINK	Leeds United	18	1	0	1	20
Nicolas ANELKA	Arsenal	17	0	0	1	18
Hamilton RICARD	Middlesbrough	15	0	3	0	18

P=Premier League, F=FA Cup, W=Worthington Cup, E=Europe

FA Carling Premiership Top Scorers

Player	*Club*	*Goals*
J-Floyd HASSELBAINK	Leeds United	18
Michael OWEN	Liverpool	18
Dwight YORKE	Manchester United	18
Nicolas ANELKA	Arsenal	17
Andy COLE	Manchester United	17
Hamilton RICARD	Middlesbrough	15
Dion DUBLIN	Coventry C./Aston Villa	14
Robbie FOWLER	Liverpool	14
Julian JOACHIM	Aston Villa	14
Alan SHEARER	Newcastle United	14
Gianfranco ZOLA	Chelsea	13
Dennis BERGKAMP	Arsenal	12
Ole Gunnar SOLSKJAER	Manchester United	12
Gustavo POYET	Chelsea	11
Tony COTTEE	Leicester City	10
Jason EUELL	Wimbledon	10
Tore Andre FLO	Chelsea	10
Marcus GAYLE	Wimbledon	10
Noel WHELAN	Coventry City	10

FA Carling Premiership Club Top Scorers

Club	*Scorers*
Arsenal	Anelka (17), Bergkamp (12)
Aston Villa	Joachim (14), Dublin (11), Merson (5)
Blackburn Rovers	Gallacher (5), Ward (5)
Charlton Athletic	Mendonca (8), Hunt (6)
Chelsea	Zola (13), Poyet (11), Flo (10)
Coventry City	Whclan (10), Huckerby (9), Aloisi (5)
Derby County	Burton (9), Wanchope (9)
Everton	Campbell (9), Jeffers (6)
Leeds United	Hasselbaink (18), Bowyer (9), Smith (7)
Leicester City	Cottee (10), Heskey (6), Izzet (5)
Liverpool	Owen (18), Fowler (14), Redknapp (8)
Manchester United	Yorke (18), Cole (17), Solskjaer (12)
Middlesbrough	Ricard (15), Deane (6), Beck (5)
Newcastle United	Shearer (14), Solano (6), Ketsbaia (5)
Nottingham Forest	Freedman (9), Van Hooijdonk (6), Rogers (4)
Sheffield Wednesday	Carbone (8), Booth (6), Rudi (6)
Southampton	Le Tissier (7), Ostenstad (7)
Tottenham Hotspur	Iversen (9), Armstrong (7), Campbell (6)
West Ham United	Wright (9), Sinclair (7), Lampard (5), Keller (5)
Wimbledon	Euell (10), Gayle (10), Ekoku (6)

FA Carling Premiership Hat-tricks

Player	*Goals*	*Match (result)*	*Date*
MENDONCA, C.	3*	CHARLTON A. v Southampton (5-0)	22-Aug
OWEN, M.	3	Newcastle U. v LIVERPOOL (1-4)	30-Aug
OWEN, M.	4	LIVERPOOL v N.Forest (5-1)	24-Oct
DUBLIN, D.	3	Southampton v ASTON VILLA (1-4)	14-Nov
FOWLER, R.	3	Aston Villa v LIVERPOOL (2-4)	21-Nov
HUCKERBY, D.	3	COVENTRY C. v N.Forest (4-0)	09-Jan
YORKE, D.	3	Leicester C. v MANCHESTER U. (2-6)	16-Jan
FOWLER, R.	3	LIVERPOOL v Southampton (7-1)	16-Jan
SOLSKJAER, OG	4	N.Forest v MANCHESTER U. (1-8)	06-Feb
ANELKA, N.	3	ARSENAL v Leicester C.	20-Feb
CAMPBELL, K.	3	EVERTON v West Ham U. (6-0)	08-May

** Includes one penalty*

ATTENDANCES

Top Attendances by Club and Number

Club	*Posn*	*Total*	*Ave*
Manchester United	1	1,048,580	55,188
Liverpool	7	823,105	43,321
Arsenal	2	722,450	38,024
Aston Villa	6	701,795	36,937
Newcastle United	13	696,631	36,665
Everton	14	687,856	36,203
Leeds United	4	681,074	35,846
Chelsea	3	660,273	34,751
Middlesbrough	9	653,393	34,389
Tottenham Hotspur	11	650,298	34,226
Derby County	8	554,998	29,210
Sheffield Wednesday	12	508,521	26,764
Blackburn Rovers	19	493,341	25,965
West Ham United	5	487,996	25,684
Nottingham Forest	20	465,894	24,521
Coventry City	15	394,791	20,778
Leicester City	10	388,910	20,469
Charlton Athletic	18	376,637	19,823
Wimbledon	16	346,468	18,235
Southampton	17	287,653	15,140
Totals		*11,636,664*	*30,622*

CLUBS BY LEAST NUMBER OF PLAYERS USED IN SEASON

		Total	*Start*	*Sub*	*Snu*	*Ps*	*Ply*
1	West Ham United	470	418	52	138	52	29
2	Leeds United	479	418	61	129	61	24
3	Sheffield Wednesday	481	418	63	127	63	31
4	Coventry City	486	418	68	122	68	28
5	Aston Villa	489	418	71	119	71	24
6	Leicester City	490	418	72	118	72	24
7	Blackburn Rovers	492	418	74	116	74	30
=	Tottenham Hotspur	492	418	74	116	74	29

9	Everton	493	418	75	115	75	34
10	Middlesbrough	494	418	76	114	76	29
11	Liverpool	497	418	79	111	79	25
12	Southampton	499	418	81	109	81	31
=	Wimbledon	499	418	81	108	81	23
14	Arsenal	502	418	84	106	84	26
15	Newcastle United	504	418	86	104	86	34
16	Nottingham Forest	506	418	88	102	88	34
17	Charlton Athletic	507	418	89	101	89	27
18	Chelsea	509	418	91	99	91	26
19	Derby County	510	418	92	98	92	30
=	Manchester United	510	418	92	98	92	23

Manchester United made the most number of changes on the pitch during the course of the season, yet they used the fewest number of players – just 23 in all, the same as Wimbledon.

BOOKINGS & DISMISSALS

Players Sent Off

Player	*Match*	*Date*	*Official*
RUFUS	Newcastle U. v CHARLTON A.	15-Aug	D.Gallagher
JONES, P.	Charlton A. v SOUTHAMPTON	22-Aug	R.Harris
PETIT †	ARSENAL v Charlton A.	28-Aug	G.Poll
DIXON †	Chelsea v ARSENAL	9-Sep	S.Lodge
DACOURT †	EVERTON v Leeds U.	12-Sep	N.Barry
DOAD	Newcastle U. v SOUTHAMPTON	12-Sep	M.Riley
LEABURN	Aston Villa v WIMBLEDON	12-Sep	D.Elleray
BUTT	Arsenal v MANCHESTER U.	20-Sep	G.Barber
PEREZ †	BLACKBURN R. v Chelsea	21-Sep	P.Jones
LE SAUX	Blackburn R. v CHELSEA	21-Sep	P.Jones
KEOWN	Sheffield W. v ARSENAL	27-Sep	P.Alcock
DAHLIN	Everton v BLACKBURN R.	27-Sep	M.Riley
DI CANIO	SHEFFIELD W. v Arsenal	27-Sep	P.Alcock
HINCHCLIFFE	Middlesbrough v SHEFFIELD W.	3-Oct	R.Harris
DABIZAS †	Arsenal v NEWCASTLE U.	4-Oct	M.Reed
GRANVILLE †	N. Forest v LEEDS U.	17-Oct	A.Wilkie
LEBOEUF †	Leeds U. v CHELSEA	24-Oct	M.Reed
CALDERWOOD †	TOTTENHAM H. v Newcastle U.	24-Oct	N.Barry
SUTTON †	BLACKBURN R. v Arsenal	25-Oct	D.Gallagher

MCATEER †	Leicester C. v LIVERPOOL	31-Oct	M.Reed
PEARCE, S.	NEWCASTLE U. v West Ham U.	31-Oct	G.Poll
MUSTOE †	Southampton v MIDDLESBRO'	7-Nov	P.Alcock
STAMP	Southampton v MIDDLESBRO'	7-Nov	P.Alcock
SHERWOOD	Manchester U. v BLACKBURN R.	14-Nov	M.Reed
COLLYMORE †	ASTON VILLA v Liverpool	21-Nov	P.Jones
STONE †	Tottenham H. v N. FOREST	21-Nov	S.Lodge
SINCLAIR †	COVENTRY C. v LEICESTER C.	28-Nov	M.Riley
WISE †	Everton v CHELSEA	5-Dec	G.Willard
DUNNE †	EVERTON v Chelsea	5-Dec	G.Willard
RUDDOCK	Leeds U. v WEST HAM U.	5-Dec	J.Winter
NEVILLE, G. †	Tottenham H. v MANCHESTER U.	12-Dec	U.Rennie
VAN HOOIJDONK	Leicester C. v N. FOREST	12-Dec	M.Riley
ARMSTRONG †	Chelsea v TOTTENHAM H.	19-Dec	G.Poll
GRIMANDI	ARSENAL v Leeds U.	20-Dec	P.Durkin
VIEIRA	Charlton A. v ARSENAL	28-Dec	U.Rennie
WANCHOPE	DERBY CO. v Middlesbrough	28-Dec	R.Harris
HAMANN †	Liverpool v NEWCASTLE U.	28-Dec	S.Lodge
STEFANOVIC †	Aston Villa v SHEFFIELD W.	28-Dec	G.Barber
SHERWOOD †	BLACKBURN R. v Leeds U.	9-Jan	R.Harris
DABIZAS †	Charlton A. v NEWCASTLE U.	17-Jan	P.Jones
CLELAND †	Aston Villa v EVERTON	18-Jan	N.Barry
WILCOX	BLACKBURN R. v Tottenham H.	30-Jan	N.Barry
SRNICEK	SHEFFIELD W. v Derby Co.	30-Jan	D.Elleray
OAKES	ASTON VILLA v Blackburn R.	6-Feb	D.Gallagher
MATTEO	LIVERPOOL v Middlesbrough	6-Feb	P.Jones
CARRAGHER	Charlton A. v LIVERPOOL	13-Feb	M.Reed
BROOMES	Chelsea v BLACKBURN R.	17-Feb	U.Rennie
VIALLI	CHELSEA v Blackburn R.	17-Feb	U.Rennie
EDINBURGH †	TOTTENHAM H. v Derby Co.	27-Feb	J.Winter
ALOISI	COVENTRY C. v Charlton A.	6-Mar	J.Winter
LOUIS-JEAN †	N. FOREST v Newcastle U.	10-Mar	J.Winter
PETIT †	Everton v ARSENAL	13-Mar	U.Rennie
JONES, K. †	Leicester C. v CHARLTON A.	13-Mar	A.Wilkie
HUTCHINSON	EVERTON v Arsenal	13-Mar	U.Rennie
PALMER †	Leeds U. v N. FOREST	3-Apr	P.Alcock
KEOWN †	ARSENAL v Blackburn R.	6-Apr	G.Poll
GILLESPIE †	Arsenal v BLACKBURN R.	6-Apr	G.Poll
HOULT	DERBY CO. v N.Forest	10-Apr	G.Barber
GOUGH †	Derby Co. v N. FOREST	10-Apr	G.Barber
LUNDEKVAM †	Aston Villa v SOUTHAMPTON	10-Apr	N.Barry

MATERAZZI †	EVERTON v Coventry C.	11-Apr	R.Harris
RUFUS	CHARLTON A. v Leeds U.	14-Apr	A.Wilkie
MONCUR †	Tottenham H. v WEST HAM U.	24-Apr	U.Rennie
TILER †	CHARLTON A. v Blackburn R.	1-May	G.Willard
TARICCO †	Liverpool v TOTTENHAM H.	1-May	S.Lodge
WRIGHT †	WEST HAM U. v Leeds U.	1-May	R.Harris
HISLOP	WEST HAM U. v Leeds U.	1-May	R.Harris
LOMAS	WEST HAM U. v Leeds U.	1-May	R.Harris
IRWIN †	Liverpool v MANCHESTER U.	5-May	D.Elleray
WATSON	ASTON VILLA v Charlton A.	8-May	M.Riley
PETTERSON	Aston Villa v CHARLTON A.	8-May	M.Riley
CHETTLE	Blackburn R. v N. FOREST	8-May	G.Poll
ATHERTON †	Charlton A. v SHEFFIELD W.	16-May	M.Reed

† indicates player sent off for two Yellow Cards, otherwise player Red-carded.

Referees by Average Number of Bookings

	Referee	*Matches*	*Yellow*	*Red*	*Ave Y*	*Ave Y+R*
1	Graham BARBER	25	115	5	4.60	5.00
2	Uriah RENNIE	23	105	7	4.57	5.17
3	Mike REED	22	97	6	4.41	4.95
4	Steve LODGE	22	95	4	4.32	4.68
5	Gary WILLARD	22	92	3	4.18	4.45
6	Graham POLL	25	104	6	4.16	4.64
7	Rob HARRIS	22	91	8	4.14	4.86
8	Neale BARRY	21	82	4	3.90	4.29
9	Steve DUNN	19	74	0	3.89	3.89
10	Alan WILKIE	19	73	3	3.84	4.16
11	Peter JONES	22	81	5	3.68	4.14
12	Mike RILEY	20	69	6	3.45	4.05
13	Jeff WINTERS	22	75	4	3.451	3.77
14	Dermot GALLAGHER	24	79	3	3.29	3.54
15	Paul ALCOCK	18	53	5	2.94	3.50
16	Paul DURKIN	19	55	1	2.89	3.00
17	Keith BURGE	18	47	0	2.61	2.61
18	David ELLERAY	17	42	3	2.47	2.82
	Totals	*380*	*1429*	*73*		

Referees – Who They Sent Off

Referee	*No.*	*Players*
HARRIS	8	Sherwood (Blackburn R.), Wanchope (Derby Co.), Hinchcliffe (Everton), P.Jones (Southampton), Materazzi (Everton), Wright (West Ham U.), Hislop (West Ham U.), Lomas (West Ham U.)
RENNIE	7	Vieira (Arsenal), Petit (Arsenal), Broomes (Blackburn), Vialli (Chelsea), G.Neville (Manchester U.), Hutchinson (Everton), Moncur (West Ham U.)
POLL	6	Petit (Arsenal), Keown (Arsenal), Gillespie (Blackburn R.), S.Pearce (Newcastle U.), Armstrong (Tottenham H.), Chettle (N.Forest)
RILEY	6	Dahlin (Blackburn R.), Sinclair (Leicester C.), Van Hooijdonk (N.Forest), Dodd (Southampton), Petterson (Charlton A.), Watson (Aston Villa)
REED	6	Sherwood (Blackburn R.), Leboeuf (Chelsea), McAteer (Liverpool), DAbizas (Newcastle U.), Carragher (Liverpool), Atherton (Sheffield W.)
ALCOCK	5	Keown (Arsenal), Mustoe (Middlesbrough), Stamp (Middlesbrough), Palmer (N.Forest), Di Canio (Sheffield W.)
BARBER	5	Hoult (Derby Co.), Butt (Manchester U.) Gough (N.Forest), Stefanovic (Sheffield W.), Calderwood (Tottenham H.)
JONES	5	Collymore (Aston Villa), Perez (Blackburn R.), Le Saux (Chelsea), Dabizas (Newcastle U.), Matteo (Liverpool)
BARRY	4	Wilcox (Blackburn R.), Dacourt (Everton), Lundekvam (Southampton), Cleland (Everton)
LODGE	4	Dixon (Arsenal), Hamann (Newcastle U.), Stone (N.Forest), Tarrico (Tottenham H.)
GALLAGHER	3	Oakes (Aston Villa), Sutton (Newcastle U.), Rufus (Charlton A.)
WILKIE	3	K.Jones (Charlton A.), Rufus (Charlton A.), Granville (Leeds U.)
WILLARD	3	Wise (Chelsea), Dunne (Everton), Tiler (Charlton A.)
WINTER	3	Aloisi (Coventry C.), Louis-Jean (N.Forest), Edinburgh (Tottenham H.), Ruddock (West Ham U.)

ELLERAY	3	Srnicek (Sheffield W.), Leaburn (Wimbledon), Irwin (Manchester U.)
DURKIN	1	Grimandi (Arsenal)

SCORES

Highest Aggregate Scorers

9	1-8	Nottingham Forest v Manchester United
8	2-6	Leicester City v Manchester United
	7-1	Liverpool v Southampton

Biggest Home Wins

7-1	Liverpool v Southampton
6-0	Everton v West Ham United

Biggest Away Wins

1-8	Nottingham Forest v Manchester United
2-6	Leicester City v Manchester United
1-6	Middlesbrough v Arsenal

Highest Score Draw

3-3	Liverpool v Charlton Athletic
	Tottenham Hotspur v Leeds United
	Southampton v Middlesbrough
	Southampton v Blackburn

FA PREMIER LEAGUE ALL-TIME RECORDS

Premiership Titles by Number

5	Manchester United	1992-93, 1993-94, 1995-96, 1996-97, 1998-99
1	Arsenal	1997-98
1	Blackburn Rovers	1994-95

Premiership Runners-up by Number

2	Manchester United	1994-95, 1997-98
2	Newcastle United	1995-96, 1996-97
1	Arsenal	1998-99
1	Aston Villa	1992-93
1	Blackburn Rovers	1993-94

Championship Records

	Season	*Champions*	*P*	*W*	*D*	*L*	*F*	*A*	*Pts*	*%*
1	1992-93	Manchester United	42	24	12	6	67	31	84	66.67
2	1993-94	Manchester United	42	27	11	4	80	38	92	73.02
3	1994-95	Blackburn Rovers	42	27	8	7	80	39	89	70.63
4	1995-96	Manchester United	38	25	7	6	73	35	82	71.93
5	1996-97	Manchester United	38	21	12	5	76	44	75	65.79
6	1997-98	Arsenal	38	23	9	6	68	33	78	68.42
7	1998-99	Manchester United	38	22	13	3	80	37	79	69.30

All-Time Biggest Home Wins

9-0	Manchester United v Ipswich Town	04/03/95
7-0	Blackburn Rovers v Nottingham Forest	18/11/95
7-0	Manchester United v Barnsley	25/10/97
7-1	Aston Villa v Wimbledon	11/02/93
7-1	Blackburn Rovers v Norwich City	02/10/92
7-1	Newcastle United v Swindon Town	12/03/94
7-1	Everton v Southampton	28/12/96
7-1	Newcastle United v Tottenham Hotspur	05/03/97
7-1	Liverpool v Southampton	16/01/99
7-2	Blackburn Rovers v Sheffield Wednesday	28/08/97

All-Time Biggest Away Wins

1-8	Nottingham Forest v Manchester United	06/02/99
1-7	Sheffield Wednesday v Nottingham Forest	01/04/95
0-6	Bolton Wanderers v Manchester United	25/02/96
1-6	Crystal Palace v Liverpool	20/08/94
1-6	Tottenham Hotspur v Chelsea	02/05/98
1-6	Middlesbrough v Arsenal	24/04/99
2-6	Wimbledon v Tottenham Hotspur	06/12/97
2-6	Leicester City v Manchester United	16/01/99

All-Time Highest Aggregate Scores

9 Goals

9-0	Manchester United v Ipswich Town	04/03/95
1-8	Nottingham Forest v Manchester United	06/02/99
7-2	Blackburn Rovers v Sheffield United	11/03/98
6-3	Southampton v Manchester United	26/10/96

All-Time Highest Score Draw

4-4	Aston Villa v Leicester City	22/02/95

All-Time Season General Records

Record	*Team*	*No*	*Season*	*P*
Most Goals Scored	Newcastle United	84	1993-94	42
	Manchester United	80	1998-99	38
Fewest Goals Scored	Crystal Palace	34	1994-95	42
	Manchester City	31	1996-97	38
Most Goals Conceded	Swindon Town	100	1993-94	42
	Barnsley	82	1997-98	38
Fewest Goals Conceded	Arsenal	28	1993-94	42
	Manchester United	28	1994-95	42
	Arsenal	17	1998-99	38
Most Points	Manchester United	92	1993-94	42
	Manchester United	82	1995-96	38
Fewest Points	Ipswich Town	27	1994-95	42
Most Wins	Manchester United	27	1993-94	42
	Blackburn Rovers	27	1994-95	42
Fewest Wins	Swindon Town	5	1993-94	42
Fewest Defeats	Manchester United	4	1993-94	42
	Manchester United	3	1998-99	38
	Chelsea	3	1998-99	38

Most Defeats	Ipswich Town	29	1994-95	42
	Bolton Wanderers	25	1995-96	38
Most Draws	Manchester City	18	1993-94	42
	Sheffield United	18	1993-94	42
	Southampton	18	1994-95	42
	Nottingham Forest	16	1996-97	38
	Coventry City	16	1997-98	38

NB: 38 or 42 refers to the number of games played in that season.

Record Attendances by Club

Club	*Att*	*Opponents*	*Date*
Arsenal	38,377	Tottenham Hotspur	29/04/95
Aston Villa	45,347	Liverpool	07/05/94
Blackburn Rovers	30,895	Liverpool	24/02/95
Bolton Wanderers	25,000	multiple occasions	1997-98
Charlton Athletic	20,046	Chelsea	03/04/99
Chelsea	37,064	Manchester United	11/09/93
Coventry City	24,410	Manchester United	12/04/94
Crystal Palace	30,115	Manchester United	21/04/93
Derby County	32,913	Liverpool	13/03/99
Everton	40,185	Liverpool	17/10/98
Ipswich Town	22,559	Manchester United	01/05/94
Leeds United	41,125	Manchester United	27/04/94
Leicester City	21,837	Liverpool	31/10/98
Liverpool	44,702	Manchester United	05/05/99
Manchester City	37,136	Manchester United	20/03/93
Manchester United	55,316	Southampton	27/02/99
Middlesbrough	34,687	Tottenham Hotspur	20/02/99
Newcastle United	36,783	Aston Villa	23/08/97
Norwich City	21,843	Liverpool	29/04/95
Nottingham Forest	30,025	Manchester United	06/02/99
Queens Park Rangers	21,267	Manchester United	05/02/94
Sheffield United	30,044	Sheffield Wednesday	23/10/93
Sheffield Wednesday	39,427	Manchester United	97-98
Southampton	19,654	Tottenham Hotspur	15/08/92
Sunderland	22,512	Derby County	26/12/96
Swindon Town	18,108	Manchester United	19/03/94
Tottenham Hotspur	36,878	Chelsea	10/05/99
West Ham United	28,832	Manchester United	25/02/94
Wimbledon	30,115	Manchester United	08/05/93

Top 10 Attendances

Psn	*Att*	*Match*	*Date*
1	55,316	Manchester United v Southampton	27/02/99
2	55,314	Manchester United v Wimbledon	29/01/97
3	55,306	Manchester United v Wimbledon	28/03/98
4	55,281	Manchester United v Tottenham Hotspur	10/01/98
5	55,270	Manchester United v Sheffield Wednesday	17/04/99
6	55,269	Manchester United v Southampton	01/02/97
7	55,267	Manchester United v Sheffield Wednesday	15/03/97
8	55,265	Manchester United v Wimbledon	17/10/98
9	55,259	Manchester United v Sheffield Wednesday	01/11/97
10	55,256	Manchester United v Leeds United	28/12/96
Biggest attendance not at Old Trafford			
	45,347	Aston Villa v Liverpool	07/05/94

Lowest Attendances by Club

Club	*Att*	*Opponents*	*Date*
Arsenal	18,253	Wimbledon	10/02/92
Aston Villa	16,180	Southampton	24/11/93
Barnsley	17,102	Wimbledon	28/02/98
Blackburn Rovers	13,505	Sheffield United	18/10/93
Bolton Wanderers	16,216	Wimbledon	13/01/96
Charlton Athletic	16,488	Southampton	22/08/98
Chelsea	8,923	Coventry City	04/05/94
Coventry City	9,526	Ipswich Town	10/10/94
Crystal Palace	10,422	Sheffield Wednesday	14/03/95
Derby County	17,022	Wimbledon	28/09/96
Everton	13,660	Southampton	04/12/93
Ipswich Town	10,747	Sheffield United	21/08/93
Leeds United	25,774	Wimbledon	15/08/92
Leicester City	15,489	Wimbledon	01/04/95
Liverpool	24,561	QPR	08/12/93
Manchester City	19,150	West Ham United	24/08/85
Manchester United	29,736	Crystal Palace	02/09/92
Middlesbrough	12,290	Oldham Athletic	22/03/93
Newcastle United	32,067	Southampton	22/01/94
Norwich City	12,452	Southampton	05/09/92
Nottingham Forest	17,525	Blackburn Rovers	25/11/96
Oldham Athletic	9,633	Wimbledon	28/08/93
Queens Park Rangers	9,875	Swindon Town	30/04/94
Sheffield United	13,646	West Ham United	28/03/94

Sheffield Wednesday	16,390	Nottingham Forest	18/11/96
Southampton	9,028	Ipswich Town	08/12/93
Sunderland	18,642	West Ham United	08/09/96
Swindon Town	11,970	Oldham Athletic	18/08/93
Tottenham Hotspur	17,452	Aston Villa	02/03/94
West Ham United	15,777	Swindon Town	11/09/93
Wimbledon	3,039	Everton	26/01/93

Lowest 10 Attendances

Psn	*Att*	*Match*	*Date*
1	3,039	Wimbledon v Everton	26/01/93
2	3,386	Wimbledon v Oldham Athletic	12/12/92
3	3,759	Wimbledon v Coventry City	22/08/92
4	3,979	Wimbledon v Sheffield United	20/02/93
5	4,534	Wimbledon v Southampton	06/03/93
6	4,714	Wimbledon v Manchester City	01/09/92
7	4,739	Wimbledon v Coventry City	26/12/93
8	4,954	Wimbledon v Ipswich Town	18/08/92
9	5,268	Wimbledon v Manchester City	21/03/95
10	5,536	Wimbledon v Sheffield Wednesday	15/01/94

THE GOALSCORERS

Top Goalscorers by Player/Total

This lists players by Total number of goals scored in the Premiership. The club listed is the club he last made an appearance for in the Premiership. S/R=Strike rate – number of games per goal, ie Alan Shearer has a S/R of 1.41 – he scores a goal every 1.41 games on average.

Player	*Club*	*Goals*	*Tot*	*S/R*	*St*	*Sub*
SHEARER Alan	Newcastle U.	153	216	1.41	207	9
WRIGHT Ian	West Ham U.	113	213	1.88	202	11
FERDINAND Les	Tottenham H.	111	223	2.01	217	6
FOWLER Robbie	Liverpool	106	185	1.75	179	6
COLE Andy	Manchester U.	105	195	1.86	174	21
LE TISSIER Matthew	Southampton	98	240	2.45	223	17
SHERINGHAM Teddy	Manchester U.	86	217	2.52	201	16
SUTTON Chris	Blackburn R.	80	209	2.61	198	11
YORKE Dwight	Manchester U.	78	211	2.71	192	19
DUBLIN Dion	Aston Villa	75	181	2.41	172	9

CANTONA Eric	Manchester U.	70	156	2.23	154	2
COTTEE Tony	Leicester C.	65	185	2.85	163	22
HOLDSWORTH Dean	Wimbledon	61	189	3.10	165	24
HUGHES Mark	Southampton	61	238	3.90	230	8
BEARDSLEY Peter	Newcastle U.	60	185	3.08	179	6
COLLYMORE Stan	Aston Villa	56	144	2.57	125	19
ARMSTRONG Chris	Tottenham H.	55	176	3.20	160	16
DEANE Brian	Middlesbrough	53	205	3.87	196	9
EKOKU Efan	Wimbledon	52	160	3.08	128	32
GALLACHER Kevin	Blackburn R.	52	159	3.06	148	11
BERGKAMP Dennis	Arsenal	51	119	2.33	117	2
BRIGHT Mark	Charlton A.	50	143	2.86	118	25

Top Goalscorers by Player/Club

This lists players who have scored the most goals for individual clubs in the Premiership.

Player	*Club*	*Goals*	*Tot*	*St*	*Sub*
SHEARER Alan	Blackburn R.	112	138	132	6
FOWLER Robbie	Liverpool	106	185	179	6
WRIGHT Ian	Arsenal	104	191	182	9
LE TISSIER Matthew	Southampton	98	240	223	17
SHERINGHAM Teddy	Tottenham H.	74	166	163	3
CANTONA Eric	Manchester U.	64	143	142	1
COLE Andy	Manchester U.	62	137	116	21
DUBLIN Dion	Coventry C.	62	145	144	1
FERDINAND Les	QPR	60	110	109	1
YORKE Dwight	Aston Villa	60	179	160	19
HOLDSWORTH Dean	Wimbledon	58	169	148	21
BERGKAMP Dennis	Arsenal	51	119	117	2
BEARDSLEY Peter	Newcastle U.	48	129	126	3
BRIGHT Mark	Sheffield W.	48	133	112	21
GIGGS Ryan	Manchester U.	48	220	204	16
SUTTON Chris	Blackburn R.	47	130	125	5
GALLACHER Kevin	Blackburn R.	46	139	129	10
RUSH Ian	Liverpool	45	130	118	12
COLE Andy	Newcastle U.	43	58	58	0
EARLE Robbie	Wimbledon	42	219	217	2
WALLACE Rod	Leeds United	42	178	153	25
FERDINAND Les	Newcastle U.	41	68	67	1
McMANAMAN Steve	Liverpool	41	240	232	8
SHEARER Alan	Newcastle U.	41	78	75	3

All-Time Player: Most Goals in One Game

Gls	*Player*	*Match*	*Date*	*Res*
5	COLE Andy	**Manchester U.** v Ipswich T.	04/03/95	9-0
4	EKOKU Efan	Everton v **Norwich C.**	25/09/93	1-5
	FOWLER Robbie	**Liverpool** v Middlesbrough	14/12/96	5-1
	VIALLI Gianluca	Barnsley v **Chelsea**	24/08/97	6-0
	KLINSMANN Jurgen	Wimbledon v **Tottenham H.**	02/05/98	6-2
	OWEN Michael	**Liverpool** v N.Forest	14/10/98	5-1
	SOLSKJAER Ole Gunnar	N.Forest v **Manchester U.**	06/02/99	1-8

Player: Consecutive Games with Goals

7 Mark Stein, Chelsea 1993-94

Dec 27	Southampton	Away	1-3	Stein
Dec 28	Newcastle United	Home	1-0	Stein
Jan 1	Swindon Town	Away	3-0	Stein
Jan 3	Everton	Home	4-2	Stein x 2 (1 penalty)
Jan 15	Norwich City	Away	1-1	Stein
Jan 22	Aston Villa	Home	1-1	Stein
Feb 5	Everton	Away	2-4	Stein x 2 (1 penalty)

(Stein actually scored 9 goals – inc. two penalties – in this sequence. These goals were scored in consecutive Chelsea matches as well.)

7 Alan Shearer, Newcastle United 1996-97

Sep 14	Blackburn Rovers	Home	2-1	Shearer (penalty)
Sep 21	Leeds United	Away	1-0	Shearer
Sep 30	Aston Villa	Home	4-3	Shearer
Oct 12	Derby Co.	Away	1-0	Shearer
Oct 20	Manchester United	Home	5-0	Shearer
Nov 23	Chelsea	Away	1-1	Shearer
Nov 30	Arsenal	Home	1-2	Shearer

(Newcastle played Leicester City, Middlesbrough and West Ham after playing Man. United and before Chelsea but Shearer was injured for these matches.)

Fastest Goals in a Game

April fools? Two of the fastest goals to have been scored in the Premier League have both come on the 1st April!

13 seconds	SUTTON Chris	**Blackburn R.** v Everton	01/04/94
17 seconds	SPENCER John	**Chelsea** v Leicester C.	08/10/94
25 seconds	HASSELBAINK JF	West Ham U. v **Leeds U.**	01/04/99

Fastest Hat-trick in a Game

4 mins 33 secs	FOWLER Robbie	**Liverpool** v Arsenal	28/08/94

Player: Most Hat-tricks in a Season

5 Alan Shearer, Blackburn Rovers 1995-96
v Coventry City, Nottingham Forest, West Ham United, Bolton Wanderers and Tottenham Hotspur

Player: Most Hat-tricks – All-time

No.	*Player*	*Hat-tricks Scored For*
9	Alan Shearer	Blackburn Rovers and Newcastle United
7	Robbie Fowler	Liverpool
5	Ian Wright	Arsenal
4	Matt Le Tissier	Southampton
4	Andy Cole	Newcastle United and Manchester United
4	Kevin Campbell	Arsenal, Nottingham Forest and Everton

THE GOALKEEPERS

Goalkeepers by Total App-Goals Ratio

Surname	*Club*	*Start*	*Sub*	*GA*	*GkA*	*GaR*
SEAMAN	Arsenal	232	0	229	182	0.78
SCHMEICHEL	Manchester United	252	0	239	222	0.87
DE GOEY	Chelsea	67	0	73	59	0.88
BOSNICH	Aston Villa	178	0	309	179	1.01
JAMES	Liverpool	213	1	309	217	1.01
SRNICEK	Sheffield Wednesday	120	1	251	125	1.03
MIMMS	Blackburn Rovers	59	2	168	66	1.08
FLOWERS	Blackburn Rovers	229	2	396	260	1.13

MARTYN	Leeds United	187	0	228	212	1.13
COTON	Sunderland	103	1	217	118	1.13
HISLOP	West Ham United	90	0	174	104	1.16
SPINK	Aston Villa	51	4	181	64	1.16
LUKIC	Arsenal	144	0	228	169	1.17
HITCHCOCK	Chelsea	57	4	291	72	1.18
POOM	Derby County	55	2	152	70	1.23
KELLER	Leicester City	67	0	100	84	1.25
MYRHE	Everton	60	0	103	76	1.27
THORSTVEDT	Tottenham Hotspur	58	2	183	76	1.27
WOODS	Southampton	69	1	279	89	1.27
KHARINE	Chelsea	114	0	334	147	1.29
SEGERS	Tottenham Hotspur	117	2	293	155	1.30

Key: GA=Goals conceded by team overall; GkA=Goals conceded by goalkeeper; CS=number of Clean Sheets; GaR=GkA divided by total appearances (App+Sub) to give number of goals conceded per game on average. Only players with a ratio of 1.30 or less are listed. A minimum of 50 games are required to qualify for the rating. Club listed is the last club played for in the Premiership.

Goalkeepers by Total Most Clean Sheets

Surname	*Club*	*CS*	*Start*	*Sub*	*%*
SCHMEICHEL	Manchester United	115	252	0	45.28
SEAMAN	Arsenal	104	232	0	44.83
JAMES	Liverpool	74	213	1	34.58
FLOWERS	Blackburn Rovers	70	229	2	30.30
MARTYN	Leeds United	69	187	0	36.90
BOSNICH	Aston Villa	64	178	0	35.96
SOUTHALL	Everton	63	207	0	30.43
LUKIC	Arsenal	49	144	0	34.03
MIKLOSKO	West Ham United	47	170	0	27.65
PRESSMAN	Sheffield Wednesday	47	187	1	25.00
OGRIZOVIC	Coventry City	46	188	0	24.47
WALKER	Tottenham Hotspur	45	172	1	26.01
SULLIVAN	Wimbledon	41	141	1	28.87
SRNICEK	Sheffield Wednesday	40	120	1	33.06

Goalkeepers by Consecutive Shut-outs

Surname	*Club*	*CSO*	*CS*	*Season*
SOUTHALL	Everton	7	14	1994-95
MANINGER	Arsenal	6	6	1997-98
SCHMEICHEL	Manchester United	5	18	1992-93
SEAMAN	Arsenal	5	20	1993-94
WALKER	Tottenham Hotspur	5	11	1994-95
WALKER	Tottenham Hotspur	5	11	1995-96
JAMES	Liverpool	5	12	1996-97
SEAMAN	Arsenal	5	10	1996-97
SCHMEICHEL	Manchester United	5	17	1997-98
BOSNICH	Aston Villa	5	9	1998-99
SEAMAN	Arsenal	5	19	1998-99

CSO=Consecutive shut-outs (number of full games without conceding a goal); CS=Clean Sheets; Season=Season it was performed.

Goalkeepers by Most Clean Sheets/Season

Surname	*Club*	*CS*	*Apps*	*%*	*GkA*	*Season*
SCHMEICHEL	Manchester United	24	32	75.00	22	1994-95
SEAMAN	Arsenal	20	39	51.28	24	1993-94
MARTYN	Leeds United	20	37	54.05	38	1996-97
MIMMS	Blackburn Rovers	19	42	45.24	46	1992-93
SEAMAN	Arsenal	19	32	59.38	15	1998-99
SCHMEICHEL	Manchester United	18	42	42.86	31	1992-93
SCHMEICHEL	Manchester United	18	36	50.00	30	1995-96
JAMES	Liverpool	17	42	40.48	37	1994-95
LUKIC	Leeds United	17	42	40.48	38	1994-95
SCHMEICHEL	Manchester United	17	34	50.00	24	1997-98
FLOWERS	Blackburn Rovers	16	39	41.03	30	1994-95
JAMES	Liverpool	16	38	42.11	34	1995-96
SEAMAN	Arsenal	16	38	42.11	32	1995-96
SEAMAN	Arsenal	15	39	38.46	32	1992-93
SOUTHALL	Everton	15	38	39.47	44	1995-96
MIKLOSKO	West Ham United	14	42	33.33	58	1993-94
SCHMEICHEL	Manchester United	14	40	35.00	38	1993-94
MARTYN	C.Palace	14	37	37.84	41	1994-95
SOUTHALL	Everton	14	41	34.15	51	1994-95
DE GOEY	Chelsea	14	35	40.00	27	1998-99
HISLOP	West Ham United	14	37	37.84	50	1998-99
KELLER	Leicester City	14	36	38.89	43	1998-99
MYRHE	Everton	14	38	36.84	47	1998-99

THE PLAYERS

Top Appearances by Player

Maximum number of games possible is 278.
NB: Clubs listed are those that player played last Premiership match with.

Player	*Club*	*Tot*	*Start*	*Sub*	*Gls*
ATHERTON Peter	Sheffield W.	257	256	1	8
SPEED Gary	Newcastle U.	252	247	5	43
SCHMEICHEL Peter	Manchester U.	252	252	0	0
SHERWOOD Tim	Tottenham H.	249	244	5	27
WINTERBURN Nigel	Arsenal	242	241	1	4
LE TISSIER Matthew	Southampton	240	223	17	98
McMANAMAN Steve	Liverpool	240	232	8	41
HUGHES Mark	Southampton	238	230	8	61
IRWIN Denis	Manchester U.	238	231	7	15
KENNA Jeff	Blackburn R.	236	232	4	5
DIXON Lee	Arsenal	235	231	4	5
McALLISTER Gary	Coventry C.	232	232	0	33
PALLISTER Gary	Middlesbrough	232	232	0	8
SEAMAN David	Arsenal	232	232	0	0
PALMER Carlton	N.Forest	231	227	4	14
PEACOCK Darren	Blackburn R.	231	223	8	8
FLOWERS Tim	Blackburn R.	231	229	2	0
WALKER Des	Sheffield W.	227	227	0	0
FERDINAND Les	Tottenham H.	223	217	6	111
GIGGS Ryan	Manchester U.	220	204	16	48
EARLE Robbie	Wimbledon	219	217	2	42
SHERINGHAM Teddy	Manchester U.	217	201	16	86
WATSON Dave	Everton	217	215	2	6
SHEARER Alan	Newcastle U.	216	207	9	153
JAMES David	Liverpool	214	213	1	0
WRIGHT Ian	West Ham U.	213	202	11	113
KEOWN Martin	Arsenal	212	194	18	3
YORKE Dwight	Manchester U.	211	192	19	78

Top Substitute Appearances by Player

NB: Clubs listed are those that player played last Premiership match with.

Player	*Club*	*Sub*	*Tot*	*Start*	*Gls*
CLARKE Andy	Wimbledon	70	124	54	11
McCLAIR Brian	Manchester U.	56	162	106	18
FENTON Graham	Leicester C.	54	91	37	13
ROSENTHAL Ronny	Tottenham H.	47	118	71	10
BARLOW Stuart	Everton	41	62	21	10
JOACHIM Julian	Aston Villa	40	103	63	29
WATSON Gordon	Southampton	40	94	54	21
SCHOLES Paul	Manchester U.	39	129	90	32

THE MANAGERS

Length of Tenure – Current Tenants

	Club	*Manager*	*Arrived*
1	Manchester United	Alex Ferguson	November '86
2	Middlesbrough	Bryan Robson	May '94
3	West Ham United	Harry Redknapp	August '94
4	Sunderland	Peter Reid	March '95
5	Derby County	Jim Smith	June '95
6	Leicester City	Martin O'Neill	December '95
7	Arsenal	Arsène Wenger	August '96
8	Coventry City	Gordon Strachan	November '96
9	Watford	Graham Taylor	May '97
10	Southampton	Dave Jones	June '97
11	Chelsea	Gianluca Vialli	February '98
12	Aston Villa	John Gregory	February '98
13	Bradford City	Paul Jewell	May '98
14	Everton	Walter Smith	July '98
15	Sheffield Wednesday	Danny Wilson	July '98
16	Newcastle United	Ruud Gullitt	August '98
17	Leeds United	David O'Leary	October '98
18	Tottenham Hotspur	George Graham	October '98
19	Liverpool	Gerard Houllier	November '98
20	Wimbledon	Egil Olsen	June '99

Managers: Most Games in Charge

Manager	Clubs	P	W	D	L	F	A	PTS	PPG
FERGUSON Alex	1	278	168	73	37	526	239	577	2.08
KINNEAR Joe	1	278	92	82	104	338	398	358	1.29
GRAHAM George	3	221	78	75	68	259	213	309	1.40
ATKINSON Ron	4	201	69	51	81	220	256	258	1.28
REDKNAPP Harry	1	194	69	49	76	228	258	256	1.32
DALGLISH Kenny	2	182	91	47	44	280	182	320	1.76
ROYLE Joe	2	181	58	54	69	241	258	228	1.26
FRANCIS Gerry	2	175	67	50	58	244	227	251	1.43
WILKINSON Howard	1	174	66	53	55	231	214	250	1.44
EVANS Roy †	1	172	83	46	43	280	173	295	1.72
LITTLE Brian	2	144	53	39	52	173	162	198	1.38
KEEGAN Kevin	1	143	78	30	35	253	147	264	1.85

† Does not include games as Joint Manager with Gerard Houllier.

Managers by Total Points Won

Manager	Clubs	P	W	D	L	F	A	Pts	PPG
FERGUSON Alex	1	278	168	73	37	526	239	577	2.08
KINNEAR Joe	1	278	92	82	104	338	398	358	1.29
DALGLISH Kenny	2	182	91	47	44	280	182	320	1.76
GRAHAM George	3	221	78	75	68	259	213	309	1.40
EVANS Roy †	1	172	83	46	43	280	173	295	1.72
KEEGAN Kevin	1	143	78	30	35	253	147	264	1.85
ATKINSON Ron	4	201	69	51	81	220	256	258	1.28
REDKNAPP Harry	1	194	69	49	76	228	258	256	1.32
FRANCIS Gerry	2	175	67	50	58	244	227	251	1.43
WILKINSON Howard	1	174	66	53	55	231	214	250	1.44
ROYLE Joe	2	181	58	54	69	241	258	228	1.26
WENGER Arsène	1	106	59	30	17	172	74	207	1.95

Managers by Average Points/Game

Manager	Clubs	P	W	D	L	F	A	Pts	PPG
FERGUSON Alex	1	278	168	73	37	526	239	577	2.08
WENGER Arsène	1	106	59	30	17	172	74	207	1.95
KEEGAN Kevin	1	143	78	30	35	253	147	264	1.85
VIALLI Gianluca	1	51	26	15	10	76	46	93	1.82
BASSETT Dave	2	104	24	35	45	114	149	107	1.77
DALGLISH Kenny	2	182	91	47	44	280	182	320	1.76

EVANS Roy	1	172	83	46	43	280	173	295	1.72
GREGORY John	1	49	24	10	15	62	56	82	1.67
RIOCH Bruce	1	38	17	12	9	49	32	63	1.66
CLARK Frank	1	97	38	31	28	136	126	145	1.49
GULLITT Ruud	2	100	41	25	33	157	135	148	1.48
WILKINSON Howard	1	174	66	53	55	231	214	250	1.44
FRANCIS Gerry	2	175	67	50	58	244	227	251	1.43
WALKER Mike	2	96	37	25	34	126	143	136	1.42
LIVERMORE/CLEMENCE Doug/Ray	1	42	16	11	15	60	66	59	1.40
GRAHAM George	3	221	78	75	68	259	213	309	1.40
FRANCIS Trevor	1	126	44	42	40	180	162	174	1.38
LITTLE Brian	2	144	53	39	52	173	162	198	1.38
SOUNESS Graeme	2	106	38	29	39	156	143	143	1.35
SMITH Jim	1	114	40	33	41	137	152	153	1.34
REDKNAPP Harry	1	194	69	49	76	228	258	256	1.32
O'NEILL Martin	1	114	37	38	39	137	151	149	1.31

SEASON BY SEASON

Crime Count – Year-by-Year

Season	*Games*	*Red Cards*	*Ave*	*Yellow Cards*	*Ave*
1992-93	462	34	0.077	760	1.65
1993-94	462	25	0.054	599	1.30
1994-95	462	65	0.140	1294	2.80
1995-96	380	57	0.150	1180	3.11
1996-97	380	31	0.082	1211	3.18
1997-98	380	69	0.182	1238	3.26
1998-99	380	73	0.192	1429	3.76

Last Day Championships

The FA Premier League Championship has been decided on the last day of the season three times.

1994-95

	P	*W*	*D*	*L*	*F*	*A*	*Pts*	*GD*
Blackburn Rovers	41	27	8	6	79	37	89	+42
Manchester United	41	26	9	6	76	27	87	+48

On the last day of the season Blackburn travelled to Liverpool needing a win to secure the title. Manchester United went to Upton Park needing three points from West Ham and hoping that Rovers would fail to win. A last minute goal gave Liverpool a 2-1 win over Blackburn, but despite a succession of missed chances Manchester United could only draw and the title went to Blackburn Rovers.

1995-96

	P	*W*	*D*	*L*	*F*	*A*	*Pts*	*GD*
Manchester United	41	24	7	6	70	35	79	+35
Newcastle United	41	24	5	8	65	36	77	+29

At one point Newcastle led the table by 12 points but a string of last-minute reversals and a relentless attack by the Red Devils allowed them to peg the Magpies back. On the final day of the season the United of Manchester travelled to the north-east to play Middlesbrough, needing a point to take the title. Newcastle entertained Spurs at home and needed to win and look a few miles south for a result. The United of Manchester prevailed, winning 3-0 at the Riverside as Newcastle drew 1-1 with Spurs.

1998-99

	P	*W*	*D*	*L*	*F*	*A*	*Pts*	*GD*
Manchester United	41	21	13	3	78	36	76	+42
Arsenal	41	21	12	4	58	17	75	+41

It was so close that the two protagonists went into the final day of the season with only a goal difference of one separating them. Manchester United knew a win over Tottenham would ensure the title. Arsenal knew a win over Aston Villa wouldn't be sufficient and that they needed arch-rivals Tottenham Hotspur to get some sort of result at Old Trafford. Tottenham – involved in the final day drama for the second time – took the lead at Old Trafford and raised the Highbury hopes. But goals either side of the interval from Beckham and Cole meant that Kanu's second-half winner for Arsenal didn't re-direct the championship outcome.

Final Table 1996-97 Season

		P	W	D	L	F	A	Pts	
1	Manchester United	38	21	12	5	76	44	75	
2	Newcastle United	38	19	11	8	73	40	68	
3	Arsenal	38	19	11	8	62	32	68	
4	Liverpool	38	19	11	8	62	37	68	
5	Aston Villa	38	17	10	11	47	34	61	
6	Chelsea	38	16	11	11	58	55	59	
7	Sheffield Wednesday	38	14	15	9	50	51	57	
8	Wimbledon	38	15	11	12	49	46	56	
9	Leicester City	38	12	11	15	46	54	47	
10	Tottenham Hotspur	38	13	7	18	44	51	46	
11	Leeds United	38	11	13	14	28	38	46	
12	Derby County	38	11	13	14	45	58	46	
13	Blackburn Rovers	38	9	15	14	42	43	42	
14	West Ham United	38	10	12	16	39	48	42	
15	Everton	38	10	12	16	44	57	42	
16	Southampton	38	10	11	17	50	56	41	
17	Coventry City	38	9	14	15	38	54	41	
18	Sunderland	38	10	10	18	35	53	40	R
19	Middlesbrough †	38	10	12	16	51	60	39	R
20	Nottingham Forest	38	6	16	16	31	59	34	R

† Deducted 3 points for failing to fulfil fixture.

Promoted: Bolton Wanderers – Champions
Barnsley – Runners-up
Crystal Palace – Play-off Winners

Final Table 1997-98 Season

		P	W	D	L	F	A	Pts	
1	Arsenal	38	23	9	6	68	33	78	
2	Manchester United	38	23	8	7	73	26	77	
3	Liverpool	38	18	11	9	68	42	65	
4	Chelsea	38	20	3	15	71	43	63	
5	Leeds United	38	17	8	13	57	46	59	
6	Blackburn Rovers	38	16	10	12	57	52	58	
7	Aston Villa	38	17	6	15	49	48	57	
8	West Ham United	38	16	8	14	56	57	56	
9	Derby County	38	16	7	15	52	49	55	
10	Leicester City	38	13	14	11	51	41	53	
11	Coventry City	38	12	16	10	46	44	52	
12	Southampton	38	14	6	18	50	55	48	
13	Newcastle United	38	11	11	16	35	44	44	
14	Tottenham Hotspur	38	11	11	16	44	56	44	
15	Wimbledon	38	10	14	14	34	46	44	
16	Sheffield Wednesday	38	12	8	18	52	67	44	
17	Everton	38	9	13	16	41	56	40	
18	Bolton Wanderers	38	9	13	16	41	61	40	R
19	Barnsley	38	10	5	23	37	82	35	R
20	Crystal Palace	38	8	9	21	37	71	33	R

Promoted: Nottingham Forest – Champions
Middlesbrough – Runners-up
Charlton Athletic – Play-off Winners

FA CHALLENGE CUP

1998-99 Sponsored by AXA

Third Round

Aston Villa	v	Hull C.	3-0	39,217
Blackburn R.	v	Charlton A.	2-0	16,631
Bolton Wanderers	v	Wolverhampton W.	1-2	18,269
Bournemouth	v	WBA	1-0	10,881
Bradford C.	v	Grimsby T.	2-1	13,870
Bristol C.	v	Everton	0-2	19,608
Bury	v	Stockport Co.	0-3	5,325
Cardiff C.	v	Yeovil T.	1-1	12,561
Coventry C.	v	Macclesfield T.	7-0	14,197
Crewe Alexandra	v	Oxford U.	1-3	4,207
Leicester C.	v	Birmingham C.	4-2	19,846
Lincoln C.	v	Sunderland	0-1	10,408
Newcastle U.	v	Crystal Palace	2-1	36,536
N.Forest	v	Portsmouth	0-1	10,092
Oldham A.	v	Chelsea	0-2	12,770
Plymouth Argyle	v	Derby Co.	0-3	16,730
QPR	v	Huddersfield T.	0-1	11,685
Rotherham U.	v	Bristol R.	0-1	6,056
Rushden & Diamonds	v	Leeds U.	0-0	6,431
Sheffield U.	v	Notts Co.	1-1	12,264
Southampton	v	Fulham	1-1	12,549
Southport	v	Leyton Orient	0-2	4,950
Swindon T.	v	Barnsley	0-0	8,016
Tottenham H.	v	Watford	5-2	36,022
Tranmere R.	v	Ipswich T.	0-1	7,223
West Ham U.	v	Swansea C.	1-1	26,039
Wimbledon	v	Manchester C.	1-0	11,226
Wrexham	v	Scunthorpe U.	4-3	4,429
Manchester U.	v	Middlesbrough	3-1	52,232
Port Vale	v	Liverpool	0-3	16,557
Sheffield W.	v	Norwich C.	4-1	18,737
Preston NE	v	Arsenal	2-4	21,099

Third Round Replays

Fulham	v	Southampton	1-0	17,448
Leeds U.	v	Rushden & Diamonds	3-1	39,159
Swansea C.	v	West Ham U.	1-0	10,116
Barnsley	v	Swindon T.	3-1	10,510
Notts County	v	Sheffield U.	3-4	7,489
Yeovil T.	v	Cardiff C.	1-2	8,101

Fourth Round

Aston Villa	v	Fulham	0-2	35,260
Barnsley	v	Bournemouth	3-1	11,982
Blackburn R.	v	Sunderland	1-0	30,125
Bristol Rovers	v	Leyton Orient	3-0	9,274
Everton	v	Ipswich T.	1-0	28,854
Leicester C.	v	Coventry C.	0-3	21,207
Newcastle U.	v	Bradford C.	3-0	36,698
Portsmouth	v	Leeds U.	1-5	18,864
Sheffield W.	v	Stockport Co.	2-0	20,984
Swansea C.	v	Derby Co.	0-1	11,383
Wimbledon	v	Tottenham H.	1-1	22,229
Wrexham	v	Huddersfield T.	1-1	8,714
Manchester U.	v	Liverpool	2-1	54,591
Wolverhampton W.	v	Arsenal	1-2	27,511
Oxford United	v	Chelsea	1-1	9,059
Sheffield United	v	Cardiff C.	4-1	13,296

Fourth Round Replays

Chelsea	v	Oxford U.	4-2	32,106
Huddersfield T.	v	Wrexham	2-1	15,427
Tottenham H.	v	Wimbledon	3-0	24,049

Fifth Round

* *Arsenal*	*v*	*Sheffield U.*	*2-1*	*38,020*
Arsenal	v	Sheffield U.	2-1	37,161
Barnsley	v	Bristol R.	4-1	17,508
Everton	v	Coventry C.	2-1	33,907
Huddersfield T.	v	Derby Co.	2-2	22,129
Leeds U.	v	Tottenham H.	1-1	39,696
Sheffield W.	v	Chelsea	0-1	29,410
Manchester U.	v	Fulham	1-0	54,798
Newcastle U.	v	Blackburn R.	0-0	36,295

***** *First game declared void after unsportsmanlike goal.***

Fifth Round Replays

Blackburn R.	v	Newcastle U.	0-1	27,483
Derby Co.	v	Huddersfield T.	3-1	28,704
Tottenham H.	v	Leeds U.	2-0	32,307

Sixth Round

Arsenal	v	Derby Co.	1-0	38,046
Manchester U.	v	Chelsea	0-0	54,587
Newcastle U.	v	Everton	4-1	36,584
Barnsley	v	Tottenham H.	0-1	18,793

Sixth Round Replay

Chelsea	v	Manchester U.	0-2	33,075

Semi-Finals

Manchester U.	v	Arsenal	0-0	39,217
		After extra time. Played at Villa Park.		
Newcastle U.	v	Tottenham H.	2-0	53,609
		After extra time. Played at Old Trafford.		

Semi-Final Replay

Arsenal	v	Manchester U.	1-2	30,223
		After extra time. Played at Villa Park.		

Final – 22 May 1999 at Wembley Stadium

Manchester United	v	Newcastle United	2-0	79,101

Sheringham (11); Scholes (53)

Manchester United: Schmeichel, G.Neville, May, Johnsen, Beckham, Scholes (Stam 77), Keane (Sheringham 8), Giggs, Cole (Yorke 60), Solskjaer.

Newcastle United: Harper, Griffin, Dabizas, Charvet, Domi, Lee, Hamann (Ferguson 46), Speed, Salano (Maric 68), Ketsbaia (Glass 78), Shearer.

Referee: Mr. Paul Jones.

Final Facts

- This was the first time that the FA Cup Final had been contested by two teams called 'United'.
- Manchester United's win ensured they became the first team to complete the Double three times. All these have come in the 1990s.

FA CUP FINALS 1971-1999

Year	*Winners*	*Runners-up*	
1971	Arsenal	Liverpool	2-1 †
1972	Leeds United	Arsenal	1-0
1973	Sunderland	Leeds United	1-0
1974	Liverpool	Newcastle United	3-0
1975	West Ham United	Fulham	2-0
1976	Southampton	Manchester United	1-0
1977	Manchester United	Liverpool	2-1
1978	Ipswich T.	Arsenal	1-0
1979	Arsenal	Manchester United	3-2
1980	West Ham United	Arsenal	1-0
1981	Tottenham Hotspur	Manchester C.	1-1 †
	Tottenham Hotspur	Manchester C.	3-2
1982	Tottenham Hotspur	Queens Park Rangers	1-1 †
	Tottenham Hotspur	Queens Park Rangers	1-0
1983	Manchester United	Brighton & Hove Albion	2-2 †
	Manchester United	Brighton & Hove Albion	4-0
1984	Everton	Watford	2-0
1985	Manchester United	Everton	1-0 †
1986	Liverpool	Everton	3- 1
1987	Coventry C.	Tottenham Hotspur	3-2 †
1988	Wimbledon	Liverpool	1-0
1989	Liverpool	Everton	3-2 †
1990	Manchester United	Crystal Palace	3-3 †
	Manchester United	Crystal Palace	1-0
1991	Tottenham Hotspur	Nottingham Forest	2-1 †
1992	Liverpool	Sunderland	2-0
1993	Arsenal	Sheffield Wednesday	1-1 †
	Arsenal	Sheffield Wednesday	2-1 †
1994	Manchester United	Chelsea	4-0
1995	Everton	Manchester United	1-0
1996	Manchester United	Liverpool	1-0
1997	Chelsea	Middlesbrough	2-0
1998	Arsenal	Newcastle United	2-0
1999	Manchester United	Newcastle United	2-0

† *after extra time.*

WORTHINGTON CUP 1998-99

Second Round

			1st	*2nd*	*Agg*
AFC Bournemouth	v	Wolverhampton W.	1-1	2-1	3-2
Barnsley	v	Reading	3-0	1-1	4-1
Blackpool	v	Tranmere R.	2-1	1-3	3-4
Bolton W.	v	Hull City	3-1	3-2	6-3
Brentford	v	Tottenham H.	2-3	2-3	4-6
Bristol C.	v	Crewe Alexandra	1-1	0-1	1-2
Bury	v	Crystal Palace	3-0	1-2	4-2
Coventry C.	v	Southend U.	1-0	4-0	5-0
Derby Co.	v	Manchester C.	1-1	1-0	2-1
Fulham	v	Southampton	1-1	1-0	2-1
Halifax T.	v	Bradford C.	1-2	1-3	2-5
Huddersfield T.	v	Everton	1-1	1-2	2-3
Ipswich T.	v	Luton T.	2-1	2-4 †	4-5
Leicester C.	v	Chesterfield	3-0	3-1	6-1
Leyton Orient	v	N.Forest	1-5	0-0	1-5
Macclesfield T.	v	Birmingham C.	0-3	0-6	0-9
Middlesbrough	v	Wycombe W.	2-0	1-1	3-1
Northampton T.	v	West Ham U.	2-0	0-1	2-1
Norwich C.	v	Wigan A.	1-0	3-2	4-2
Portsmouth	v	Wimbledon	2-1	1-4	3-5
QPR	v	Charlton A.	0-2	0-1	0-3
Sheffield U.	v	Grimsby T.	2-1	0-2 †	2-3
Sheffield W.	v	Cambridge U.	0-1	1-1	1-2
Sunderland	v	Chester C.	3-0	1-0	4-0

Byes: Arsenal, Aston Villa, Chelsea, Liverpool, Manchester United and Newcastle United.

Third Round

Barnsley	v	AFC Bournemouth	2-1		8,560
Charlton A.	v	Leicester C.	1-2		19,671
Liverpool	v	Fulham	3-1		22,296
Luton Town	v	Coventry C.	2-0		9,051
Northampton T.	v	Tottenham H.	1-3		7,422
Norwich C.	v	Bolton W.	1-1	†	14,189

Bolton Wanderers win on penalties

N.Forest	v	Cambridge U.	3-3	†	9,192

Nottingham Forest win on penalties

Sunderland	v	Grimsby T.	2-1	†	18,676
Tranmere R.	v	Newcastle U.	0-1		12,017
Birmingham C.	v	Wimbledon	1-2		11,845
Chelsea	v	Aston Villa	4-1		26,790
Crewe Alexandra	v	Blackburn R.	0-1		5,403
Derby Co.	v	Arsenal	1-2		25,621
Leeds U.	v	Bradford C.	1-0		27,561
Manchester U.	v	Bury	2-0	†	52,495
Middlesbrough	v	Everton	2-3	†	20,748

Fourth Round

Bolton W.	v	Wimbledon	1-2		7,868
Liverpool	v	Tottenham H.	1-3		20,772
Luton Town	v	Barnsley	1-0		8,435
Arsenal	v	Chelsea	0-5		37,562
Everton	v	Sunderland	1-1	†	28,132

Sunderland win on penalties

Leicester C.	v	Leeds U.	2-1		20,161
Manchester U.	v	N.Forest	2-1		37,237
Newcastle U.	v	Blackburn R.	1-1	†	34,702

Blackburn Rovers win on penalties

Quarter-Finals

Sunderland	v	Luton T.	3-0	35,472
Wimbledon	v	Chelsea	2-1	19,286
Leicester C.	v	Blackburn R.	1-0	19,442
Tottenham H.	v	Manchester U.	3-1	35,702

Semi-Finals First Leg

Sunderland	v	Leicester C.	1-2	38,332
Tottenham H.	v	Wimbledon	0-0	

Semi-Finals Second Leg

Leicester C.	v	Sunderland	1-1	21,231

Leicester City win 3-2 on aggregate

Wimbledon	v	Tottenham H.	0-1	25,204

Tottenham Hotspur win 1-0 on aggregate

Final – 21 March 1999 at Wembley Stadium

Leicester C.	v	Tottenham H. Nielsen (90)	0-1	77,892

Leicester City: Keller, Savage (Zagorakis 90), Guppy, Elliott, Taggart, Walsh, Ullathorne, Izzet, Lennon, Heskey (Marshall 75), Cottee.
Subs Not Used: Arphexad, Campbell, Kaamark. Booked: Elliott, Savage.

Tottenham Hotspur: Walker, Carr, Campbell, Vega, Edinburgh, Anderton, Freund, Nielsen, Ginola (Sinton 90), Ferdinand, Iversen.
Subs Not Used: Armstrong, Dominguez, Young, Baardsen.
Sent Off: Edinburgh (63). Booked: Vega.
Referee: Mr T. Heilbron (Newton Aycliffe).

† = after extra time.

FINALS 1993-1999

Coca-Cola Cup

Year	*Winners*	*Runners-up*		
1993	Arsenal	Sheffield Wednesday	2-1	
1994	Aston Villa	Manchester United	3-1	
1995	Liverpool	Bolton Wanderers	2-1	
1996	Aston Villa	Leeds United	3-0	
1997	Leicester C. *after 1-1 aet draw at Wembley*	Middlesbrough	1-0	†
1998	Chelsea	Middlesbrough	2-0	†

Worthington Cup

Year	*Winners*	*Runners-up*	
1999	Tottenham H.	Leicester C.	1-0

† after extra time

FWA FOOTBALLER OF THE YEAR WINNERS

Season	*Winner*	*Club*
1947-48	Stanley Matthews	Blackpool & England
1948-49	Johnny Carey	Manchester U. & Rep. of Ireland
1949-50	Joe Mercer	Arsenal & England
1950-51	Harry Johnston	Blackpool & England
1951-52	Billy Wright	Wolverhampton W. & England
1952-53	Nat Lofthouse	Bolton W. & England
1953-54	Tom Finney	Preston NE & England
1954-55	Don Revie	Manchester C. & England
1955-56	Bert Trautmann	Manchester C.
1956-57	Tom Finney	Preston NE & England
1957-58	Danny Blanchflower	Tottenham H. & Northern Ireland
1958-59	Syd Owen	Luton T. & England
1959-60	Bill Slater	Wolverhampton W. & England
1960-61	Danny Blanchflower	Tottenham H. & Northern Ireland
1961-62	Jimmy Adamson	Burnley
1962-63	Stanley Matthews	Stoke C. & England
1963-64	Bobby Moore	West Ham U. & England
1964-65	Bobby Collins	Leeds U. & Scotland
1965-66	Bobby Charlton	Manchester U. & England
1966-67	Jack Charlton	Leeds U. & England
1967-68	George Best	Manchester U. & Northern Ireland
1968-69	Dave Mackay	Derby Co. & Scotland
	Tony Book	Manchester C.
1969-70	Billy Bremner	Leeds U. & Scotland
1970-71	Frank McLintock	Arsenal & Scotland
1971-72	Gordon Banks	Stoke C. & England
1972-73	Pat Jennings	Tottenham H. & Northern Ireland
1973-74	Ian Callaghan	Liverpool & England
1974-75	Alan Mullery	Fulham & England
1975-76	Kevin Keegan	Liverpool & England
1976-77	Emlyn Hughes	Liverpool & England
1977-78	Kenny Burns	N.Forest & Scotland
1978-79	Kenny Dalglish	Liverpool & Scotland
1979-80	Terry McDermott	Liverpool & England
1980-81	Frans Thijssen	Ipswich T. & Holland
1981-82	Steve Perryman	Tottenham H. & England

1982-83	Kenny Dalglish	Liverpool & Scotland
1983-84	Ian Rush	Liverpool & Wales
1984-85	Neville Southall	Everton & Wales
1985-86	Gary Lineker	Everton & England
1986-87	Clive Allen	Tottenham H. & England
1987-88	John Barnes	Liverpool & England
1988-89	Steve Nicol	Liverpool & England
1989-90	John Barnes	Liverpool & England
1990-91	Gordon Strachan	Leeds U. & Scotland
1991-92	Gary Lineker	Tottenham H. & England
1992-93	Chris Waddle	Sheffield W. & England
1993-94	Alan Shearer	Blackburn R. & England
1994-95	Jurgen Klinsmann	Tottenham H. & Germany
1995-96	Eric Cantona	Manchester U. & France
1996-97	Gianfranco Zola	Chelsea & Italy
1997-98	Dennis Bergkamp	Arsenal & Holland
1998-99	David Ginola	Tottenham Hotspur & France

PFA AWARDS 1998-99

Player of the Year

1. David Ginola (Tottenham Hotspur)
2. Dwight Yorke (Manchester United)
3. Emmanuel Petit (Arsenal)

Young Player of the Year

1. Nicolas Anelka (Arsenal)
2. Michael Owen (Liverpool)
3. Harry Kewell (Leeds United)

Premiership Team

Goalkeeper	Nigel Martyn (Leeds United)
Defenders	Gary Neville (Manchester United)
	Denis Irwin (Manchester United)
	Sol Campbell (Tottenham Hotspur)
	Japp Stam (Manchester United)
Midfield	Patrick Vieira (Arsenal)
	David Beckham (Manchester United)
	Emmanuel Petit (Arsenal)
Forwards	Nicolas Anelka (Arsenal)
	Dwight Yorke (Manchester United)
	David Ginola (Tottenham Hotspur)

CLUB DIRECTORY 1999-2000

KEY TO CLUB DIRECTORY ABBREVIATIONS
Stats relating to FA Carling Premiership Season

Tot	Total appearances in season – this is St + Sb.
St	Total number of times player was in starting line-up.
Sb	Total number of times player came on as sub.
Snu	Total number of times player was sub but not used (Sub not used).
PS	Total number of times player was substituted (Player Subbed).
Gls	Total number of goals scored.
Y	Total number of Yellow cards received.
R	Total number of Red cards received. (Note: A red card issued due to a second yellow card is recorded as 1Y and 1R.)
Fa/La	Total number of appearances in FA Cup and League Cup.
Fg/Lg	Total number of goals scored in FA Cup and League Cup.
†	Player no longer with club at time of going to press.
CM	Caretaker Manager.
PM	Player-Manager.
DOF	Director of Football.
1Rf/1Rs	1st Round First Leg/ 1st Round Second Leg.
CL	Champions' League.
CWC	Cup-Winners' Cup.
UEFA	UEFA Cup.
Note:	Record wins and defeats listed by number of goals not by margin.

Arsenal

Formed as Dial Square, a workshop in Woolwich Arsenal with a sundial over the entrance, in October 1886, becoming Royal Arsenal, the 'Royal' possibly from a local public house, later the same year. Turned professional and became Woolwich Arsenal in 1891. Selected for an expanded Football League Division Two in 1893, the first southern team to join. Moved from the Manor Ground, Plumstead, south-east London, to Highbury, north London, in 1913, changing name again at the same time. Elected from fifth in Division Two to the expanded First Division for the 1919-20 season and never relegated. Premier League founder members 1992. In 1997-98 performed the Double for the second time.

Ground: Arsenal Stadium, Avenell Road, Highbury, London N5 1BU
Club No.: 0171-704-4000 **Information:** 0171-704-4242
Box Office: 0171-704-4040 **CC Bookings:** 0171-413-3370
News: 0891 20 20 21 **Nickname:** Gunners
Capacity: 39,497 **Pitch size:** 110 yds x 71 yds
Colours: Red/White sleeves, White, Red
Radio: 1548AM Capital Radio
Internet: www.arsenal.co.uk

Chairman: P.D. Hill-Wood **Vice-Chairman:** David Dein
MD: Ken Friar **Manager:** Arsène Wenger
Assistant/Coach: Pat Rice **Physio:** Gary Lewin MCSP SRP

League History: 1893 Elected to Division 2; 1904-13 Division 1; 1913-19 Division 2; 1919-92 Division 1; 1992- FA Premier League.

Honours: *FA Premier League: Champions* 1997-98; *Runners-up* 1998-99; *Football League: Division 1 Champions* 1930-31, 1932-33, 1933-34, 1934-35, 1937-38, 1947-48, 1952-53, 1970-71, 1988-89, 1990-91; *Runners-up* 1925-26, 1931-32, 1972-73; *Division 1 Runners-up* 1903-04. *FA Cup: Winners* 1929-30, 1935-36, 1949-50, 1970-71, 1978-79, 1992-93, 1997-98; *Runners-up* 1926-27, 1931-32, 1951-52, 1971-72, 1977-78, 1979-80. *Football League Cup: Winners* 1986-87, 1992-93; *Runners-up* 1967-68, 1968-69, 1987-88. *League-Cup Double Performed:* 1970-71, 1997-98. *Cup-Cup Double Performed:* 1992-93. *Cup-Winners' Cup Winners* 1993-94; *Runners-up* 1979-80, 1994-95. *Fairs Cup: Winners* 1969-70. *European Super Cup: Runners-up* 1994-95.

European Record: Champions' League (3): 71-72 (QF), 91-92 (2), 98-99 (L); Cup-Winners' Cup (3): 79-80 (F), 93-94 (W), 94-95 (F); UEFA Cup (8): 63-64 (2), 69-70 (W), 71-70 (Q), 78-79 (3), 81-82 (2), 82-83 (1), 96-97 (1), 97-98 (1).

Managers: Sam Hollis 1894-97; Tom Mitchell 1897-98; George Elcoat 1898-99; Harry Bradshaw 1899-1904; Phil Kelso 1904-08; George Morrell 1908-15; Leslie Knighton 1919-25; Herbert Chapman 1925-34; George Allison 1934-47; Tom Whittaker 1947-56; Jack Crayston 1956-58; George Swindin 1958-62; Billy Wright 1962-66; Bertie Mee 1966-76; Terry Neill 1976-83; Don Howe 1984-86; *(FAPL)* George Graham May 1986-Feb 1995; Stewart Houston (caretaker) Feb 1995-May 1995; Bruce Rioch May 1995-Aug 1996; Stewart Houston (CM) Aug 1996; Pat Rice (CM) Sept 1996; Arsène Wenger Sept 1996-.

All-Time Records

Record FAPL Win: 6-1 v Middlesbrough, Away, 24/04/99
Record FAPL Defeat: 0-4 v Liverpool, Away, 05/05/98
2-4 v Norwich City, Home, 15/08/92
Record FL Win: 12-0 v Loughborough T., Div 2, 12/3/1900
Record FL Defeat: 0-8 v Loughborough T., Div 2, 12/12/1896
Record Cup Win: 11-1 v Darwen, FA Cup R3, 9/1/32
Record Fee Received: £5m from West Ham U. for John Hartson, 3/97
Record Fee Paid: £7.5m to Internazionale for Dennis Bergkamp, 6/95
Most FL Apps: 547 – David O'Leary, 1975-92
Most FAPL Apps: 242 – Nigel Winterburn, 1992-99
Most FAPL Goals: 104 – Ian Wright, 1992-98
Highest Scorer in FAPL Season: 30: Ian Wright, 1992-93
Record Attendance: 73,295 v Sunderland, D1, 9/3/35 (at Highbury)
73,707 v RC Lens, CL 25/11/98 (at Wembley)
Record Attendance (FAPL): 38,377 v Tottenham Hotspur 29/4/95
Most FAPL Goals in Season: 68, 1997-98 – 38 games
Most FAPL Points in Season: 78, 1997-98 and 1998-99 – 38 games

5-Year Record

	Div.	*P*	*W*	*D*	*L*	*F*	*A*	*Pts*	*Pos*	*FAC*	*FLC*
94-95	PL	42	13	12	17	52	49	51	12	3	5
95-96	PL	38	17	12	9	49	32	63	5	3	SF
96-97	PL	38	19	11	8	62	32	68	3	4	4
97-98	PL	38	23	9	6	68	33	78	1	W	SF
98-99	PL	38	22	12	4	59	17	78	2	SF	4

Summary 1998-99

Player	*Tot*	*St*	*Sb*	*Snu*	*PS*	*Gls*	*Y*	*R*	*Fa*	*Fg*	*La*	*Lg*
ADAMS	26	26	0	0	0	1	4	0	5	0	0	0
ANELKA	35	34	1	2	15	17	1	0	5	0	0	0
BERGKAMP	29	28	1	1	6	12	5	0	6	3	1	0
BOA MORTE	8	2	6	4	1	0	0	0	1	1	2	0
BOULD	19	14	5	9	1	0	3	0	4	0	0	0
CABALLERO †	1	0	1	2	0	0	0	0	1	0	1	0
CROWE	0	0	0	0	0	0	0	0	0	0	1	0
DIAWARA †	12	2	10	4	2	0	0	0	3	0	0	0
DIXON	36	36	0	0	3	0	6	1	5	0	0	0
GARDE †	10	6	4	8	2	0	2	0	4	0	2	0
GRIMANDI	8	3	5	14	0	0	1	1	2	0	2	0
GROUDIN	1	1	0	0	0	0	0	0	0	0	2	0
HUGHES	13	4	9	7	0	1	2	0	4	0	2	0
KANU	12	5	7	2	3	6	0	0	5	1	0	0
KEOWN	34	34	0	0	3	1	6	2	4	0	0	0
LJUNDBERG	16	10	6	1	8	1	4	0	3	0	2	0
LUKIC	0	0	0	13	0	0	0	0	0	0	0	0
MANNINGER	6	6	0	24	0	0	1	0	2	0	2	0
MENDEZ	1	0	1	3	0	0	0	0	1	0	2	0
OVERMARS	37	37	0	0	19	6	2	0	7	4	0	0
PARLOUR	35	35	0	0	6	6	4	0	7	0	0	0
PETIT	27	26	1	0	2	4	6	2	3	2	0	0
RIZA	0	0	0	0	0	0	0	0	0	0	1	0
SEAMAN	32	32	0	0	0	0	0	0	5	0	0	0
TAYLOR	0	0	0	1	0	0	0	0	0	0	0	0
UPSON	5	0	5	4	0	0	0	0	1	0	2	0
VERNAZZA	0	0	0	0	0	0	0	0	0	0	0	0
VIEIRA	34	34	0	0	5	3	7	1	5	1	0	0
VIVAS	23	10	13	2	1	0	5	0	6	0	2	1
WREH	12	3	9	4	4	0	0	0	0	0	2	0
WINTERBURN	30	30	0	1	3	0	8	0	6	0	0	0
Own Goals						1						1
32 Players	502	418	84	106	84	59	67	7	95	12	26	2

Paying the Penalty

While Manchester United walked into the record books, Arsenal were left to reflect on what might have been. The Gunners matched the 78 points collected the previous season when they won the Premier League and, had Dennis Bergkamp successfully beaten Peter Schmeichel from the penalty spot in their FA Cup semi-final replay, Arsène Wenger's side could have faced Newcastle in the final for a second successive year.

Arsenal made a steady, if not spectacular, start to the season and were unbeaten for the opening six games, although four were drawn. Indeed just one of 13 games were lost but six draws stopped them from taking charge at the top. While United ended the season with a run of 20 unbeaten Premiership matches, Arsenal were undefeated for 19 games until going down to a crucial defeat at Leeds during the final week of the season. But it was the last game before the long unbeaten run which probably accounted for the Gunners' downfall as a comfortable 2-0 lead at Villa Park was swapped for a shock 3-2 defeat. This was a pivotal point in the season and the only occasion in which they conceded three goals in a Premiership match. In best Arsenal traditions Wenger's side set a new Premiership record by conceding just 17 goals while Nicolas Anelka followed a good first season with the club by notching 17 goals to be the joint second highest scorer in the Premiership. Arsenal were the only Premiership side to complete the league season unbeaten at home.

Arsenal's grip on the FA Cup was maintained through a fortunate win at Preston and a more straightforward success at Wolves before a highly controversial meeting with Sheffield United which, at Wenger's insistence, resulted in the game being replayed after Marc Overmars scored a discredited winner. But after defeating Derby in the quarter-final through Kanu's late goal, the Gunners bowed out to Manchester United after Schmeichel saved a Bergkamp penalty.

If there was a competition in which Arsenal did under-achieve then it was the Champions' League where they fell out at the Group stage, thanks in the main to a poor home record – one win in three games – when the distinction of playing 'home' matches at Wembley was not a total success although attendances supported the move. Arsenal's lack of experienced strength in depth was highlighted more by the results than performances. In reality it was goals conceded in injury time in games against RC Lens and Dynamo Kyiv that cost a place in the later stages.

Wenger was busy strengthening his squad during the close season and having to deal with the winging Nicolas Anelka. ■

Results 1998-99

FA Carling Premiership

Date	*Opponents*	*Ven*	*Res*	*Atten*	*Scorers*
17-Aug	N.Forest	H	2-1	38,064	Petit (58); Overmars (80)
22-Aug	Liverpool	A	0-0	44,429	
29-Aug	Charlton A.	H	0-0	38,014	
09-Sep	Chelsea	A	0-0	34,644	
12-Sep	Leicester C.	A	1-1	21,628	S.Hughes (90)
20-Sep	Manchester U.	H	3-0	38,142	Adams (13); Anelka (44); Ljungberg (84)
27-Sep	Sheffield W.	A	0-1	27,949	
04-Oct	Newcastle U.	H	3-0	38,102	Bergkamp (22, 66 pen); Anelka (29)
17-Oct	Southampton	H	1-1	38,027	Anelka (34)
25-Oct	Blackburn R.	A	2-1	30,867	Anelka (25); Petit (39)
31-Oct	Coventry C.	A	1-0	23,040	Anelka (63)
08-Nov	Everton	H	1-0	38,088	Anelka (6)
14-Nov	Tottenham H.	H	0-0	38,278	
21-Nov	Wimbledon	A	0-1	26,003	
29-Nov	Middlesbrough	H	1-1	38,075	Anelka (89)
05-Dec	Derby Co.	A	0-0	29,018	
13-Dec	Aston Villa	A	2-3	39,217	Bergkamp (14, 45)
20-Dec	Leeds U.	H	3-1	38,025	Bergkamp (28); Vieira (53); Petit (82)
26-Dec	West Ham U.	H	1-0	38,098	Overmars (7)
28-Dec	Charlton A.	A	1-0	20,043	Overmars (53 pen)
09-Jan	Liverpool	H	0-0	38,107	
16-Jan	N.Forest	A	1-0	26,021	Keown (34)
31-Jan	Chelsea	H	1-0	38,121	Bergkamp (32)
06-Feb	West Ham U.	A	4-0	26,042	Bergkamp (35); Overmars (45); Anelka (83); Parlour (87)
17-Feb	Manchester U.	A	1-1	55,171	Anelka (48)
20-Feb	Leicester C.	H	5-0	38,069	Anelka (23, 27, 44); Parlour (42, 48)
28-Feb	Newcastle U.	A	1-1	36,708	Anelka (36)
09-Mar	Sheffield W.	H	3-0	37,792	Bergkamp (83, 88): Kanu (86)
13-Mar	Everton	A	2-0	38,049	Parlour (16); Bergkamp (69 pen)
21-Mar	Coventry C.	H	2-0	38,073	Parlour (16); Overmars (80)
03-Apr	Southampton	A	0-0	15,255	
06-Apr	Blackburn R.	H	1-0	37,762	Bergkamp (42)

19-Apr	Wimbledon	H	5-1	37,982	Parlour (34); Vieira (49); OG (56, Thatcher); Bergkamp (57); Kanu (59)
24-Apr	Middlesbrough	A	6-1	34,630	Overmars (4 pen); Anelka (38, 78); Vieira (58); Kanu (45,60)
02-May	Derby Co.	H	1-0	37,323	Anelka (14)
05-May	Tottenham H.	A	3-1	36,019	Petit (17); Anelka (33); Kanu (85)
11-May	Leeds U.	A	0-1	40,142	
16-May	Aston Villa	H	1-0	38,308	Kanu (66)

UEFA Champions' League

Date	*Opponents*	*Vn*	*Rnd*	*Res*	*Atten*	*Scorers*
16-Sep	RC Lens	A	GpE	1-1	36,000	Overmars (51)
30-Sep	Panathinaikos	H	GpE	2-1	73,455	Adams (65); Keown (73)
21-Oct	Dynamo Kyiv	H	GpE	1-1	73.256	Bergkamp (74)
04-Nov	Dynamo Kyiv	A	GpE	1-3	80,000	Hughes (83)
25-Nov	RC Lens	H	GpE	0-1	73,707	
09-Dec	Panathinaikos	A	GpE	3-1	45,000	OG (65, Asanovic); Anelka (80); Boa Morte (86)

FA Challenge Cup

Sponsored by AXA

Date	*Opponents*	*Vn*	*Rnd*	*Res*	*Atten*	*Scorers*
04-Jan	Preston NE	A	3R	4-2	21,099	Boa Morte (44); Petit (60, 79); Overmars (81)
24-Jan	Wolves	A	4R	2-1	27,511	Overmars (10); Bergkamp (70)
13-Feb	Sheffield U.	H	5R†	2-1	38,020	Vieira (28); Overmars (76)
23-Feb	Sheffield U.	H	5R	2-1	37,161	Overmars (15); Bergkamp (37)
06-Mar	Derby Co.	H	QF	1-0	38,046	Kanu (89)
12-Apr	Manchester U.		SF	0-0	39,217	*(aet. at Villa Park)*
14-Apr	Manchester U.		SFR	1-2	30,223	Bergkamp (69) *(aet. at Villa Park)*

† *Void match*

Worthington Cup

Date	*Opponents*	*Vn*	*Rnd*	*Res*	*Atten*	*Scorers*
28-Oct	Derby Co.	A	3R	2-1	25,621	OG (Carsley, 21); Vivas (55)
11-Nov	Chelsea	H	4R	0-5	37,562	

Aston Villa

Founded in 1874 by cricketers from the Aston Wesleyan Chapel, Lozells, who played on Aston Park, moving to a field in Wellington Road, Perry Barr in 1876. Prominent nationally, the club was a founder member of the Football League in 1888.

The landlord at Perry Barr made such demands that the club sought its own ground and eventually moved back to Aston occupying the Aston Lower Grounds, which had already been used for some big games. Not known as Villa Park until some time later, the ground first saw league football in 1897. Premier League founder members 1992.

Ground: Villa Park, Trinity Rd, Birmingham, B6 6HE
Club No.: 0121-327 2299 **Fax:** 0121-322 2107
Box Office: 0121-327 5353 **CC Bookings:** 0121-607 8000
News: 0891 12 11 48 **Ticket:** 0891 12 18 48
Capacity: 40,530 **Pitch:** 115 yds x 75 yds
Colours: Claret/Blue, White, Blue/Claret
Nickname: The Villains
Radio: 1152AM Sport Extra
Internet: –

President: J.A. Alderson **Chairman:** Doug Ellis
Secretary: Steven Stride
Manager: John Gregory **Assistant:** Allan Evans
Coaches: Steve Harrison, Kevin McDonald
Physio: Jim Walker

League History: 1888 Founder Member of the League; 1936-38 Division 2; 1938-59 Division 1; 1959-60 Division 2; 1960-67 Division 1; 1967-70 Division 2; 1970-72 Division 3; 1972-75 Division 2; 1975-87 Division 1; 1987-88 Division 2; 1988-92 Division 1; 1992- FA Premier League.

Honours: *FA Premier League: Runners-up* 1992-93; *Football League: Division 1 Champions* 1893-94, 1895-96, 1896-97, 1898-99, 1899-1900, 1909-10, 1980-81; *Runners-up* 1888-89, 1902-03, 1907-08, 1910-11, 1912-13, 1913-14, 1930-31, 1932-33, 1989-90; *Division 1 Champions* 1937-38, 1959-60; *Runners-up* 1974-75, 1987-88; *Division 3 Champions* 1971-72. *FA Cup: Winners* 1887, 1895, 1897, 1905, 1913, 1920, 1957; *Runners-up* 1892, 1924. *League-Cup Double Performed:* 1896-97. *Football League Cup: Winners* 1961, 1975, 1977, 1994, 1996; *Runners-*

up 1963, 1971. *Champions' Cup: Winners* 1981-82. *European Super Cup: Winners* 1982-83. *World Club Championship: Runners-up* 1982-83.

European Record: CC (2): 81-82 (W), 82-83 (QF); CWC (0); UEFA (9): 75-76 (1), 77-78 (Q), 83-84 (2), 90-91 (2), 93-94 (2), 94-95 (2), 96-97 (1), 97-98 (QF), 98-99 (2)

Managers: George Ramsay 1884-1926; W.J. Smith 1926-34; Jimmy McMullan 1934-35; Jimmy Hogan 1936-44; Alex Massie 1945-50; George Martin 1950-53; Eric Houghton 1953-58; Joe Mercer 1958-64; Dick Taylor 1965-67; Tommy Cummings 1967-68; Tommy Docherty 1968-70; Vic Crowe 1970-74; Ron Saunders 1974-82; Tony Barton 1982-84; Graham Turner 1984-86; Billy McNeill 1986-87; Graham Taylor 1987-91; Dr Jozef Venglos 1990-91; *(FAPL)* Ron Atkinson June 1991-Nov 1994; Brian Little Nov 94-Feb 98; John Gregory Feb 1998-.

All-Time Records

Record FAPL Win: 7-1 v Wimbledon, Home, 11/02/95
Record FAPL Defeat: 0-5 v Blackburn Rovers, Away, 17/01/96
1-5 v Newcastle United, Away, 27/04/94
Record FL Win: 12-2 v Accrington, Div 1, 12/3/1892
Record FL Defeat: 1-8 v Blackburn Rovers, FAC R3, 16/2/1889
Record Cup Win: 13-0 v Wednesbury Old Athletic, FAC R1, 30/10/1886
Record Fee Received: £12.6m from Manchester United for Dwight Yorke, 8/98
Record Fee Paid: £7m to Liverpool for Stan Collymore, 5/97
Most FL Apps: Charlie Aitken, 561, 1961-76
Most FAPL Apps: 196 – Ugo Ehiogu, 1992-99
Most FAPL Goals: 60 – Dwight Yorke, 1992-99
Highest Scorer in FAPL Season: 17 – Dean Saunders, 1992-93; Dwight Yorke, 1995-96 and 1996-97
Record Attendance (all-time): 76,588 v Derby Co., FAC R6, 2/2/46
Record Attendance (FAPL): 45,347 v Liverpool, 7/5/94
Most FAPL Goals in Season: 57, 1992-93 – 42 games
Most FAPL Points in Season: 74, 1992-93 – 42 games

Summary 1998-99

Player	*Tot*	*St*	*Sb*	*Snu*	*PS*	*Gls*	*Y*	*R*	*Fa*	*Fg*	*La*	*Lg*
BARRY	32	27	5	4	4	2	3	0	2	0	0	0
BOSNICH †	15	15	0	2	0	0	1	0	0	0	0	0
BYFIELD	0	0	0	1	0	0	0	0	0	0	1	0
CALDERWOOD	8	8	0	0	2	0	0	0	0	0	0	0
CHARLES	11	10	1	5	3	1	2	0	1	0	1	0
COLLYMORE	20	11	9	1	3	1	6	1	1	2	0	0
DELANEY	2	0	2	3	0	0	0	0	0	0	0	0
DRAPER	23	13	10	6	7	2	4	0	1	0	1	1
DUBLIN	24	24	0	0	7	11	4	0	0	0	0	0
EHIOGU	25	23	2	1	1	2	3	0	2	0	1	0
ENCKELMAN	0	0	0	6	0	0	0	0	0	0	0	0
FERRARESI	0	0	0	5	0	0	0	0	0	0	0	0
GHENT	0	0	0	2	0	0	0	0	0	0	0	0
GRAYSON	15	4	11	13	1	0	2	0	1	0	1	0
HENDRIE	32	31	1	0	5	3	8	0	2	0	0	0
HUGHES	0	0	0	2	0	0	0	0	0	0	0	0
JASZCZUN	0	0	0	0	0	0	0	0	0	0	1	0
JOACHIM	36	29	7	2	7	14	1	0	2	1	1	0
LEE	0	0	0	1	0	0	0	0	0	0	0	0
LESCOTT	0	0	0	3	0	0	0	0	1	0	0	0
MERSON	26	21	5	1	6	5	2	0	1	0	0	0
OAKES	23	23	0	15	0	0	0	1	2	0	1	0
PETTY	0	0	0	1	0	0	0	0	0	0	0	0
RACHEL	1	0	1	12	0	0	0	0	0	0	0	0
SAMUEL	0	0	0	8	0	0	0	0	0	0	0	0
SCIMECA	18	16	2	4	5	2	3	0	2	0	1	0
SOUTHGATE	38	38	0	0	0	1	5	0	2	0	0	0
STANDING	0	0	0	1	0	0	0	0	0	0	0	0
STONE	10	9	1	0	1	0	1	0	0	0	0	0
TAYLOR	33	31	2	0	5	4	6	0	1	0	1	0
THOMPSON	25	20	5	4	7	2	6	0	0	0	1	0
VASSELL	6	0	6	15	0	0	0	0	1	0	1	0
WATSON	27	26	1	1	6	0	2	1	2	0	1	0
WRIGHT	38	38	0	0	1	0	3	0	2	0	1	0
YORKE †	1	1	0	0	0	0	0	0	0	0	0	0
Own Goals						1						
35 Players	489	418	71	119	71	51	62	3	26	3	14	1

Villa Fizzle Out

Rated as no better than seventh favourites for the championship pre-season, Aston Villa enjoyed a sensational star to the season, with manager John Gregory being the darling of the national media as his humour was in stark contrast to the serious air exuded by many of his contemporaries. By the time new signing Dion Dublin, a £5.75m capture from Coventry, had scored a hat-trick in his second match, taking his total of goals to five in two games, Villa were still undefeated and two points clear of champions Arsenal with a game in hand. Villa's form, though, was not sustained and a run of four winless games, starting with a 4-2 home defeat by Liverpool, signalled the beginning of the end of their championship aspirations. Although Villa had a flurry of three successive wins during April, results following the good start were not impressive as just six of the final 26 games were won. Still, Villa did prove the bookies wrong, albeit by one place, as they finished inside the top seven for a fourth consecutive year.

Dublin's early weeks with the club were sensational as he rattled in nine goals in seven games while Julian Joachim had his most productive season yet at Villa Park with 14 Premiership goals. The youngster, aided and abetted by Dublin took the opportunity thrust his way by the departure of Dwight Yorke to Old Trafford for a mind-boggling £12.6 million.

Looking to the future, Villa can take heart from Gregory's very English-based side which includes a number of highly promising youngsters, amongst them Gareth Barry, Lee Hendrie and Michael Oakes. Another possible star of the future was uncovered in the UEFA Cup when local-born teenager Darius Vassell scored two injury-time goals to clinch a 3-2 home win over Stromsgodset.

But Villa were not without problematical players, none more so than Stan Collymore who virtually left the club, citing stress, which led to a prolonged spell away from Villa Park. Even Paul Merson, re-emerging as an England player, had problems settling at Villa Park following his £6.75m transfer from Middlesbrough in the autumn.

Villa's European venture was brief with Celta Vigo wrapping up a 2nd Round UEFA Cup clash with a 3-1 win at Villa Park and it was also on home soil that Gregory's side was humbled by Fulham in the 4th Round of the FA Cup. The Worthington Cup was exited at the first hurdle with a 4-1 defeat at Chelsea. The season ended with another high-profile departure to Old Trafford, this time in the form of Mark Bosnich whose position was re-filled by David James from Liverpool. ■

Results 1998-99

FA Carling Premiership

Date	*Opponents*	*Ven*	*Res*	*Atten*	*Scorers*
15-Aug	Everton	A	0-0	40,112	
23-Aug	Middlesbrough	H	3-1	29,559	Joachim (6); Charles (52); Thompson (78)
29-Aug	Sheffield W.	A	1-0	25,989	Joachim (37)
09-Sep	Newcastle U.	H	1-0	39,241	Hendrie (63 pen)
12-Sep	Wimbledon	H	2-0	32,959	Merson (45); Taylor (57)
19-Sep	Leeds U.	A	0-0	33,446	
27-Sep	Derby Co.	H	1-0	38,007	Merson (15)
03-Oct	Coventry C.	A	2-1	22,654	Taylor (29, 39)
17-Oct	West Ham U.	A	0-0	26,002	
24-Oct	Leicester C.	H	1-1	39,241	Ehiogu (68)
07-Nov	Tottenham H.	H	3-2	39,241	Dublin (31, 35); Collymore (48)
14-Nov	Southampton	A	4-1	15,242	Dublin (3, 56, 85); Merson
21-Nov	Liverpool	H	2-4	39,241	Dublin (47, 63)
28-Nov	N.Forest	A	2-2	25,753	Joachim (58, 63)
05-Dec	Manchester U.	H	1-1	39,241	Joachim (55)
09-Dec	Chelsea	A	1-2	34,765	Hendrie (31)
13-Dec	Arsenal	H	3-2	39,217	Joachim (62); Dublin (65, 83)
21-Dec	Charlton A.	A	1-0	20,043	OG (3, Rufus)
26-Dec	Blackburn R.	A	1-2	27,536	Scimeca (81)
28-Dec	Sheffield W.	H	2-1	39,217	Southgate (7); Ehiogu (85)
09-Jan	Middlesbrough	A	0-0	34,643	
18-Jan	Everton	H	3-0	32,488	Joachim (40, 51); Merson (78)
30-Jan	Newcastle U.	A	1-2	36,766	Merson (61)
06-Feb	Blackburn R.	H	1-3	37,404	Joachim (69)
17-Feb	Leeds U.	H	1-2	37,510	Scimeca (76)
21-Feb	Wimbledon	A	0-0	15,582	
27-Feb	Coventry C.	H	1-4	38,799	Dublin (55 pen)
10-Mar	Derby Co.	A	1-2	26,836	Thompson (44)
13-Mar	Tottenham H.	A	0-1	35,963	
22-Mar	Chelsea	H	0-3	39,217	
02-Apr	West Ham U.	H	0-0	36,813	
06-Apr	Leicester C.	A	2-2	20,652	Hendrie (2); Joachim (49)
10-Apr	Southampton	H	3-0	32,203	Draper (13); Joachim (66); Dublin (89)
17-Apr	Liverpool	A	1-0	44,306	Taylor (33)
24-Apr	N.Forest	H	2-0	34,492	Draper (45); Barry (57)
01-May	Manchester U.	A	1-2	55,189	Joachim (33)

08-May	Charlton A.	H	3-4	37,705	Barry (7); Joachim (66, 79)
16-May	Arsenal	A	0-1	38,308	

UEFA Cup

Date	*Opponents*	*Vn*	*Rnd*	*Res*	*Atten*	*Scorers*
15-Sep	Strømsgodset	H	1Rf	3-2	28,893	Charles (83); Vassell (90,90)
29-Sep	Strømsgodset	A	1Rs	3-0	5,500	Collymore (19, 23, 64)
		Aston Villa win 6-2 on aggregate				
20-Oct	Celta Vigo	A	2Rf	1-0	27,500	Joachim (15)
03-Nov	Celta Vigo	H	2Rs	1-3	29,910	Collymore (30 pen)
		Celta Vigo win 3-2 on aggregate				

FA Challenge Cup

Sponsored by AXA

Date	*Opponents*	*Vn*	*Rnd*	*Res*	*Atten*	*Scorers*
02-Jan	Hull City	H	3R	3-0	39,217	Collymore (44, 66); Joachim (51)
23-Jan	Fulham	H	4R	0-2	35,260	

Worthington Cup

Date	*Opponents*	*Vn*	*Rnd*	*Res*	*Atten*	*Scorers*
28-Oct	Chelsea	A	3R	1-4	26,790	Draper (10)

5-Year Record

	Div.	*P*	*W*	*D*	*L*	*F*	*A*	*Pts*	*Pos*	*FAC*	*FLC*
94-95	PL	42	11	15	16	51	56	48	18	4	4
95-96	PL	38	18	9	11	52	35	63	4	SF	W
96-97	PL	38	17	10	11	47	34	61	5	4	4
97-98	PL	38	17	6	15	49	48	57	7	5	3
98-99	PL	38	15	10	13	51	46	44	6	4	3

Bradford City

Founded as a football club in 1903 after the club had started life as a rugby side – Manningham RC – which had got into financial difficulties. It worked as the club were immediately voted into the Football League not least because the organising body wished to get a foothold in that part of the country. The club immediately turned professional and within five years were in Division 1 and three years later lifted the FA Cup. Following relegation in 1922 the club bounced around the lower divisions and as recently as 1992 were playing in Division 3. In 1985, 56 people died when the old Main Stand was consumed by flames, after a discarded cigarette butt turned litter into tinder. In 1996 the club won promotion to Division 1 and on the last day of the 1999 season confirmed promotion to the Premier League for the first time since the rugby club played its first game at Valley Parade all those years ago.

Ground: Valley Parade, Bradford, BD8 7DY
Club No.: 01274 773355 **Fax:** 01274 773356
Box Office: 01274 770022 **Info:** 0891 888 640
Capacity: 18,018 **Pitch:** 110 x 73 yards
Colours: Claret and Amber, Black, Black
Nickname: The Bantams
Radio: Bantams 1566 AM; BBC Radio Leeds 92.4FM

Chairman: Geoffrey Richmond **Vice-Chairman:** David Thompson
Secretary: Jon Pollard
Manager: Paul Jewell **Assistant:** Chris Hutchings
Coach: Terry Yorath
Physio: Steve Redmond

League History: 1903-1908 Division 2; 1908-22 Division 1; 1922-27 Division 2; 1927-29 Division 3N; 1929-37 Division 2; 1937-61 Division 3; 1961-69 Division 4; 1969-72 Division 3; 1972-77 Division 4; 1977-78 Division 3; 1978-82 Division 4; 1982-85 Division 3; 1985-90 Division 2; 1990-92 Division 3; 1992-96 Division 2; 1996-99 Division 1; 1999- FAPL.

Honours: *Division 1 Runners-up* 1998-99; *Division 2 Champions* 1907-08; *Division 3 Champions* 1984-85; *Division 3N Champions* 1928-29; *Division 4 Runners-up* 1981-82; *FA Cup Winners* 1910-11.

European Record: Never qualified.

Managers: Robert Campbell 1903-05; Peter O'Rouke 1905-21; David Menzies 1921-26; Colin Veitch 1926-28; Peter O'Rouke 1928-30; Jack Peart 1930-35; Dick Ray 1935-37; Fred Westgarth 1938-43; Bob Sharp 1943-46; Jack Barker 1946-47; John Milburn 1947-48; David Steele 1948-52; Albert Harris 1952; Ivor Powell 1952-55; Peter Jackson 1955-61; Bob Brocklebank 1961-64; Bill Harris 1965-66; Willie Watson 1966-69; Grenville Hair 1967-68; Jimmy Wheeler 1968-71; Bryan Edwards 1971-75; Bobby Kennedy 1975-78; John Napier 1978; George Mulhall 1978-81; Roy McFarland 1981-82; Trevor Cherry 1982-87; Terry Dolan 1987-89; Terry Yorath 1989-90; John Docherty 1990-91; Frank Stapleton 1991-94; Lennie Lawrence 1994-95; Chris Kamara 1995-98; Paul Jewell May 1999-.

All-Time Records

Record FAPL Win: –
Record FAPL Defeat: –
Record FL Win: 11-1 v Rotherham United, Div 3N, 25/08/28
Record FL Defeat: 1-9 v Colchester United, Div 4, 30/12/61
Record Cup Win: 11-3 v Walker Celtic, FAC 1RR, 01/12/37
Record Fee Received: £2m from Newcastle United for Des Hamilton, 3/97
Record Fee Paid: £1.3m to Arsenal for Isaiah Rankin, 8/98
Most FL Apps: 502: Cec Podd, 1970-84
Most FAPL Apps: –
Most FAPL Goals: –
Highest Scorer in FAPL Season: –
Record Attendance (all-time): 39,146 v Burnley, FAC 4R, 11/03/1911
Record Attendance (FAPL): –
Most FAPL Goals in Season: –
Most FAPL Points in Season: –

5-Year Record

	Div.	*P*	*W*	*D*	*L*	*F*	*A*	*Pts*	*Pos*	*FAC*	*FLC*
94-95	2	46	16	12	18	57	64	60	14	1	2
95-96	2	46	22	7	17	71	69	73	6	3	5
96-97	1	46	12	12	22	47	72	48	21	5	1
97-98	1	46	14	15	17	46	59	57	13	3	1
98-99	1	46	26	9	11	82	47	87	2	4	3

Summary 1998-99

Player	*Tot*	*St*	*Sb*	*Snu*	*PS*	*Gls*	*Y*	*R*	*Fa*	*Fg*	*La*	*Lg*
BEAGRIE	43	43	0	0	5	12	4	0	2	0	5	3
BLAKE	39	35	4	0	11	16	1	0	2	0	3	1
BOLLAND	2	2	0	2	1	0	0	0	0	0	2	0
BOWER	0	0	0	1	0	0	0	0	0	0	0	0
DREYER	21	19	2	3	0	0	2	1	0	0	5	0
EDINHO	3	1	2	1	1	0	0	0	0	0	1	0
GRANT	5	1	4	3	1	0	0	0	0	0	2	0
JACOBS	44	42	2	0	3	3	4	0	2	0	3	0
LAWRENCE	35	33	2	0	2	2	3	0	2	1	3	0
MCCALL	43	43	0	0	3	3	8	0	2	0	3	0
MILLS	44	44	0	0	9	24	2	2	2	1	4	0
MOORE	44	44	0	0	0	3	6	0	2	0	5	1
O'BRIEN	31	19	12	13	3	0	2	0	1	0	3	0
PEPPER	9	5	4	6	1	1	2	0	0	0	2	1
PRUDHOE	0	0	0	1	0	0	0	0	0	0	0	0
RAMAGE	3	0	3	8	0	0	1	0	0	0	1	0
RANKIN	27	15	12	11	7	5	0	0	1	0	2	1
SHARPE	9	6	3	0	2	2	0	0	0	0	0	0
STEINER	0	0	0	1	0	0	0	0	0	0	1	0
TODD	14	13	1	5	3	0	0	0	0	0	2	0
VERITY	0	0	0	1	0	0	0	0	0	0	0	0
WALSH	46	46	0	0	0	0	2	0	2	0	5	0
WATSON	18	5	13	4	6	4	0	0	0	0	4	0
WESTWOOD	19	17	2	5	3	2	2	1	2	0	0	0
WHALLEY	45	45	0	0	3	2	1	0	2	0	5	0
WINDASS	12	6	6	0	4	3	2	0	0	0	0	0
WRIGHT	23	22	1	0	5	0	1	0	2	0	3	0
27 Players	579	506	73	65	73	82	43	4	24	2	64	7

Jewell Valley

The bookies took a dim view of Bradford City's chances of playing top-flight football for the first time since 1922 and rated them no higher than 12th favourites for promotion to the Premiership. Bantams chairman Geoffrey Richmond took a different view, however, and insisted that the club from the ninth biggest city in England should be at the cutting edge of English football.

Manager Paul Jewell brought in five players, of whom Stuart McCall was the most experienced and Gareth Whalley, from Crewe, the most expensive at £600,000. But early in the season Jewell soon smashed City's transfer record to bring in Isaiah Rankin from Arsenal for £1.3m and Lee Mills from Port Vale for £1m. Mills wasted little time in settling at Valley Parade and, with 25 goals, was City's top scorer.

Bradford's start to the season was highly unimpressive as just one point was collected from four games, which left Jewell's side rooted to the foot of the table. A win at home to Birmingham on the final day of August got the bandwagon going. Such was the transition that a 3-0 win over Bury on 9 October took Bradford to seventh but City had to wait another month before clambering into the top six on the back of Peter Beagrie's winning penalty at Tranmere. Bradford didn't move into the automatic promotion places until 16 January when Mills became the first City player for five years to score a hat-trick as Crewe were beaten 4-1. Birmingham ended the eight-match undefeated run but Bradford confirmed their promotion push when taking four points from Watford and Ipswich.

Such was the intensity of the promotion race that five wins in six matches still only had Bradford ahead of Ipswich in second place on goals scored in mid-April and it was with a thrilling last day of the season 3-2 victory at Wolves that promotion was finally secured. That result, in turn, denied the home side a shot at the play-offs.

As with the other two promoted sides, Bradford came up against Premier League opposition in the knock-out competitions but failed to notch a victory as Newcastle removed them from the 4th Round of the FA Cup and Leeds did likewise in the Worthington Cup.

In preparation for their first ever season in the Premier League, manager Jewell was quick off the mark to add experience to his squad by snapping up Gunnar Halle from Leeds United for a bargain £200,000. What other deals he will have done by the start of the 1999-2000 season will go a long way to deciding if Bradford City are to have any chance of remaining a Premiership club past the first year of the century. ■

Results 1998-99

Nationwide Division 1

Date	*Opponents*	*Ven*	*Res*	*Atten*	*Scorers*
08-Aug	Stockport Co.	H	1-2	14,360	Beagrie (75 pen)
15-Aug	Watford	A	0-1	10,731	
23-Aug	Bolton W.	H	2-2	13,163	Rankin (42); Mills (89)
28-Aug	Crewe Alex.	A	1-2	5,759	McCall (38);
31-Aug	Birmingham C.	H	2-1	13,910	Mills (60); Moore (73)
08-Sep	Ipswich T.	A	0-3	11,596	
12-Sep	Sheffield U.	H	2-2	13,169	McCall (17); Blake (28)
20-Sep	WBA	A	2-0	12,426	Mills (4, 16)
26-Sep	Barnsley	H	2-1	15,887	Watson (86, 89)
29-Sep	Port Vale	H	4-0	13,245	Blake (31); Moore (57); Mills (60); OG (90, Beesley)
03-Oct	Sunderland	A	0-0	37,828	
09-Oct	Bury	H	3-0	15,697	Blake (15); McCall (55); Beagrie (67)
17-Oct	Grimsby T.	A	0-2	7,473	
20-Oct	Portsmouth	A	4-2	10,062	Whalley (22); Rankin (32); Mills (33); Beagrie (80)
31-Oct	Bristol C.	H	5-0	14,468	Mills (7); OG (14,Carey); Rankin (51); Beagrie (57); Blake (90)
07-Nov	Norwich C.	A	2-2	14,722	Rankin (19); Mills (89)
10-Nov	Tranmere R.	A	1-0	6,002	Beagrie (44 pen)
14-Nov	Swindon T.	H	3-0	14,897	Beagrie (48 pen); Pepper (79); Jacobs (90)
21-Nov	Huddersfield T.	A	1-2	18,173	Blake (18)
28-Nov	QPR	H	0-3	15,037	
05-Dec	Oxford U.	A	1-0	5,969	Mills (22)
12-Dec	Swindon T.	A	4-1	7,447	Blake (20, 83); Mills (48, 61)
19-Dec	Wolverhampton	H	2-1	13,846	Blake (20); Mills (50)
26-Dec	Bolton W.	A	0-0	24,625	
28-Dec	Tranmere R.	H	2-0	14,076	Blake (27); Mills (61)
09-Jan	Stockport Co.	A	2-1	8,975	Blake (9); Beagrie (72)
16-Jan	Crewe Alex.	H	4-1	12,595	Mills (24, 41, 55); Blake (67)
19-Jan	Crystal Palace	H	2-1	14,368	Westwood (75); Beagrie (87 pen)
31-Jan	Birmingham C.	A	1-2	19,291	Lawrence (27)
06-Feb	Watford	H	2-0	14,142	McCall (8); Mills (62)
13-Feb	Ipswich T.	H	0-0	15,024	
19-Feb	Sheffield U.	A	2-2	14,675	Blake (32, 82)

27-Feb	WBA	H	1-0	14,278	Jacobs (2)
03-Mar	Barnsley	A	1-0	16,866	Watson (75)
09-Mar	Sunderland	H	0-1	15,124	
13-Mar	Norwich C.	H	4-1	13,331	Moore (12); Beagrie (25 pen); Mills (34); Lawrence (45)
20-Mar	Bristol C.	A	3-2	10,870	Mills (30); Jacobs (40); Whalley (83)
28-Mar	Crystal Palace	A	0-1	15,626	
03-Apr	Grimsby T.	H	3-0	14,522	Blake (11); Sharpe (76); Beagrie (90)
05-Apr	Bury	A	2-0	8,000	Windass (28, 43)
10-Apr	Portsmouth	H	2-1	13,552	Mills (26); Sharpe (35)
13-Apr	Port Vale	A	1-1	6,998	Mills (33)
17-Apr	Huddersfield T.	H	2-3	15,124	Blake (8); Windass (71)
24-Apr	QPR	A	3-1	11,641	Beagrie (33); Westwood (62); Watson (90)
01-May	Oxford U.	H	0-0	15,064	
09-May	Wolves	A	3-2	27,589	Beagrie (25); Mills (40); Blake (65)

FA Challenge Cup

Sponsored by AXA

Date	*Opponents*	*Vn*	*Rnd*	*Res*	*Atten*	*Scorers*
02-Jan	Grimsby T.	H	3R	2-1	13,870	Mills (29); Lawrence (66)
23-Jan	Newcastle U.	A	4R	0-3	36,698	

Worthington Cup

Date	*Opponents*	*Vn*	*Rnd*	*Res*	*Atten*	*Scorers*
11-Aug	Lincoln C.	H	1Rf	1-1	4,481	Beagrie (89)
18-Aug	Lincoln C.	A	1Rs	1-0	3,066	Rankin (74)
	Bradford City win 2-1 on aggregate					
15-Sep	Halifax T.	A	2Rf	2-1	5,714	Moore (32); Beagrie (68)
22-Sep	Halifax T.	H	2Rs	3-1	6,237	Blake (56); Beagrie (77 pen); Pepper (82)
	Bradford City win 5-2 on aggregate					
28-Oct	Leeds U.	A	3R	0-1	27,561	

Chelsea

Founded in 1905. The Mears brothers developed Stamford Bridge Athletic Ground, which they owned, into a football stadium for prestigious matches and, prospectively, nearby Fulham FC. But Fulham did not take up the chance so the Mears brothers established their own club, rejecting possible names such as 'London' and 'Kensington' in favour, eventually, of Chelsea. Judging that the club would not be accepted into the Southern League, it sought membership of the Football League. This was gained at the first attempt and it started the 1906-07 season in Division Two. Premier League founder members 1992. Completed League Cup and Cup-Winners' Cup double in 1997-98.

Ground: Stamford Bridge, London SW6 1HS
Phone: 0171-385 5545
Box Office: 0171-386 7799 **CC Booking:** 0171-386 7799
News: 0891 12 11 59 **Tickets:** 0891 12 10 11
Capacity: 34,900 > 41,000 **Pitch:** 113 yds x 74 yds
Colours: Royal Blue, Royal Blue, White
Nickname: The Blues
Radio: 1548AM Capital Gold
Internet: www.chelseafc.co.uk

Patron: Ruth Harding **Chairman:** Ken Bates
MD: Colin Hutchinson **Secretary:** Keith Lacy
Manager: Gianluca Vialli **Assistant:** Gwyn Williams
Coach: Graham Rix **Physio:** Mike Banks

League History: 1905 Elected to Division 2; 1907-10 Division 1; 1910-12 Division 2; 1912-24 Division 1; 1924-30 Division 2; 1930-62 Division 1; 1962-63 Division 2; 1963-75 Division 1; 1975-77 Division 2; 1977-79 Division 1; 1979-84 Division 2; 1984-88 Division 1; 1988-89 Division 2; 1989-92 Division 1; 1992- FA Premier League.

Honours: *Football League: Division 1 Champions* 1954-55; *Division 2 Champions* 1983-84, 1988-89; *Runners-up* 1906-07, 1911-12, 1929-30,1962-63, 1976-77. *FA Cup: Winners* 1969-70, 1996-97; *Runners-up* 1914-15, 1966-67, 1993-94. *Football League Cup: Winners* 1964-65, 1997-98; *Runners-up* 1971-72. *Cup-Winners' Cup: Winners* 1970-71, 1997-98. *Full Members' Cup: Winners* 1985-86. *Zenith Data Systems Cup: Winners* 1989-90.

European Record: CC (0) – ; CWC (5): 70-71 (W), 71-72 (2), 94-95 (SF), 97-98 (W), 99-98 (F); UEFA (3): 58-60(QF), 65-66 (SF), 68-69 (2).

Managers: John Tait Robertson 1905-07; David Calderhead 1907-33; A. Leslie Knighton 1933-39; Billy Birrell 1939-52; Ted Drake 1952-61; Tommy Docherty 1962-67; Dave Sexton 1967-74; Ron Stuart 1974-75; Eddie McCreadie 1975-77; Ken Shellito 1977-78; Danny Blanchflower 1978-79; Geoff Hurst 1979-81; John Neal 1981-85 (Director to 1986); John Hollins 1985-88; Bobby Campbell 1988-91; *(FAPL)* Ian Porterfield June 1991-1993; Dave Webb 1993; Glenn Hoddle July 1993-June 1996; Ruud Gullit June 96-Feb 98; Gianluca Vialli Feb 1998-.

All-Time Records

Record FAPL Win: 6-0 v Barnsley, Away, 24/08/97
6-1 v Tottenham H., Away, 06/12/97
6-2 v Crystal Palace, Home, 11/03/98
Record FAPL Defeat: 1-4 v Leeds United, Away, 06/11/93,
1-4 v Manchester United, Home, 21/10/95
2-4 on five separate occasions
Record FL Win: 9-2 v Glossop NE, Div 2, 01/09/1906
Record FL Defeat: 1-8 v Wolverhampton W., Div 1, 26/09/53
Record Cup Win: 13-0 v Jeunesse Hautcharage (Lux), CWC 1Rf, 29/09/71
Record Fee Received: £2.5m from QPR for John Spencer, 11/96
Rccord Fee Paid: £5.4m to Lazio for Pierluigi Casiraghi, 7/98
Most FL Apps: Ron Harris, 655, 1962-80
Most FAPL Apps: 195 – Dennis Wise, 1992-99
Most FAPL Goals: 36 – John Spencer, 1992-97
Highest Scorer in FAPL Season: 13 – Mark Stein, 1993-94 and John Spencer, 1995-96
Record Attendance (all-time): 82,905 v Arsenal, Div 1, 12/10/35
Record Attendance (FAPL): 37,064 v Manchester United, 11/9/93
Most FAPL Goals in Season: 71, 1997-98 – 38 games
Most FAPL Points in Season: 75, 1998-99 – 38 games

5-Year Record

	Div.	*P*	*W*	*D*	*L*	*F*	*A*	*Pts*	*Pos*	*FAC*	*FLC*
94-95	PL	42	13	15	14	50	55	54	11	4	3
95-96	PL	38	12	14	12	46	44	50	11	SF	2
96-97	PL	38	16	11	11	58	55	59	6	W	3
97-98	PL	38	20	3	15	71	43	63	4	3	W
98-99	PL	38	20	15	3	57	30	75	3	QF	QF

Summary 1998-99

Player	Tot	St	Sb	Snu	PS	Gls	Y	R	Fa	Fg	La	Lg
BABAYARO	28	26	2	0	3	3	6	0	5	0	3	0
CASIRAGHI	10	10	0	0	7	1	2	0	0	0	0	0
CLEMENT	0	0	0	0	0	0	0	0	0	0	2	0
DE GOEY	35	35	0	1	1	0	2	0	6	0	0	0
DESAILLY	31	30	1	0	2	0	5	0	6	0	0	0
DI MATTEO	30	26	4	1	7	2	9	0	6	1	2	0
DUBERRY	25	18	7	6	2	0	8	0	2	0	3	0
FERRER	30	30	0	1	2	0	9	0	2	0	1	0
FLO	30	18	12	2	4	10	2	0	3	0	3	1
FORSSELL	10	4	6	4	3	1	0	0	3	2	0	0
GOLDBAEK	23	13	10	3	4	5	2	0	6	0	2	0
HARLEY	0	0	0	0	0	0	0	0	0	0	1	0
HITCHCOCK	3	2	1	35	0	0	0	0	0	0	0	0
KHARINE	1	1	0	1	0	0	0	0	0	0	3	0
LAMBOURDE	17	12	5	7	2	0	3	0	2	0	3	0
LAUDRUP	7	5	2	0	3	0	0	0	0	0	0	0
LEBOEUF	33	33	0	0	3	4	8	1	4	1	2	2
LE SAUX	31	30	1	0	6	0	4	1	6	0	0	0
MORRIS	18	14	4	8	8	1	4	0	5	0	2	0
MYERS	1	1	0	1	1	0	0	0	2	0	0	0
NEWTON	7	1	6	7	0	0	0	0	1	0	0	0
NICHOLLS	9	0	9	11	0	0	0	0	3	0	2	0
PERCASSI	0	0	0	0	0	0	0	0	0	0	1	0
PETRESCU	32	23	9	1	7	4	8	0	4	0	3	0
POYET	28	21	7	0	7	11	4	0	0	0	2	2
TERRY	2	0	2	8	0	0	0	0	3	0	1	0
VIALLI	9	9	0	0	1	1	3	1	3	2	3	5
WISE	22	21	1	1	1	0	8	1	5	1	3	0
ZOLA	37	35	2	1	17	13	1	0	6	1	0	0
Own Goals						1						
29 Players	509	418	91	99	91	57	88	4	83	8	42	10

Entertaining Blues

Managed by an Italian, Gianluca Vialli, and packed with nationals from more than a dozen different countries, Chelsea provided the most cosmopolitan and entertaining side in the Premier League during the 1998-99 season. But unlike the two previous seasons, the team failed to bring any silverware to Stamford Bridge. Vialli made six summer signings to bolster the club's championship push with Pierluigi Casiraghi, World Cup winner Marcel Desailly and Albert Ferrer leading the way at a combined cost of £12.2m; Casiraghi's campaign was swiftly ended by a serious injury.

For the second successive year Chelsea lost on the opening day to Coventry but it was to be their last reversal until going down 1-0 to Arsenal at the end of January. That result, coupled with Manchester United winning at Charlton, conspired to topple Chelsea from the top of the table after a 21-match unbeaten run had threatened to end a 44-year wait to be crowned English champions. A spell of five wins in six games to mid-April kept the dream alive but three successive draws, including a 2-2 draw with Leicester after leading 2-0, effectively saw the title slip away, as Vialli was quick to acknowledge.

The overseas influence was highlighted no better than by Jody Morris who scored Chelsea's first league goal of the season by an Englishman on 17 February! The brilliant Zola was top scorer and he was followed closely by Poyet and Flo.

Chelsea lost as few games as the eventual champions, conceded the second least goals and were just four points adrift of the top spot. Nevertheless they will be disappointed not to have weakened United's grip on the domestic game, which they would have had a better chance of doing had they not lost the highly influential Poyet to injury for a large chunk of the season.

Chelsea were fancied to retain the Cup Winners' Cup but, after seeing off pretty much second-rate opposition, they surprisingly fell in the semi-finals to Real Mallorca. The Blues progressed to the last eight of the FA Cup before Manchester United, against whom they drew both league matches, soaked up endless pressure before winning 2-0 at the Bridge. Vialli, who announced his retirement from playing at the end of the season, scored in three rounds of the Worthington Cup before his side lost at Wimbledon in the quarter-finals.

The ill-discipline of club captain Dennis Wise remains a worry as he added four more red cards to his already unimpressive poor record. ■

Results 1998-99

FA Carling Premiership

Date	*Opponents*	*Ven*	*Res*	*Atten*	*Scorers*
15-Aug	Coventry C.	A	1-2	23,042	Poyet (37)
22-Aug	Newcastle U.	H	1-1	34,795	Babayaro (23)
09-Sep	Arsenal	H	0-0	34,644	
12-Sep	N.Forest	H	2-1	34,809	Zola (1); Poyet (35)
21-Sep	Blackburn R.	A	4-3	23,113	Zola (15); Leboeuf (51 pen); Flo (82, 86)
27-Sep	Middlesbrough	H	2-0	34,811	OG (26, Pallister); Zola (81)
04-Oct	Liverpool	A	1-1	44,404	Casiraghi (10)
17-Oct	Charlton A.	H	2-1	34,639	Leboeuf (18 pen); Poyet (88)
24-Oct	Leeds U.	A	0-0	36,292	
08-Nov	West Ham U.	A	1-1	26,023	Babayaro (76)
14-Nov	Wimbledon	H	3-0	34,757	Zola (32); Poyet (55); Petrescu (70)
21-Nov	Leicester C.	A	4-2	21,401	Zola (28, 90); Poyet (39); Flo (56)
28-Nov	Sheffield W.	H	1-1	34,451	Zola (27)
05-Dec	Everton	A	0-0	36,430	
09-Dec	Aston Villa	H	2-1	34,765	Zola (29); Flo (90)
12-Dec	Derby Co.	A	2-2	29,056	Flo (55); Poyet (59)
16-Dec	Manchester U.	A	1-1	55,159	Zola (83)
19-Dec	Tottenham H.	H	2-0	34,881	Poyet (80); Flo (90)
26-Dec	Southampton	A	2-0	15,253	Flo (20); Poyet (48)
29-Dec	Manchester U.	H	0-0	34,741	
09-Jan	Newcastle U.	A	1-0	36,711	Petrescu (39)
16-Jan	Coventry C.	H	2-1	34,869	Leboeuf (45); DiMatteo (90)
31-Jan	Arsenal	A	0-1	38,121	
06-Feb	Southampton	H	1-0	34,920	Zola (11)
17-Feb	Blackburn R.	H	1-1	34,382	Morris (43)
20-Feb	N.Forest	A	3-1	26,351	Forssell (6); Goldbaek (25, 83)
27-Feb	Liverpool	H	2-1	34,822	Leboeuf (7 pen); Goldbaek (38)
13-Mar	West Ham U.	H	0-1	34,765	
22-Mar	Aston Villa	A	3-0	39,217	Flo (59, 90); Goldbaek (86)
03-Apr	Charlton A.	A	1-0	20,046	Di Matteo (11)
11-Apr	Wimbledon	A	2-1	21,577	Flo (24); Poyet (53)
14-Apr	Middlesbrough	A	0-0	34,406	
18-Apr	Leicester C.	H	2-2	34,535	Zola (30); Petrescu (69)
25-Apr	Sheffield W.	A	0-0	21,652	
01-May	Everton	H	3-1	34,909	Zola (25, 81); Petrescu (50)
05-May	Leeds U.	H	1-0	34,762	Poyet (68)

10-May	Tottenham H.	A	2-2	36,878	Poyet (4); Goldbaek (72)
16-May	Derby Co.	H	2-1	35,016	Babayaro (40); Vialli (68)

Cup-Winners' Cup

Date	*Opponents*	*Vn*	*Rnd*	*Res*	*Atten*	*Scorers*
17-Sep	Helsingborgs	H	1f	1-0	17,714	Leboeuf (43)
01-Oct	Helsingborgs	A	1s	0-0	12,348	
			Chelsea win 1-0 on aggregate			
22-Oct	FC København	H	2f	1-1	21,207	Desailly (90)
05-Nov	FC København	A	2s	1-0	25,118	Laudrup (32)
			Chelsea win 2-1 on aggregate			
04-Mar	Vålerenga IF	H	QFf	3-0	34,177	Babayaro (9); Zola (30); Wise (85)
18-Mar	Vålerenga IF	A	QFs	3-2	17,936	Vialli (12); Lambourde (15); Flo (33)
			Chelsea win 6-2 on aggregate			
08-Apr	R.Mallorca	H	SFf	1-1	32,524	Flo (50)
22-Apr	R.Mallorca	A	SFs	0-1	10,848	
			Real Mallorca win 2-1 on aggregate			

FA Challenge Cup

Sponsored by AXA

Date	*Opponents*	*Vn*	*Rnd*	*Res*	*Atten*	*Scorers*
02-Jan	Oldham A.	A	3R	2-0	12,770	Vialli (68, 75)
25-Jan	Oxford U.	A	4R	1-1	9,059	Leboeuf (90 pen)
03-Feb	Oxford U.	H	4RR	4-2	32,106	Wise (12); Zola (39); Forssell (46, 53)
13-Feb	Sheffield W.	A	5R	1-0	29,410	Di Matteo (85)
07-Mar	Manchester U.	A	QF	0-0	54,587	
10-Mar	Manchester U.	H	QFR	0-2	33,075	

Worthington Cup

Date	*Opponents*	*Vn*	*Rnd*	*Res*	*Atten*	*Scorers*
28-Oct	Aston Villa	H	3R	4-1	26,790	Vialli (32, 67, 85); Flo (71)
11-Nov	Arsenal	A	4R	5-0	37,562	Leboeuf (pen 34, 73); Vialli (49); Poyet (65, 80)
01-Dec	Wimbledon	A	QF	1-2	19,286	Vialli (85)

Coventry City

Founded as Singer's FC, cycle manufacturers, in 1883. Joined the Birmingham and District League in 1894; in 1898 changed name to Coventry City; and in 1905 moved to the Athletic Ground, Highfield Road. Elected to Division One of the Southern League in 1908, but relegated to the Second in 1914.

Joined the Wartime Midland Section of the Football League in 1918 and elected to an expanded Second Division of the Football League for 1919-20. Founder members of the Fourth Division in 1958. Promoted to Division One for the first time in 1967 and never relegated. Premier League founder members 1992.

Ground:	Highfield Road Stadium, King Richard St, Coventry, CV2 4FW	
Phone:	01203-234000	**Fax:** 01203-234099
Box Office:	01203-234020	**CC Booking:** 01203-578000
News:	0891 12 11 66	
Capacity:	24,021	**Pitch:** 110 yds x 75 yds
Colours:	All Sky Blue	**Nickname:** Sky Blues
Radio:	95.6FM BBC Radio West Midlands	
Internet:	www.ccfc.co.uk	

President:	Eric Grove	
Chairman:	Bryan Richardson	**Secretary:** Graham Hover
Manager:	Gordon Strachan OBE	**Assistant:** Alec Miller
Physio:	George Dalton	

League History: 1919 Elected to Division 2; 1925-26 Division 3 (N); 1926-36 Division 3 (S); 1936-52 Division 2; 1952-58 Division 3 (S); 1958-59 Division 4; 1959-64 Division 3; 1964-67 Division 2; 1967-92 Division 1; 1992- FA Premier League.

Honours: *Football League: Division 2 Champions* 1966-67; *Division 3 Champions* 1963-64; *Division 3 (S) Champions* 1935-36; *Runners-up* 1933-34; *Division 4 Runners-up* 1958-59. *FA Cup: Winners* 1986-87.

European Record: CC (0) – ; CWC (0) – ; UEFA (1): 70-71 (2)

Managers: H.R. Buckle 1909-10; Robert Wallace 1910-13; Frank Scott-Walford 1913-15; William Clayton 1917-19; H. Pollitt 1919-20; Albert Evans 1920-24; Jimmy Kerr 1924-28; James McIntyre 1928-31; Harry

Storer 1931-45; Dick Bayliss 1945-47; Billy Frith 1947-48; Harry Storer 1948-53; Jack Fairbrother 1953-54; Charlie Elliott 1954-55; Jesse Carver 1955-56; Harry Warren 1956-57; Billy Frith 1957-61; Jimmy Hill 1961-67; Noel Cantwell 1967-72; Bob Dennison 1972; Joe Mercer 1972-75; Gordon Milne 1972-81; Dave Sexton 1981-83; Bobby Gould 1983-84; Don Mackay 1985-86; George Curtis 1986-87 (became MD); John Sillett 1987-90; Terry Butcher 1990-92; Don Howe 1992; *(FAPL)* Bobby Gould July 1992-93; Phil Neal Nov 1993-Feb 1995; Ron Atkinson Feb 1995-Nov 1996; Gordon Strachan Nov 1996-.

All-Time Records

Record FAPL Win: 5-0 v Blackburn Rovers, Home, 09/12/95
5-1 v Liverpool, Home, 19/12/92
5-1 v Bolton Wanderers 97-98, 31/1/98
Record FAPL Defeat: 0-5 v Manchester United, 28/12/92
1-5 v QPR, Away, 23/10/93
1-5 v Sheffield W., Away, 27/10/94
1-5 v Newcastle United, 19/09/98
Record FL Win: 9-0 v Bristol C, Div 3(S), 28/4/34
Record FL Defeat: 2-10 v Norwich C, Div 3(S), 15/3/30
Record Cup Win: 7-0 v Scunthorpe U, FAC R1, 24/11/34
Record Fee Received: £6m from Aston Villa for Dion Dublin
Record Fee Paid: £3.25m to Grasshopper-Club for Viorel Moldovan, 12/97
Most FL+PL Apps: Steve Ogrizovic, 504, 1998-99
Most FAPL Apps: 188 – Steve Ogrizovic, 1992-99
Most FAPL Goals: 62 – Dion Dublin, 1992-99
Highest Scorer in FAPL Season: 18 – Dion Dublin, 1997-98
Record Attendance (all-time): 51,455 v Wolves, Div 2, 29/4/67
Record Attendance (FAPL): 24,410 v Manchester United 12/04/93
Most FAPL Goals in Season: 62, 1992-93 – 42 games
Most FAPL Points in Season: 56, 1993-94 – 42 games

5-Year Record

	Div.	*P*	*W*	*D*	*L*	*F*	*A*	*Pts*	*Pos*	*FAC*	*FLC*
94-95	PL	42	12	14	16	44	62	50	16	4	3
95-96	PL	38	8	14	16	42	60	38	16	4	4
96-97	PL	38	9	14	15	38	54	41	17	5	3
97-98	PL	38	12	16	10	46	44	52	11	6	4
98-99	PL	38	11	9	18	39	51	42	15	5	3

Summary 1998-99

Player	*Tot*	*St*	*Sb*	*Snu*	*PS*	*Gls*	*Y*	*R*	*Fa*	*Fg*	*La*	*Lg*
ALOISI	16	7	9	2	3	5	0	1	2	0	0	0
BOATENG	33	29	4	1	4	4	10	0	3	1	3	1
BOLAND	0	0	0	0	0	0	0	0	0	0	1	0
BREEN	25	21	4	6	5	0	3	0	1	0	2	0
BRIGHTWELL	0	0	0	0	0	0	0	0	0	0	1	0
BURROWS	23	23	0	0	6	0	7	0	3	0	2	0
CLEMENT	12	6	6	6	3	0	1	0	2	0	2	0
DAISH	0	0	0	1	0	0	0	0	0	0	0	0
DELORGE	0	0	0	1	0	0	0	0	0	0	0	0
DUBLIN	10	10	0	0	0	3	1	0	0	0	2	1
EDWORTHY	22	16	6	7	3	0	3	0	1	0	0	0
FROGGATT	23	23	0	0	0	1	3	0	3	2	0	0
GIOACCHINI	3	0	3	3	0	0	0	0	0	0	0	0
M. HALL	5	2	3	3	0	0	1	0	0	0	1	0
P. HALL	9	2	7	4	2	0	0	0	0	0	2	1
HAWORTH	1	1	0	2	0	0	0	0	0	0	0	0
HEDMAN	36	36	0	1	0	0	2	0	3	0	3	0
HUCKERBY	34	31	3	0	10	9	7	0	3	3	2	0
JACKSON	3	0	3	3	0	0	0	0	0	0	0	0
KIRKLAND	0	0	0	9	0	0	0	0	0	0	0	0
KONJIC	4	3	1	7	1	0	2	0	0	0	0	0
McALLISTER	29	29	0	0	8	3	5	0	3	1	1	0
McSHEFFREY	1	0	1	0	0	0	0	0	0	0	0	0
NILSSON	28	28	0	1	6	0	0	0	2	0	0	0
OGRIZOVIC	2	2	0	27	0	0	0	0	0	0	0	0
QUINN	7	6	1	3	1	0	1	0	0	0	1	0
SHAW	37	36	1	1	0	0	2	0	3	0	3	0
SHILTON	5	1	4	11	1	0	0	0	1	0	2	0
SOLTVEDT	27	21	6	11	6	2	2	0	3	0	3	1
STRACHAN	0	0	0	0	0	0	0	0	0	0	1	0
TELFER	32	30	2	2	4	2	11	0	3	1	2	0
WALLEMME	6	4	2	2	1	0	2	0	0	0	2	0
WHELAN	31	31	0	0	2	10	9	0	3	2	2	1
WILLIAMS	22	20	2	8	2	0	3	0	2	0	2	0
Own Goals										1		
34 Players	486	418	68	122	68	39	75	1	41	11	40	5

Last Day Pleasure

Coventry City had the rare pleasure of playing their final league match of the season knowing that their Premier League status was not under threat. But it was far from plain sailing for Gordon Strachan's side who went into the New Year just two points above the relegation pack, having lost exactly half of their opening 20 league games. By the time of a trip to Midlands rivals Aston Villa at the end of February, the Sky Blues had slipped into the bottom three when their fortunes changed dramatically with a 4-1 success which was followed by a home win over fellow strugglers Charlton. Victories over Sheffield Wednesday and Southampton over Easter just about ended the relegation fears, only for three successive defeats to bring about more furrowed brows before four points from games with Wimbledon and Derby ensured Premier League survival.

Manager Gordon Strachan delved little in the transfer market during the summer with Phillippe Clement and Jean-Guy Wallemme being his major signings for a combined fee of just £1.3m. The Sky Blues had money in the bank following the £4m sale of Viorel Moldovan after less than a season at Highfield Road and in November almost £6m was gathered from Dion Dublin's move to Villa. Following Dublin's departure the mantle of top goalscorer passed to Noel Whelan while Darren Huckleby's star failed to glow as brightly as a year before and he ended the season with nine Premiership goals but will undoubtedly come good again. He did have the honour of scoring City's only hat-tricks of the season as Forest were thrashed 4-0 in the league and Macclesfield 7-0 in the FA Cup. Injuries again blighted the form of veteran midfielder Gary McAllister but Swedish goalkeeper Marcus Hedman firmly established himself as the club's number one keeper and enhanced his reputation in two internationals against England. Coventry were involved in a bizarre transfer deal which saw Robert Jarni join from Real Betis for £2.6m but then sign for Real Madrid a week later for £3.25m.

City's most embarrassing moment came in a 2-0 Worthington Cup defeat at Luton while in the FA Cup the thrashing of Macclesfield was followed by a commendable 3-0 win at Leicester before a seven-match unbeaten record at Highfield Road was cut short by Everton.

Having moved one step away from the normal last-day nail-biter, Coventry fans will be hoping that that small but considerable building blocks can be built upon with a 'safe' season to help calm their jangled nerves. Other building blocks will be reserved for the new stadium the club have announced. ■

Results 1998-99

FA Carling Premiership

Date	*Opponents*	*Ven*	*Res*	*Atten*	*Scorers*
15-Aug	Chelsea	H	2-1	23,042	Huckerby (10); Dublin (16)
22-Aug	N.Forest	A	0-1	22,546	
29-Aug	West Ham U.	H	0-0	20,818	
09-Sep	Liverpool	A	0-2	47,771	
12-Sep	Manchester U.	A	0-2	55,193	
19-Sep	Newcastle U.	H	1-5	22,656	Whelan (4)
27-Sep	Charlton A.	A	1-1	20,043	Whelan (69)
03-Oct	Aston Villa	H	1-2	22,654	Soltvedt (71)
18-Oct	Sheffield W.	H	1-0	16,006	Dublin (74)
24-Oct	Southampton	A	1-2	15,152	Dublin (60)
31-Oct	Arsenal	H	0-1	23,040	
07-Nov	Blackburn R.	A	2-1	23,779	Huckerby (54); Whelan (74)
15-Nov	Everton	H	3-0	19,290	Froggatt (15); Huckerby (48); Whelan (89)
21-Nov	Middlesbrough	A	0-2	34,293	
28-Nov	Leicester C.	H	1-1	19,894	Huckerby (78)
05-Dec	Wimbledon	A	1-2	11,717	McAllister (54 pen)
14-Dec	Leeds U.	A	0-2	31,802	
19-Dec	Derby Co.	H	1-1	16,627	Whelan (16)
26-Dec	Tottenham H.	H	1-1	23,098	Aloisi (81)
28-Dec	West Ham U.	A	0-2	25,662	
09-Jan	N.Forest	H	4-0	17,172	Huckerby (45, 46, 75); Telfer (54)
16-Jan	Chelsea	A	1-2	34,869	Huckerby (9)
30-Jan	Liverpool	H	2-1	23,056	Boateng (60); Whelan (71)
06-Feb	Tottenham H.	A	0-0	34,376	
17-Feb	Newcastle U.	A	1-4	36,352	Whelan (17)
20-Feb	Manchester U.	H	0-1	22,596	
27-Feb	Aston Villa	A	4-1	38,799	Aloisi (25, 73); Boateng (51, 84)
06-Mar	Charlton A.	H	2-1	20,259	Whelan (67); Soltvedt (85)
13-Mar	Blackburn R.	H	1-1	19,701	Aloisi (22)
21-Mar	Arsenal	A	0-2	38,073	
03-Apr	Sheffield W.	A	2-1	28,136	McAllister (19 pen); Whelan (84)
05-Apr	Southampton	H	1-0	21,402	Boateng (64)
11-Apr	Everton	A	0-2	32,341	
17-Apr	Middlesbrough	H	1-2	19,231	McAllister (72)
24-Apr	Leicester C.	A	0-1	20,224	
01-May	Wimbledon	H	2-1	21,200	Huckerby (16); Whelan (29)

08-May	Derby Co.	A	0-0	32,450	
16-May	Leeds U.	H	2-2	23,049	Aloisi (63); Telfer (72)

FA Challenge Cup

Sponsored by AXA

Date	*Opponents*	*Vn*	*Rnd*	*Res*	*Atten*	*Scorers*
02-Jan	Macclesfield	H	3R	7-0	14,197	Froggatt (28); Whelan (36); OG (Payne, 44); Huckerby (60, 71, 89); Boateng (88)
23-Jan	Leicester C.	A	4R	3-0	21,207	Whelan (17); Telfer (89); Froggatt (90)
13-Feb	Everton	A	5R	1-2	33,907	McAllister (84)

Worthington Cup

Date	*Opponents*	*Vn*	*Rnd*	*Res*	*Atten*	*Scorers*
16-Sep	Southend U.	H	2R1L	1-0	6,631	Hall (64)
22-Sep	Southend U.	A	2R2L	4-0	6,292	Boateng (6); Dublin (27); Whelan (44); Soltvedt (83)
27-Oct	Luton Town	A	3R	0-2	9,051	

Derby County

In 1884 members of the Derbyshire County Cricket team formed the football club as a way of boosting finances in the cricket close season. They played their first season at the Racecourse Ground and entered the FA Cup. A year later the club moved to the Baseball Ground where they remained until a move to Pride Park Stadium for the 1997-98 season. In 1888 they became founder members of the Football League. Since their formation they have fluctuated through the top divisions, but enjoyed a sparkling spell during the 1970s.

Ground: Pride Park Stadium, Derby, DE24 8XL
Phone: 01332-202202 **Fax:** 01332-667540
Box Office: 01332 209999 **News:** 0891 12 11 87
Capacity: 33,000 **Pitch:** 110 yds x 74 yds
Colours: White & Black, Black, White & Black
Nickname: The Rams
Radio: BBC Radio Derby 1116AM/104.5FM
Internet: www.dcfc.co.uk

Chairman: Lionel Pickering **Vice-Chairman:** Peter Gadsby
CEO: Keith Loring **Secretary:** Keith Pearson
Manager: Jim Smith **Coach:** Steve McClaren
Physio: Peter Melville

League History: 1888 Founder members of Football League; 107-12 Division 1; 1912-14 Division 2; 1914-15 Division 1; 1915-21 Division 1; 1921-26 Division 2; 1926-53 Division 1; 1953-55 Division 2; 1955-57 Division 3N; 1957-69 Division 2; 1969-80 Division 1; 1980-84 Division 2; 1984-86 Division 3; 1986-87 Division 2; 1987-91 Division 1; 1991-92 Division 2; 1992-96 Division 1; 1996- FA Premier League.

Honours: *Football League: Division 1 Champions* 1971-72, 1974-75; *Runners-up* 1895-96, 1929-30, 1935-36, 1995-96; *Division 2 Champions* 1911-12, 1914-15, 1968-69, 1986-87; *Runners-up* 1925-26; *Division 3N Champions* 1956-57; *Runners-up* 1955-56. *FA Cup: Winners* 1945-46; *Runners-up* 1897-98, 1888-89, 1902-03. *Anglo Italian Cup: Runners-up* 1992-93.

European Record: CC (2): 1972-73 (SF), 1975-76 (2); CWC (0) – ; UEFA (2): 1974-75 (3), 1976-77 (2).

Managers: Harry Bradshaw 1904-09; Jimmy Methven 1906-22; Cecil Potter 1922-25; George Jobey 1925-41; Ted Manger 1944-46; Stuart McMillan 1946-53; Jack Barker 1953-55; Harry Storer 1955-62; Tim Ward 1962-67; Brian Clough 1967-73; Dave Mackay 1973-76; Colin Murphy 1977; Tommy Docherty 1977-79; Colin Addison 1979-82; Johnny Newman 1982; Peter Taylor 1982-84; Roy McFarland 1984, Arthur Cox 1984-93; Roy McFarland 1993-95; *(FAPL)* Jim Smith June 1995-.

All-Time Records

Record FAPL Win: 5-2 v Sheffield W., Away, 24/09/97
Record FAPL Defeat: 1-6 v Middlesbrough, 05/03/97
Record FL Win: 9-0 v Wolverhampton W., Div. 1 10/1/1891
Record Cup Win: 12-0 v Finn Harps, UEFA Cup 1Rf, 15/9/76
Record Fee Received: £2.9m from Liverpool for Dean Saunders, 7/91
Record Fee Paid: £5.3m to Blackburn Rovers for Christian Dailly, 8/98
Most FL Apps: Kevin Hector, 486, 1966-78, 1980-82
Most FAPL Apps: 101 – Jacob Laursen, 1996-99
Most FAPL Goals: 25 – Dean Sturridge, 1996-99
Highest Scorer in FAPL Season: 13 – Paulo Wanchope, 1997-98
Record Attendance (all-time): 41,826 v Tottenham H., Div 1, 20/9/69
Record Attendance (FAPL): 32,913 v Liverpool, 13/03/99
Most FAPL Goals in Season: 52, 1997-98 – 38 games
Most FAPL Points in Season: 55, 1997-98 – 38 games

5-Year Record

	Div.	*P*	*W*	*D*	*L*	*F*	*A*	*Pts*	*Pos*	*FAC*	*FLC*
94-95	1	46	18	12	16	66	51	66	9	3	4
95-96	1	46	21	16	9	71	51	79	2	3	3
96-97	PL	38	11	13	14	45	58	46	12	6	2
97-98	PL	38	16	7	15	52	49	55	9	4	4
98-99	PL	38	13	13	12	40	45	52	8	QF	3

Summary 1998-99

Player	*Tot*	*St*	*Sb*	*Snu*	*PS*	*Gls*	*Y*	*R*	*Fa*	*Fg*	*La*	*Lg*
BAIANO	22	17	5	3	14	4	3	0	3	3	3	0
BECK	7	6	1	0	3	1	0	0	0	0	0	0
BOERTIEN	1	0	1	0	0	0	0	0	0	0	0	0
BOHINEN	32	29	3	0	11	0	6	0	3	0	0	0
BORBOKIS	4	3	1	0	1	0	0	0	0	0	0	0
BRIDGE-WILKINSON	1	0	1	4	0	0	0	0	0	0	0	0
BURTON	21	14	7	4	3	9	3	0	5	3	1	0
CARBONARI	29	28	1	3	5	5	4	0	4	0	0	0
CARSLEY	22	20	2	1	0	1	5	0	5	0	3	0
CHRISTIE	2	0	2	9	0	0	0	0	0	0	0	0
DAILLY	1	1	0	0	0	0	0	0	0	0	0	0
DELAP	23	21	2	0	5	0	6	0	1	0	3	1
DORIGO	18	17	1	1	3	1	3	0	3	2	1	0
ELLIOTT	11	7	4	8	2	0	3	0	2	0	2	0
ERANIO	25	18	7	3	7	0	3	0	4	0	2	0
HARPER	27	6	21	4	5	1	1	0	3	1	3	0
HOULT	23	23	0	11	1	0	2	1	3	0	0	0
HUNT	6	0	6	3	0	1	0	0	3	0	0	0
JACKSON	0	0	0	5	0	0	0	0	0	0	0	0
KNIGHT	0	0	0	9	0	0	0	0	0	0	0	0
KOSLUK	7	3	4	1	2	0	1	0	2	0	1	0
LAUNDERS	1	0	1	2	0	0	0	0	0	0	0	0
LAURSEN	37	37	0	0	5	0	7	0	4	0	3	0
MURRAY	4	0	4	2	0	0	1	0	0	0	0	0
POOM	17	15	2	16	0	0	0	0	2	0	3	0
POWELL	33	30	3	0	3	0	8	0	2	0	3	0
PRIOR	34	33	1	0	1	1	4	0	4	0	2	0
ROBINSON	1	0	1	2	0	0	0	0	0	0	0	0
SCHNOOR	23	20	3	5	7	2	6	0	3	0	2	0
STIMAC	14	14	0	0	2	0	6	0	3	0	1	0
STURRIDGE	29	23	6	2	9	5	3	0	4	0	3	1
WANCHOPE	35	33	2	0	3	9	9	1	2	0	3	1
32 Players	510	418	92	98	92	40	84	2	65	9	39	3

Forty Towers

The fixture computer decreed that Derby County's first six matches of the 1998-99 season would not be against sides considered to be the most difficult in the Premier League and Jim Smith's team took the opportunity to kick off their campaign with six unbeaten matches, three of which were won. After two goalless matches to start the campaign, Costa Rican Paulo Wanchope opened his, and the club's, account in a 1-1 draw with Middlesbrough. Wanchope finished the campaign with nine league goals, a total matched by joint top scorer Deon Burton, but Derby's 40 goals was the lowest of any side in the top half of the table. The bright start was soured by three straight defeats and, with just two wins from 13 games, the Rams slipped from second place – their highest position since the mid-seventies – to 11th by Boxing Day following a draw at Everton, their fourth consecutive draw. Consistency continued to be a problem for Derby throughout the remainder of the season, a point highlighted by good 2-1 and 3-2 home wins over Aston Villa and Liverpool respectively, being followed by 4-1 and 4-3 defeats at Leeds and at home to Newcastle. Although the Rams claimed their highest finish in three seasons of Premier League football they failed to beat any of the top five clubs. Home draws were achieved against the top four while reversals were suffered away to all of the top six clubs.

In the knock-out competitions Arsenal completed a domestic cup double over Smith's side after Derby had beaten Nationwide League opposition in both tournaments. After being held at home by Manchester City in the Worthington Cup, the Rams won the return at Maine Road before losing at home to Arsenal. Plymouth, Swansea and Huddersfield, after a replay, were removed from the FA Cup before Arsenal scored a last-minute winner in the quarter final.

A great wheeler-dealer in the transfer market down the years, Smith was conspicuous by his absence this season as his three major signings during the campaign cost a combined fee of just £1.8m although his pre-season capture of Horacio Carbonari set the club back £2.7m. That deal was more than offset by the sale of Christian Dailly, Gary Rowett and Lee Carsley for around £9m during the course of the season.

The close season came with the Rams coaching staff looking to freshen-up their squad from home and abroad and with the future of a number of players in the balance. ■

Results 1998-99

FA Carling Premiership

Date	*Opponents*	*Ven*	*Res*	*Atten*	*Scorers*
15-Aug	Blackburn R.	A	0-0	24,007	
22-Aug	Wimbledon	H	0-0	25,747	
29-Aug	Middlesbrough	A	1-1	34,121	Wanchope (31)
09-Sep	Sheffield W.	H	1-0	26,209	Sturridge (23)
12-Sep	Charlton A.	A	2-1	19,516	Wanchope (5); Baiano (60)
19-Sep	Leicester C.	H	2-0	26,738	Schnoor (34); Wanchope (51)
27-Sep	Aston Villa	A	0-1	38,007	
03-Oct	Tottenham H.	H	0-1	30,083	
17-Oct	Newcastle U.	A	1-2	36,750	Burton (73)
24-Oct	Manchester U.	H	1-1	30,867	Burton (74)
31-Oct	Leeds U.	H	2-2	27,034	Schnoor (3 pen); Sturridge (56)
07-Nov	Liverpool	A	2-1	44,020	Harper (6); Wanchope (27)
16-Nov	N.Forest	A	2-2	24,014	Dorigo (56 pen); Carbonari (72)
22-Nov	West Ham U.	H	0-2	31,666	
28-Nov	Southampton	A	1-0	14,762	Carbonari (33)
05-Dec	Arsenal	H	0-0	29,018	
12-Dec	Chelsea	H	2-2	29,056	Carbonari (26); Sturridge (90)
19-Dec	Coventry C.	A	1-1	16,627	Carsley (50)
26-Dec	Everton	A	0-0	39,206	
28-Dec	Middlesbrough	H	2-1	32,726	Sturridge (29); Hunt (85)
09-Jan	Wimbledon	A	1-2	12,732	Wanchope (76)
16-Jan	Blackburn R.	H	1-0	27,386	Burton (84)
30-Jan	Sheffield W.	A	1-0	24,440	Prior (54)
03-Feb	Manchester U.	A	0-1	55,174	
07-Feb	Everton	H	2-1	27,603	Burton (51, 85)
20-Feb	Charlton A.	H	0-2	27,853	
27-Feb	Tottenham H.	A	1-1	35,392	Burton (46)
10-Mar	Aston Villa	H	2-1	26,836	Baiano (17); Burton (21)
13-Mar	Liverpool	H	3-2	32,913	Burton (12); Wanchope (44, 49)
21-Mar	Leeds U.	A	1-4	38,971	Baiano (4 pen)
03-Apr	Newcastle U.	H	3-4	32,039	Burton (8); Baiano (22 pen); Wanchope (90)
10-Apr	N.Forest	H	1-0	32,217	Carbonari (85)
17-Apr	West Ham U.	A	1-5	25,485	Wanchope (89)
24-Apr	Southampton	H	0-0	26,557	
02-May	Arsenal	A	0-1	37,323	
05-May	Leicester C.	A	2-1	20,535	Sturridge (17); Beck (60)
08-May	Coventry C.	H	0-0	32,450	
16-May	Chelsea	A	1-2	35,016	Carbonari (87)

FA Challenge Cup

Sponsored by AXA

Date	*Opponents*	*Vn*	*Rnd*	*Res*	*Atten*	*Scorers*
02-Jan	Plymouth Ar.	A	3R	3-0	16,730	Burton (15, 82); Eranio (21 pen)
23-Jan	Swansea C.	A	4R	1-0	11,383	Harper (81)
13-Feb	Huddersfield	A	5R	2-2	22,129	Burton (55); Dorigo (59 pen)
24-Feb	Huddersfield	H	5RR	3-1	28,704	Dorigo (34); Baiano (73, 82)
06-Mar	Arsenal	A	QF	0-1	38,046	

Worthington Cup

Date	*Opponents*	*Vn*	*Rnd*	*Res*	*Atten*	*Scorers*
16-Sep	Manchester C.	H	2Rf	1-1	22,986	Delap (9)
23-Sep	Manchester C.	A	2Rs	1-0	19,622	Wanchope (28)
28-Oct	Arsenal	H	3R	1-2	25,621	Sturridge (83)

Everton

The cricket team of St Domingo's Church turned to football around 1878. Playing in Stanley Park, in late 1879 changed name to Everton FC, the name of the district to the west of the park. Moved to a field at Priory Road in 1882 and then, in 1884, moved to a site in Anfield Road. As one of the country's leading teams, became founder members of the Football League in 1888. Moved to Goodison Park, a field on the north side of Stanley Park, in 1892 following a dispute with the ground's landlord. Premier League founder members 1992.

Ground: Goodison Park, Liverpool, L4 4EL
Phone: 0151 330 2200
Box Office: 0151 330 2300 **CC Bookings:** 0151 471 8000
Info: 0891 12 11 99
Colours: Royal Blue, White, Blue **Nickname:** The Toffees
Capacity: 40,160 **Pitch:** 112 yds x 78 yds
Radio: Radio Everton 1602AM
Internet: www.evertonfc.com

Chairman: Peter Johnson **Secretary:** Michael Dunford
Manager: Walter Smith **Assistant:** Archie Knox
Coach: Dave Watson **Physio:** Les Helm

League History: 1888 Founder Member of the Football League; 1930-31 Division 2; 1931-51 Division 1; 1951-54 Division 2; 1954-92 Division 1; 1992- FA Premier League.

Honours: *Football League: Division 1 Champions* 1890-91, 1914-15, 1927-28, 1931-32, 1938-39, 1962-63, 1969-70, 1984-85, 1986-87; *Runners-up* 1889-90, 1894-95, 1901-02, 1904-05, 1908-09, 1911-12, 1985-86; *Division 2 Champions* 1930-31; *Runners-up* 1953-54. *FA Cup: Winners* 1906, 1933, 1966, 1984, 1995; *Runners-up* 1893, 1897, 1907, 1968, 1985, 1986, 1989. *Football League Cup: Runners-up* 1976-77, 1983-84. *League Super Cup: Runners-up* 1986. *Cup-Winners' Cup: Winners* 1984-85. *Simod Cup: Runners-up* 1989. *Zenith Data Systems Cup: Runners-up* 1991.

European Record: CC (2): 63-64 (1), 70-71 (QF); CWC (3): 66-67 (2), 84-85 (W), 95-96 (2); UEFA (6): 62-63 (1), 64-65 (3), 65-66 (2), 75-76 (1), 78-79 (2), 79-80 (1).

Managers: W.E. Barclay 1888-89; Dick Molyneux 1889-1901; William C. Cuff 1901-18; W.J. Sawyer 1918-19; Thomas H. McIntosh 1919-35; Theo Kelly 1936-48; Cliff Britton 1948-56; Ian Buchan 1956-58; Johnny Carey 1958-61; Harry Catterick 1961-73; Billy Bingham 1973-77; Gordon Lee 1977-81; Howard Kendall 1981-87; Colin Harvey 1987-90; *(FAPL)* Howard Kendall Nov 1990-93; Mike Walker Jan 1993-Nov 1994; Joe Royle Nov 1994-Mar 1997; Dave Watson (Caretaker) Apr 1997-July 1997; Howard Kendall July 1997-July 1998; Walter Smith Jul 1998-.

All-Time Records

Record FAPL Win: 7-1 v Southampton, Home, 16/11/96
Record FAPL Defeat: 1-5 v Norwich City, Home, 25/09/93
1-5 v Sheffield W., Away, 02/04/94
3-5 v QPR, Home, 12/04/93
Record FL Win: 9-1 v Manchester City, Div 1, 3/9/06;
Plymouth Argyle, Div 2, 27/12/30
Record FL Defeat: 4-10 v Tottenham H, Div 1, 11/10/58
Record Cup Win: 11-2 v Derby County, FAC R1, 18/1/90
Record Fee Received: £8m from Fiorentina for Andrei Kanchelskis, 1/97 and £8m for Duncan Ferguson from Newcastle United 11/99 (includes £1m payable after 60 appearances)
Record Fee Paid: £5.75m to Middlesbrough for Nick Barmby, 10/96
Most FL+PL Apps: Neville Southall, 578, 1981-98
Most FAPL Apps: 217 – Dave Watson, 1992-99
Most FAPL Goals: 37 – Duncan Ferguson, 1994-99
Highest Scorer in FAPL Season: 16 – Tony Cottee, 93-94
Andrei Kanchelskis, 95-96
Record Attendance (all-time): 78,299 v Liverpool, Division 1, 18/9/48
Record Attendance (FAPL): 40,185 v Liverpool, 17/10/98
Most FAPL Goals in Season: 64, 1995-96 – 38 games
Most FAPL Points in Season: 61, 1995-96 – 38 games

5-Year Record

	Div.	*P*	*W*	*D*	*L*	*F*	*A*	*Pts*	*Pos*	*FAC*	*FLC*
94-95	PL	42	11	17	14	44	51	50	15	W	2
95-96	PL	38	17	10	11	64	44	61	6	4	2
96-97	PL	38	10	12	16	44	57	42	15	4	2
97-98	PL	38	9	13	16	41	56	40	17	3	3
98-99	PL	38	11	10	17	42	47	43	14	QF	4R

Summary 1998-99

Player	Tot	St	Sb	Snu	PS	Gls	Y	R	Fa	Fg	La	Lg
BAKAYOKO†	23	17	6	3	10	4	3	0	3	2	2	1
BALL	37	36	1	0	1	3	8	0	3	0	4	0
BARMBY	24	20	4	2	9	3	4	0	4	1	2	0
BILIC	4	4	0	2	0	0	1	0	1	0	0	0
BRANCH	7	1	6	5	1	0	0	0	2	0	0	0
CADAMARTERI	30	11	19	4	4	4	6	0	4	0	4	0
CAMPBELL	8	8	0	0	1	9	1	0	0	0	0	0
CLELAND	18	16	2	3	4	0	3	1	1	0	3	0
COLLINS	20	19	1	0	2	1	4	0	0	0	4	1
DACOURT	30	28	2	1	1	2	14	1	2	0	4	1
DEGN	4	0	4	3	0	0	0	0	0	0	0	0
DUNNE	15	15	0	1	1	0	6	1	2	0	2	0
FARLEY	1	0	1	0	0	0	0	0	0	0	0	0
FARRELLY	1	0	1	6	0	0	0	0	0	0	0	0
FERGUSON	13	13	0	0	1	4	3	0	0	0	4	1
GEMMILL	7	7	0	0	1	1	3	0	0	0	0	0
GERRARD	0	0	0	15	0	0	0	0	0	0	1	0
GRANT	16	13	3	7	9	0	0	0	4	0	2	0
HUTCHISON	33	29	4	0	2	3	8	1	4	0	4	1
JEFFERS	15	11	4	2	5	6	0	0	2	1	0	0
JEVONS	1	0	1	5	0	0	0	0	0	0	0	0
MADAR	2	2	0	1	2	0	0	0	0	0	1	0
MATERAZZI	27	26	1	1	4	1	7	1	2	0	4	1
MILLIGAN	3	0	3	3	0	0	0	0	0	0	0	0
MYRHE	38	38	0	0	0	0	3	0	4	0	3	0
O'KANE	2	2	0	2	2	0	0	0	3	0	0	0
OSTER	9	6	3	1	4	0	1	0	4	1	2	0
PHELAN	0	0	0	1	0	0	0	0	0	0	0	0
SHORT	22	22	0	4	3	0	5	0	0	0	2	0
SIMONSEN	0	0	0	22	0	0	0	0	0	0	0	0
SPENCER	3	2	1	2	2	0	0	0	0	0	0	0
THOMAS	1	0	1	1	0	0	0	0	0	0	0	0
TILER	2	2	0	3	0	0	1	0	0	0	1	0
UNSWORTH	34	33	1	0	1	1	8	0	3	1	3	0
WARD	7	4	3	8	3	0	2	0	2	0	1	0
WATSON	22	22	0	7	2	0	0	0	3	0	1	1
WEIR	14	11	3	0	0	0	2	0	1	0	0	0
37 Players	493	418	75	115	75	42	93	5	54	6	54	7

New Manager, Same Story

With a succession of managers having failed to come anywhere near to repeating the phenomenal success Everton enjoyed under Howard Kendall during the 1980s, the Toffeemen pinned their hopes for an upturn in fortunes on the most successful manager in Scottish club football in recent years, Walter Smith. But despite forking out £10.5m on summer signings and a further £8m on Ibrahim Bakayoko and Steve Simonsen by October, Everton still endured another season of misery and an all too familiar relegation tussle. Furthermore, to the dismay of the fans, striker Duncan Ferguson was sold to Newcastle in a £7m deal without Smith's knowledge. That transfer precipitated a boardroom revolt which was expected to result in Smith's early departure but in fact ended with the manager's position strengthened. Despite the changes 'upstairs', Smith's transfer activity was limited although in March he pulled a master stroke in taking the former Arsenal and Nottingham Forest striker Kevin Campbell on loan from Trabzonspor, Campbell responded with an outstanding nine goals in eight games which ensured Premiership survival.

Everton's most acute problem was an inability to score goals at Goodison Park where the opposition net was located just three times in the first 12 matches. After starting the season with five home blank scoresheets, Everton's first goal encouraged visitors Manchester United to add four of their own. The drought was ended by a 5-0 thrashing of Middlesbrough on 17 February and by the end of the season West Ham had also been humbled, this time 6-0.

Since winning the FA Cup in 1995, Everton have experienced short runs in both domestic cup competitions but there were signs of an improvement during 1998-99. In the FA Cup, Bristol City and Ipswich Town were removed before the emerging talent of Francis Jeffers got one of the goals that defeated Coventry, only for Newcastle to end the run with a 4-1 quarter-final hammering on Merseyside. The long-serving Dave Watson scored his only goal of the season during a two-legged victory over Huddersfield Town in the Worthington Cup while Ferguson scored his penultimate goal for the club during an extra-time victory win over Middlesbrough, only for promotion-bound Sunderland to win a penalty shoot-out at Goodison Park in Round Four.

During the close season Walter Smith continued the restructuring of his squad. Ibrahim Bakayoko departed for Marseille while veteran, and fellow Scot, Richard Gough arrived from Forest. A case of new for old? ■

Results 1998-99

FA Carling Premiership

Date	*Opponents*	*Ven*	*Res*	*Atten*	*Scorers*
15-Aug	Aston Villa	H	0-0	40,112	
22-Aug	Leicester C.	A	0-2	21,037	
29-Aug	Tottenham H.	H	0-1	39,378	
08-Sep	N.Forest	A	2-0	25,610	Ferguson (72, 84)
12-Sep	Leeds U.	H	0-0	36,687	
19-Sep	Middlesbrough	A	2-2	34,563	Ball (47 pen); Collins (48)
27-Sep	Blackburn R.	H	0-0	36,404	
03-Oct	Wimbledon	A	2-1	16,054	Cadamarteri (32); Ferguson (59)
17-Oct	Liverpool	H	0-0	40,185	
24-Oct	Sheffield W.	A	0-0	26,952	
31-Oct	Manchester U.	H	1-4	40,079	Ferguson (30)
08-Nov	Arsenal	A	0-1	38,088	
15-Nov	Coventry C.	A	0-3	19,290	
23-Nov	Newcastle U.	H	1-0	30,357	Ball (18)
28-Nov	Charlton A.	A	2-1	20,043	Cadamarteri (45,73)
05-Dec	Chelsea	H	0-0	36,430	
12-Dec	Southampton	H	1-0	32,073	Bakayoko (31)
19-Dec	West Ham U.	A	1-2	25,998	Cadamarteri (71)
26-Dec	Derby Co.	H	0-0	39,206	
28-Dec	Tottenham H.	A	1-4	36,053	Bakayoko (31)
9-Jan	Leicester C.	H	0-0	32,792	
18-Jan	Aston Villa	A	0-3	32,488	
30-Jan	N.Forest	H	0-1	34,175	
07-Feb	Derby Co.	A	1-2	27,603	Barmby (37)
17-Feb	Middlesbrough	H	5-0	31,606	Barmby (1, 16); Dacourt (61); Materazzi (67); Unsworth (73)
20-Feb	Leeds U.	A	0-1	36,344	
27-Feb	Wimbledon	H	1-1	32,574	Jeffers (57)
10-Mar	Blackburn R.	A	2-1	27,219	Bakayoko (15, 65)
13-Mar	Arsenal	H	0-2	38,049	
22-Mar	Manchester U.	A	1-3	55,182	Hutchison (80)
03-Apr	Liverpool	A	2-3	44,852	Dacourt (1); Jeffers (84)
05-Apr	Sheffield W.	H	1-2	35,270	Jeffers (12)
11-Apr	Coventry C.	H	2-0	32,341	Campbell (29, 88)
17-Apr	Newcastle U.	A	3-1	36,775	Campbell (1,44); Gemmill (88)
24-Apr	Charlton A.	H	4-1	40,089	Hutchison (24); Campbell (31, 60); Jeffers (75)
01-May	Chelsea	A	1-3	34,909	Jeffers (69)

08-May	West Ham U.	H	6-0	40,049	Campbell (14,52,77); Ball (25pen); Hutchison (38); Jeffers (87)
16-May	Southampton	A	0-2	15,254	

FA Challenge Cup

Sponsored by AXA

Date	*Opponents*	*Vn*	*Rnd*	*Res*	*Atten*	*Scorers*
02-Jan	Bristol City	A	3R	2-0	19,608	Bakayoko (86, 88)
23-Jan	Ipswich T.	H	4R	1-0	28,854	Barmby (39)
13-Feb	Coventry C.	H	5R	2-1	33,907	Jeffers (20); Oster (77)
7-Mar	Newcastle U.	A	QF	1-4	36,584	Unsworth (57)

Worthington Cup

Date	*Opponents*	*Vn*	*Rnd*	*Res*	*Atten*	*Scorers*
15-Sep	Huddersfield	A	2Rf	1-1	15,395	Watson (37)
23-Sep	Huddersfield	H	2Rs	2-1	18,718	Dacourt (29); Materazzi (42)
	Everton win 3-2 on aggregate					
28-Oct	Middlesbro'	A	3R	3-2	20,748	Ferguson (67); Bakayoko (102); Hutchison (108). *aet*
11-Nov	Sunderland	H	4R	1-1	28,132	Collins (74)

Leeds United

Leeds City, founded in 1904, took over the Elland Road ground of the defunct Holbeck Club and in 1905 gained a Football League Division Two place. The club was, however, expelled in 1919 for disciplinary reasons associated with payments to players during the War. The club closed down. Leeds United FC, a new professional club, emerged the same year and competed in the Midland League. The club was elected to Football League Division Two for season 1920-21. The club has subsequently never been out of the top two divisions. Premier League founder members 1992.

Ground: Elland Road, Leeds, LS11 0ES
Phone: 0113-226 6000
Box Office: 0113-226 1000 **CC Bookings**: 0113-271 0710
Info: 0891 12 11 80
Colours: All White **Nickname:** United
Capacity: 40,204 **Pitch:** 110 yds x 72 yds
Radio: Radio Leeds United 1323AM
Internet: www.lufc.co.uk

President: Rt Hn The Earl of Harewood
Chairman: Peter Ridsdale **MD:** Jeremy Fenn
Secretary: Nigel Pleasants
Manager: David O'Leary **Assistant:** Eddie Gray
Physios: David Swift and Alan Sutton

League History: 1920 Elected to Division 2; 1924-27 Division 1; 1927-28 Division 2; 1928-31 Division 1; 1931-32 Division 2; 1932-47 Division 1; 1947-56 Division 2; 1956-60 Division 1; 1960-64 Division 2; 1964-82 Division 1; 1982-90 Division 2; 1990-92 Division 1; 1992- FA Premier League.

Honours: *Football League: Division 1 Champions* 1968-69, 1973-74, 1991-92; *Runners-up* 1964-65, 1965-66, 1969-70, 1970-71, 1971-72; *Division 2 Champions* 1923-24, 1963-64, 1989-90; *Runners-up* 1927-28, 1931-32, 1955-56. *FA Cup: Winners* 1971-72; *Runners-up* 1964-65, 1969-70, 1972-73. *Football League Cup: Winners* 1967-68. *Runners-up* 1995-96 *Champions' Cup: Runners-up* 1974-75. *Cup-Winners' Cup: Runners-up* 1972-73. *UEFA Cup: Winners* 1967-68, 1970-71; *Runners-up* 1966-67.

European Record: CC (3): 69-70 (SF), 74-75 (F), 92-93 (2); CWC (1): 72-73 (F); UEFA (10): 65-66 (SF), 66-67 (F), 67-68 (W), 68-69 (QF), 70-71 (W), 71-72 (1), 73-74 (3), 79-80 (2), 95-96 (2), 98-99 (2).

Managers: Dick Ray 1919-20; Arthur Fairclough 1920-27; Dick Ray 1927-35; Bill Hampson 1935-47; Willis Edwards 1947-48; Major Frank Buckley 1948-53; Raich Carter 1953-58; Bill Lambton 1958-59; Jack Taylor 1959-61; Don Revie 1961-74; Brian Clough 1974; Jimmy Armfield 1974-78; Jock Stein 1978; Jimmy Adamson 1978-80; Allan Clarke 1980-82; Eddie Gray 1982-85; Billy Bremner 1985-88; *(FAPL)* Howard Wilkinson Oct 1988-Sept 1996; George Graham Sept 1996-Sept 1998; David O'Leary Sept 1998-.

All-Time Records

Record FAPL Win: 5-0 v Tottenham H, Home, 25/08/92,
5-0 v Swindon Town, Away, 07/05/94
5-0 v Derby County, Away, 15/03/98
5-1 v West Ham United, Away, 01/05/99
5-2 v Blackburn Rovers, Home, 10/03/93
Record FAPL Defeat: 2-6 v Sheffield Wednesday, Away, 16/12/95
Record FL Win: 8-0 v Leicester City, Div 1, 7/4/1934
Record FL Defeat: 1-8 v Stoke City, Div 1, 27/8/1934
Record Cup Win: 10-0 v Lyn (Oslo), CL 1Rf, 17/09/69
Record Fee Received: £3.5m from Everton for Gary Speed, 6/96
Record Fee Paid: £4.5m to Parma for Tomas Brolin, 11/95
Most FL Apps: Jack Charlton, 629, 1953-73
Most FAPL Apps: 201 – David Wetherall, 1992-99
Most FAPL Goals: 42 – Rod Wallace, 1992-98
Highest Scorer in FAPL Season: 18 – J-F Hasselbaink, 1998-99
Record Attendance (all-time): 57,892 v Sunderland, FAC 5RR, 15/3/67
Record Attendance (FAPL): 41,125 v Manchester United, 27/4/94
Most FAPL Goals in Season: 65, 1993-94 – 42 games
Most FAPL Points in Season: 73, 1994-95 – 42 games

5-Year Record

	Div.	*P*	*W*	*D*	*L*	*F*	*A*	*Pts*	*Pos*	*FAC*	*FLC*
94-95	PL	42	20	13	9	59	38	73	5	5	2
95-96	PL	38	12	7	19	40	57	43	13	QF	F
96-97	PL	38	11	13	14	28	38	46	11	5	3
97-98	PL	38	17	8	13	57	46	59	5	6	4
98-99	PL	38	18	13	7	62	34	67	4	5	4

Summary 1998-99

Player	*Tot*	*St*	*Sb*	*Snu*	*PS*	*Gls*	*Y*	*R*	*Fa*	*Fg*	*La*	*Lg*
BATTY	10	10	0	0	1	0	6	0	0	0	0	0
BEENEY	0	0	0	4	0	0	0	0	0	0	0	0
BOWYER	35	35	0	0	2	9	8	0	4	0	2	0
GRANVILLE	9	7	2	8	3	0	1	1	3	0	1	0
HAALAND	29	24	5	4	1	1	10	0	4	0	0	0
HALLE †	17	14	3	15	1	2	0	0	3	0	1	0
HARTE	35	34	1	0	1	4	7	0	5	2	1	0
HASSELBAINK	36	36	0	0	7	18	8	0	5	1	2	0
HIDEN	14	14	0	0	1	0	3	0	0	0	1	0
HOPKIN	34	32	2	0	2	4	6	0	5	0	2	0
JACKSON	0	0	0	1	0	0	0	0	0	0	0	0
JONES	8	3	5	5	1	0	0	0	1	0	0	0
KEWELL	38	36	2	0	9	6	3	0	5	1	2	2
KNARVIK	0	0	0	2	0	0	0	0	1	0	0	0
KORSTEN	7	4	3	0	1	2	0	0	3	0	0	0
LILLEY	2	0	2	1	0	0	0	0	0	0	0	0
McPHAIL	17	11	6	3	4	0	0	0	0	0	1	0
MARTYN	34	34	0	1	1	0	0	0	5	0	1	0
MOLENAAR	17	17	0	0	2	2	4	0	0	0	2	0
RADEBE	29	29	0	0	3	0	2	0	3	0	0	0
RIBEIRO	13	7	6	11	6	1	1	0	1	1	1	0
ROBINSON	5	4	1	29	0	0	0	0	0	0	1	0
SANTOS	0	0	0	3	0	0	0	0	0	0	0	0
SHARPE	4	2	2	5	1	0	0	0	0	0	1	0
SMITH	22	15	7	2	3	7	6	0	4	2	0	0
WETHERALL	21	14	7	17	1	0	3	0	4	1	0	0
WIJNHARD	18	11	7	16	8	3	5	0	2	1	1	0
WOODGATE	25	25	0	2	2	2	5	0	5	0	2	0
Own Goals						1						
28 Players	479	418	61	129	61	62	78	1	63	9	22	2

No Kidding from O'Leary

What could have been a turbulent season for Leeds United following manager George Graham's defection to Tottenham, turned out to be one of the more promising campaigns for the Elland Road club in recent years as they claimed their highest finish since winning the championship in 1992. Following Graham's departure, Leeds took an eternity before finally handing permanent control of team matters to assistant manager David O'Leary who oversaw a seven-match winning run – the club's best since the war – and a place in the UEFA Cup.

Star of the show was Jimmy Floyd Hasselbaink who, with 18 goals, was joint top scorer in the Premier League, while young Australian Harry Kewell, teenage English striker Alan Smith and Eire defender Ian Harte all made giant forward strides. Goalkeeper Nigel Martyn was again in terrific form as Leeds conceded the second least number of home goals in the Premier League and at the other end of the pitch only two sides scored more freely than Leeds.

The team kicked off with a six-match unbeaten run and conceded just one goal in the first five games until drawing 3-3 at Spurs in Graham's final match. Despite letting in few goals, Leeds only won two of their opening 11 games although a further eight finished all square. Of the three sides to finish above them, Leeds defeated Arsenal at Elland Road – a result which virtually gave Manchester United the title – and drew with United and Chelsea but lost to all three on their travels.

If there was one result which disappointed the club, it came in the FA Cup where Spurs, after drawing at Elland Road, won a 5th Round Replay. Leeds took revenge in the league match in Yorkshire. United's UEFA Cup venture proved to be short as a 1st Round penalty shoot-out win over Maritimo was followed by a single goal defeat against Roma. Hopes of ending a 31-year wait since last lifting the Worthington (League) Cup floundered in the 4th Round at Leicester.

Last season Leeds, generally, stayed clear of the transfer market although £4.4m was handed to Newcastle to bring David Batty back home while prior to the start of the season Danny Glanville and Clyde Wijnhard were signed at a cost of £3.1m. For this season, O'Leary was less stringent with the cheque book and made an immediate swoop for Charlton's Danny Mills in exchange for £4m readies.

The Leeds manager has placed great faith in his youngsters – this season will be their real test as they will no longer be the unknowns and will need to show they can last the pace and take the pressure to maintain the high standards they have already set themselves. ■

Results 1998-99

FA Carling Premiership

Date	*Opponents*	*Ven*	*Res*	*Atten*	*Scorers*
15-Aug	Middlesbrough	A	0-0	34,162	
24-Aug	Blackburn R.	H	1-0	30,652	Hasselbaink (18)
29-Aug	Wimbledon	A	1-1	16,437	Bowyer (61)
08-Sep	Southampton	H	3-0	30,637	OG (38, Marshall); Harte (52); Wijnhard (86)
12-Sep	Everton	A	0-0	36,687	
19-Sep	Aston Villa	H	0-0	33,446	
27-Sep	Tottenham H.	A	3-3	35,535	Halle (4); Hasselbaink (26); Wijnhard (61)
03-Oct	Leicester C.	H	0-1	32,606	
17-Oct	N.Forest	A	1-1	23,911	Halle (53)
24-Oct	Chelsea	H	0-0	36,292	
31-Oct	Derby Co.	A	2-2	27,034	Molenaar (16); Kewell (43)
08-Nov	Sheffield W.	H	2-1	30,012	Hasselbaink (40); Woodgate (61)
14-Nov	Liverpool	A	3-1	44,305	Smith (79); Hasselbaink (81, 86)
21-Nov	Charlton A.	H	4-1	32,487	Hasselbaink (34); Bowyer (51); Smith (67); Kewell(87)
29-Nov	Manchester U.	A	2-3	55,172	Hasselbaink (29); Kewell (52)
05-Dec	West Ham U.	H	4-0	36,320	Bowyer (8,61); Molenaar (68); Hasselbaink (79)
14-Dec	Coventry C.	H	2-0	31,802	Hopkin (40); Bowyer (90)
20-Dec	Arsenal	A	1-3	38,025	Hasselbaink (66)
26-Dec	Newcastle U.	A	3-0	36,783	Kewell (38); Bowyer (62); Hasselbaink (90)
29-Dec	Wimbledon	H	2-2	39,816	Ribeiro (26); Hopkin (57)
09-Jan	Blackburn R.	A	0-1	27,620	
16-Jan	Middlesbrough	H	2-0	37,473	Smith (21); Bowyer (27)
30-Jan	Southampton	A	0-3	15,236	
06-Feb	Newcastle U.	H	0-1	40,202	
17-Feb	Aston Villa	A	2-1	37,510	Hasselbaink (7,31)
20-Feb	Everton	H	1-0	36,344	Korsten (55)
01-Mar	Leicester C.	A	2-1	18,101	Kewell (24); Smith (60)
10-Mar	Tottenham H.	H	2-0	34,521	Smith (42); Kewell (68)
13-Mar	Sheffield W.	A	2-0	28,142	Hasselbaink (4); Hopkin (73)
21-Mar	Derby Co.	H	4-1	38,971	Bowyer (18); Hasselbaink (32); Korsten (45); Harte (85)

03-Apr	N.Forest	H	3-1	39,645	Hasselbaink (43); Harte (60); Smith (84)
12-Apr	Liverpool	H	0-0	39,451	
17-Apr	Charlton A.	A	1-1	20,043	Woodgate (24)
25-Apr	Manchester U.	H	1-1	40,255	Hasselbaink (32)
01-May	West Ham U.	A	5-1	25,997	Hasselbaink (1); Smith (45); Harte (62 pen); Bowyer (78); Haaland (79)
05-May	Chelsea	A	0-1	34,762	
11-May	Arsenal	H	1-0	40,142	Hasselbaink (86)
16-May	Coventry C.	A	2-2	23,049	Wijnhard (43); Hopkin (90)

UEFA Cup

Date	*Opponents*	*Vn*	*Rnd*	*Res*	*Atten*	*Scorers*
15-Sep	CS Maritimo	H	1Rf	1-0	38,033	Hasselbaink (84)
29-Sep	CS Maritimo	A	1Rs	0-1	14,000	
1-1 on aggregate. Leeds United win on penalties						
20-Oct	Roma	A	2Rf	0-1	40,003	
03-Oct	Roma	H	2Rs	0-0	39,161	
Roma win 1-0 on aggregate						

FA Challenge Cup

Sponsored by AXA

Date	*Opponents*	*Vn*	*Rnd*	*Res*	*Atten*	*Scorers*
02-Jan	Rushden D.	A	3R	0-0	6,431	
13-Jan	Rushden D.	H	3RR	3-1	39,159	Smith (22, 51); Hasselbaink (67)
23-Jan	Portsmouth	A	4R	5-1	18,864	Wetherall (11); Harte (17); Kewell (51); Ribeiro (73); Wijnhard (82)
13-Feb	Tottenham H.	H	5R	1-1	39,696	Harte (73)
24-Feb	Tottenham H.	A	5RR	0-2	32,307	

Worthington Cup

Date	*Opponents*	*Vn*	*Rnd*	*Res*	*Atten*	*Scorers*
28-Oct	Bradford C.	H	3R	1-0	27,561	Kewell (28)
11-Nov	Leicester C.	A	4R	1-2	20,161	Kewell (17)

Leicester City

Founded in 1884 as Leicester Fosse by former pupils of the Wyggeston School from the western part of the city near the old Roman Fosse Way. Moved to their present ground in 1891 and from the Midland League joined Division Two of the Football League in 1894. Promoted for the first time in 1908, they have been relegated seven times from the top flight. FA Cup runners-up four times, they gained European Cup-Winners' Cup experience in 1961-62. Members of the new Division One in its first season, 1992-93, and promoted to the Premier League following play-off success in 1994. Relegated straight back but repromoted, again via the play-offs at the end of the 1995-96 season. Won the League Cup in 1997 and were losing finalists in 1999.

Ground: City Stadium, Filbert Street, Leicester LE2 7FL
Phone: 0116-255 5000 **Fax:** 0116-247 0585
Box Office: 0116- 291 5232 **CC Bookings:** 0116-291 5232
Info: 0891-12 11 85
Colours: All Blue **Nickname:** Filberts or Foxes
Capacity: 22,517 **Pitch:** 112 x 75 yds

Head of Committee: Sir Rodney Walker
CEO: Barrie Pierpoint **Secretary:** tba
Manager: Martin O'Neill **Assistant:** John Robertson
Coaches: Paul Franklin, Steve Walford
Physios: Alan Smith, Mick Yeomans
Radio: 104.9FM BBC Radio Leicester
Internet: www.lcfc.co.uk

League History: 1894 Elected to Division 2; 1908-09 Division 1; 1909-25 Division 2; 1925-35 Division 1; 1935-37 Division 2; 1937-39 Division 1; 1946-54 Division 2; 1954-55 Division 1; 1955-57 Division 2; 1957-69 Division 1; 1969-71 Division 2; 1971-78 Division 1; 1978-80 Division 2; 1980-81 Division 1; 1981-83 Division 2; 1983-87 Division 1; 1987-92 Division 2; 1992-94 Division 1; 1994-95 FA Premier League; 1995-96 Division 1; 1996- FA Premier League.

Honours: *Football League: Division 1 Runners-up* 1928-29; *Division 2 Champions* 1924-25, 1936-37, 1953-54, 1956-57, 1970-71, 1979-80;

Runners-up 1907-08. *FA Cup: Runners-up* 1949, 1961, 1963, 1969. *Football League Cup: Winners* 1964, 1997; *Runners-up* 1965, 1999.

European Competitions: CC (0) – ; CWC (1): 61-62 (1); UEFA (1) 97-98 (1).

Managers (and secretary-managers): William Clarke 1896-97, George Johnson 1898-1907, James Blessington 1907-09, Andy Aitkin 1909-11, J.W. Bartlett 1912-14, Peter Hodge 1919-26, William Orr 1926-32, Peter Hodge 1932-34, Andy Lochhead 1934-36, Frank Womack 1936-39, Tom Bromilow 1939-45, Tom Mather 1945-46, Johnny Duncan 1946-49, Norman Bullock 1949-55, David Halliday 1955-58, Matt Gillies 1959-68, Frank O'Farrell 1968-71, Jimmy Bloomfield 1971-77, Frank McLintock 1977-78, Jock Wallace 1978-82, Gordon Milne 1982-86, Bryan Hamilton 1986-87, David Pleat 1987-91, Brian Little May 1991-Nov 94; Mark McGhee Dec 1994-Dec 95; *(FAPL)*: Martin O'Neill Dec 1995 -.

All-Time Records

Record FAPL Win:	4-0 v Derby County, Away, 24/04/98
	4-2 v Derby County, 22/2/97
	4-2 v Blackburn Rovers, 11/5/97
	4-3 v Southampton, Home, 14/10/94
Record FAPL Defeat:	2-6 v Manchester U. Home, 16/01/99
	0-5 v Arsenal, Away, 20/02/99
Record FL Win:	10-0 v Portsmouth, Div 1, 20/10/28
Record FL Defeat:	0-12 v Nottingham Forest, Div 1, 21/4/09
Record Cup Win:	8-1 v Coventry City (A), LC R5, 1/12/64
Record Fee Received:	£3.5m from Aston Villa for Mark Draper, 7/95
Record Fee Paid:	£1.6m to Oxford U. for Matt Elliott, 1/97
Most FL Apps:	Adam Black, 528, 1920-35
Most FAPL Apps:	109 – Neil Lennon, 1996-99
Most FAPL Goals:	26 – Emile Heskey , 1997-99

Highest Scorer in FAPL Season: 12 – Steve Claridge, 1996-97
Record Attendance (all-time): 47,298 v Tottenham H., FAC 5R, 18/2/28
Record Attendance (FAPL): 21,837 v Liverpool, 31/10/98
Most FAPL Goals in Season: 51, 1997-98 – 38 games
Most FAPL Points in Season: 49, 1998-99 – 38 games

Summary 1998-99

Player	*Tot*	*St*	*Sb*	*Snu*	*PS*	*Gls*	*Y*	*R*	*Fa*	*Fg*	*La*	*Lg*
ARPHEXAD	4	2	2	34	0	0	0	0	0	0	1	0
CAMPBELL	12	1	11	6	2	0	1	0	1	0	2	0
COTTEE	31	29	2	0	8	10	1	0	1	1	5	5
ELLIOTT	37	37	0	0	2	3	7	0	2	0	8	0
FENTON	9	3	6	12	3	0	0	0	0	0	2	1
GUNNLAUGSSON	9	5	4	3	5	0	1	0	0	0	0	0
GUPPY	38	38	0	0	0	4	4	0	2	1	8	0
HESKEY	30	29	1	0	3	6	3	0	2	0	8	3
IMPEY	18	17	1	2	4	0	0	0	1	0	0	0
IZZET	31	31	0	0	4	5	2	0	2	0	5	1
KAAMARK	19	15	4	8	3	0	0	0	0	0	2	0
KELLER	36	36	0	2	2	0	2	0	2	0	7	0
LENNON	37	37	0	0	2	1	6	0	2	0	8	1
McMAHON	0	0	0	1	0	0	0	0	0	0	0	0
MARSHALL	10	6	4	5	2	3	0	0	1	0	1	0
MILLER	4	1	3	5	1	0	0	0	0	0	0	0
OAKES	3	2	1	3	1	0	0	0	0	0	0	0
PARKER	7	2	5	11	2	0	0	0	2	0	4	1
SAVAGE	34	29	5	0	6	1	3	0	0	0	7	0
SINCLAIR	31	30	1	1	2	1	10	1	2	1	6	0
TAGGART	15	9	6	9	2	0	3	0	2	0	6	1
ULLATHORNE	25	25	0	0	2	0	3	0	2	1	8	0
WALSH	22	17	5	1	4	3	2	0	1	0	5	0
WILSON	9	1	8	2	1	0	0	0	0	0	5	1
ZAGORAKIS	19	16	3	13	11	1	4	0	2	0	5	0
Own Goals						2						
25 Players	490	418	72	118	72	40	52	1	27	4	103	14

Foxes Slippery Glacier

For the second time in three seasons Leicester City reached the final of the Worthington (League) Cup but this was very much a mixed bag of a campaign for the Foxes. After drawing 2-2 at Old Trafford on the opening day of the season – having led 2-0 – Leicester defeated Everton but then went six matches without victory until the evergreen Tony Cottee scored the winner against Leeds at a time when the Yorkshire club were courting Martin O'Neill as a possible replacement for George Graham. O'Neill, who will doubtless be the centre of further such speculation during the 1999-2000 season, rejected Leeds' overtures and even had the pleasure of seeing his side complete the double over Graham's new club. Despite ending in a familiar safe midtable position, 10th, consistency was not Leicester's strength – as underlined by heavy defeats when facing all of the top three sides whilst drawing the return matches. On the other hand the Premier League status was secured on the back of an eight-match unbeaten run during March and April.

That run was all the more commendable as it came either side of the Worthington Cup final which saw the Foxes go down to a 1-0 defeat through a last-minute goal at the end of a pretty dismal game. After defeating Chesterfield in the 2nd Round, Leicester reached the final with some notable victories over Charlton, Leeds – courtesy of two goals in the last three minutes – Blackburn and Sunderland. Such success was not repeated in the FA Cup where a 3rd Round win over Birmingham was followed by a 3-0 home reversal against Coventry.

Cottee made light of the passing of time to have his most productive campaign in the Premier League for three years while his five Worthington Cup goals also played a significant part in Leicester's progress to Wembley. Emile Heskey scored the first Premiership goal of the season and ended the campaign with an England call-up while Rob Ullathorne's amazing ill fortune with injury persisted as he suffered a broken leg; his end of season dispute with the club will have done little for moral and his future at Filbert Street.

Cash isn't the most fluid of commodities at Filbert Street and O'Neill may find he is strapped for it while the bricks and mortar are bought for the new 40,000-seat stadium the club have announced.

Leicester's discipline was a credit to the club as just one red card was issued in league games and the total of 52 yellow cards was only bettered by one club. ■

Results 1998-99

FA Carling Premiership

Date	*Opponents*	*Ven*	*Res*	*Atten*	*Scorers*
15-Aug	Manchester U.	A	2-2	55,052	Heskey (7); Cottee (76)
22-Aug	Everton	H	2-0	21,037	Cottee (10); Izzet (38)
29-Aug	Blackburn R.	A	0-1	22,544	
09-Sep	Middlesbrough	H	0-1	20,635	
12-Sep	Arsenal	H	1-1	21,628	Heskey (28)
19-Sep	Derby Co.	A	0-2	26,738	
28-Sep	Wimbledon	H	1-1	17,725	Elliott (86)
03-Oct	Leeds U.	A	1-0	32,606	Cottee (76)
19-Oct	Tottenham H.	H	2-1	20,787	Heskey (37); Izzet (85)
24-Oct	Aston Villa	A	1-1	39,241	Cottee (36)
31-Oct	Liverpool	H	1-0	21,837	Cottee (59)
07-Nov	Charlton A.	A	0-0	20,021	
14-Nov	West Ham U.	A	2-3	25,642	Izzet (28); OG (87, Lampard)
21-Nov	Chelsea	H	2-4	21,401	Izzet (40); Guppy (60)
28-Nov	Coventry C.	A	1-1	19,894	Heskey (89)
05-Dec	Southampton	H	2-0	18,423	Heskey (61); Walsh (63)
12-Dec	N.Forest	H	3-1	20,891	Heskey (43); Elliott (55 pen); Guppy (75)
19-Dec	Newcastle U.	A	0-1	36,718	
26-Dec	Sheffield W.	A	1-0	33,513	Cottee (34)
28-Dec	Blackburn R.	H	1-1	21,083	Walsh (44)
09-Jan	Everton	A	0-0	32,792	
16-Jan	Manchester U.	H	2-6	22,091	Zagorakis (35); Walsh (73)
30-Jan	Middlesbrough	A	0-0	34,631	
06-Feb	Sheffield W.	H	0-2	20,113	
20-Feb	Arsenal	A	0-5	38,069	
01-Mar	Leeds U.	H	1-2	18,101	Cottee (76)
06-Mar	Wimbledon	A	1-0	11,801	Guppy (6)
13-Mar	Charlton A.	H	1-1	20,220	Lennon (60)
03-Apr	Tottenham H.	A	2-0	35,415	Elliott (43); Cottee (67)
06-Apr	Aston Villa	H	2-2	20,652	Savage (63); Cottee (71)
10-Apr	West Ham U.	H	0-0	20,402	
18-Apr	Chelsea	A	2-2	34,535	OG (82, Duberry); Guppy (88)
21-Apr	Liverpool	A	1-0	36,019	Marshall (90)
24-Apr	Coventry C.	H	1-0	20,224	Marshall (45)
01-May	Southampton	A	1-2	15,228	Marshall (17)
05-May	Derby Co.	H	1-2	20,535	Sinclair (28)
08-May	Newcastle U.	H	2-0	21,125	Izzet (20); Cottee (41)
16-May	N.Forest	A	0-1	25,353	

FA Challenge Cup

Sponsored by AXA

Date	*Opponents*	*Vn*	*Rnd*	*Res*	*Atten*	*Scorers*
02-Jan	Birm'ham C.	H	3R	4-2	19,846	Sinclair (21); Ullathorne (27); Cottee (51); Guppy (72)
23-Jan	Coventry C.	H	4R	0-3	21,207	

Worthington Cup

Date	*Opponents*	*Vn*	*Rnd*	*Res*	*Atten*	*Scorers*
16-Sep	Chesterfield	H	2Rf	3-0	13,480	Heskey (41, 51); Taggart (61)
22-Sep	Chesterfield	A	2Rs	3-1	4,565	Heskey (57); Fenton (87); Wilson (90)
	Leicester City win 6-1 on aggregate					
27-Oct	Charlton A.	A	3R	2-1	19,671	Cottee (51, 60)
11-Nov	Leeds U.	H	4R	2-1	20,161	Izzet (88); Parker (90 pen)
2-Dec	Blackburn R.	H	QF	1-0	19,442	Lennon (67)
26-Jan	Sunderland	A	SFf	2-1	38,332	Cottee (31,62)
17-Feb	Sunderland	H	SFs	1-1	21,231	Cottee (54)
	Leicester City win 3-2 on aggregate					
21-Mar	Tottenham H.		F	0-1	77,892	
	Played at Wembley					

5-Year Record

	Div.	*P*	*W*	*D*	*L*	*F*	*A*	*Pts*	*Pos*	*FAC*	*FLC*
94-95	PL	42	6	11	25	45	80	29	21	5	2
95-96	1	46	19	14	13	66	60	71	5	3	3
96-97	PL	38	12	11	15	46	54	47	9	5	W
97-98	PL	38	13	14	11	51	41	53	10	4	3
98-99	PL	38	12	13	13	40	46	49	10	4	F

Liverpool

Following a dispute between Everton and its Anfield landlord a new club, Liverpool AFC, was formed in 1892 by the landlord, former Everton committee-man John Houlding, with its headquarters at Anfield. An application for Football League membership was rejected without being put to the vote. Instead the team joined the Lancashire League and immediately won the Championship. After that one campaign, when the Liverpool Cup was won but there was early FA Cup elimination, Liverpool was selected to fill one of two vacancies in an expanded Football League Second Division in 1893. Premier League founder members 1992.

Ground: Anfield Road, Liverpool L4 0TH
Phone: 0151-263 2361 **Match Info:** 0151-260 9999
Box Office: 0151-260 8680 **CC Bookings:** 0151-263 5727
News: 0891 12 11 84 **Ticket Info:** 0891 12 15 85
Capacity: 45,362 **Pitch:** 110 yds x 75 yds
Colours: All Red/White Trim **Nickname:** Reds or Pool
Radio: 1485AM/95.8FM BBC Radio Merseyside
Internet: –

Chairman: David Moores **Vice-Chairman:** P.B.Robinson
CEO: Rick Parry **Secretary:** Bryce Morrison
Manager: Gerard Houllier **Assistant:** Phil Thompson
Physio: Mark Leather

League History: 1893 Elected to Division 2; 1894-95 Division 1; 1895-96 Division 2; 1896-1904 Division 1; 1904-05 Division 2; 1905-54 Division 1; 1954-62 Division 2; 1962-92 Division 1; 1992- FA Premier League.

Honours: *Football League: Division 1 Champions* 1900-01, 1905-06, 1921-22, 1922-23, 1946-47, 1963-64, 1965-66, 1972-73, 1975-76, 1976-77, 1978-79, 1979-80, 1981-82, 1982-83, 1983-84, 1985-86, 1987-88, 1989-90; *Runners-up* 1898-99, 1909-10, 1968-69, 1973-74, 1974-75, 1977-78, 1984-85, 1986-87, 1988-89, 1990-91; *Division 2 Champions* 1893-94, 1895-96, 1904-05, 1961-62. *FA Cup: Winners* 1964-65, 1973-74, 1985-86, 1988-89, 1991-92; *Runners-up* 1913-14, 1949-50, 1970-71, 1976-77, 1987-88, 1995-96. *Football League Cup: Winners* 1980-81, 1981-82, 1982-83, 1983-84, 1994-95; *Runners-up* 1977-78, 1986-87,

1995-96 *League Super Cup: Winners* 1985-86. *Champions' Cup: Winners* 1976-77; 1977-78, 1980-81; 1983-84; *Runners-up* 1984-85. *Cup-Winners' Cup: Runners-up* 1965-66. *UEFA Cup: Winners* 1972-73, 1975-76. *European Super Cup: Winners* 1977; *Runners-up* 1984. *World Club Championship: Runners-up* 1981, 1984.

European Record: CC (12): 64-65 (SF), 66-67 (2), 73-74 (2), 76-77 (W), 77-78 (W), 78-79 (1), 79-80 (1), 80-81 (W), 81-82 (QF), 82-83 (QF), 83-84 (W), 84-85 (F); CWC (5): 65-66 (F), 71-72 (2), 74-75 (2), 92-93 (2), 96-97 (SF); UEFA (10) 67-68 (3), 68-69 (1), 69-70 (2), 70-71 (SF), 72-73 (W), 75-76 (W), 91-92 (QF), 94-95 (2), 97-98 (2), 98-99 (3).

Managers: W.E. Barclay 1892-96; Tom Watson 1896-1915; David Ashworth 1920-22; Matt McQueen 1923-28; George Patterson 1928-36 (continued as secretary); George Kay 1936-51; Don Welsh 1951-56; Phil Taylor 1956-59; Bill Shankly 1959-74; Bob Paisley 1974-83; Joe Fagan 1983-85; Kenny Dalglish 1985-91; *(FAPL)* Graeme Souness 1991-94; Roy Evans Jan 1994-July 1998; Roy Evans & Gerard Houllier July 1998-Nov 1998; Gerard Houllier Nov 1998–.

All-Time Records

Record FAPL Win: 7-1 v Southampton, Home, 16/01/99
Record FAPL Defeat: 1-5 v Coventry City, Away, 19/12/92
Record FL Win: 10-1 v Rotherham T., Div 2, 18/2/1896 and
9-0 v Crystal Palace, Div 1, 12/9/89
Record FL Defeat: 1-9 v Birmingham City, Div 2, 11/12/54
Record Cup Win: 11-0 v Stromsgodset Drammen, CWC 1R1L, 17/9/74
Record Fee Received: £7m from Aston Villa for Stan Collymore, 5/97
Record Fee Paid: £8.5m to N. Forest for Stan Collymore, 6/95
Most FL Apps: Ian Callaghan, 640, 1960-78
Most FAPL Apps: 240 – Steve McManaman, 1992-99
Most FAPL Goals: 106 – Robbie Fowler, 1993-99
Highest Scorer in FAPL Season: 28 – Robbie Fowler, 1995-96
Record Attendance (all-time): 61,905 v Wolves, FAC 4R, 2/2/52
Record Attendance (FAPL): 44,702 v Manchester U., 05/05/99
Most FAPL Goals in Season: 68, 1997-98 – 38 games
Most FAPL Points in Season: 74, 1994-95 – 42 games

Summary 1998-99

Player	*Tot*	*St*	*Sb*	*Snu*	*PS*	*Gls*	*Y*	*R*	*Fa*	*Fg*	*La*	*Lg*
BARB –	25	24	1	2	3	0	6	0	1	0	0	0
BERGER	32	30	2	0	9	7	4	0	2	0	1	0
BYORNEBYE	23	20	3	6	4	0	5	0	2	0	2	0
CARRAGHER	34	34	0	0	2	1	5	1	2	0	2	0
DUNDEE †	3	0	3	1	0	0	0	0	0	0	1	0
FERRI	2	0	2	6	0	0	0	0	0	0	0	0
FOWLER	25	23	2	1	5	14	4	0	2	1	2	1
FRIEDEL	12	12	0	24	0	0	0	0	0	0	2	0
GERRARD	12	4	8	1	3	0	1	0	0	0	0	0
HARKNESS	6	4	2	11	3	0	2	0	2	0	0	0
HEGGEM	29	27	2	1	8	2	2	0	1	0	1	0
INCE –	34	34	0	0	2	6	9	0	2	1	2	1
JAMES †–	26	26	0	12	0	0	1	0	2	0	0	0
KVARME	7	2	5	12	1	0	0	0	0	0	0	0
LEONHARDSEN	9	7	2	4	2	1	0	0	0	0	1	0
McATEER †	13	6	7	5	1	0	1	1	2	0	2	0
McMANAMAN †	28	25	3	0	5	4	2	0	0	0	0	0
MATTEO	20	16	4	4	0	1	2	1	1	0	0	0
MURPHY	1	0	1	3	0	0	0	0	0	0	2	0
NIELSON	0	0	0	1	0	0	0	0	0	0	0	0
OWEN	30	30	0	0	9	18	0	0	2	2	2	1
REDKNAPP	34	33	1	0	4	8	6	0	2	0	0	0
RIEDLE	34	16	18	1	3	5	7	0	1	0	1	0
SONG	13	10	3	1	5	0	3	0	0	0	0	0
STAUNTON	31	31	0	4	8	0	2	0	1	0	2	0
THOMPSON	14	4	10	10	2	1	3	0	0	0	2	0
WARNER	0	0	0	1	0	0	0	0	0	0	0	0
Own Goals												1
27 Players	497	418	79	111	79	68	65	3	25	4	25	4

5-Year Record

	Div.	*P*	*W*	*D*	*L*	*F*	*A*	*Pts*	*Pos*	*FAC*	*FLC*
94-95	PL	42	21	11	10	65	37	74	4	QF	W
95-96	PL	38	20	11	7	70	34	71	3	F	4
96-97	PL	38	19	11	8	62	37	68	4	4	QF
97-98	PL	38	18	11	9	68	42	65	3	3	SF
98-99	PL	38	15	9	14	68	49	54	7	4	4

Bootroom Retired

The era of the famed Liverpool bootroom came to an end with the appointment of Gerard Houllier as manager, following the departure of the long-serving Roy Evans on 12 November. Evans's exit came on the back of just one win in eight Premier League matches as Liverpool lost interest in the race for the championship at an unusually early stage. The jury is still out as to whether Houllier, whose position was often questioned by the media, can halt the Reds' gradual decline but the new manager is pinning his hopes on overseas talent as he brought in Jean-Michel Ferri, Robert Song, Frode Kippe and Djimi Troare for around £5m. Out went the more local Jason McAteer, to Blackburn for £4m, and Steve Harkness. Further extensive changes can be anticipated.

Liverpool gave occasional reminders of their quality. Michael Owen scored a hat-trick as Newcastle were beaten 4-1 and he added four more during a 5-1 romp over Nottingham Forest. Robbie Fowler scored a trio of goals during a 7-1 slaughter of Southampton but both players, despite being the second most prolific partnership in the top flight, suffered injury problems and the latter, although reclaiming his England place at the end of the season, was frequently in trouble with the authorities. Steve McManaman announced his departure to Real Madrid for a personal fortune estimated at £12m, a staggering price for a player who still fails to turn genuine potential to rich fulfilment by running up too many blind alleys. Paul Ince was central to the midfield but didn't always dominate in his familiar way, Jamie Redknapp's quality continued to sparkle. Liverpool suffered the rare indignity of ten away league defeats but on the plus side were the second highest scorers in the Premier League.

In the UEFA Cup, the Reds had an easy ride past Kosice and an away-goals win over Valencia before being well beaten by Celta Vigo. In the domestic knock-out competitions, Liverpool won through one round in both tournaments before being tipped out by the eventual winners. The FA Cup defeat at Old Trafford was particularly galling as Manchester United scored twice in the final two minutes to overturn Owen's early goal but 'Pool did slow United's title surge with a draw at Anfield in early May courtesy of Ince's late strike.

At the start of last season Houliier was in joint control. This time round he has the reins to himself. If he is to continue to hold them beyond the end of the coming year there will need to be big improvements all-round. With some £10 million spent on new signings before June was out, matters would seem to be well in hand. ■

Results 1998-99

FA Carling Premiership

Date	*Opponents*	*Ven*	*Res*	*Atten*	*Scorers*
16-Aug	Southampton	A	2-1	15,202	Riedle (39); Owen (72)
22-Aug	Arsenal	H	0-0	44,429	
30-Aug	Newcastle U.	A	4-1	36,740	Owen (17, 18, 32); Berger (45)
09-Sep	Coventry C.	H	2-0	41,771	Berger (26); Redknapp (48)
12-Sep	West Ham U.	A	1-2	26,029	Riedle (88)
19-Sep	Charlton A.	H	3-3	44,526	Fowler (33 pen, 82); Berger (67)
24-Sep	Manchester U.	A	0-2	55,181	
04-Oct	Chelsea	H	1-1	44,404	Redknapp (83)
17-Oct	Everton	A	0-0	40,185	
24-Oct	N.Forest	H	5-1	44,595	Owen (10, 38, 71 pen, 77); McManaman (23)
31-Oct	Leicester C.	A	0-1	21,837	
07-Nov	Derby Co.	H	1-2	44,020	Redknapp (84)
14-Nov	Leeds U.	H	1-3	44,305	Fowler (68 pen)
21-Nov	Aston Villa	A	4-2	39,241	Ince (2); Fowler (7, 58, 66)
29-Nov	Blackburn R.	H	2-0	41,753	Ince (29); Owen (32)
05-Dec	Tottenham H.	A	1-2	36,521	Berger (55)
13-Dec	Wimbledon	A	0-1	26,080	
19-Dec	Sheffield W.	H	2-0	40,003	Berger (19); Owen (34)
26-Dec	Middlesbrough	A	3-1	34,626	Owen (17); Redknapp (35); Heggem (88)
28-Dec	Newcastle U.	H	4-2	44,605	Owen (67, 80); Riedle (71, 84)
09-Jan	Arsenal	A	0-0	38,107	
16-Jan	Southampton	H	7-1	44,011	Fowler (21, 36, 47); Matteo (35); Carragher (54); Owen (63); Thompson (73)
30-Jan	Coventry C.	A	1-2	23,056	McManaman (86)
06-Feb	Middlesbrough	H	3-1	44,384	Owen (9); Heggem (44); Ince (45)
13-Feb	Charlton A.	A	0-1	20,043	
20-Feb	West Ham U.	H	2-2	44,511	Fowler (22); Owen (45)
27-Feb	Chelsea	A	1-2	34,822	Owen (77)
13-Mar	Derby Co.	A	2-3	32,913	Fowler (36 pen, 57)
03-Apr	Everton	H	3-2	44,852	Fowler (15 pen, 21); Berger (82)
05-Apr	N.Forest	A	2-2	28,374	Redknapp (15); Owen (72)
12-Apr	Leeds U.	A	0-0	39,451	
17-Apr	Aston Villa	H	0-1	44,306	

21-Apr	Leicester C.	H	0-1	36,019	
24-Apr	Blackburn R.	A	3-1	29,944	McManaman (23); Redknapp (32); Leonhardsen (32)
01-May	Tottenham H.	H	3-2	44,007	Redknapp (49 pen); Ince (77); McManaman (79)
05-May	Manchester U.	H	2-2	44,702	Redknapp (69 pen); Ince (89)
08-May	Sheffield W.	A	0-1	27,383	
16-May	Wimbledon	H	3-0	41,902	Berger (12); Riedle (50); Ince (65)

UEFA Cup

Date	*Opponents*	*Vn*	*Rnd*	*Res*	*Atten*	*Scorers*
15-Sep	1.FC Kosice	A	1Rf	3-0	3,783	Berger (18); Riedle (23); Owen (59)
29-Sep	1.FC Kosice	H	1Rs	5-0	22,792	Redknapp (23, 55); Ince (52); Fowler (53, 90)
	Liverpool win 8-0 on aggregate					
20-Oct	Valencia	H	2Rf	0-0	26,004	
03-Nov	Valencia	A	2Rs	2-2	50,000	McManaman (80); Berger (85)
	2-2 on aggregate. Liverpool win on away goals rule					
24-Nov	Celta Vigo	A	3Rf	1-3	32,000	Owen (35)
08-Dec	Celta Vigo	H	3Rs	0-1	30,289	
	Celta Vigo win 4-1 on aggregate					

FA Challenge Cup

Sponsored by AXA

Date	*Opponents*	*Vn*	*Rnd*	*Res*	*Atten*	*Scorers*
03-Jan	Port Vale	A	3R	3-0	16,557	Owen (34 pen); Ince (38); Fowler (90)
24-Jan	Manchester U.	A	4R	1-2	54,591	Owen (3)

Worthington Cup

Date	*Opponents*	*Vn*	*Rnd*	*Res*	*Atten*	*Scorers*
27-Oct	Fulham	H	3R	3-1	22,296	OG (55, Morgan); Fowler (66 pen); Ince (76)
10-Nov	Tottenham H.	H	4R	1-3	20,772	Owen (81)

Manchester United

Came into being in 1902 upon the bankruptcy of Newton Heath. Predecessors appear to have been formed in 1878 as Newton Heath (LYR) when workers at the Carriage and Wagon Department at the Lancashire and Yorkshire Railway formed a club. This soon outgrew railway competition. Turned professional in 1885 and founder members of Football Alliance in 1889. In 1892 Alliance runners-up Newton Heath were elected to an enlarged Division One of the Football League. In 1902 the club became Manchester United and, in February 1910, moved from Bank Street, Clayton, to Old Trafford. Premier League founder members 1992. Five times Premiership champions and the only side to have completed the Treble to cap off their greatest season in 1998-99.

Ground: Old Trafford, Manchester, M16 0RA
Phone: 0161-872 1661 **Box Office:** 0161-872 0199
Info: 0891 12 11 61
Capacity: 56,320 > 67,000 **Pitch:** 116 yds x 76 yds
Colours: Red, White, Black **Nickname:** Red Devils
Radio: Manchester United Radio 1413AM
Internet: www.manutd.com

Chair/CEO: Martin Edwards **Secretary:** Kenneth Merrett
Manager: Alex Ferguson **Assistant:** Steve McClaren

League History: 1892 Newton Heath elected to Division 1; 1894-1906 Division 2; 1906-22 Division 1; 1922-25 Division 2; 1925-31 Division 1; 1931-36 Division 2; 1936-37 Division 1; 1937-38 Division 2; 1938-74 Division 1; 1974-75 Division 2; 1975-92 Division 1; 1992- FA Premier League.

Honours: *FA Premier League: Champions* 1992-93, 1993-94, 1995-96, 1996-97, 1998-99; *Runners-up* 1994-95, 1997-98. *Football League: Division 1 Champions* 1907-8, 1910-11, 1951-52, 1955-56, 1956-57, 1964-65, 1966-67; *Runners-up* 1946-47, 1947-48, 1948-49, 1950-51, 1958-59, 1963-64, 1967-68, 1979-80, 1987-88, 1991-92; *Division 2 Champions* 1935-36, 1974-75; *Runners-up* 1896-97, 1905-06, 1924-25, 1937-38. *FA Cup: Winners* 1908-09, 1947-48, 1962-63, 1976-77, 1982-83, 1984-85, 1989-90, 1993-94, 1995-96, 1998-99; *Runners-up* 1957, 1958, 1976, 1979, 1995. *Football League Cup: Winners* 1991-92; *Runners-up* 1982-83, 1990-91, 1993-94. *Champions' League: Winners* 1967-68, 1998-99. *Cup-Winners' Cup: Winners* 1990-91. *League/Cup*

Double Performed: 1993-94, 1995-96, 1998-99. *Treble Performed:* 1998-99.

European Record: CC (10): 56-57 (SF), 57-58 (SF), 65-66 (SF), 67-68 (W), 68-69 (SF), 93-94 (SF), 94-95 (CL), 96-97 (SF), 97-98 (QF), 98-99 (W); CWC (5): 63-64 (QF), 77-78 (2), 83-84 (SF), 90-91 (W), 91-92 (2); UEFA (7): 64-65 (SF), 76-77 (2), 80-81 (1), 82-83 (1), 84-85 (QF), 92-93 (1), 95-96 (1).

Managers: Ernest Mangnall 1900-12; John Robson 1914-21; John Chapman 1921-26; Clarence Hilditch 1926-27; Herbert Bamlett 1927-31; Walter Crickmer 1931-32; Scott Duncan 1932-37; Jimmy Porter 1938-44; Walter Crickmer 1944-45; Matt Busby 1945-69 (continued as GM then Director); Wilf McGuinness 1969-70; Frank O'Farrell 1971-72; Tommy Docherty 1972-77; Dave Sexton 1977-81; Ron Atkinson 1981-86; *(FAPL)* Alex Ferguson Nov 1986-.

All-Time Records

Record FAPL Win: 9-0 v Ipswich Town, Home, 04/03/95
Record FAPL Defeat: 3-6 v Southampton, Away, 26/10/96
Record FL Win: 10-1 v Wolverhampton W., Div 2, 15/10/1892
Record FL Defeat: 0-7 v Blackburn R., Div. 1, 10/4/26;
Aston Villa, Div. 1, 27/12/30;
Wolverhampton W.,Div. 2, 26/12/31
Record Cup Win: 10-0 v RSC Anderlecht, Champions Cup, Preliminary Round 2nd Leg, 26/9/56
Record Fee Received: £7m from Internazionale for Paul Ince, 6/95
Record Fee Paid: £12.6m to Aston Villa for Dwight Yorke, 8/98
Most FL Apps: Bobby Charlton, 606, 1956-73
Most FAPL Apps: 252 – Peter Schmeichel, 1992-99
Most FAPL Goals: 64 – Eric Cantona, 1992-97
Highest Scorer in FAPL Season: 18 – Eric Cantona, 1993-94
OG Solskjaer, 1996-97
Dwight Yorke, 1998-99
Record Attendance (all-time): 70,504 v Aston Villa, Div 1, 27/12/20
Record Attendance (FAPL): 55,316 v Southampton, 27/02/99
Most FAPL Goals in Season: 80, 1993-94 – 42 games
80, 1998-99 – 38 games
Most FAPL Points in Season: 92, 1993-94 – 42 games

Summary 1998-99

Player	*Tot*	*St*	*Sb*	*Snu*	*PS*	*Gls*	*Y*	*R*	*Fa*	*Fg*	*La*	*Lg*
BECKHAM	34	33	1	3	6	6	6	0	7	1	1	0
BERG	16	10	6	8	0	0	1	0	5	0	3	0
BLOMQVIST	25	20	5	6	14	1	2	0	5	0	1	0
BROWN	14	11	3	6	3	0	1	0	2	0	1	0
BUTT	31	22	9	1	5	2	3	1	5	0	2	0
CLEGG	0	0	0	0	0	0	0	0	0	0	3	0
COLE	32	26	6	2	7	17	3	0	7	2	0	0
CRUYFF	5	0	5	4	1	2	0	0	0	0	2	0
CULKIN	0	0	0	3	0	0	0	0	0	0	0	0
CURTIS	4	1	3	2	0	0	0	0	0	0	3	0
GIGGS	24	20	4	1	8	3	1	0	6	2	1	0
GREENING	3	0	3	1	0	0	0	0	1	0	3	0
IRWIN	29	26	3	1	4	2	3	1	6	1	0	0
JOHNSEN	22	19	3	4	2	3	2	0	5	0	1	0
KEANE	35	33	2	0	6	2	8	0	7	0	0	0
MAY	6	4	2	5	1	0	1	0	1	0	2	0
MULRYNE	0	0	0	0	0	0	0	0	0	0	2	0
NEVILLE, G.	34	34	0	0	3	1	6	1	7	0	0	0
NEVILLE, P.	28	19	9	7	5	0	5	0	7	0	2	0
NEVLAND	0	0	0	0	0	0	0	0	0	0	1	1
NOTMAN	0	0	0	0	0	0	0	0	0	0	1	0
SCHMEICHEL	34	34	0	0	1	0	0	0	8	0	0	0
SCHOLES	31	24	7	3	9	6	7	0	6	1	1	0
SHERINGHAM	17	7	10	2	2	2	4	0	4	1	1	1
SOLSKJAER	19	9	10	9	5	12	0	0	8	1	3	3
STAM	30	30	0	0	5	1	5	0	7	0	0	0
VAN DER GOUW	5	4	1	27	0	0	0	0	0	0	3	0
WALLWORK	0	0	0	0	0	0	0	0	0	0	1	0
WILSON	0	0	0	2	0	0	0	0	0	0	2	0
YORKE	32	32	0	1	5	18	3	0	8	3	0	0
Own Goals						2						
30 Players	510	418	92	98	92	80	61	3	112	12	10	5

Money Talks – Threefold!

As befitting the richest club in the world, Manchester United swept all before them during the 1998-99 season as they achieved what many believed to be impossible by adding the Champions' Cup to the domestic double. The dominant force in English football throughout the nineties, United, courtesy of a last day of the season victory over Tottenham, lifted the Premiership title for the fifth time in seven seasons, and with a comfortable 2-0 victory over Newcastle in the FA Cup final completed an unprecedented third double.

Their record-breaking campaign saw several players enhance their reputations, none more so than David Beckham who, in the aftermath of his World Cup nightmare, led the Reds' bid for honours. There wasn't a better player in England, perhaps the world, than the Leytonstone kid, and he will be a main contender for World Footballer of the Year this time round – even if we cannot recognise his talent in our more local award polls. It was Beckham who supplied the two corners from which Teddy Sheringham and Ole Gunnar Solskjaer poached the goals which secured United's sensational Champions' League final victory over Bayern Munich deep into injury time. Sheringham's end of season form earned him an England recall.

Roy Keane, in spite of disciplinary problems on and off the pitch, was outstanding while Peter Schmeichel ended his Old Trafford career by playing a significant part in the equalising goal against Bayern as he moved into the opposition penalty area to cause mayhem. Andy Cole and £12.6m early season signing from Aston Villa, Dwight Yorke, forged the most profitable partnership in the Premiership while Dutch defender Jaap Stam bounced back from an indifferent World Cup to become the linchpin of United's backline following his £10m transfer.

High-points were numerous but there were also games during which the dream could have died, particularly in the cups. In the FA Cup Liverpool were stunned at Old Trafford as Yorke and Solskjaer scored last-minute goals to reverse a seemingly lost cause while Schmeichel's semi-final penalty save from Bergkamp also proved decisive prior to Ryan Giggs's breathtaking solo goal. United's European venture looked destined to end in failure as Juventus, after drawing at Old Trafford, took a two-goal semi-final lead in Italy before Ferguson's side seized an historic 3-2 triumph. But the most astonishing comeback was saved for the final itself when the 90th anniversary of Sir Matt Busby's birth was celebrated in momentous fashion with the winning of the Champions' Cup in Barcelona. ■

Results 1998-99

FA Carling Premiership

Date	*Opponents*	*Ven*	*Res*	*Atten*	*Scorers*
15-Aug	Leicester C.	H	2-2	55,052	Sheringham (79); Beckham (90)
22-Aug	West Ham U.	A	0-0	26,039	
09-Sep	Charlton A.	H	4-1	55,147	Solskjaer (38, 63); Yorke (45, 48)
12-Sep	Coventry C.	H	2-0	55,193	Yorke (21); Johnsen (48)
20-Sep	Arsenal	A	0-3	38,142	
24-Sep	Liverpool	H	2-0	55,181	Irwin (18 pen); Scholes (79)
03-Oct	Southampton	A	3-0	15,251	Yorke (11); Cole (59); Cruyff (74)
17-Oct	Wimbledon	H	5-1	55,265	Cole (19, 88); Giggs (45); Beckham (48); Yorke (54)
24-Oct	Derby Co.	A	1-1	30,867	Cruyff (86)
31-Oct	Everton	A	4-1	40,079	Yorke (14); OG (23, Short); Cole (59); Blomqvist (64)
08-Nov	Newcastle U.	H	0-0	55,174	
14-Nov	Blackburn R.	H	3-2	55,198	Scholes (32, 58); Yorke (44)
21-Nov	Sheffield W.	A	1-3	39,475	Cole (29)
29-Nov	Leeds U.	H	3-2	55,172	Solskjaer (45); Keane (46); Butt (77)
05-Dec	Aston Villa	A	1-1	39,241	Scholes (47)
12-Dec	Tottenham H.	A	2-2	36,070	Solskjaer (11, 18)
16-Dec	Chelsea	H	1-1	55,159	Cole (45)
19-Dec	Middlesbrough	H	2-3	55,152	Butt (62); Scholes (70)
26-Dec	N.Forest	H	3-0	55,216	Johnsen (28, 59); Giggs (62)
29-Dec	Chelsea	A	0-0	34,741	
10-Jan	West Ham U.	H	4-1	55,180	Yorke (10); Cole (39, 68); Solskjaer (80)
16-Jan	Leicester C.	A	6-2	22,091	Yorke (10, 63, 84); Cole (49, 61); Stam (89)
31-Jan	Charlton A.	A	1-0	20,043	Yorke (89)
03-Feb	Derby Co.	H	1-0	55,174	Yorke (65)
06-Feb	N.Forest	A	8-1	30,025	Yorke (2,66); Cole (7, 49); Solskjaer (80, 87, 90, 90)
17-Feb	Arsenal	H	1-1	55,171	Cole (60)
20-Feb	Coventry C.	A	1-0	22,596	Giggs (78)
27-Feb	Southampton	H	2-1	55,316	Keane (79); Yorke (83)
13-Mar	Newcastle U.	A	2-1	36,500	Cole (25, 51)
22-Mar	Everton	H	3-1	55,182	Solskjaer (55); G.Neville (63); Beckham (67)

03-Apr	Wimbledon	A	1-1	26,121	Beckham (44)
17-Apr	Sheffield W.	H	3-0	55,270	Solskjaer (35); Sheringham (44); Scholes (62)
25-Apr	Leeds U.	A	1-1	40,255	Cole (56)
01-May	Aston Villa	H	2-1	55,189	OG (20, Watson); Beckham (46)
05-May	Liverpool	A	2-2	44,702	Yorke (23); Irwin (56 pen)
09-May	Middlesbrough	A	1-0	34,665	Yorke (45)
12-May	Blackburn R.	A	0-0	30,463	
16-May	Tottenham H.	H	2-1	55,189	Beckham (42); Cole (47)

UEFA Champions' League

Date	*Opponents*	*Vn*	*Rnd*	*Res*	*Atten*	*Scorers*
12-Aug	LKS Lódz	H	2Qf	2-0	50,906	Giggs (16); Cole (81)
26-Aug	LKS Lódz	A	2Qs	0-0	9,000	
	Manchester United win 2-0 on aggregate					
16-Sep	Barcelona	H	D	3-3	53,601	Giggs (17); Scholes (25); Beckham (64)
30-Sep	B.München	A	D	2-2	55,000	Yorke (30); Scholes (49)
21-Oct	Brøndby IF	A	D	6-2	40,315	Giggs (2, 21); Cole (27); Keane (54); Yorke (59); Solskjaer (61)
04-Nov	Brøndby IF	H	D	5-0	53,250	Beckham (7); Cole (13); P.Neville (16); Yorke (28); Scholes (62)
25-Nov	Barcelona	A	D	3-3	70,000	Yorke (25, 67); Cole (52)
09-Dec	B.München	H	D	1-1	54,334	Keane (43)
	Manchester United qualify as one of two best runners-up					
03-Mar	Internazionale	H	QFf	2-0	54,430	Yorke (7, 45)
17-Mar	Internazionale	A	QFs	1-1	79,518	Scholes (88)
	Manchester United win 3-1 on aggregate					
	Juventus	H	SFf	1-1	54,487	Giggs (90)
	Juventus	A	SFs	3-2	60,806	Keane (24); Yorke (34); Cole (84)
	Manchester United win 4-3 on aggregate					
26-May	B.München	n	F	2-1		Sheringham (90): Solskjaer (90)

FA Cup, Worthington Cup and 5-Year Records can be found on Page 204

Middlesbrough

Formed in 1876 and played first game in 1877. Turned professional in 1889, but reverted to amateur status shortly afterwards, being early winners of the FA Amateur Cup. League football was first played in Middlesbrough by the Ironpolis side for one season, 1893-94. Middlesbrough turned professional again, were elected to Division Two in 1899, and moved to Ayresome Park in 1903. They were founder members of the Premier League in 1993 but were relegated in their first season. Moved to purpose-built stadium in 1995 coinciding with return to Premiership. Reached and lost both Cup Finals in 1997 in addition to being relegated to Division 1.

Ground: The Cellnet Riverside Stadium, Middlesbrough, TS3 6RS
Phone: 01642-877700 **Fax:** 0164-877840
Box Office: 01642-877745
Info: 0891 42 42 00 **Club Shop:** 01642-877720
Colours: Red with Black, White with Black, Red with Black
Capacity: 34,500 **Pitch:** 115 yds x 74 yds
Nickname: The Boro
Radio: 100.7FM Century Radio
Internet: –

Chairman: Steve Gibson **CEO:** Keith Lamb
Secretary: Karen Nelson
Manager: Bryan Robson **Assistant:** Viv Anderson
Coach: Gordon McQueen
Physios: Bob Ward, Tommy Johnson

League History: 1899 Elected to Division 2; 1902-24 Division 1; 1924-27 Division 2; 1927-28 Division 1; 1928-29 Division 2; 1929-54 Division 1; 1954-66 Division 2; 1966-67 Division 3; 1967-74 Division 2; 1974-82 Division 2; 1982-86 Division 2; 1986-87 Division 3; 1988-89 Division 1; 1989-92 Division 2; 1992-93 FAPL; 1993-95 Division 1; 1995-97 FAPL; 1997- Division 1

Honours: *Football League: Division 1 (new) Champions* 1994-95; *Runners-up* 1997-98; *Division 2 Champions* 1926-27, 1928-29, 1973-74; *Runners-up* 1901-02, 1991-92; *Division 3 Runners up* 1966-67, 1986-87. *FA Cup: Runners-up* 1996-97. *League Cup: Runners-up* 1996-97, 1997-

98. *FA Amateur Cup: Winners* 1895, 1898. *Anglo-Scottish Cup: Winners* 1975-76.

European Record: Never qualified

Managers: John Robson 1899-05; Alex Massie 1905-06; Andy Atkin 1906-09; J. Gunter 1908-10; Andy Walker 1910-11; Tom McIntosh 1911-19; James Howie 1920-23; Herbert Bamlett 1923-26; Peter McWilliam 1927-34; Wilf Gillow 1933-44; David Jack 1944-52; Walter Rowley 1952-54; Bob Dennison 1954-63; Raich Carter 1963-66; Stan Anderson 1966-73; Jack Charlton 1973-77; John Neal 1977-81; Bobby Murdoch 1981-82; Malcolm Allison 1982-84; Willie Maddren 1984-86; Bruce Rioch 1986-90; Colin Todd 1990-91; Lennie Lawrence 1991-94; *(FAPL)* Bryan Robson May 1994-.

All-Time Records

Record FAPL Win: 4-0 v Sheffield Wednesday, Home, 03/10/98
4-1 v Leeds United, Home, 22/08/92
4-1 v Manchester City, Home, 09/12/95
4-2 v West Ham United, Home, 22/12/95
Record FAPL Defeat: 1-6 v Arsenal, Home, 24/05/99
Record FL Win: 9-0 v Brighton & HA, Div 2 23/8/58
Record FL Defeat: 0-9 v Blackburn Rovers, Div 2 6/11/54
Record Cup Win: 9-3 v Goole Town, FAC R1, 9/1/15
Record Fee Received: £12m from Atletico Madrid for Juninho, 7/97
Record Fee Paid: £7m to Juventus for Fabrizio Ravanelli, 7/96
Record Attendance (all-time): 53,596 v Newcastle Utd, Div 1 27/12/49
at Ayresome Park
Record Attendance (FAPL): 34,687 v Tottenham Hotspur, 20/02/99
at Riverside Stadium
Most FL Apps: Tim Williamson, 563, 1902-23
Most FAPL Apps: 108 – Robbie Mustoe, 1992-99
Most FAPL Goals: 16 – Fabrizio Ravanelli, 1996-97
Highest Scorer in FAPL Season: 16 – Fabrizio Ravanelli, 1996-97
Most FAPL Goals in Season: 54, 1992-93 – 42 games,
1998-99 – 38 games
Most FAPL Points in Season: 51, 1998-99 – 38 games

Summary 1998-99

Player	*Tot*	*St*	*Sb*	*Snu*	*PS*	*Gls*	*Y*	*R*	*Fa*	*Fg*	*La*	*Lg*
ARMSTRONG	6	0	6	2	0	1	0	0	0	0	0	0
BAKER	1	1	0	5	0	0	0	0	0	0	0	0
BECK †	27	13	14	2	5	5	2	0	1	0	2	0
BERESFORD	4	4	0	31	0	0	0	0	0	0	3	0
BLACKMORE	0	0	0	9	0	0	0	0	0	0	1	0
BRANCA	1	0	1	0	0	0	0	0	0	0	0	0
CAMPBELL	8	1	7	4	1	0	1	0	0	0	3	0
COOPER	32	31	1	0	2	1	6	0	1	0	1	0
CUMMINS	1	1	0	0	0	0	0	0	0	0	0	0
DEANE	26	24	2	0	6	6	2	0	1	0	1	0
FESTA	25	25	0	0	2	2	9	0	0	0	2	1
FLEMING	14	12	2	0	1	1	2	0	1	0	1	0
GASCOIGNE	26	25	1	1	12	3	12	0	1	0	2	0
GAVIN	2	2	0	0	1	0	0	0	0	0	0	0
GORDON	38	38	0	0	0	3	3	0	1	0	2	0
HARRISON	4	3	1	2	0	0	0	0	0	0	2	0
KINDER	5	0	5	8	1	2	1	0	0	0	1	0
MADDISON	20	10	10	10	5	0	1	0	1	0	1	0
MERSON †	3	3	0	0	0	0	0	0	0	0	0	0
MOORE	4	3	1	7	3	0	0	0	0	0	1	0
MUSTOE	33	32	1	0	3	4	8	1	1	0	1	0
O'NEILL	6	4	2	1	2	0	2	0	0	0	0	0
ORMEROD	0	0	0	0	0	0	0	0	0	0	1	0
PALLISTER	26	26	0	0	2	0	5	0	1	0	0	0
RICARD	36	32	4	1	14	15	5	0	1	0	3	3
ROBERTS	0	0	0	3	0	0	0	0	0	0	0	0
SCHWARZER	34	34	0	3	0	0	1	0	1	0	0	0
STAMP	16	5	11	3	3	2	1	1	1	0	3	0
STOCKDALE	19	17	2	9	5	0	3	0	0	0	3	0
SUMMERBELL	11	7	4	9	1	0	4	0	0	0	2	1
TOWNSEND	35	35	0	0	6	1	10	0	1	1	1	0
VICKERS	31	30	1	4	1	1	4	0	0	0	3	0
Own Goals						1						
32 Players	494	418	76	114	76	48	82	2	13	1	40	5

Consistency Gap

A case of deja vu engulfed Middlesbrough for the second half of the 1998-99 season as Bryan Robson's side fell away alarmingly in a fashion not too dissimilar to the one which led to their relegation two seasons earlier. Thoughts of relegation were the furthest things from the minds of Boro supporters though on 19 December as goals from Hamilton Ricard, Dean Gordon and Brian Deane clinched a 3-2 win at Old Trafford as the Teesiders rose to fourth place having lost only two of their opening 18 Premier League fixtures. That was the good news.

What followed next was a nightmare as Boro went nine matches without a win which included a spell in which they scored just once in six games, losing twice to Liverpool and being thrashed 5-0 at Everton. During this time Middlesbrough also returned to Old Trafford for a 3rd Round FA Cup tie and made a controversial 3-1 exit. Boro brought the famine to a close with an undefeated seven-match run but again that came to a shuddering end as Arsenal won 6-1 at the Riverside, inflicting not just their heaviest Premiership defeat but also handing out a football lesson. The season closed with a 4-0 drubbing at West Ham. Boro's final three home games of the season were against the top three sides and the Arsenal reversal, followed by a 1-0 success for Manchester United came after a goalless draw with Chelsea and all conspired to dent an otherwise good home record.

Whilst the form of Paul Gascoigne brought a mixed reaction, the Colombian Hamilton Ricard was a success as his 18 league and cup goals made him one of the hottest properties in the Premier League, and defender Steve Vickers took his total of league appearances past 500. Gary Pallister made a very welcome £2.5m return to Boro after nine years away when he became one of two pre-season signings, Gordon being the other. But overall Boro were less active in the transfer market than in recent seasons with Deane, £3m from Benfica, and Keith O'Neill, £700,000 from Norwich, being the only major captures after the start of the season. Paul Merson's stay at the Riverside was terminated in September with a £6.75m move to Aston Villa while Mikkel Beck made a transfer deadline-day move to Derby.

Boro's Worthington Cup venture was brief with a 2nd Round success over Wycombe being followed by an extra-time defeat at home to Everton.

Boro will need another great start to the 1999-2000 season, or some overall consistency if they are to continue in the top flight. ■

Results 1998-99

FA Carling Premiership

Date	Opponents	Ven	Res	Atten	Scorers
15-Aug	Leeds U.	H	0-0	34,162	
23-Aug	Aston Villa	A	1-3	29,559	Beck (62)
29-Aug	Derby Co.	H	1-1	34,121	Ricard (48)
09-Sep	Leicester C.	A	1-0	20,635	Gascoigne (45)
13-Sep	Tottenham H.	A	3-0	30,437	Ricard (25, 32); Kinder (87)
19-Sep	Everton	H	2-2	34,563	Ricard (27, 35)
27-Sep	Chelsea	A	0-2	34,811	
03-Oct	Sheffield W.	H	4-0	34,163	Beck (27, 45); Ricard (49); Gascoigne (90)
17-Oct	Blackburn R.	H	2-1	34,413	Ricard (83 pen); Fleming (90)
24-Oct	Wimbledon	A	2-2	14,114	Mustoe (23); Ricard (37)
01-Nov	N.Forest	H	1-1	34,223	Deane (22)
07-Nov	Southampton	A	3-3	15,202	Gascoigne (47); OG (66, Lundekvam); Festa (90)
14-Nov	Charlton A.	A	1-1	20,043	Stamp (74)
21-Nov	Coventry C.	H	2-0	34,293	Gordon (66); Ricard (83)
29-Nov	Arsenal	A	1-1	38,075	Deane (5)
06-Dec	Newcastle U.	H	2-2	34,629	Townsend (13); Cooper (59)
12-Dec	West Ham U.	H	1-0	34,623	Deane (40)
19-Dec	Manchester U.	A	3-2	55,152	Ricard (23); Gordon (31); Deane (59)
26-Dec	Liverpool	H	1-3	34,626	Deane (32)
28-Dec	Derby Co.	A	1-2	32,726	Beck (77)
09-Jan	Aston Villa	H	0-0	34,643	
16-Jan	Leeds U.	A	0-2	37,473	
30-Jan	Leicester C.	H	0-0	34,631	
06-Feb	Liverpool	A	1-3	44,384	Stamp (86)
17-Feb	Everton	A	0-5	31,606	
20-Feb	Tottenham H.	H	0-0	34,687	
27-Feb	Sheffield W.	A	1-3	24,534	Mustoe (78)
14-Mar	Southampton	H	3-0	33,387	Beck (44); Ricard (45); Vickers (62)
21-Mar	N.Forest	A	2-1	21,468	Ricard (30); Deane (87)
03-Apr	Blackburn R.	A	0-0	27,482	
05-Apr	Wimbledon	H	3-1	33,999	Ricard (1, 29); Festa (8)
10-Apr	Charlton A.	H	2-0	34,529	Ricard (35); Mustoe (60)
14-Apr	Chelsea	H	0-0	34,406	
17-Apr	Coventry C.	A	2-1	19,231	Kinder (64); Gordon (82)
24-Apr	Arsenal	H	1-6	34,630	Armstrong (87)

01-May	Newcastle U.	A	1-1	36,552	Mustoe (60)
09-May	Manchester U.	H	0-1	34,665	
16-May	West Ham U.	A	0-4	25,902	

FA Challenge Cup

Sponsored by AXA

Date	*Opponents*	*Vn*	*Rnd*	*Res*	*Atten*	*Scorers*
03-Jan	Manchester U.	A	3R	1-3	52,232	Townsend (52)

Worthington Cup

Date	*Opponents*	*Vn*	*Rnd*	*Res*	*Atten*	*Scorers*
16-Sep	Wycombe W.	H	2Rf	2-0	11,531	Ricard (37); Festa (90)
22-Sep	Wycombe W.	A	2Rs	1-1	5,698	Ricard (53)
	Middlesbrough win 3-1 on aggregate					
28-Oct	Everton	H	3R	2-3	20,748	Summerbell (64); Ricard (117)

5-Year Record

	Div.	*P*	*W*	*D*	*L*	*F*	*A*	*Pts*	*Pos*	*FAC*	*FLC*
94-95	1	46	23	13	10	67	40	82	1	3	3
95-96	PL	38	11	10	17	35	50	43	12	4	4
96-97	PL	38	10	12	16	51	60	39	19	F	F
97-98	1	46	27	10	9	77	41	91	2	4	F
98-99	PL	38	12	15	11	48	54	51	9	3	3

Newcastle United

Formed 1882 as Newcastle East End on the amalgamation of Stanley and Rosewood. Founder members, as a professional club, of the Northern League in 1889. Moved from Chillington Road, Heaton, in 1892 to take over the home of the defunct Newcastle West End, with several of those associated with the West End side joining the newcomers.

Applied for Football League Division One membership in 1892, failed and decided against a place in the new Second Division, staying in the Northern League. Later in 1892 changed name to Newcastle United. Elected to an expanded Football League Division Two in 1893.

Ground: St James's Park, Newcastle-upon-Tyne, NE1 4ST
Phone: 0191-201 8400 **Fax:** 0191-201 8600
Box Office: 0191-261 1571 **CC Bookings:** 0191-261 1571
Info: 0891 12 11 90 **Club Shop:** 0191-201 8426
Colours: Black/White, Black, Black **Nickname:** Magpies
Capacity: 36,672 > 51,000 **Pitch:** 115 yds x 75 yds
Radio: 97.1FM Metro Radio
Internet: www.newcastle-utd.co.uk

CEO: Freddy Shepherd **Secretary:** Russell Cushing
Manager: Ruud Gullitt **Assistant:** Steve Clark
Coaches: Chris McMenemy, Alan Irvine
Physio: Derek Wright, Paul Ferris

League History: 1893 Elected to Division 2; 1898-1934 Division 1; 1934-48 Division 2; 1948-61 Division 1; 1961-65 Division 2; 1965-78 Division 1; 1978-84 Division 2; 1984-89 Division 1; 1989-92 Division 2; 1992-1993 Division 1; 1993- FA Premier League.

Honours: *FA Premier League: Runners-up* 1995-96, 1996-97. *Football League: Division 1 Champions* 1904-05, 1906-07, 1908-09, 1926-27, 1992-93; *Division 2 Champions* 1964-65; *Runners-up* 1897-98, 1947-48. *FA Cup: Winners* 1909-10, 1923-24, 1931-32, 1950-51, 1951-52, 1954-55; *Runners-up* 1904-05, 1905-06, 1907-08, 1910-11, 1973-74, 1997-98. *Football League Cup: Runners-up* 1975-76. *Texaco Cup: Winners* 1973-74, 1974-75. *UEFA Cup: Winners* 1968-69.

European Record: CC (1) 97-98 (CL); CWC (1): 98-99 (1); UEFA (7): 68-69 (W), 69-70 (QF), 70-71 (2), 77-78 (2), 94-95 (2), 96-97 (QF).

Managers: Frank Watt 1895-1932 (secretary until 1932); Andy Cunningham 1930-35; Tom Mather 1935-39; Stan Seymour 1939-47 (hon. manager); George Martin 1947-50; Stan Seymour 1950-54 (hon. manager); Duggie Livingstone; 1954-56, Stan Seymour (hon. manager) 1956-58; Charlie Mitten 1958-61; Norman Smith 1961-62; Joe Harvey 1962-75; Gordon Lee 1975-77; Richard Dinnis 1977; Bill McGarry 1977-80; Arthur Cox 1980-84; Jack Charlton 1984; Willie McFaul 1985-88; Jim Smith 1988-91; Ossie Ardiles 1991-92; *(FAPL)* Kevin Keegan Feb 1992-Jan 1997; Kenny Dalglish Jan 1997-Aug 1998; Ruud Gullitt Aug 1998–.

All-Time Records

Record FAPL Win: 7-1 v Swindon Town, Home, 12/03/94
7-1 v Tottenham Hotspur, Home, 28/12/96
Record FAPL Defeat: 1-4 v Liverpool, Home, 30/08/98
2-4 v Liverpool, Away, 28/12/98
Record FL Win: 13-0 v Newport County, Div 2, 05/10/46
Record FL Defeat: 0-9 v Burton Wanderers, Div 2, 15/4/1895
Record Cup Win: 9-0 v Southport, FAC4R, 1/2/32
Record Fee Received: £7m from Manchester United for Andy Cole, 1/95 (inc. part exchange)
Record Fee Paid: £15m to Blackburn R. for Alan Shearer, 7/97
Most FL Apps: Jim Lawrence, 432, 1904-22
Most FAPL Apps: 199 – Robert Lee, 1993-99
Most FAPL Goals: 48 – Peter Beardsley, 1993-97
Highest Scorer in FAPL Season: 34 – Andy Cole, 1993-94
Record Attendance (all-time): 68,386 v Chelsea, Div 1, 3/9/30
Record Attendance (FAPL): 36,783 v Aston Villa, 23/08/97
Most FAPL Goals in Season: 82, 1993-94 – 42 games
Most FAPL Points in Season: 78, 1995-96 – 38 games

5-Year Record

	Div.	*P*	*W*	*D*	*L*	*F*	*A*	*Pts*	*Pos*	*FAC*	*FLC*
94-95	PL	42	20	12	10	67	47	72	6	QF	4
95-96	PL	38	24	6	8	66	37	78	2	3	QF
96-97	PL	38	19	11	8	73	40	68	2	4	4
97-98	PL	38	11	11	16	35	44	44	13	F	QF
98-99	PL	38	11	13	14	48	54	46	13	F	4

Summary 1998-99

Player	*Tot*	*St*	*Sb*	*Snu*	*PS*	*Gls*	*Y*	*R*	*Fa*	*Fg*	*La*	*Lg*
ALBERT	6	3	3	4	0	0	2	0	0	0	0	0
ANDERSSON	15	11	4	3	7	2	0	0	1	0	0	0
BARNES †	1	0	1	3	1	0	0	0	0	0	0	0
BARTON	24	17	7	11	4	0	3	0	5	0	1	0
BATTY †	8	6	2	0	0	0	2	0	0	0	2	0
BEHARALL	4	4	0	3	0	0	0	0	0	0	0	0
BRADY	9	3	6	3	2	0	0	0	3	0	0	0
CALDWELL	0	0	0	1	0	0	0	0	0	0	0	0
CHARVET	31	30	1	0	0	1	3	0	5	0	1	0
DABIZAS	30	25	5	1	1	3	8	2	6	0	2	0
DALGLISH	11	6	5	2	4	1	1	0	0	0	2	1
DOMI	14	14	0	0	0	0	1	0	4	0	0	0
FERGUSON	7	7	0	0	3	2	0	0	2	0	0	0
GEORGIADIS	10	7	3	2	3	0	1	0	2	1	1	0
GILLESPIE	7	5	2	1	1	0	0	0	0	0	1	0
GIVEN	31	31	0	4	1	0	0	0	6	0	2	0
GLASS	22	18	4	0	8	3	0	0	4	0	2	0
GRIFFIN	14	14	0	2	2	0	0	0	3	0	1	0
GUI'VARCH	4	2	2	1	1	1	0	0	0	0	0	0
HAMANN	23	22	1	3	3	4	6	1	7	1	1	0
HARPER	8	7	1	20	0	0	0	0	2	0	0	0
HOWEY	14	14	0	1	1	0	1	0	4	0	0	0
HUGHES	14	12	2	10	1	0	1	0	2	0	1	0
KEEN	0	0	0	1	0	0	0	0	0	0	0	0
KETSBAIA	26	14	12	2	8	5	2	0	6	3	0	0
LEE	26	20	6	0	2	0	6	0	3	0	0	0
McCLEN	1	1	0	3	1	0	0	0	0	0	0	0
MARIC	10	9	1	0	5	0	1	0	3	0	0	0
PEARCE	12	12	0	3	0	0	1	1	0	0	2	0
PEREZ	0	0	0	12	0	0	0	0	0	0	0	0
PISTONE	3	2	1	2	1	0	1	0	0	0	0	0
SAHA	11	5	6	0	3	1	1	0	1	1	0	0
SERRANT	4	3	1	0	2	0	1	0	0	0	0	0
SHEARER	30	29	1	0	2	14	6	0	6	5	2	1
SOLANO	29	24	5	6	14	6	0	0	7	0	1	0
SPEED	38	34	4	0	3	4	6	0	6	1	2	0
WATSON †	7	7	0	0	2	0	0	0	0	0	0	0
Own Goals						1						
37 Players	504	418	86	104	86	48	54	4	88	12	24	2

Double Trouble

Lightning, as Newcastle United proved at Wembley in the FA Cup, does indeed strike twice as the Magpies, in losing 2-0 to Manchester United, put in a performance every bit as disappointing as the one which saw Arsenal triumph by the same score a year earlier. What should have been a celebration at the end of Ruud Gullitt's first season in charge at St. James's Park following the departure of Kenny Dalglish, instead became a detraction from another season of under-achievement as far as Premier League results were concerned. Finishing a lowly 13th, Newcastle lost six times on their own soil and just how far they trailed behind the leading sides can be gauged from the fact that Gullitt's team beat just one of the top seven sides on Tyneside.

Comparisons between Newcastle and the failings at Blackburn are inevitable given that United have frequently resorted to the cheque book in recent years but Newcastle, for all their shortcomings in the league, have reached two cup finals and, in Alan Shearer, still possess one of the game's great goalscorers although injury restricted his total of Premiership goals to 14. On the plus side Shearer did score the two goals that took United to Wembley in the semi-final victory over Spurs.

Gullitt is certainly not afraid to ship out fans' favourites if the sale of Steve Watson and David Batty is anything to go by but the £16.65m recouped from their departures plus fees from three other players, did help finance incoming deals totalling £19.9m, of which £7m went on Duncan Ferguson whose history of injury problems surfaced again following his surprise November move from Everton.

Newcastle made a slow start to the season and when a run of three successive wins, including respective 4-0 and 5-1 thrashings of Southampton and Coventry, was not maintained, there was a possibility of the Magpies being sucked into a relegation battle, a position not helped by two sequences of just two wins in 13 games.

European success was thwarted at the first hurdle by Partizan Belgrade while Worthington Cup progress ended in the 3rd Round when Blackburn won a penalty shoot-out at St. James's Park. Newcastle at least had the satisfaction of revenge at Ewood Park in the FA Cup on their way to Wembley.

There will have been a good number of changes at Newcastle during the close season – the fans will be even more vehement that they deliver the silverware in the coming year. But they may find that even though more and more clubs spend bigger and bigger – there are still only the same number of pots to be handed out at the end of any one season. ■

Results 1998-99

FA Carling Premiership

Date	*Opponents*	*Ven*	*Res*	*Atten*	*Scorers*
15-Aug	Charlton A.	H	0-0	36,719	
22-Aug	Chelsea	A	1-1	34,795	Andersson (42)
30-Aug	Liverpool	H	1-4	36,740	Guivarc'h (28)
09-Sep	Aston Villa	A	0-1	39,241	
12-Sep	Southampton	H	4-0	36,454	Shearer (8, 38 pen); Ketsbaia (90); OG (90, Marshall)
19-Sep	Coventry C.	A	5-1	22,656	Dabizas (14); Shearer (42, 90); Speed (43); Glass (58)
27-Sep	N.Forest	H	2-0	36,760	Shearer (11, 89 pen)
04-Oct	Arsenal	A	0-3	38,102	
17-Oct	Derby Co.	H	2-1	36,750	Dabizas (13); Glass (17)
24-Oct	Tottenham H.	A	0-2	36,047	
31-Oct	West Ham U.	H	0-3	36,744	
08-Nov	Manchester U.	A	0-0	55,174	
14-Nov	Sheffield W.	H	1-1	36,698	Dalglish (4)
23-Nov	Everton	A	0-1	30,357	
28-Nov	Wimbledon	H	3-1	36,623	Solano (38); Ferguson (59, 90)
06-Dec	Middlesbrough	A	2-2	34,629	Charvet (38); Dabizas (83)
12-Dec	Blackburn R.	A	0-0	27,569	
19-Dec	Leicester C.	H	1-0	36,718	Glass (66)
26-Dec	Leeds U.	H	0-3	36,783	
28-Dec	Liverpool	A	2-4	44,605	Solano (29); Andersson (56)
09-Jan	Chelsea	H	0-1	36,711	
17-Jan	Charlton A.	A	2-2	20,043	Ketsbaia (13); Solano (55)
30-Jan	Aston Villa	H	2-1	36,766	Shearer (4); Ketsbaia (27)
06-Feb	Leeds U.	A	1-0	40,202	Solano (63)
17-Feb	Coventry C.	H	4-1	36,352	Shearer (18, 75); Speed (55); Saha (58)
20-Feb	Southampton	A	1-2	15,244	Hamann (86)
28-Feb	Arsenal	H	1-1	36,708	Hamann (77)
10-Mar	N.Forest	A	2-1	22,852	Shearer (45 pen); Hamann (73)
13-Mar	Manchester U.	H	1-2	36,500	Solano (16)
21-Mar	West Ham U.	A	0-2	25,997	
03-Apr	Derby Co.	A	4-3	32,039	Speed (11, 24); Ketsbaia (39); Solano (60)
05-Apr	Tottenham H.	H	1-1	36,655	Ketsbaia (78)
17-Apr	Everton	H	1-3	36,775	Shearer (82 pen)
21-Apr	Sheffield W.	A	1-1	21,545	Shearer (45 pen)
24-Apr	Wimbledon	A	1-1	21,172	Shearer (18)

01-May	Middlesbrough	H	1-1	36,552	Shearer (64 pen)
08-May	Leicester C.	A	0-2	21,125	
16-May	Blackburn R.	H	1-1	36,623	Hamann (51)

Cup-Winners' Cup

Date	*Opponents*	*Vn*	*Rnd*	*Res*	*Atten*	*Scorers*
17-Sep	P.Beograd	H	1f	2-1	26,599	Shearer (12); Dabizas (71)
01-Oct	P.Beograd	A	1s	0-1	28,000	

2-2 on aggregate. Partizan Beograd win on away goals rule

FA Challenge Cup

Sponsored by AXA

Date	*Opponents*	*Vn*	*Rnd*	*Res*	*Atten*	*Scorers*
02-Jan	C.Palace	H	3R	2-1	36,536	Speed (47); Shearer (69)
23-Jan	Bradford C.	H	4R	3-0	36,698	Hamann (33); Shearer (51); Ketsbaia (85)
14-Feb	Blackburn R.	H	5R	0-0	36,295	
24-Feb	Blackburn R.	A	5RR	1-0	27,483	Saha (39)
07-Mar	Everton	H	QF	4-1	36,584	Ketsbaia (21, 73); Georgiadis (62); Shearer (81)
12-Apr	Tottenham H. *At Old Trafford. aet*	H	SF	2-0	53,609	Shearer (109 pen, 118)
22-May	Manchester U. *At Wembley*		F	0-2	79,101	

Worthington Cup

Date	*Opponents*	*Vn*	*Rnd*	*Res*	*Atten*	*Scorers*
27-Oct	Tranmere R.	A	3R	1-0	12,017	Dalglish (31)
11-Nov	Blackburn R.	H	4R	1-1	34,702	Shearer (9)

Sheffield Wednesday

Founded in 1867 by members of the Wednesday Cricket Club and played at Highfield before moving to Myrtle Road. Were first holders of the Sheffield FA Cup. The club played at Sheaf House then Endcliff and became professionals in 1886. In 1887 moved to Olive Grove. Refused admission to the Football League, the club was founder member, and first champions, of the Football Alliance in 1889. In 1892 most Alliance clubs became founder members of Football League Division Two, but Wednesday were elected to an enlarged top division. The club moved to Hillsborough in 1899. Founder members of the Premier League 1992.

Ground: Hillsborough, Sheffield, S6 1SW
Phone: 0114-221 2121 **News:** 0891 12 11 86
Box Office: 0114-221 2400 **Fax:** 0114-221 2401
Info: 0891 12 11 86
Capacity: 36,020 **Pitch:** 115 yds x 77 yds
Colours: Blue/White, Blue, Blue **Nickname:** The Owls
Radio: BBC Radio Sheffield 88.6 and 104.1FM
Internet: www.swfc.co.uk

Chairman: D.G. Richards **Vice-Chairman:** K.T. Addy
Secretary: Alan Sykes
Manager: Danny Wilson **Assistant:** Frank Barlow
Coach: Chris Waddle **Physio:** David Galley

League History: 1892 Elected to Division 1; 1899-1900 Division 2; 1900-20 Division 1; 1920-26 Division 2; 1926-37 Division 1; 1937-50 Division 2; 1950-51 Division 1; 1951-52 Division 2; 1952-55 Division 1; 1955-56 Division 2; 1956-58 Division 1; 1958-59 Division 2; 1959-70 Division 1; 1970-75 Division 2; 1975-80 Division 3; 1980-84 Division 2; 1984-90 Division 1; 1990-91 Division 2; 1991-92 Division 1; 1992- FA Premier League.

Honours: *Football League: Division 1 Champions* 1902-03, 1903-04, 1928-29, 1929-30; *Runners-up* 1960-61; *Division 2 Champions* 1899-1900, 1925-26, 1951-52, 1955-56, 1958-59; *Runners-up* 1949-50, 1983-84. *FA Cup: Winners* 1895-96, 1906-07, 1934-35; *Runners-up* 1889-90, 1965-66, 1992-93; *Football League Cup: Winners* 1990-91; *Runners-up* 1992-93.

European Record: CC (0): –; CWC (0): – ; UEFA (3): 61-62 (QF), 63-64 (2), 92-93 (2).

Managers: Arthur Dickinson 1891-1920; Robert Brown 1920-33; Billy Walker 1933-37; Jimmy McMullan 1937-42; Eric Taylor 1942-58 (continued as GM to 1974); Harry Catterick 1958-61; Vic Buckingham 1961-64; Alan Brown 1964-68; Jack Marshall 1968-69; Danny Williams 1969-71; Derek Dooley 1971-73; Steve Burtenshaw 1974-75; Len Ashurst 1975-77; Jackie Charlton 1977-83; Howard Wilkinson 1983-88; Peter Eustace 1988-89; Ron Atkinson 1989-91; *(FAPL)* Trevor Francis June 1991-May 1995; David Pleat July 1995-Nov 97; Ron Atkinson Nov 1997-Jun 98; Danny Wilson Aug-98–.

All-Time Records

Record FAPL Win: 6-2 v Leeds United, Home, 16/12/95
Record FAPL Defeat: 1-7 v Nottingham Forest, Away, 01/04/95
Record FL Win: 9-1 v Birmingham, Div 1, 13/12/30
Record FL Defeat: 0-10 v Aston Villa, Div 1, 5/10/12
Record Cup Win: 12-0 v Halliwell, FAC R1, 17/1/1891
Record Fee Received: £2.7m from Blackburn Rovers for Paul Warhurst, 9/93
Record Fee Paid: £4.7m to Celtic for Paolo Di Canio, 8/97
Most FL Apps: Andy Wilson, 502, 1900-20
Most FAPL Apps: 227 – Des Walker, 1992-99
Most FAPL Goals: 48 – Mark Bright, 1992-97
Highest Scorer in FAPL Season: 19 – Bright, 1993-94
Record Attendance (all-time): 72,841 v Man City, FA Cup R5, 17/2/34
Record Attendance (FAPL): 39,427 v Manchester United, 97-98
Most FAPL Goals in Season: 76, 1993-94 – 42 games
Most FAPL Points in Season: 64, 1993-94 – 42 games

5-Year Record

	Div.	*P*	*W*	*D*	*L*	*F*	*A*	*Pts*	*Pos*	*FAC*	*FLC*
94-95	PL	42	13	12	17	49	57	51	13	4	4
95-96	PL	38	10	10	18	48	61	40	15	3	4
96-97	PL	38	14	15	9	50	51	57	7	6	2
97-98	PL	38	12	8	18	52	67	44	16	4	2
98-99	PL	38	13	7	18	41	42	46	12	5	2

Summary 1998-99

Player	Tot	St	Sb	Snu	PS	Gls	Y	R	Fa	Fg	La	Lg
AGOGO	1	0	1	4	0	0	1	0	1	0	0	0
ALEXANDERSSON	32	31	1	0	9	3	0	0	3	0	1	0
ATHERTON	38	38	0	0	0	2	4	1	3	0	2	0
BARRETT ⁃	5	0	5	3	0	0	0	0	0	0	1	0
BOOTH	34	34	0	0	7	6	7	0	2	0	2	0
BRISCOE	16	5	11	12	2	1	0	0	2	0	1	0
CARBONE	31	31	0	0	6	8	9	0	3	1	2	0
CLARKE	0	0	0	22	0	0	0	0	0	0	0	0
COBIAN	9	7	2	4	5	0	2	0	0	0	1	0
CRESSWELL	7	1	6	1	0	1	0	0	0	0	0	0
DI CANIO	6	5	1	0	2	3	0	1	0	0	2	0
HASLAM	2	2	0	2	2	0	0	0	0	0	0	0
HIGGINS	0	0	0	1	0	0	0	0	0	0	0	0
HINCHCLIFFE	32	32	0	0	2	3	4	1	2	0	2	0
HUMPHREYS	19	10	9	7	4	1	1	0	2	2	0	0
HYDE	1	0	1	4	0	0	0	0	0	0	0	0
JONK	38	38	0	0	6	2	4	0	3	0	2	0
McKEEVER	3	1	2	2	0	0	0	0	0	0	0	0
MAGILTON	6	1	5	9	1	0	0	0	0	0	0	0
MORRISON	1	0	1	0	0	0	0	0	0	0	0	0
NEWSOME	4	2	2	14	0	0	0	0	1	0	1	0
OAKES	1	0	1	3	0	0	0	0	0	0	0	0
PRESSMAN	15	14	1	15	0	0	0	0	1	0	2	0
QUINN	1	1	0	0	1	0	0	0	0	0	0	0
RUDI	34	33	1	0	7	6	2	0	3	1	1	0
SANETTI	3	0	3	5	0	0	0	0	0	0	2	0
SCOTT	4	0	4	0	0	1	0	0	0	0	0	0
SONNER	26	24	2	3	6	3	6	0	3	0	0	0
SRNICEK	24	24	0	0	0	0	1	1	2	0	0	0
STEFANOVIC	11	8	3	11	0	0	3	1	2	1	0	0
THOME	38	38	0	0	1	1	3	0	3	1	2	0
WALKER ⁃	37	37	0	0	1	0	2	0	3	0	2	0
WHITTINGHAM	2	1	1	5	1	0	0	0	0	0	1	0
Own Goals												1
33 Players	481	418	63	127	63	41	49	5	39	6	27	1

Seasonal Anomalies

Possibly the club to endure the most bizarre season was Sheffield Wednesday who were at the centre of the ludicrous Paolo Di Canio incident when a moment's sheer stupidity led to a prolonged absence from the game. Yet the Owls finished the campaign accused of going through the motions in search of a UEFA Cup place through the nonsensical UEFA Fair Play system. Wednesday collected 48 bookings, the fewest in the Premier League, but only three sides received more than their five red cards. As it was, two clubs finished above them as talk of Europe petered away.

In between those anomalies, it was a tough baptism for manager Danny Wilson following his summer move from Barnsley. Seven players departed from Hillsborough before the season started while Wilson made four new signings, of which Wim Jonk was thc most expensive at £2.5m. Wednesday were one of few clubs not to spend big money during the season, with deadline-day signing Richard Cresswell from York being the Owls' next most cxpensive signing at £950,000. He repaid a slice of that fee with his first goal for the club, against Liverpool, which clinched Wednesday's Premier League status for another year. The club recouped £1.75m in January with the sale of Di Canio to West Ham to bring a conclusion to a saga that started the previous September following his dismissal during a 1-0 win over Arsenal. Di Canio received an extended ban for then shoving to the ground referee Paul Alcock but increased his absence from the game by staying in his native Italy, claiming to be suffering from stress.

Only one side scored less home goals than Wednesday who did net a good number of their goals against the lower sides. That said, Niclas Alexandersson scored twice as Manchester United were beaten 3-1 at Hillsborough and West Ham were crushed 4-0 at Upton Park. Benito Carbone was top scorer with eight league goals followed by local favourite Andy Booth who went 18 games without a goal before scoring against Leeds in November.

Wednesday's best hope for success was likely to be in the cups but a humiliating defeat was suffered in the Worthington Cup as Division Three side Cambridge United clinched a 2-1 aggregate victory. Nationwide League sides Norwich and Stockport were removed from the FA Cup before Chelsea won a 5th Round tie in Yorkshire. ■

Results 1998-99

FA Carling Premiership

Date	Opponents	Ven	Res	Atten	Scorers
15-Aug	West Ham U.	H	0-1	30,236	
22-Aug	Tottenham H.	A	3-0	32,129	Atherton (26); Di Canio (35); Hinchcliffe (78)
29-Aug	Aston Villa	H	0-1	25,989	
09-Sep	Derby Co.	A	0-1	26,209	
12-Sep	Blackburn R.	H	3-0	20,846	Atherton (18); Hinchcliffe (33); Di Canio (87)
19-Sep	Wimbledon	A	1-2	13,163	Di Canio (84)
27-Sep	Arsenal	H	1-0	27,949	Briscoe (89)
03-Oct	Middlesbrough	A	0-4	34,163	
18-Oct	Coventry C.	A	0-1	16,006	
24-Oct	Everton	H	0-0	26,952	
31-Oct	Southampton	H	0-0	30,078	
08-Nov	Leeds U.	A	1-2	30,012	Booth (3)
14-Nov	Newcastle U.	A	1-1	36,698	Rudi (80)
21-Nov	Manchester U.	H	3-1	39,475	Alexandersson (14, 73); Jonk (55)
28-Nov	Chelsea	A	1-1	34,451	Booth (67)
07-Dec	N.Forest	H	3-2	19,321	Alexandersson (22); Carbone (53,58)
12-Dec	Charlton A.	H	3-0	26,010	Booth (13); Carbone (64); Rudi (77)
19-Dec	Liverpool	A	0-2	40,003	
26-Dec	Leicester C.	H	0-1	33,513	
28-Dec	Aston Villa	A	1-2	39,217	Carbone (8)
09-Jan	Tottenham H.	H	0-0	28,204	
16-Jan	West Ham U.	A	4-0	25,642	Hinchcliffe (26); Rudi (31); Humphreys (68); Carbone (73 pen)
30-Jan	Derby Co.	H	0-1	24,440	
06-Feb	Leicester C.	A	2-0	20,113	Jonk (48); Carbone (78)
20-Feb	Blackburn R.	A	4-1	24,643	Sonner (20); Rudi (40, 43); Booth (82)
27-Feb	Middlesbrough	H	3-1	24,534	Booth (11, 80); Sonner (77)
03-Mar	Wimbledon	H	1-2	24,116	Thome (60)
09-Mar	Arsenal	A	0-3	37,792	
13-Mar	Leeds U.	H	0-2	28,142	
21-Mar	Southampton	A	0-1	15,201	
03-Apr	Coventry C.	H	1-2	28,136	Rudi (51)

05-Apr	Everton	A	2-1	35,270	Carbone (52, 68)
17-Apr	Manchester U.	A	0-3	55,270	
21-Apr	Newcastle U.	H	1-1	21,545	Scott (52)
25-Apr	Chelsea	H	0-0	21,652	
01-May	N.Forest	A	0-2	20,480	
08-May	Liverpool	H	1-0	27,383	Cresswell (87)
16-May	Charlton A.	A	1-0	20,043	Sonner (79)

FA Challenge Cup

Sponsored by AXA

Date	*Opponents*	*Vn*	*Rnd*	*Res*	*Atten*	*Scorers*
03-Jan	Norwich C.	H	3R	4-1	18,737	Humphreys (17, 33); Rudi (40); Stefanovic (72)
23-Jan	Stockport C.	H	4R	2-0	20,984	Thome (16); Carbone (57)
13-Feb	Chelsea	H	5R	0-1	29,410	

Worthington Cup

Date	*Opponents*	*Vn*	*Rnd*	*Res*	*Atten*	*Scorers*
16-Sep	Cambridge U.	H	2Rf	0-1	8,921	
22-Sep	Cambridge U.	A	2Rs	1-1	8,502	OG (69, Campbell)

Cambridge United win 2-1 on aggregate

Southampton

Formed 1885 by members of the St Mary's Young Men's Association, St Mary's FC. The church link was dropped, though the name retained, in 1893. In 1895 applied for a Southern League place, but were refused, only to be invited to fill a subsequent vacancy. 'St Mary's' was dropped after two seasons. Moved from the County Cricket Ground to the Dell in 1898.

Six times Southern League champions, Southampton were founder members of Football League Division Three in 1920 (this becoming Division Three (South) the following season), of Division Three at the end of regionalisation in 1958, and of the Premier League, 1992.

Ground: The Dell, Milton Road, Southampton, SO9 4XX
Phone: 01703-220505 Fax: 01703 330360
Box Office: 01703-228575 **News:** 0891 12 15 93
Capacity: 15,288 **Pitch:** 110 yds x 72 yds
Colours: Red/White, Black, Black **Nickname:** The Saints
Radio: Radio Solent 96.1FM
Internet: www.saintsfc.co.uk

President: Ted Bates **Chairman:** Rupert Lowe
Secretary: Brian Truscott
Manager: David Jones **Coach:** Stuart Gray
Assistants: John Sainty, John Mortimore
Physio: Don Taylor, Jim Joyce

League History: 1920 Original Member of Division 3; 1921 Division 3 (S); 1922-53 Division 2; 1953-58 Division 3 (S); 1958-60 Division 3; 1960-66 Division 2; 1966-74 Division 1; 1974-78 Division 2; 1978-92 Division 1; 1992- FA Premier League.

Honours: *Football League: Division 1 Runners-up* 1983-84; *Division 2 Runners-up* 1965-66, 1977-78; *Division 3 (S) Champions* 1921-22; *Runners-up* 1920-21; *Division 3 Champions* 1959-60. *FA Cup: Winners* 1975-76; *Runners-up* 1900, 1902. *Football League Cup: Runners-up* 1978-79. *Zenith Data Systems Cup: Runners-up* 1991-92.

European Record: CWC (1): 76-77 (QF); UEFA (5): 69-70 (3), 71-72 (1), 81-82 (2), 82-83 (1), 84-85 (1).

Managers: Cecil Knight 1894-95; Charles Robson 1895-97; E. Arnfield 1897-1911 (continued as secretary); George Swift 1911-12; E. Arnfield

1912-19; Jimmy McIntyre 1919-24; Arthur Chadwick 1925-31; George Kay 1931-36; George Cross 1936-37; Tom Parker 1937-43; (J.R. Sarjantson stepped down from the board to act as secretary-manager 1943-47 with the next two listed being team managers during this period); Arthur Dominy 1943-46; Bill Dodgin Snr 1946-49; Sid Cann 1949-51; George Roughton 1952-55; Ted Bates 1955-73; Lawrie McMenemy 1973-85; Chris Nicholl 1985-91; *(FAPL)* Ian Branfoot 1991-94; Alan Ball Jan 1994-July 1995; Dave Merrington July 1995-June 1996; Graeme Souness July 1996-May 1997; David Jones July 1997-.

All-Time Records

Record FAPL Win: 6-3 v Manchester United, Home, 20/10/96
Record FAPL Defeat: 1-7 v Everton, Away, 16/11/96
1-7 v Liverpool, Away, 16/01/99
Record FL Win: 9-3 v Wolverhampton W., Div 2, 18/9/65
Record FL Defeat: 0-8 v Tottenham Hotspur, Div 2, 28/3/36;
0-8 v Everton, Division 1, 20/11/71
Record Cup Win: 7-1 v Ipswich Town, FAC R3, 7/1/61
Record Fee Received: £7.5m from Blackburn R. for Kevin Davies, 7/97
Record Fee Paid: £2.0m to Sheffield W. for David Hirst, 10/97
Most FL Apps: Terry Payne, 713, 1956-74
Most FAPL Apps: 240 – Matt Le Tissier, 1992-99
Most FAPL Goals: 98 – Matt Le Tissier, 1992-99
Highest Scorer in FAPL Season: 25 – Matt Le Tissier, 1993-94
Record Attendance (all-time): 31,044 v Manchester United, Div 1, 08/10/69
Record Attendance (FAPL): 19,654 v Tottenham Hotspur, 15/8/92
Most FAPL Goals in Season: 61, 1994-95 – 42 games
Most FAPL Points in Season: 54, 1994-95 – 42 games

5-Year Record

	Div.	*P*	*W*	*D*	*L*	*F*	*A*	*Pts*	*Pos*	*FAC*	*FLC*
94-95	PL	42	12	18	12	61	63	54	10	5	3
95-96	PL	38	9	11	18	34	52	38	17	QF	4
96-97	PL	38	10	11	17	50	56	41	16	3	QF
97-98	PL	38	14	6	18	50	55	48	12	3	4
98-99	PL	28	11	8	19	37	64	41	17	3	2

Summary 1998-99

Player	*Tot*	*St*	*Sb*	*Snu*	*PS*	*Gls*	*Y*	*R*	*Fa*	*Fg*	*La*	*Lg*
BASHAM	4	0	4	5	0	1	0	0	0	0	1	0
BEATTIE	35	22	13	3	8	5	4	0	2	0	2	1
BENALI	23	19	4	1	1	0	2	0	0	0	2	0
BERESFORD	4	1	3	1	1	0	0	0	0	0	0	0
BEVAN	0	0	0	1	0	0	0	0	0	0	0	0
BRADLEY	3	0	3	2	0	0	0	0	0	0	0	0
BRIDGE	23	15	8	9	6	0	0	0	0	0	1	0
COLLETER	16	16	0	1	3	1	4	0	2	0	0	0
DODD	28	27	1	1	0	1	4	1	2	0	2	0
DRYDEN	4	4	0	6	0	0	1	0	0	0	0	0
GIBBENS	4	2	2	4	1	0	0	0	0	0	2	0
HILEY	29	27	2	8	4	0	2	0	1	0	0	0
HIRST	2	0	2	0	0	0	0	0	0	0	0	0
HOWELLS	9	8	1	5	4	1	1	0	1	0	1	0
HUGHES, D.	9	6	3	2	3	0	1	0	0	0	0	0
HUGHES, M.	32	32	0	0	4	1	14	0	2	0	2	0
JONES	31	31	0	1	0	0	1	1	2	0	2	0
KACHLOUL	22	18	4	3	5	5	5	0	2	0	0	0
LE TISSIER	30	20	10	0	7	7	10	0	1	0	2	0
LUNDEKVAM	33	30	3	2	2	0	4	1	2	0	2	0
MARSDEN	14	14	0	0	1	2	4	0	0	0	0	0
MARSHALL	2	2	0	2	0	0	1	0	0	0	0	0
MONK	4	4	0	6	0	0	0	0	1	0	0	0
MONKOU	22	22	0	1	1	1	6	0	2	0	0	0
MOSS	7	7	0	23	0	0	0	0	0	0	0	0
OAKLEY	22	21	1	0	8	2	2	0	2	0	0	0
OSTENSTAD	34	27	7	1	8	7	1	0	2	1	2	0
PAHARS	6	4	2	0	3	3	2	0	0	0	0	0
PALMER	19	18	1	0	0	0	6	0	1	0	2	0
PAUL	0	0	0	1	0	0	0	0	0	0	0	0
RIPLEY	22	16	6	2	9	0	2	0	1	0	1	0
STEUSGAARD	0	0	0	13	0	0	0	0	0	0	0	0
WARNER	5	5	0	2	2	0	0	0	0	0	1	0
WILLIAMS	1	0	1	3	0	0	0	0	0	0	0	0
34 Players	499	418	81	109	81	37	77	3	26	1	25	1

Something in the Locker

Dave Jones's first season as Southampton manager kicked off with three successive defeats but things got worse for his second season as the Saints embarked on 1998-99 with five straight reversals, during which time they conceded 16 goals and scored twice, one of which was a Matt Le Tissier penalty. The slump was slowed by a 1-1 draw with Tottenham but the Saints' first taste of victory was not savoured until the 10th game of the season when Coventry were beaten at the Dell. Southampton went into that match six points adrift at the foot of the Premier League but it was just a further four matches before goals from Matthew Oakley and Steve Basham clinched victory at Blackburn and lifted the Saints up one place at the expense of the Lancashire club. Survival was anything but straightforward for the Saints but after the turn of the year Jones's side won seven and drew two of their final nine home matches. It was a foundation which proved just enough when supported by one solitary away win, at Wimbledon, as the Saints closed their campaign with three consecutive victories. The new year revival on home soil was not matched away as seven consecutive games were lost, with a 7-1 thrashing at Liverpool being the lowest point.

The Saints went into the season with a new strike force following Kevin Davies's remarkable £7.25m transfer to Blackburn. In came veteran Mark Hughes from Chelsea and the Blackburn pair of Stuart Ripley and James Beattie who remained as Jones's only seven-figure signings right through the season. Hughes, though, had his effectiveness reduced due to collecting an excessive number of bookings. Beattie took his chance well and chipped in with five goals while Le Tissier was as enigmatic as ever and conjured up a number of top-quality goals. Southampton's most expensive signing during the season was Marian Pahars whose £800,000 was swiftly accounted for as it was his goals on the final day of the season which ensured Southampton's continued existence in the Premier League.

Former Southampton favourite Kevin Keegan compounded the Saints' dreadful first half to the season when guiding his Fulham side to victory over the Saints in both the Worthington Cup and the FA Cup.

You can't help having the feeling that Dave Jones has something in his locker – despite a few aging stars who will surely be dispatched sooner rather than later – just maybe there is something in the wings for the Southampton faithful. ■

Results 1998-99

FA Carling Premiership

Date	Opponents	Ven	Res	Atten	Scorers
16-Aug	Liverpool	H	1-2	15,202	Ostenstad (37)
22-Aug	Charlton A.	A	0-5	16,488	
29-Aug	N.Forest	H	1-2	14,942	Le Tissier (89pen)
08-Sep	Leeds U.	A	0-3	30,637	
12-Sep	Newcastle U.	A	0-4	36,454	
19-Sep	Tottenham H.	H	1-1	15,204	Le Tissier (64)
28-Sep	West Ham U.	A	0-1	23,153	
03-Oct	Manchester U.	H	0-3	15,251	
17-Oct	Arsenal	A	1-1	38,027	Howells (67)
24-Oct	Coventry C.	H	2-1	15,152	Le Tissier (23); Ostenstad (44)
31-Oct	Sheffield W.	A	0-0	30,078	
07-Nov	Middlesbrough	H	3-3	15,202	Monkou (61); Beattie (82); Ostenstad (85)
14-Nov	Aston Villa	H	1-4	15,242	Le Tissier (53)
21-Nov	Blackburn R.	A	2-0	22,812	Oakley (4); Basham (89)
28-Nov	Derby Co.	H	0-1	14,762	
05-Dec	Leicester C.	A	0-2	18,423	
12-Dec	Everton	A	0-1	32,073	
19-Dec	Wimbledon	H	3-1	14,354	Ostenstad (11, 68); Kachloul (64)
26-Dec	Chelsea	H	0-2	15,253	
28-Dec	N.Forest	A	1-1	23,456	Kachloul (48)
09-Jan	Charlton A.	H	3-1	15,222	Kachloul (8); Colleter (52); Beattie (89)
16-Jan	Liverpool	A	1-7	44,011	Ostenstad (59)
30-Jan	Leeds U.	H	3-0	15,236	Kachloul (31); Oakley (62); Ostenstad (86)
06-Feb	Chelsea	A	0-1	34,920	
20-Feb	Newcastle U.	H	2-1	15,244	Beattie (16); Dodd (43 pen)
27-Feb	Manchester U.	A	1-2	55,316	Le Tissier (90)
02-Mar	Tottenham H.	A	0-3	28,580	
06-Mar	West Ham U.	H	1-0	15,240	Kachloul (10)
14-Mar	Middlesbrough	A	0-3	33,387	
21-Mar	Sheffield W.	H	1-0	15,201	Le Tissier (41)
03-Apr	Arsenal	H	0-0	15,255	
05-Apr	Coventry C.	A	0-1	21,402	
10-Apr	Aston Villa	A	0-3	32,203	
17-Apr	Blackburn R.	H	3-3	15,209	Marsden (22); M.Hughes (61); Pahars (85)

24-Apr	Derby Co.	A	0-0	26,557	
01-May	Leicester C.	H	2-1	15,228	Marsden (36); Beattie (74)
08-May	Wimbledon	A	2-0	24,068	Beattie (72); Le Tissier (84)
16-May	Everton	H	2-0	15,254	Pahars (24, 68)

FA Challenge Cup

Sponsored by AXA

Date	*Opponents*	*Vn*	*Rnd*	*Res*	*Atten*	*Scorers*
02-Jan	Fulham	H	3R	1-1	12,549	Ostenstad (89)
13-Jan	Fulham	A	3RR	0-1	17,448	

Worthington Cup

Date	*Opponents*	*Vn*	*Rnd*	*Res*	*Atten*	*Scorers*
15-Sep	Fulham	A	2Rf	1-1	10,222	Beattie (62)
23-Sep	Fulham	H	2Rs	0-1	11,645	
	Fulham win 2-1 on aggregate					

Sunderland

Formed in 1879 as The Sunderland and District Teachers' Association FC by James Allan, a Scottish school teacher. Originally membership was restricted to teachers only, but this requirement was soon removed. Became Sunderland AFC in 1880 and had their first ground at the Blue House pub. Played at a number of grounds until they moved to their current Roker Park site in 1898. Elected to Division 2 of the Football League in 1890 and best remembered for their famous FA Cup win over Leeds United in 1973. Had one previous season in FAPL (1996-97) but were immediately relegated.

Ground: Stadium of Light, Sunderland, SR5 1SU
Phone: 0191-551 5000 **Fax:** 0191 5515123
Box Office: 0191 551 5151 **News:** 0891 12 11 40
Capacity: 41,590 > 48,000 **Pitch:** 115 x 75 yds
Colours: Red & White stripes, Black, Red with White trim
Nickname: The Rokermen
Radio: Metro Radio 97.1FM
Internet: www.sunderland-afc.com

Chairman: Bob Murray **CEO:** John Ficking
Secretary: Mark Blackbourne
Manager: Peter Reid **Assistant:** Bobby Saxton
Physio: Neil Metcalfe

League History: 1890 Elected to Division 1; 1958-64 Division 2; 1964-70 Division 1; 1970-76 Division 2; 1976-77 Division 1; 1977-80 Division 2; 1980-85 Division 1; 1985-87 Division 2; 1987-88 Division 3; 1988-90 Division 2; 1990-91 Division 1; 1991-92 Division 2; 1992-96 Division 1; 1996-1997 FAPL; Division 1 1997–1999; FAPL 1999–.

Honours: *Football League Division 1 Champions:* 1891-92, 1892-93, 1894-95, 1901-02, 1912-13, 1935-36, 1995-96, 1998-99; *Runners-up:* 1893-94, 1897-88; 1900-01, 1922-23, 1934-35; *Division 2 Champions:* 1975-76; *Runners-up:* 1963-64, 1979-80; *Division 3 Champions:* 1987-88; *FA Cup Winners:* 1936-37, 1972-73; *Runners-up:* 1912-13, 1991-92. *Football League Cup Runners-up:* 1984-85.

European Record: CC (0): – ; CWC (1) 1973-74 (2) ; UEFA (0): –

Managers: Tom Watson 1888-96; Bob Campbell 1896-99; Alex Mackie 1899-1905; Bob Kyle 1905-28; Johnny Cochrane 1928-39; Bill Murray 1939-57; Alan Brown 1957-64; George Hardwick 1964-65; Ian McColl 1965-68; Alan Brown 1968-72; Bob Stokoe 1972-76; Jimmy Adamson 1976-78; Ken Knighton 1979-81; Alan Durban 1981-84; Len Ashurst 1984-85; Lawrie McMenemy 1985-87; Denis Smith 1987-91; Malcolm Crosby 1992-93; Terry Butcher 1993; Mick Buxton 1993-94; Lou Macari 1994-1995; Peter Reid 1995-.

All-Time Records

Record FAPL Win: 4-1 v N.Forest, Away, 21/08/96
Record FAPL Defeat: 2-6 v Chelsea, Away, 16/03/97
Record FL Win: 9-1 v Newcastle United (away), Div 1, 05/12/08
Record FL Defeat: 0-8 v West Ham United, Div 1, 19/10/68 *and* 0-8 v Watford Div 1, 25/09/82
Record Cup Win: 11-1 v Fairfield, FA Cup 1st Rd, 02/02/1895
Record Fee Received: £1.5m from Crystal Palace for Marco Gabbiadini, 9/91
Record Fee Paid: £2.5m to Newcastle United for Lee Clark, 7/97
Most FL Apps: Jim Montgomery, 537, 1966-77
Most FAPL Apps: 38 – Paul Bracewell, 1996-97
Most FAPL Goals: 4 – Craig Russell, 1996-97
Highest Scorer in FAPL Season: 4 – Craig Russell, 1996-97
Record Attendance (all-time): 75,118 v Derby County, FAC 6RR, 08/03/33
Record Attendance (FAPL): 22,512 v Derby County, 26/12/96 *(at Roker Park)*
Most FAPL Goals in Season: 35, 1996-97 – 38 games
Most FAPL Points in Season: 40, 1996-97 – 38 games

5-Year Record

	Div.	*P*	*W*	*D*	*L*	*F*	*A*	*Pts*	*Pos*	*FAC*	*FLC*
94-95	1	46	12	18	16	41	45	54	20	4	2
95-96	1	46	22	17	7	59	33	83	1	3	2
96-97	PL	38	10	10	18	35	53	40	18	3	3
97-98	1	46	26	12	8	86	50	90	3	4	3
98-99	1	46	31	12	3	91	28	105	1	4	SF

Summary 1998-99

Player	*Tot*	*St*	*Sb*	*Snu*	*PS*	*Gls*	*Y*	*R*	*Fa*	*Fg*	*La*	*Lg*
AISTON	1	0	1	0	0	0	0	0	0	0	1	0
BALL	42	42	0	1	7	2	11	1	2	0	4	0
BRIDGES	27	13	14	9	8	8	0	0	0	0	7	4
BUTLER	44	44	0	0	1	2	6	0	2	0	7	0
CLARKE	27	26	1	0	4	3	1	0	2	0	4	0
CRADDOCK	6	3	3	18	0	0	0	0	0	0	5	0
DICHIO	36	16	20	5	6	10	3	0	2	0	5	2
GRAY	36	35	1	0	6	2	2	0	2	0	5	0
HARRISON	0	0	0	0	0	0	0	0	0	0	1	0
HOLLOWAY	6	1	5	1	0	0	0	0	0	0	0	0
JOHNSTON	40	40	0	0	7	7	3	0	1	0	7	1
LUMSDON	0	0	0	0	0	0	0	0	0	0	1	0
MAKIN	38	37	1	0	1	0	5	0	2	0	7	0
MALEY	0	0	0	0	0	0	0	0	0	0	1	0
MARRIOTT	1	1	0	0	0	0	0	0	0	0	0	0
MCCANN	11	5	6	3	2	0	1	0	2	1	1	1
MELVILLE	44	44	0	0	2	2	5	0	2	0	6	1
MULLIN	10	8	2	2	2	2	2	0	0	0	5	0
PHILLIPS	26	26	0	0	4	23	1	0	1	0	5	2
PROCTOR	0	0	0	0	0	0	0	0	0	0	1	0
QUINN	39	36	3	0	14	18	4	0	2	0	5	3
RAE	16	13	3	3	4	2	2	0	1	0	2	0
SCOTT	15	14	1	1	0	2	1	0	1	0	6	1
SMITH	8	4	4	8	1	3	0	0	1	0	6	1
SORENSEN	45	45	0	0	1	0	2	0	2	0	9	0
SUMMERBEE	36	36	0	0	4	3	2	0	0	0	6	0
THIRLWELL	2	1	1	4	1	0	1	0	0	0	3	0
WAINWRIGHT	2	0	2	0	0	0	0	0	0	0	3	0
WILLIAMS	26	16	10	5	3	0	2	0	1	0	4	0
Own Goals						2						
29 Players	584	506	78	60	78	91	54	1	26	1	117	16

Lighting the Way

Having missed out on promotion through what was probably the most dramatic match ever seen at Wembley the previous May, Sunderland manager Peter Reid bolstered his squad with four close-season signings at a modest cost of £1.2m, while seven players left the Stadium of Light, including highly rated goalkeeper Lionel Perez.

Understandably installed as pre-season title favourites, Sunderland were quickly into their stride with the phenomenal Kevin Phillips opening his account on day one with the winning strike against Queens Park Rangers. That match was the first in a run of 18 unbeaten matches for the Wearsiders who first tasted defeat in mid-November when Barnsley won 3-2 at the Stadium of Light. Sunderland's first away defeat did not occur until Boxing Day, by which time Reid's side were already eight points clear at the top of the table. From then on Sunderland's promotion to the Premiership was never in doubt and following a 13-match undefeated run - later extended to 17 games – the club returned to the top flight on 16 April with Phillips scoring four times during an emphatic 5-2 win at relegation-bound Bury. The title was secured one week later as revenge was gained over Barnsley with a 3-1 success at Oakwell.

The form of Phillips was exceptional (I can't believe this is the guy I used to watch at Baldock Town!) as he netted in 16 separate league matches, scored 40 times in the calendar year and earned an England call-up as his club equalled Swindon's 13-year Football League record of 102 points and scored more goals and conceded less than any other side in the whole of the Nationwide League.

In the FA Cup Sunderland won at Lincoln City before getting a reminder that life may be tougher in the Premiership as they were put out by struggling Blackburn. Turning to the Worthington Cup, a competition the club has never won, the Rokermen defeated York, Chester and Grimsby before beating Everton in a penalty shoot-out. Luton were beaten in the quarter-final but hopes of a return to Wembley were blocked by Leicester who won on Wearside and drew at Filbert Street.

Sunderland's failure to win any of four games against Premier sides will not have been lost on Reid as the club seeks to avoid continuing to yo-yo between the top two Divisions. They have the support, they have the stadium but will they have the team? Only the cheque book will tell. ■

Results 1998-99

Nationwide League Division 1

Date	*Opponents*	*Ven*	*Res*	*Atten*	*Scorers*
08-Aug	QPR	H	1-0	41,008	Phillips (76 pen)
15-Aug	Swindon T.	A	1-1	10,207	Phillips (60)
22-Aug	Tranmere R.	H	5-0	34,155	Phillips (17); Dichio (45, 79); Mullin (48); Butler (84)
25-Aug	Watford	H	4-1	36,587	Johnston (26);Summerbee (41); Dichio (45); Melville (63)
29-Aug	Ipswich T.	A	2-0	15,813	Mullin (11); Phillips (36)
08-Sep	Bristol C.	H	1-1	34,111	Phillips (12)
12-Sep	Wolverhampton	A	1-1	26,816	Phillips (90)
19-Sep	Oxford U.	H	7-0	34,567	Bridges (3, 56); Gray (6); Dichio (36 pen, 66); Rae (54, 81)
26-Sep	Portsmouth	A	1-1	17,022	Johnston (83)
29-Sep	Norwich C.	A	2-2	17,504	Quinn (3); OG (47, Marshall)
03-Oct	Bradford C.	H	0-0	37,828	
18-Oct	WBA	A	3-2	14,761	Melville (67); Bridges (80); Ball (86)
21-Oct	Huddersfield T.	A	1-1	20,741	Ball (42)
24-Oct	Bury	H	1-0	38,049	Dichio (78)
01-Nov	Bolton W.	A	3-0	21,676	Johnston (27); Quinn (33); Bridges (83)
03-Nov	Crewe Alex.	A	4-1	5,361	Dichio (11); Gray (28); Quinn (45); Bridges (60)
07-Nov	Grimsby T.	H	3-1	40,077	Smith (64, 69); Quinn (82)
14-Nov	Port Vale	A	2-0	8,839	OG (28, Aspin); Quinn (64)
21-Nov	Barnsley	H	2-3	40,231	Scott (63 pen); Quinn (72)
28-Nov	Sheffield U.	A	4-0	25,612	Quinn (7, 75); Bridges (13,35)
05-Dec	Stockport Co.	H	1-0	36,040	Summerbee (30)
12-Dec	Port Vale	H	2-0	37,583	Smith (25); Butler (44)
15-Dec	Crystal P.	H	2-0	33,870	Scott (33 pen); Dichio (89)
19-Dec	Birmingham C.	A	0-0	22,095	
26-Dec	Tranmere R.	A	0-1	14,248	
28-Dec	Crewe Alex.	H	2-0	41,433	Dichio (16); Bridges (78)
09-Jan	QPR	A	2-2	17,128	Phillips (33); Quinn (90)
17-Jan	Ipswich T.	H	2-1	39,835	Quinn (26, 33)
30-Jan	Watford	A	1-2	20,188	Quinn (36)
06-Feb	Swindon T.	H	2-0	41,304	Quinn (28); Phillips (29)
13-Feb	Bristol C.	A	1-0	15,736	Phillips (89)
20-Feb	Wolverhampton	H	2-1	41,268	Johnston (10); Quinn (90)

27-Feb	Oxford U.	A	0-0	9,044	
02-Mar	Portsmouth	H	2-0	37,656	Dichio (9); Phillips (60)
06-Mar	Norwich C.	H	1-0	39,004	Phillips (7)
09-Mar	Bradford C.	A	1-0	15,124	Quinn (71)
13-Mar	Grimsby T.	A	2-0	9,528	Phillips (50); Clark (78)
20-Mar	Bolton W.	H	3-1	41,505	Phillips (23); Johnston (28, 55)
03-Apr	WBA	H	3-0	41,135	Phillips (22, 48); Clark (26)
05-Apr	Crystal P.	A	1-1	22,096	Phillips (23)
10-Apr	Huddersfield T.	H	2-0	41,074	Quinn (28); Johnston (41)
13-Apr	Bury	A	5-2	8,669	Phillips (10, 30, 33, 90); Quinn (23)
16-Apr	Barnsley	A	3-1	17,390	Summerbee (45); Clark (63); Phillips (90)
24-Apr	Sheffield U.	H	0-0	41,179	
01-May	Stockport Co.	A	1-0	10,548	Phillips (56)
09-May	Birmingham C.	H	2-0	41,634	Phillips (60); Quinn (68)

FA Challenge Cup

Sponsored by AXA

Date	*Opponents*	*Vn*	*Rnd*	*Res*	*Atten*	*Scorers*
02-Jan	Lincoln C.	A	3R	1-0	10,408	McCann (16)
23-Jan	Blackburn R.	A	4R	0-1	30,125	

Worthington Cup

Date	*Opponents*	*Vn*	*Rnd*	*Res*	*Atten*	*Scorers*
11-Aug	York C.	A	1Rf	2-0	6,277	Dichio (14, 29)
18-Aug	York C.	H	1Rs	2-1	22,695	Phillips (65); Smith (88)
	Sunderland win 4-1 on aggregate					
15-Sep	Chester C.	H	2Rf	3-0	20,618	Scott (32); Phillips (39); Bridges (58)
22-Sep	Chester C.	A	2Rs	1-0	2,738	Johnston (12)
	Sunderland win 4-0 on aggregate					
27-Oct	Grimsby T.	H	3R	2-1	18,676	Bridges (66); Quinn (115)
11-Nov	Everton	A	4R	1-1	28,132	Bridges (29)
1-Dec	Luton T.	H	QF	3-0	35,472	Melville (40); Bridges (89); Quinn (90)
26-Jan	Leicester C.	H	SFf	1-2	38,332	McCann (75)
17-Feb	Leicester C.	A	SFs	1-1	21,231	Quinn (34)
	Leicester City win 3-2 on aggregate					

Tottenham Hotspur

Formed in 1882 by members of the schoolboys' Hotspur CC as Hotspur FC and had early church connections. Added 'Tottenham' in 1884 to distinguish club from London Hotspur FC. Turned professional in 1895 and elected to the Southern League in 1896 having been rebuffed by the Football League.

Played at two grounds (Tottenham Marshes and Northumberland Park) before moving to the site which became known as White Hart Lane in 1899. Joined the Football League Second Division in 1908. Having failed to gain a place in the re-election voting, they secured a vacancy caused by a late resignation. Premier League founder members 1992.

Ground: 748 High Road, Tottenham, London, N17 0AP
Phone: 0181-365 5000 **News:** 0891 33 55 55
Box Office: 0181-365 5050 **Tickets:** 0891 33 55 66
Capacity: 36,900 **Pitch:** 110 yds x 73 yds
Colours: White, Navy Blue, White **Nickname:** Spurs
Radio: 1548AM Capital Gold
Internet: www.spurs.co.uk

Chairman: Alan Sugar **President:** W.E. Nicholson OBE
CEO: Claude Littner **Secretary:** Peter Barnes
DOF: David Pleat
Manager: George Graham **Assistant:** Stuart Houston
Physio: Alisdair Beattie

League History: 1908 Elected to Division 2; 1909-15 Division 1; 1919-20 Division 2; 1920-28 Division 1; 1928-33 Division 2; 1933-35 Division 1; 1935-50 Division 2; 1950-77 Division 1; 1977-78 Division 2; 1978-92 Division 1; 1992- FA Premier League.

Honours: *Football League: Division 1 Champions* 1950-51, 1960-61; *Runners-up* 1921-22, 1951-52, 1956-57, 1962-63; *Division 2 Champions* 1919-20, 1949-50; *Runners-up* 1908-09, 1932-33. *FA Cup: Winners* 1900-01, 1920-21, 1960-61, 1961-62, 1966-67, 1980-81, 1981-82, 1990-91; *Runners-up* 1986-87. *Football League Cup: Winners* 1970-71, 1972-73, 1998-99; *Runners-up* 1981-82; *Cup-Winners' Cup: Winners* 1962-63; *Runners-up:* 1981-82. *UEFA Cup: Winners* 1971-72, 1983-84; *Runners-up:* 1973-74.

European Record: CC (1): 61-62 (SF); CWC (6): 62-63 (W), 63-64 (2), 67-68 (2), 81-82 (SF), 82-83 (2), 91-92 (QF); UEFA (5): 71-72 (W), 72-73 (SF), 73-74 (F), 83-84 (W), 84-85 (QF).

Managers: Frank Brettell 1898-99; John Cameron 1899-1907; Fred Kirkham 1907-08; Peter McWilliam 1912-27; Billy Minter 1927-29; Percy Smith 1930-35; Jack Tresadern 1935-38; Peter McWilliam 1938-42; Arthur Turner 1942-46; Joe Hulme 1946-49; Arthur Rowe 1949-55; Jimmy Anderson 1955-58; Bill Nicholson 1958-74; Terry Neill 1974-76; Keith Burkinshaw 1976-84; Peter Shreeves 1984-86; David Pleat 1986-87; Terry Venables 1987-91; Peter Shreeves 1991-92; *(FAPL)* Doug Livermore 1992-June 93; Ossie Ardiles June 1993-Nov 94; Gerry Francis Nov 1994-Nov 97; Christian Gross Nov 1997-Sept 98; David Pleat (Caretaker Manager) Sept 1998; George Graham Sept 1998–.

All-Time Records

Record FAPL Win: 6-2 v Wimbledon, Away, 02/05/98
Record FAPL Defeat: 1-7 v Newcastle United, Away, 28/12/96
Record FL Win: 9-0 v Bristol Rovers, Div 2, 22/10/77
Record FL Defeat: 0-7 v Liverpool, Div 1, 02/09/1978
Record Cup Win: 13-2 v Crewe Alex., FAC 4RR, 03/02/60
Record Fee Received: £5.5m from Lazio for Paul Gascoigne, 5/92
Record Fee Paid: £6.0m to Newcastle U. for Les Ferdinand, 7/97
Most FL Apps: Steve Perryman, 655, 1969-86
Most FAPL Apps: 205 – Sol Campbell, 1992-99
Most FAPL Goals: 76 – Teddy Sheringham, 1992-97
Highest Scorer in FAPL Season: 24 – Jurgen Klinsmann, 1994-95
Record Attendance (all-time): 75,038 v Sunderland, FAC 6R, 5/3/38
Record Attendance (FAPL): 36,878 v Chelsea, 10/05/99
Most FAPL Goals in Season: 66, 1994-95 – 42 games
Most FAPL Points in Season: 62, 1994-95 – 42 games

5-Year Record

	Div.	*P*	*W*	*D*	*L*	*F*	*A*	*Pts*	*Pos*	*FAC*	*FLC*
94-95	PL	42	16	14	12	66	58	62	7	SF	3
95-96	PL	38	16	13	9	50	38	61	8	5	3
96-97	PL	38	13	7	18	44	51	46	10	3	4
97-98	PL	38	11	11	16	44	56	44	14	4	3
98-99	PL	38	11	14	13	47	50	47	11	SF	W

Summary 1998-99

Player	*Tot*	*St*	*Sb*	*Snu*	*PS*	*Gls*	*Y*	*R*	*Fa*	*Fg*	*La*	*Lg*
ALLEN	5	0	5	4	0	0	0	0	0	0	3	0
ANDERTON	32	31	1	0	4	3	6	0	7	2	7	0
ARMSTRONG	34	24	10	1	5	7	4	1	5	0	5	5
BAARDSEN	12	12	0	25	0	0	0	0	0	0	3	0
BERTI	4	4	0	3	2	0	1	0	0	0	0	0
CALDERWOOD	12	11	1	8	3	0	4	1	0	0	5	0
CAMPBELL	37	37	0	0	0	6	0	0	7	0	8	2
CARR	37	37	0	0	1	0	4	0	7	0	8	1
CLEMENCE	18	9	9	6	7	0	1	0	1	0	3	0
DOMINGUEZ	13	2	11	6	2	2	1	0	0	0	2	1
EDINBURGH	16	14	2	4	3	0	3	1	4	0	5	0
FERDINAND	24	22	2	0	7	5	5	0	7	0	4	0
FOX	20	17	3	9	7	3	1	0	2	1	3	0
FREUND	17	17	0	0	3	0	6	0	6	0	3	0
GINOLA	30	30	0	3	13	3	9	0	6	3	8	1
GOWER	0	0	0	2	0	0	0	0	0	0	2	0
IVERSON	27	22	5	1	4	9	1	0	7	2	6	2
KING	0	0	0	2	0	0	0	0	0	0	0	0
NIELSEN	28	24	4	3	2	3	6	0	4	3	7	3
NILSEN	3	3	0	4	0	0	1	0	0	0	0	0
SAIB	4	0	4	0	0	0	0	0	0	0	0	0
SCALES	7	7	0	2	1	0	1	0	0	0	2	1
SEGERS	1	1	0	2	0	0	0	0	0	0	1	0
SHERWOOD	14	12	2	0	0	2	1	0	4	1	0	0
SINTON	22	12	10	4	4	0	3	0	6	1	6	0
TARICCO	13	12	1	1	3	0	2	1	3	0	0	0
THELWELL	1	1	0	1	0	0	0	0	0	0	0	0
TREMAZZANI	6	6	0	0	1	0	1	0	0	0	1	0
VEGA	16	13	3	5	1	2	2	0	4	0	5	1
WALKER	25	25	0	11	0	0	1	0	7	0	4	0
WILSON	0	0	0	3	0	0	0	0	0	0	1	0
YOUNG	14	13	1	6	1	0	5	0	5	0	2	0
Own Goals						2						
32 Players	492	418	74	116	74	47	69	4	92	13	104	17

Cup Clues

Tipped as the 'big' club expected to struggle following their brush with relegation the previous season, Tottenham started badly and manager Christian Gross had the dubious honour of proving the bookies right as he became the first Premiership casualty of the season when Spurs sacked him on 5 September. After a prolonged wait, George Graham switched from Leeds to Tottenham and now sought to emulate the consistent success he achieved with neighbours Arsenal, a possibility strengthened by the appointment of Stuart Houston as his assistant.

The early signs were promising as within six months of Graham's arrival at White Hart Lane the club had its hands on the Worthington Cup, its first silverware for eight years. But despite that success and a run through to the last four of the FA Cup, this remains a transitional period although a return to European action in 1999-2000 should prove a step in the right direction. In Steffen Iversen Spurs have a striker of great potential but with Les Ferdinand and Chris Armstrong failing to produce the goods Tottenham lack a cutting edge to supplement the flair of Darren Anderton and David Ginola, the latter having walked off with the PFA and Football Writers' Footballer of the Year awards.

Spurs' poor start saw Wimbledon and Sheffield Wednesday help themselves to three goals apiece before Ferdinand's first goal of the season clinched victory in Gross's last match at Everton. Graham's arrival soon brought positive results as the club embarked on a 16-match unbeaten run and in one 17-game spell kept a dozen clean sheets. Premier League survival was virtually guaranteed as early as 2 March with a 3-0 win over Southampton but it was in the cup competitions that Tottenham excelled. After victories over Brentford and Northampton, both Liverpool and Manchester United were ousted from the Worthington Cup. Wimbledon went the same way after two gruelling semi-final encounters, and Nielsen's goal against Leicester settled a poor final. Graham, looking to repeat his 1993 domestic cup double with Arsenal, took satisfaction from a 5th Round FA Cup replay win over Leeds thanks to sublime goals from Anderton and Ginola, while the Frenchman scored another classic in the quarter-final win at Barnsley. The run ended, amidst controversy, against Newcastle in the semi-final. ■

Results 1998-99

FA Carling Premiership

Date	*Opponents*	*Ven*	*Res*	*Atten*	*Scorers*
15-Aug	Wimbledon	A	1-3	23,031	Fox (75)
22-Aug	Sheffield W.	H	0-3	32,129	
29-Aug	Everton	A	1-0	39,378	Ferdinand (5)
09-Sep	Blackburn R.	H	2-1	28,338	Ferdinand (26); Nielsen (50)
13-Sep	Middlesbrough	H	0-3	30,437	
19-Sep	Southampton	A	1-1	15,204	Fox (25)
27-Sep	Leeds U.	H	3-3	35,535	Vega (14); Iversen (71); Campbell (90)
03-Oct	Derby Co.	A	1-0	30,083	Campbell (60)
19-Oct	Leicester C.	A	1-2	20,787	Ferdinand (12)
24-Oct	Newcastle U.	H	2-0	36,047	Iversen (40, 76)
02-Nov	Charlton A.	H	2-2	32,202	Nielsen (50); Armstrong (57)
07-Nov	Aston Villa	A	2-3	39,241	Anderton (65 pen); Vega (76)
14-Nov	Arsenal	A	0-0	38,278	
21-Nov	N.Forest	H	2-0	35,832	Armstrong (59); Nielsen (69)
28-Nov	West Ham U.	A	1-2	26,044	Armstrong (72)
05-Dec	Liverpool	H	2-1	36,521	Fox (26); OG (50, Carragher)
12-Dec	Manchester U.	H	2-2	36,070	Campbell (70, 90)
19-Dec	Chelsea	A	0-2	34,881	
26-Dec	Coventry C.	A	1-1	23,098	Campbell (17)
28-Dec	Everton	H	4-1	36,053	Ferdinand (24); Armstrong (63, 76, 81)
09-Jan	Sheffield W.	A	0-0	28,204	
16-Jan	Wimbledon	H	0-0	32,422	
30-Jan	Blackburn R.	A	1-1	29,643	Iversen (61)
06-Feb	Coventry C.	H	0-0	34,376	
20-Feb	Middlesbrough	A	0-0	34,687	
27-Feb	Derby Co.	H	1-1	35,392	Sherwood (69)
02-Mar	Southampton	H	3-0	28,580	Armstrong (19); Iversen (68); Dominguez (90)
10-Mar	Leeds U.	A	0-2	34,521	
13-Mar	Aston Villa	H	1-0	35,963	Sherwood (88)
03-Apr	Leicester C.	H	0-2	35,415	
05-Apr	Newcastle U.	A	1-1	36,655	Anderton (50 pen)
17-Apr	N.Forest	A	1-0	25,181	Iversen (62)
20-Apr	Charlton A.	A	4-1	20,043	Iversen (58); Campbell (78); Dominguez (89); Ginola (90)
24-Apr	West Ham U.	H	1-2	36,089	Ginola (73)
01-May	Liverpool	A	2-3	44,007	OG (13, Carragher); Iversen (35)

05-May	Arsenal	H	1-3	36,019	Anderton (43)
10-May	Chelsea	H	2-2	36,878	Iversen (38); Ginola (64)
16-May	Manchester U.	A	1-2	55,189	Ferdinand (24)

FA Challenge Cup

Sponsored by AXA

Date	*Opponents*	*Vn*	*Rnd*	*Res*	*Atten*	*Scorers*
02-Jan	Watford	H	3R	5-2	36,022	Iversen (10, 19); Anderton (13pen); Nielsen (42); Fox (86)
23-Jan	Wimbledon	A	4R	1-1	22,229	Ginola (70)
02-Feb	Wimbledon	H	4RR	3-0	24,049	Sinton (2); Nielsen (56, 84)
13-Feb	Leeds U.	A	5R	1-1	39,696	Sherwood (53)
24-Feb	Leeds U.	H	5RR	2-0	32,307	Anderton (59); Ginola (67)
16-Mar	Barnsley	A	QF	1-0	18,793	Ginola (68)
12-Apr	Newcastle U.		SF	0-2	53,609	
	At Old Trafford. Aet					

Worthington Cup

Date	*Opponents*	*Vn*	*Rnd*	*Res*	*Atten*	*Scorers*
15-Sep	Brentford	A	2Rf	3-2	11,831	Carr (44); Dominguez (53); Vega (82)
23-Sep	Brentford	H	2Rs	3-2	22,980	Nielsen (24); Campbell (46); Armstrong (53)
	Tottenham Hotspur win 6-4 on aggregate					
27-Oct	Northampton	A	3R	3-1	7,422	Armstrong (39, 83); Campbell (47)
10-Nov	Liverpool	A	4R	3-1	20,772	Iversen (2); Scales (20); Nielsen (62)
2-Dec	Manchester U.	H	QF	3-1	35,702	Armstrong (48, 55); Ginola (86)
27-Jan	Wimbledon	H	SFf	0-0	35,997	
16-Feb	Wimbledon	A	SFs	1-0	25,204	Iversen (39)
	Tottenham Hotspur win 1-0 on aggregate					
21-Mar	Leicester C.		F	1-0	77,892	Neilsen (90)
	Played at Wembley					

Watford

Founded in 1881 as Watford Rovers, they became West Herts in 1893 and then 'absorbed' Watford St Mary's FC in 1898 to become Watford FC. The club played its early football at the West Herts Sports Ground in Cassio Road. Playing in the Southern League they gained entry to the newly formed Football League Division 3 in 1920. In 1922 the team moved into a new ground at the Vicarage Road site, where they have played ever since. From 1982-88 they played in the old Division 1, finishing runners-up in their first season, when they were managed by current manager Graham Taylor. Taylor returned to the club and became team manager in May 1997 and immediately led them to successive promotions and a place in the Premier League via the play-offs.

Ground: Vicarage Road Stadium, Watford, WD1 8ER
Club No.: 01923 496000 **Fax:** 01923 496001
Box Office: 01923 496010
News: 0891 104104 **Ticket:** 01923 496010
Capacity: 22,000 **Pitch:** 115 x 75 yards
Colours: Yellow with Red sleeves, Red, Red and Yellow
Nickname: The Hornets
Radio: BBC Three Counties 103.8FM/630 AM
Internet: www.watfordfc.co.uk

Chairman: Sir Elton John CBE
CEO: Howard Wells **Secretary:** John Alexander
Manager: Graham Taylor **Assistant:** Kenny Jackett
Coach: Luther Blissett
Physio: Paul Rastick

League History: 1920 Division 3 Founder; 1921-58 Division 3S; 1958-60 Division 4; 1960-69 Division 3; 1969-72 Division 2; 1972-75 Division 3; 1975-78 Division 4; 1978-79 Division 3; 1979-82 Division 2; 1982-88 Division 1; 1988-92 Division 2; 1992-96 Division 1; 1996-98 Division 2; 1998-99 Division 1; 1999– FAPL.

Honours: *Football League: Division 1 Runners-up* 1982-83; *Division 2 Champions* 1997-98; *Runners-up* 1981-82; *Division 3 Champions 1968-69; Runners-up* 1978-79; *Division 4 Champions* 1977-78; *FA Cup Runners-up* 1983-84.

European Record: CL (0) –; CWC (0) –; UEFA (1) 1983-84

Managers: John Goodall 1903-10; Harry Kent 1910-26; Fred Pagham 1926-29; Neil McBain 1929-37; Bill Findlay 1938-47; Jack Bray 1947-48; Eddie Hapgood 1948-50; Ron Gray 1950-51; Haydn Gray 1950-51; Len Goulden 1952-55; Johnn Y Paton 1955-56; Neil McBain 1956-59; Ron Burgess 1959-63; Bill McGarry 1963-64; Ken Furphy 1964-71; George Kirby 1971-73; Mike Keen 1973-77; Graham Taylor 1977-87; Dave Bassett 1987-88; Steve Harrison 1988-90; Colin Lee 1990; Steve Perryman 1990-93; Glenn Roeder 1993-96; Kenny Jackett 1996-97; Graham Taylor May 1997–.

All-Time Records

Record FAPL Win: –
Record FAPL Defeat: –
Record FL Win: 8-0 v Sunderland, Div 1, 25/08/92
Record FL Defeat: 1-8 v Crystal Palace, Div 4, 23/09/59
Record Cup Win: 10-1 v Lowestoft Town, FAC 1R, 27/11/26
Record Fee Received: £2.3m from Chelsea for Paul Furlong, 05/94
Record Fee Paid: £550,000 to Milan for Luthur Blissett, 08/84
Most FL Apps: 415: Luther Blissett, 1976-83, 1984-88, 1991-92
Most FAPL Apps: –
Most FAPL Goals: –
Highest Scorer in FAPL Season: –
Record Attendance (all-time): 34,099 v Manchester United, FAC 4RR, 03/02/69
Record Attendance (FAPL): –
Most FAPL Goals in Season: –
Most FAPL Points in Season: –

5-Year Record

	Div.	*P*	*W*	*D*	*L*	*F*	*A*	*Pts*	*Pos*	*FAC*	*FLC*
94-95	1	46	19	13	14	52	46	70	7	5	3
95-96	1	46	10	18	18	62	70	48	23	3	5
96-97	2	46	16	19	11	45	38	67	13	4	2
97-98	2	46	24	16	6	67	41	88	1	3	2
98-99	1	46	21	14	11	65	56	77	5	3	1

Summary 1998-99

Player	*Tot*	*St*	*Sb*	*Snu*	*PS*	*Gls*	*Y*	*R*	*Fa*	*Fg*	*La*	*Lg*
BAZELEY	40	36	4	1	1	2	1	0	1	0	2	0
BONNOT	4	1	3	1	0	0	0	0	0	0	0	0
CHAMBERLAIN	46	46	0	0	0	0	0	0	1	0	2	0
DALEY	12	6	6	0	6	1	1	0	0	0	2	0
DAY	0	0	0	1	0	0	0	0	0	0	0	0
EASTON	7	7	0	5	2	0	1	0	0	0	2	0
GIBBS	10	9	1	2	1	0	0	0	0	0	0	0
GUDMUNDSSON	13	6	7	5	3	2	0	0	0	0	0	0
HAZAN	23	8	15	5	5	2	0	0	0	0	2	0
HYDE	44	43	1	0	5	2	5	0	1	0	2	0
IROHA	10	8	2	0	4	0	4	0	1	0	0	0
JOHNSON	40	40	0	0	0	4	7	1	1	1	0	0
KENNEDY	46	46	0	0	1	6	5	0	1	1	2	0
LEE	1	1	0	0	0	1	0	0	0	0	1	0
MILLEN	11	10	1	0	2	1	1	0	0	0	2	0
MOONEY	36	20	16	4	3	9	3	0	0	0	1	0
NGONGE	22	13	9	1	9	4	2	0	0	0	1	1
NOEL-WILLIAMS	26	19	7	2	4	10	2	0	1	0	0	0
PAGE	39	37	2	3	0	0	4	0	1	0	1	0
PALMER	41	40	1	2	1	2	2	0	1	0	2	0
PERPETUINI	1	1	0	0	1	0	1	0	0	0	0	0
PLUCK	0	0	0	3	0	0	0	0	0	0	0	0
ROBINSON	29	26	3	4	1	0	8	0	1	0	2	0
ROSENTHAL	5	1	4	1	0	0	0	0	1	0	2	0
SLATER	0	0	0	1	0	0	0	0	0	0	0	0
SMART	35	34	1	1	18	7	6	1	1	0	1	0
SMITH	8	3	5	2	2	2	0	0	0	0	0	0
WARD	1	1	0	0	0	0	0	0	0	0	0	0
WHITTINGHAM	5	4	1	0	3	0	0	0	0	0	0	0
WRIGHT	33	31	2	3	19	6	3	0	1	0	0	0
YATES	9	9	0	0	0	1	0	0	0	0	1	0
Own Goals						3						
31 Players	597	506	91	47	91	65	56	2	13	2	28	1

Just Follow the Yellow Brick Road!

The partnership of rock superstar Elton John as chairman and Graham Taylor as manager will go down as one of the all-time great football collaborations as the duo paired up for a second time to guide Watford into the Premier League. Following the Hornets' dramatic rise through the ranks 20 years earlier and Taylor's subsequent success at Aston Villa, he was appointed England manager but his career appeared to be in decline after being reviled in that position and branded a failure during a brief spell as Wolves manager. A return to Watford seemed a natural move and almost as if to defy the critics he has led the club to two successive promotions and a place back among the elite. Talk of sticking by those who won the club promotion and not introducing players with Premier League experience, however, appears on the face of it to be misguided given the frequency with which promoted clubs have been swiftly despatched back to the Nationwide League. However, if there is one person who can achieve it – then Graham Taylor is your man.

Watford's route to promotion was a bizarre one. The season started with three straight wins and then three successive defeats, then more wins ensued before the Hornets went four more games without winning. Between the end of September and 20 March Watford failed to win back to back matches and were four points adrift of the play-off places having played a game more than three of the sides battling above them. A run of six consecutive victories followed by a draw at Barnsley and a 1-0 win over Grimsby which, ironically, condemned Wolves to another season of Nationwide League football, carried the Hornets into the play-offs. During this sequence Tom Mooney scored seven times, including scoring in six successive matches.

A goal from free signing Michel Ngonge earned a 1st leg victory over Birmingham but the sides were locked together at 1-1 after the second meeting before Watford won through with a dramatic penalty shoot-out success at St. Andrews. Making their first Wembley appearance since the 1984 FA Cup final, Watford clinched promotion with a 2-0 win over Bolton with Nick Wright scoring a spectacular overhead effort.

Despite their league success, Watford made no impact in the cups and went out of the FA and Worthington cups at the first hurdles, to Tottenham and Cambridge United respectively.

It was great to be at Wembley and see my local club do so well – can Taylor get more out of his players and unearth additional talent? In Mica Hyde he has, to my mind, a potential star of the future. It will be a fascinating season for all at Vicarage Road. ■

Results 1998-99

Nationwide Division 1

Date	*Opponents*	*Ven*	*Res*	*Atten*	*Scorers*
08-Aug	Portsmouth	A	2-1	15,275	OG (80, Thomson); Lee (84)
15-Aug	Bradford C.	H	1-0	10,731	Ngonge (62)
22-Aug	Bristol C.	A	4-1	13,063	Johnson (8, 61); Yates (58); Hazan (79)
25-Aug	Sunderland	A	1-4	36,587	Smart (11)
28-Aug	Wolverhampton	H	0-2	12,016	
08-Sep	Huddersfield T.	A	0-2	9,811	
12-Sep	QPR	H	2-1	14,251	Millen (4); Smart (84)
19-Sep	Swindon T.	A	4-1	8,781	Smart (37, 58); Wright (44); Hazan (50)
26-Sep	Ipswich T.	H	1-0	13,109	Kennedy (4 pen)
29-Sep	Sheffield U.	H	1-1	9,090	Noel-Williams (44)
04-Oct	WBA	A	1-4	11,840	Kennedy (32 pen)
10-Oct	Birmingham C.	H	1-1	10,090	OG (68, Rowett)
17-Oct	Tranmere	A	2-3	6,753	Smart (15); Noel-Williams (81)
20-Oct	Bolton W.	A	2-1	15,921	Noel-Williams (42); Kennedy (86)
24-Oct	Port Vale	H	2-2	8,750	Gudmundsson (27, 53)
31-Oct	Bury	A	3-1	4,342	Bazeley (26); Ngonge (42); Smart (84)
03-Nov	Norwich C.	H	1-1	10,011	OG (8, Jackson)
07-Nov	Oxford U.	H	2-0	10,137	Palmer (24); Noel-Williams (76)
14-Nov	Stockport Co.	A	1-1	8,019	Johnson (9)
21-Nov	Crewe Alex.	H	4-2	9,405	Noel-Williams (38, 68); Bazeley (43); Wright (45)
28-Nov	Crystal Palace	A	2-2	19,521	Wright (24); Kennedy (27)
05-Dec	Barnsley	H	0-0	10,165	
12-Dec	Stockport Co.	H	4-2	9,250	Johnson (7); Wright (17); Noel-Williams (64, 86)
19-Dec	Grimsby T.	A	1-2	6,679	Noel-Williams (73)
26-Dec	Bristol C.	H	1-0	15,081	Smart (57)
28-Dec	Norwich C.	A	1-1	19,255	Palmer (80)
09-Jan	Portsmouth	H	0-0	12,057	
16-Jan	Wolverhampton	A	0-0	23,408	
23-Jan	WBA	H	0-2	11,664	
30-Jan	Sunderland	H	2-1	20,188	Wright (18); Noel-Williams (52)
06-Feb	Bradford C.	A	0-2	14,142	

16-Feb	Huddersfield T.	H	1-1	10,303	Mooney (70)
20-Feb	QPR	A	2-1	14,918	Wright (16); Smith (70);
26-Feb	Swindon T.	H	0-1	8,692	
02-Mar	Ipswich T.	A	2-3	18,818	Smith (82); Mooney (84)
06-Mar	Sheffield U.	A	0-3	15,943	
13-Mar	Oxford U.	A	0-0	8,137	
20-Mar	Bury	H	0-0	9,336	
03-Apr	Tranmere	H	2-1	8,682	Kennedy (66); Ngonge (86)
05-Apr	Birmingham C.	A	2-1	24,877	Mooney (26); Daley (58)
10-Apr	Bolton W.	H	2-0	13,001	Hyde (23); Mooney (53)
17-Apr	Crewe Alex.	A	1-0	5,461	Mooney (25)
24-Apr	Crystal Palace	H	2-1	15,590	Hyde (6); Mooney (5);
27-Apr	Port Vale	A	2-1	7,126	Mooney (24, 60)
01-May	Barnsley	A	2-2	17,098	Ngonge (43); Mooney (67)
09-May	Grimsby T.	H	1-0	20,303	Kennedy (41)

Division 1 Play-offs

16-May	Birmingham C.	H	1-0	18,535	Ngonge (5)
20-May	Birmingham C.	A	0-1	29,100	

Aet. 1-1 on aggregate. Watford win 7-6 on penalties.

31-May	Bolton W.		2-0	70,343	Wright (37); Smart (89)

Played at Wembley

FA Challenge Cup

Sponsored by AXA

Date	*Opponents*	*Vn*	*Rnd*	*Res*	*Atten*	*Scorers*
02-Jan	Tottenham H.	A	3R	2-5	36,022	Johnson (1); Kennedy (34)

Worthington Cup

Date	*Opponents*	*Vn*	*Rnd*	*Res*	*Atten*	*Scorers*
11-Aug	Cambridge U.	A	1Rf	0-1	3,073	
18-Aug	Cambridge U.	H	1Rs	1-1	6,817	Ngonge (48)

Cambridge United win 2-1 on aggregate

West Ham United

Thames Ironworks founded 1895, to give recreation for the shipyard workers. Several different grounds were used as the club entered the London League (1896) and won the championship (1898). In 1899, having become professional, won the Southern League Second Division (London) and moved into Division One.

On becoming a limited liability company the name was changed to West Ham United. Moved from the Memorial Ground to a pitch in the Upton Park area, known originally as 'The Castle', in 1904. Elected to an expanded Football League Division Two for the 1919-20 season and never subsequently out of the top two divisions.

Ground: Boleyn Ground, Green Street, Upton Park, London E13 9AZ
Phone: 0181-548 2748 **News:** 0891 12 11 65
Box Office: 0181-548 2700
Capacity: 25,985 **Pitch:** 112 yds x 72 yds
Colours: Claret, White, White **Nickname:** The Hammers
Radio: 1548AM Capital Gold
Internet: westhamunited.co.uk

Chairman: Terence Brown **Vice-Chairman:** Martin Cearns
Secretary: Graham Mackrell
Manager: Harry Redknapp **Assistant:** Frank Lampard
Coach: Roger Cross
Physios: John Green and Josh Collins

League History: 1919 Elected to Division 2; 1923-32 Division 1; 1932-58 Division 2; 1958-78 Division 1; 1978-81 Division 2; 1981-89 Division 1; 1989-91 Division 2; 1991-1993 Division 1; 1993- FA Premier League.

Honours: *Football League: Division 1 Runners-up* 1992-93; *Division 2 Champions* 1957-58, 1980-81; *Runners-up* 1922-23, 1990-91. *FA Cup: Winners* 1964, 1975, 1980; *Runners-up* 1922-23. *Football League Cup: Runners-up* 1966, 1981. *Cup-Winners' Cup: Winners* 1964-65; *Runners-up* 1975-76.

European Record: CC (0): –; CWC (4): 64-65 (W), 65-66 (SF), 75-76 (F), 80-81 (QF); UEFA (0): –

Managers: Syd King 1902-32; Charlie Paynter 1932-50; Ted Fenton 1950-61; Ron Greenwood 1961-74 (continued as GM to 1977); John Lyall 1974-89; Lou Macari 1989-90; *(FAPL)* Billy Bonds Feb 1990-Aug 1994; Harry Redknapp Aug 1994-.

All-Time Records

Record FAPL Win: 6-0 v Barnsley, Home, 10/1/98
Record FAPL Defeat: 0-6 v Everton, Away, 08/05/99
Record FL Win: 8-0 v Rotherham United, Div 2, 8/3/58
8-0 v Sunderland, Div 1, 19/10/68
Record FL Defeat: 2-8 v Blackburn Rovers, Div 1, 26/12/63
Record Cup Win: 10-0 v Bury, FLC 2Rs, 25/10/83
Record Fee Received: £6m from Wimbledon for John Hartson, 1/99 (£3m down, £3m after appearances)
Record Fee Paid: £5m to Arsenal for John Hartson, 3/97 (£3.2m down, balance paid on transfer to Wimbledon)
Most FL Apps: Billy Bonds, 663, 1967-88
Most FAPL Apps: 179 – Steve Potts, 1993-99
Most FAPL Goals: 24 – John Hartson, 1996-99
Highest Scorer in FAPL Season: 15 – John Hartson, 1997-98
Record Attendance (all-time): 42,322 v Tottenham H., Div 1, 17/10/70
Record Attendance (FAPL): 28,832 v Manchester United, 26/2/94
Most FAPL Goals in Season: 56, 1997-98 – 38 games
Most FAPL Points in Season: 57, 1998-99 – 38 games

5-Year Record

	Div.	*P*	*W*	*D*	*L*	*F*	*A*	*Pts*	*Pos*	*FAC*	*FLC*
94-95	PL	42	13	11	18	44	48	50	14	4	4
95-96	PL	38	14	9	15	43	52	51	10	4	3
96-97	PL	38	10	12	16	39	48	42	14	3	4
97-98	PL	38	16	8	14	56	57	56	8	6	QF
98-99	PL	38	16	9	13	46	53	57	5	3	2

Summary 1998-99

Player	*Tot*	*St*	*Sb*	*Snu*	*PS*	*Gls*	*Y*	*R*	*Fa*	*Fg*	*La*	*Lg*
ABOU	3	2	1	7	1	0	0	0	1	0	1	0
ALEXANDER	0	0	0	1	0	0	0	0	0	0	0	0
BERKOVIC	30	28	2	4	12	3	3	0	2	0	1	0
BOYLAN	0	0	0	1	0	0	0	0	0	0	0	0
BREACKER	3	2	1	9	1	0	0	0	1	0	1	0
BULLARD	0	0	0	2	0	0	0	0	0	0	0	0
COLE	8	2	6	4	2	0	1	0	1	0	0	0
COYNE	1	0	1	4	0	0	0	0	0	0	0	0
DI CANIO	13	12	1	0	2	4	1	0	0	0	0	0
DICKS	9	9	0	0	0	0	2	0	2	1	1	0
ETHERINGTON	0	0	0	1	0	0	0	0	0	0	0	0
FERDINAND	31	31	0	0	2	0	5	0	1	0	1	0
FOE	13	13	0	1	1	0	8	0	0	0	0	0
FORREST	2	1	1	31	0	0	0	0	0	0	0	0
HALL	0	0	0	0	0	0	0	0	1	0	0	0
HARTSON †	17	16	1	1	1	4	3	0	2	0	1	0
HISLOF	37	37	0	0	0	0	0	1	2	0	2	0
HODGES	1	0	1	3	0	0	0	0	0	0	0	0
HOLLIGAN	1	0	1	0	0	0	0	0	0	0	0	0
IMPEY	8	6	2	3	1	0	2	0	0	0	1	0
IRIEKPEN	0	0	0	1	0	0	0	0	0	0	0	0
KELLER	21	17	4	11	5	5	3	0	0	0	1	0
KITSON	17	13	4	1	4	3	2	0	0	0	0	0
LAMPARD	38	38	0	0	0	5	3	0	1	0	2	1
LAZARIDIS	15	11	4	9	3	0	3	0	2	0	1	0
LOMAS	30	30	0	0	2	1	4	1	2	0	0	0
MARGAS	3	3	0	5	0	0	0	0	0	0	0	0
MEAN	0	0	0	3	0	0	0	0	0	0	0	0
MINTO	15	14	1	2	1	0	2	0	0	0	0	0
MONCUR	14	6	8	12	0	0	8	1	0	0	1	0
OMOYIMNI	3	0	3	4	0	0	0	0	2	0	1	0
PARTRIDGE	0	0	0	1	0	0	0	0	0	0	0	0
PEARCE	33	33	0	0	1	2	4	0	1	0	2	0
POTTS	19	11	8	11	2	0	4	0	1	0	2	0
RUDDOCK	27	27	0	0	2	2	8	1	2	0	1	0
SEALEY	0	0	0	6	0	0	0	0	0	0	0	0
SINCLAIR	36	36	0	0	3	7	7	0	2	0	2	0
WRIGHT	22	20	2	0	6	9	9	1	1	0	2	0
Own Goals						1						
38 Players	470	418	52	138	52	46	82	5	27	1	24	1

InterToto's Poor Reward

By finishing fifth, West Ham United enjoyed their best season yet in the Premier League but they were the only side in the top seven to have a negative goal difference and a total of eight league games in which they conceded four goals or more was by far the worst of any side in the Premiership. Such a statistic is in stark contrast to how the Hammers started the season when they were one of two sides to have an unblemished defensive record after three games. Twenty-seven minutes into the fourth game and West Ham looked to be off to a flier as they led Wimbledon 3-0, only to crash to a remarkable 4-3 defeat. Successive home wins over Liverpool and Southampton, either side of a draw at Forest, suggested that West Ham were back on course for a memorable season but, following a 3-0 defeat at Blackburn at the start of November, the defensive record began to take a battering. Even so, the Hammers still enjoyed a couple of decent runs although their end of season form seemed to sum up the entire season as a 2-1 win over Spurs was sandwiched between wins of 5-1 and 4-0, and defeats of 5-1 and 6-0, the latter at goal-shy Everton. The 5-1 home defeat by Leeds saw West Ham have three players sent off and Ian Wright reported to the FA for damaging the referee's personal property after being dismissed. Wright's disciplinary problem, and a lengthy injury lay-off, didn't stop him being the Hammers' top goalscorer. Further controversy came West Ham's way when John Hartson kicked Eyal Berkovic in the face at a training session and was duly fined and suspended prior to a £3m, possibly £4.5m, move to Wimbledon. Despite some problems down the years with overseas signings, Harry Redknapp increased his foreign legion during the season with Javier Margas, Marc-Vivien Foe and Paolo Di Canio all joining the club for a total of almost £8m.

West Ham's participation in the cup competitions was nothing short of a disaster. In the FA Cup, Third Division Swansea, after drawing at Upton Park, won a 3rd Round replay 1-0 at Vetch Field and in the Worthington Cup, Division Two Northampton won 2-1 on aggregate in the 2nd Round.

There was a time when fifth would get you into Europe – now it doesn't while a place is open to the League Cup winners – something that will change in due course. So the Hammers were due to get their season well under way by mid-July with the InterToto Cup, in a bid to qualify for one of the three UEFA Cup spots open to the regional winners.■

Results 1998-99

FA Carling Premiership

Date	*Opponents*	*Ven*	*Res*	*Atten*	*Scorers*
15-Aug	Sheffield W.	A	1-0	30,236	Wright (85)
22-Aug	Manchester U.	H	0-0	26,039	
29-Aug	Coventry C.	A	0-0	20,818	
09-Sep	Wimbledon	H	3-4	25,311	Hartson (7); Wright (14, 27)
12-Sep	Liverpool	H	2-1	26,029	Hartson (4); Berkovic (51)
19-Sep	N.Forest	A	0-0	28,463	
28-Sep	Southampton	H	1-0	23,153	Wright (60)
03-Oct	Blackburn R.	A	0-3	25,213	
17-Oct	Aston Villa	H	0-0	26,002	
24-Oct	Charlton A.	A	2-4	20,043	OG (17, Rufus); Berkovic (40)
31-Oct	Newcastle U.	A	3-0	36,744	Wright (56, 90); Sinclair (76)
08-Nov	Chelsea	H	1-1	26,023	Ruddock (4)
14-Nov	Leicester C.	H	3-2	25,642	Kitson (37); Lomas (56); Lampard (76)
22-Nov	Derby Co.	A	2-0	31,666	Hartson (7); Keller (72)
28-Nov	Tottenham H.	H	2-1	26,044	Sinclair (39, 46)
05-Dec	Leeds U.	A	0-4	36,320	
12-Dec	Middlesbrough	A	0-1	34,623	
19-Dec	Everton	H	2-1	25,998	Keller (19); Sinclair (75)
26-Dec	Arsenal	A	0-1	38,098	
28-Dec	Coventry C.	H	2-0	25,662	Wright (7); Hartson (68)
10-Jan	Manchester U.	A	1-4	55,180	Lampard (89)
16-Jan	Sheffield W.	H	0-4	25,642	
30-Jan	Wimbledon	A	0-0	23,035	
06-Feb	Arsenal	H	0-4	26,042	
13-Feb	N.Forest	H	2-1	25,458	Pearce (35); Lampard (39)
20-Feb	Liverpool	A	2-2	44,511	Lampard (24 pen); Keller (74)
27-Feb	Blackburn R.	H	2-0	25,529	Pearce (28); Di Canio (31)
06-Mar	Southampton	A	0-1	15,240	
13-Mar	Chelsea	A	1-0	34,765	Kitson (75)
21-Mar	Newcastle U.	H	2-0	25,997	Di Canio (17); Kitson (82)
02-Apr	Aston Villa	A	0-0	36,813	
05-Apr	Charlton A.	H	0-1	26,041	
10-Apr	Leicester C.	A	0-0	20,402	
17-Apr	Derby Co.	H	5-1	25,485	Di Canio (19); Berkovic (28); Wright (55); Ruddock (64); Sinclair (68)
24-Apr	Tottenham H.	A	2-1	36,089	Wright (5); Keller (66)
01-May	Leeds U.	H	1-5	25,997	Di Canio (48)

08-May	Everton	A	0-6	40,049	
16-May	Middlesbrough	H	4-0	25,902	Lampard (4); Keller (26); Sinclair (75); Di Canio (78)

FA Challenge Cup

Sponsored by AXA

Date	*Opponents*	*Vn*	*Rnd*	*Res*	*Atten*	*Scorers*
02-Jan	Swansea C.	H	3R	1-1	26,039	Dicks (86)
13-Jan	Swansea C.	A	3RR	0-1	10,116	

Worthington League Cup

Date	*Opponents*	*Vn*	*Rnd*	*Res*	*Atten*	*Scorers*
15-Sep	Northampton	A	2Rf	0-2	7,254	
22-Sep	Northampton	H	2Rs	1-0	25,435	Lampard (90)

Northampton Town win 2-1 on aggregate

Wimbledon

Founded 1889 as Wimbledon Old Centrals, an old boys' side of the Central School playing on Wimbledon Common. Member of the Southern Suburban League, the name was changed to Wimbledon in 1905. Moved to Plough Lane in 1912. Athenian League member for two seasons before joining the Isthmian League in 1921.

FA Amateur Cup winners 1963 and seven times Isthmian League champions. Turned professional in 1965, joining the Southern League, of which they were champions three times before being elected to Football League Division Four in 1977. Started ground sharing at Selhurst Park in 1991 and founder member of the Premier League 1992.

Ground: Selhurst Park, South Norwood, London SE25 6PY
Phone: 0181-771 2233 **News:** 0891 12 11 75
Box Office: 0181-771 8841
Colours: All Blue with Yellow trim **Nickname:** The Dons
Capacity: 26,995 **Pitch:** 110 yds x 74 yds
Radio: 1548AM Capital Gold
Internet: –

Chairman: Stanley Reed **Vice-Chairman:** J. Lelliott
MD: Sam Hamman **CEO:** David Barnard
Secretary: Steve Rooke
Manager: Egil Olsen **Assistant:** tba
Coaches: tba
Physio: Steve Allen

League History: 1977 Elected to Division 4; 1979-80 Division 3; 1980-81 Division 4; 1981-82 Division 3; 1982-83 Division 4; 1983-84 Division 3; 1984-86 Division 2; 1986-92 Division 1; 1992- FA Premier League.

Honours: *Football League: Division 3 Runners-up* 1983-84; *Division 4 Champions* 1982-83. *FA Cup: Winners* 1987-88. *FA Amateur Cup: Winners* 1963.

European Record: Never qualified.

Managers: Les Henley 1955-71; Mike Everitt 1971-73; Dick Graham 1973-74; Allen Batsford 1974-78; Dario Gradi 1978-81; Dave Bassett 1981-87; Bobby Gould 1987-90; Ray Harford 1990-91; Peter Withe 1991; *(FAPL)* Joe Kinnear January 1992-June 1999; Egil Olsen June 1999–

All-Time Records

Record FAPL Win: 5-2 v Oldham Athletic, Home, 15/12/92
Record FAPL Defeat: 1-7 v Aston Villa, Away, 11/2/95
Record FL Win: 6-0 v Newport County, Div 3, 3/9/83
Record FL Defeat: 0-8 v Everton, League Cup R2, 29/8/78
Record Cup Win: 7-2 v Windsor & Eton, FAC 1R, 22/11/80
Record Fee Received: £4.5m from Newcastle for Warren Barton, 6/95
Record Fee Paid: £6m to West Ham U. for John Hartson, 1/99 (£3m down, £3m after appearances)
Most FL Apps: 430 – Alan Cork, 1977-92
Most FAPL Apps: 219 – Robbie Earle, 1992-99
Most FAPL Goals: 58 – Dean Holdsworth, 1992-97
Highest Scorer in FAPL Season: 19 – Dean Holdsworth, 1992-93
Record Attendance (all-time): 30,115 v Manchester United, 8/5/93
Record Attendance (FAPL): 30,115 v Manchester United, 8/5/93
Most FAPL Goals in Season: 56, 1992-93 – 42 games
56, 1993-94 – 42 games
Most FAPL Points in Season: 65, 1993-94 – 42 games

5-Year Record

	Div.	*P*	*W*	*D*	*L*	*F*	*A*	*Pts*	*Pos*	*FAC*	*FLC*
94-95	PL	42	15	11	16	48	65	56	9	5	3
95-96	PL	38	10	11	17	55	70	41	14	QF	2
96-97	PL	38	15	11	12	49	46	56	8	SF	SF
97-98	PL	38	10	14	14	34	46	44	15	5	3
98-99	PL	38	10	12	16	40	63	42	16	4	SF

Summary 1998-99

Player	*Tot*	*St*	*Sb*	*Snu*	*PS*	*Gls*	*Y*	*R*	*Fa*	*Fg*	*La*	*Lg*
AGYEMANG	0	0	0	1	0	0	0	0	0	0	0	0
AINSWORTH	8	5	3	2	3	0	0	0	0	0	0	0
ARDLEY	23	16	7	4	9	0	0	0	3	0	5	3
BAKKE	0	0	0	5	0	0	0	0	0	0	0	0
BLACKWELL	28	27	1	1	3	0	0	0	2	0	4	0
CASTLEDINE	1	1	0	4	1	0	0	0	0	0	0	0
CORT	16	6	10	6	3	3	1	0	3	1	3	0
CUNNINGHAM	35	35	0	0	0	0	3	0	2	0	7	0
EARLE	35	35	0	0	4	5	2	0	3	1	5	1
EKOKU	22	11	11	2	7	6	1	0	0	0	5	3
EUELL	33	31	2	0	6	10	3	0	3	0	7	0
FEAR	2	0	2	3	0	0	0	0	0	0	1	0
FRANCIS	0	0	0	6	0	0	0	0	0	0	2	0
GAYLE	35	31	4	0	7	10	1	0	1	0	4	1
GOODMAN	1	0	1	0	0	0	0	0	0	0	0	0
HARTSON	14	12	2	0	6	2	2	0	0	0	0	0
HEALD	0	0	0	33	0	0	0	0	0	0	2	0
HUGHES, C.	14	8	6	3	3	0	5	0	3	0	1	0
HUGHES, M.	30	28	2	0	9	2	7	0	2	0	4	1
JUPP	6	3	3	4	0	0	2	0	1	0	2	0
KENNEDY	17	7	10	15	2	0	0	0	2	0	5	1
KIMBLE	26	22	4	11	4	0	3	0	2	0	3	0
LEABURN	22	14	8	3	8	0	2	1	3	0	7	1
McALLISTER	0	0	0	2	0	0	0	0	0	0	1	0
PERRY	34	34	0	0	1	0	5	0	2	0	7	0
ROBERTS	28	23	5	4	3	2	9	0	3	0	4	0
SULLIVAN	38	38	0	0	0	0	4	0	3	0	5	0
THATCHER	31	31	0	0	2	0	8	0	2	0	7	0
28 Players	499	418	81	109	81	40	58	1	40	2	91	11

Kinnear gets Olsen Line

Not for the first time in the nineties, Wimbledon stood on the verge of Wembley glory and a possible place in the UEFA Cup through a good league placing. But it all fell flat for the Dons on 3 March, despite winning 2-1 at Sheffield Wednesday on that day to cement their position of sixth place in the Premier League – the club lost manager Joe Kinnear through a heart attack which kept him out of action for the remainder of the season. Wimbledon still had 11 games to play but failed to win any of them and three times lost three successive matches, the heaviest of which was a 5-1 hammering at Arsenal.

The Dons kicked off the season with a 3-1 victory over Spurs, sweet revenge for the 6-2 defeat suffered the previous spring. The unbeaten run was stretched to four games, the last of which saw Marcus Gayle score twice as the side won 4-3 at West Ham after trailing 3-0. Some fine wins were achieved at Selhurst Park, most notably over Arsenal and Liverpool, but perversely some surprising setbacks were endured on their travels as defeats were received at Southampton, Charlton and Blackburn, amongst others.

Going into his seventh season as Wimbledon manager, Kinnear stayed away from the transfer market during the close season although four squad members were released and Mick Harford retired. But in January the Dons stunned the football world with a swift move to sign West Ham striker John Hartson for an initial £3m, which could rise to £4.5m. The striker contributed two goals before the season was out. More impressive was the form of Carl Cort who finished the season by scoring his fifth goal in five England Under-21 appearances.

FA and Worthington (League) Cup semi-finalists two seasons earlier, the Dons again reached the last four of the latter in 1998-99 only to have their path blocked by Spurs who won 1-0 with a 2nd Leg victory at Selhurst Park. It was also Tottenham who cut short the Dons' FA Cup run with a 3-0 replay win after Wimbledon had beaten Manchester City in the 3rd Round.

An era came to an end at the end of the season with Kinnear stepping down as manager to be replaced by Norwegian coach Egil Olsen. His style – he was manager of the Valerenga side that lost to Chelsea in the Cup Winners' Cup last season – would seem ideally suited to the Dons. But the Premiership is a different kettle of fish. ■

Results 1998-99

FA Carling Premiership

Date	*Opponents*	*Ven*	*Res*	*Atten*	*Scorers*
15-Aug	Tottenham H.	H	3-1	23,031	Earle (48); Ekoku (60, 88)
22-Aug	Derby Co.	A	0-0	25,747	
29-Aug	Leeds U.	H	1-1	16,437	M.Hughes (72)
09-Sep	West Ham U.	A	4-3	25,311	Gayle (30, 77); Euell (64); Ekoku (81)
12-Sep	Aston Villa	A	0-2	32,959	
19-Sep	Sheffield W.	H	2-1	13,163	Euell (1, 50)
28-Sep	Leicester C.	A	1-1	17,725	Earle (74)
03-Oct	Everton	H	1-2	16,054	Roberts (8)
17-Oct	Manchester U.	A	1-5	55,265	Euell (39)
24-Oct	Middlesbrough	H	2-2	14,114	Gayle (26, 76)
31-Oct	Blackburn R.	H	1-1	12,526	Earle (76)
07-Nov	N.Forest	A	1-0	21,362	Gayle (23)
14-Nov	Chelsea	A	0-3	34,757	
21-Nov	Arsenal	H	1-0	26,003	Ekoku (77)
28-Nov	Newcastle U.	A	1-3	36,623	Gayle (34)
05-Dec	Coventry C.	H	2-1	11,717	Euell (71, 83)
13-Dec	Liverpool	H	1-0	26,080	Earle (48)
19-Dec	Southampton	A	1-3	14,354	Gayle (76)
26-Dec	Charlton A.	H	2-1	19,106	Euell (33); M.Hughes (51)
29-Dec	Leeds U.	A	2-2	39,816	Earle (41); Cort (83)
09-Jan	Derby Co.	H	2-1	12,732	Euell (8); Roberts (83)
16-Jan	Tottenham H.	A	0-0	32,422	
30-Jan	West Ham U.	H	0-0	23,035	
08-Feb	Charlton A.	A	0-2	20,002	
21-Feb	Aston Villa	H	0-0	15,582	
27-Feb	Everton	A	1-1	32,574	Ekoku (14)
03-Mar	Sheffield W.	A	2-1	24,116	Ekoku (8); Gayle (31)
06-Mar	Leicester C.	H	0-1	11,801	
13-Mar	N.Forest	H	1-3	12,149	Gayle (79)
21-Mar	Blackburn R.	A	1-3	21,754	Euell (65)
03-Apr	Manchester U.	H	1-1	26,121	Euell (5)
05-Apr	Middlesbrough	A	1-3	33,999	Cort (75)
11-Apr	Chelsea	H	1-2	21,577	Gayle (88)
19-Apr	Arsenal	A	1-5	37,982	Cort (70)
24-Apr	Newcastle U.	H	1-1	21,172	Hartson (24)
01-May	Coventry C.	A	1-2	21,200	Hartson (74)
08-May	Southampton	H	0-2	24,068	
16-May	Liverpool	A	0-3	41,902	

FA Challenge Cup

Sponsored by AXA

Date	*Opponents*	*Vn*	*Rnd*	*Res*	*Atten*	*Scorers*
02-Jan	Manchester C.	H	3R	1-0	11,226	Cort (62)
23-Jan	Tottenham H.	H	4R	1-1	22,229	Earle (60)
02-Feb	Tottenham H.	A	4RR	0-3	24,049	

Worthington Cup

Date	*Opponents*	*Vn*	*Rnd*	*Res*	*Atten*	*Scorers*
15-Sep	Portsmouth	A	2Rf	1-2	7,010	Ekoku (35)
22-Sep	Portsmouth	H	2Rs	4-1	3,756	Ardley (26); Ekoku (53, 112); Leaburn (104)
	Aet. Wimbledon win 5-3 on aggregate					
28-Oct	Birmingham	A	3R	2-1	11,845	Ardley (35, 46)
10-Nov	Bolton W.	A	4R	2-1	7,868	Gayle (16); Kennedy (63)
1-Dec	Chelsea	H	QF	2-1	19,286	Earle (20); Hughes, M (pen 75)
27-Jan	Tottenham H.	A	SFf	0-0	35,997	
16-Feb	Tottenham H.	H	SFs	0-1	25,204	
	Tottenham Hotspur win 1-0 on aggregate					

D1: Blackburn Rovers

Founded in 1875 by local school-leavers. Used several pitches, including Alexander Meadows, the East Lancashire Cricket Club ground, and became known nationally for their FA Cup exploits, eclipsing the record of Blackburn Olympic, the first club to take the trophy away from London. Three consecutive wins in the 1880s, when in the finals Queen's Park (twice) and West Bromwich Albion were beaten, brought recognition by way of a special shield awarded by the FA to commemorate the achievement. Founder members of the Football League in 1888, the club settled at Ewood Park in 1890, purchasing the ground outright in 1893-94. Premier League founder members 1992 and champions in 1994-95. Relegated to Football League at end of 1998-99.

Ground: Ewood Park, Blackburn, BB2 4JF
Phone: 01254-698888 **Fax:** 01254-671042
Box Office: 01254-671666 **CC Bookings:** 01254 671666
News: 0891 12 10 14
Capacity: 30,591 **Pitch:** 115 yds x 76 yds
Colours: Blue/White, White, Blue **Nickname:** Blue and Whites
Radio: 999AM Red Rose Gold
Internet: www.rovers.co.uk

Club President: W.H. Bancroft **Snr-Vice President:** J. Walker
Chairman: R.D. Coar **Vice-Chairman:** R. L. Matthewman
Secretary: Tom Finn
Manager: Brian Kidd **Assistant:** Brian McClair
Coach: Tony Parkes **Physio:** Steve Foster

League History: 1888 Founder member of the League; 1936-39 Division 2; 1946-48 Division 1; 1948-58 Division 2; 1958-66 Division 1; 1966-71 Division 2; 1971-75 Division 3; 1975-79 Division 2; 1979-80 Division 3; 1980-92 Division 2; 1992-99 FA Premier League. 1999- Division 1.

Honours: *FA Premier League: Champions* 1994-95; *Runners-up* 1993-94. *Football League: Division 1 Champions* 1911-12, 1913-14; *Division 2 Champions* 1938-39; *Runners-up* 1957-58; *Division 3 Champions* 1974-75; *Runners-up* 1979-1980. *FA Cup: Winners* 1884, 1885, 1886, 1890, 1891, 1928; *Runners-up* 1882, 1960. *Full Members' Cup: Winners* 1986-87.

European Record: CC (1): 95-96; CWC (0); UEFA (2): 94-95 (1), 98-99 (1).

Managers: Thomas Mitchell 1884-96; J. Walmsley 1896-1903; R.B. Middleton 1903-25; Jack Carr 1922-26 (TM under Middleton to 1925); Bob Crompton 1926-31 (Hon. TM); Arthur Barritt 1931-36 (had been Secretary from 1927); Reg Taylor 1936-38; Bob Crompton 1938-41; Eddie Hapgood 1944-47; Will Scott 1947; Jack Bruton 1947-49; Jackie Bestall 1949-53; Johnny Carey 1953-58; Dally Duncan 1958-60; Jack Marshall 1960-67; Eddie Quigley 1967-70; Johnny Carey 1970-71; Ken Furphy 1971-73; Gordon Lee 1974-75; Jim Smith 1975-78; Jim Iley 1978; John Pickering 1978-79; Howard Kendall 1979-81; Bobby Saxton 1981-86; Don Mackay 1987-91; *(FAPL)* Kenny Dalglish Oct 1991-May 1995; Ray Harford May 1995-Oct 1996; Tony Parkes (caretaker) Oct 1996-June 97; Roy Hodgson July 97-Nov 98; Tony Parkes (caretaker) Nov 1998–Dec 1998; Brian Kidd Dec 1998–.

All-Time Records

Record FAPL Win: 7-0 v Nottingham Forest, Home, 18/11/95
7-1 v Norwich City, Home, 03/10/92
7-2 v Sheffield Wednesday, Home, 25/08/97
Record FAPL Defeat: 0-5 v Coventry City, Away, 09/01/95
2-6 v Leeds United, Away, 10/03/93
Record FL Win: 9-0 v Middlesbrough, Div 2, 6/11/54
Record FL Defeat: 0-8 v Arsenal, Div 1, 25/2/33
Record Cup Win: 11-0 v Rossendale, FAC 1R, 13/10/1884
Record Fee Received: £15m from Newcastle U. for Alan Shearer, 7/96
Record Fee Paid: £7.25m to Southampton for Kevin Davies, 7/98
Most FL Apps: Derek Fazackerley, 596, 1970-86
Most FAPL Apps: 235 – Tim Sherwood, 1992-99
Most FAPL Goals: 112 – Alan Shearer, 1992-96
Highest Scorer in FAPL Season: 34 – Alan Shearer, 1994-95
Record Attendance (all-time): 61,783 v Bolton W, FAC 6R, 2/3/29
Record Attendance (FAPL): 30,895 v Liverpool, 24/2/96
Most FAPL Goals in Season: 80, 1994-95 – 42 games
Most FAPL Points in Season: 89, 1994-95 – 42 games

Summary 1998-99

Player	*Tot*	*St*	*Sb*	*Snu*	*PS*	*Gls*	*Y*	*R*	*Fa*	*Fg*	*La*	*Lg*
ANDERSON	0	0	0	2	0	0	0	0	0	0	0	0
BLAKE	11	9	2	2	0	3	0	0	3	0	0	0
BROOMES	13	8	5	8	0	0	3	1	4	0	0	0
CARSLEY	8	7	1	0	1	0	1	0	0	0	0	0
COUGHLAN	0	0	0	2	0	0	0	0	0	0	0	0
CROFT	12	10	2	14	3	0	1	0	4	0	1	0
DAHLIN	5	2	3	0	0	0	0	1	0	0	0	0
DAILLY	17	14	3	4	1	0	0	0	0	0	2	0
DAVIDSON	34	34	0	0	1	1	7	0	2	0	3	0
DAVIES	21	9	12	9	6	1	5	0	2	1	3	0
DUFF	28	18	10	5	9	1	0	0	4	0	3	0
DUNN	15	10	5	5	6	1	2	0	3	0	2	0
FETTIS	2	2	0	13	0	0	0	0	0	0	0	0
FILAN	26	26	0	7	1	0	3	0	4	0	2	0
FLITCROFT	8	8	0	1	0	2	3	0	0	0	0	0
FLOWERS	11	10	1	13	0	0	1	0	1	0	1	0
GALLAGHER	16	13	3	0	7	5	0	0	1	0	1	0
GILLESPIE	16	13	3	0	2	1	3	1	4	1	0	0
HENCHOZ †	34	34	0	0	4	0	6	0	2	0	3	0
JANSEN	11	10	1	0	9	3	0	0	0	0	0	0
JOHNSON	21	14	7	5	5	1	3	0	0	0	3	0
KENNA	23	22	1	1	1	0	1	0	3	0	3	0
KONDE	0	0	0	0	0	0	0	0	1	0	0	0
McATEER	13	13	0	0	0	1	4	0	0	0	0	0
McKINLAY	16	14	2	3	2	0	4	0	1	0	1	0
MARCOLIN	10	5	5	7	2	1	4	0	3	0	2	0
PEACOCK	30	27	3	3	2	1	7	0	3	0	2	0
PEDERSON	0	0	0	1	0	0	0	0	0	0	0	0
PEREZ	5	4	1	1	2	1	3	1	1	0	0	0
SHERWOOD	19	19	0	0	0	3	4	2	0	0	2	1
SUTTON	17	17	0	0	2	3	9	1	1	0	1	1
TAYLOR	3	1	2	5	0	0	0	0	0	0	0	0
WARD	17	17	0	0	0	5	3	0	3	0	0	0
WILCOX	30	28	2	1	8	3	6	1	3	1	0	0
WILLIAMS	0	0	0	4	0	0	0	0	0	0	0	0
Own Goals						1						
35 Players	492	418	74	116	74	38	83	8	53	3	35	2

...and Jack Came Tumbling Down

After a wait of 81 years, Blackburn Rovers were English champions in 1995. Just four years later the club that Jack Walker's millions built fell into disarray as Rovers suffered the indignity of being the first Premier League championship-winning club to be relegated. Roy Hodgson's first year as manager brought about an upturn in fortunes following a drop to 13th place in 1996-97, but with just two wins from the opening 15 league games in 1998-99, it was clear that Hodgson was living on borrowed time. To bolster an attack that relied heavily upon the goals of Chris Sutton and Kevin Gallacher, Hodgson paid Southampton £7.25m and Bolton £4.25m for strikers Kevin Davies and Nathan Blake respectively. It was a gamble which failed as the duo contributed a total of just four league goals, three of which were down to Blake.

Hodgson was relieved of his duties in November with Brian Kidd coming in for his first managerial task after eight years as Alex Ferguson's assistant. Under Kidd, Rovers enjoyed a mini revival starting with Davies's winning goal against Charlton on 5 December which ended a seven-match winless run. A further home win was recorded over Leeds and the double was completed over Villa as Rovers embarked on a run of one defeat in ten Premier matches. Sheffield Wednesday brought the run to a crushing end with a 4-1 win at Ewood Park and four days later Newcastle confirmed that the revival was over by winning a 5th Round FA Cup replay in Lancashire to avenge a penalty shoot-out defeat in the Worthington Cup. Rovers' fall from grace was limp as just one of the final 14 games ended in victory and a draw against Manchester United confirmed relegation. Kidd was a big player in the transfer market with Ashley Ward, Keith Gillespie, Jason McAteer, Matt Jansen and Lee Carsley all joining the club for a combined fee of almost £18m while Tim Sherwood joined Spurs for £3.8m.

The season had begun with great optimism at Ewood Park following a return to European football but a 1st Round UEFA Cup defeat by Lyon compounded their early season problems in the league. Rovers' Worthington Cup interest was terminated by Leicester in the 5th Round.

People kept saying Rovers were too good to go down. Really? Injury played its part, but once again the Premiership proved that good teams win championships and fighting teams avoid relegation. Blackburn were neither of these last season but will probably fight their way back the stronger for it. ■

Results 1998-99

FA Carling Premiership

Date	Opponents	Ven	Res	Atten	Scorers
15-Aug	Derby Co.	H	0-0	24,007	
24-Aug	Leeds U.	A	0-1	30,652	
29-Aug	Leicester C.	H	1-0	22,544	Gallacher (12)
09-Sep	Tottenham H.	A	1-2	28,338	Gallacher (11)
12-Sep	Sheffield W.	A	0-3	20,846	
21-Sep	Chelsea	H	3-4	23,113	Sutton (22, 79 pen); Perez (57)
27-Sep	Everton	A	0-0	36,404	
03-Oct	West Ham U.	H	3-0	25,213	Flitcroft (10, 87); Davidson (68)
17-Oct	Middlesbrough	A	1-2	34,413	Sherwood (56)
25-Oct	Arsenal	H	1-2	30,867	Johnson (64)
31-Oct	Wimbledon	A	1-1	12,526	Sutton (47 pen)
07-Nov	Coventry C.	H	1-2	23,779	Sherwood (73)
14-Nov	Manchester U.	A	2-3	55,198	Marcolin (65); Blake (74)
21-Nov	Southampton	H	0-2	22,812	
29-Nov	Liverpool	A	0-2	41,753	
05-Dec	Charlton A.	H	1-0	22,568	Davies (75)
12-Dec	Newcastle U.	H	0-0	27,569	
19-Dec	N.Forest	A	2-2	22,013	Blake (49, 90)
26-Dec	Aston Villa	H	2-1	27,536	Gallacher (44); Sherwood (88)
28-Dec	Leicester C.	A	1-1	21,083	Gallacher (38)
09-Jan	Leeds U.	H	1-0	27,620	Gillespie (22)
16-Jan	Derby Co.	A	0-1	27,386	
30-Jan	Tottenham H.	H	1-1	29,643	Jansen (43)
06-Feb	Aston Villa	A	3-1	37,404	OG (32, Southgate); Ward (62); Dunn (64)
17-Feb	Chelsea	A	1-1	34,382	Ward (83)
20-Feb	Sheffield W.	H	1-4	24,643	McAteer (68)
27-Feb	West Ham U.	A	0-2	25,529	
10-Mar	Everton	H	1-2	27,219	Ward (2)
13-Mar	Coventry C.	A	1-1	19,701	Wilcox (67)
21-Mar	Wimbledon	H	3-1	21,754	Ward (7); Jansen (18, 26)
03-Apr	Middlesbrough	H	0-0	27,482	
06-Apr	Arsenal	A	0-1	37,762	
17-Apr	Southampton	A	3-3	15,209	Ward (14); Peacock (25); Wilcox (47)
24-Apr	Liverpool	H	1-3	29,944	Duff (63)
01-May	Charlton A.	A	0-0	20,041	
08-May	N.Forest	H	1-2	24,565	Gallacher (25)

12-May	Manchester U.	H	0-0	30,463	
16-May	Newcastle U.	A	1-1	36,623	Wilcox (37)

UEFA Cup

Date	*Opponents*	*Vn*	*Rnd*	*Res*	*Atten*	*Scorers*
15-Sep	O.Lyonnais	H	1Rf	0-1	13,646	
29-Sep	O.Lyonnais	A	1Rs	2-2	24,558	Perez (36); Flitcroft (56)

Olympique Lyonnais win 3-2 on aggregate

FA Challenge Cup

Sponsored by AXA

Date	*Opponents*	*Vn*	*Rnd*	*Res*	*Atten*	*Scorers*
02-Jan	Charlton A.	H	3R	2-0	16,631	Davies (44); Wilcox (88)
23-Jan	Sunderland	H	4R	1-0	30,125	Gillespie (67)
14-Feb	Newcastle U.	A	5R	0-0	36,295	
24-Feb	Newcastle U.	H	5RR	0-1	27,483	

Worthington Cup

Date	*Opponents*	*Vn*	*Rnd*	*Res*	*Atten*	*Scorers*
28-Oct	Crewe Alex.	A	3R	1-0	5,403	Sutton (47)
11-Nov	Newcastle U.	A	4R	1-1	34,702	Sherwood (30)
2-Dec	Leicester C.	A	QF	0-1	19,442	

5-Year Record

	Div.	*P*	*W*	*D*	*L*	*F*	*A*	*Pts*	*Pos*	*FAC*	*FLC*
94-95	PL	42	27	8	7	80	39	89	1	3	4
95-96	PL	38	18	7	13	61	47	61	7	3	4
96-97	PL	38	9	15	14	42	43	42	13	4	3
97-98	PL	38	16	10	12	57	52	58	6	4	3
98-99	PL	38	7	14	17	38	52	35	19	5	QF

D1: Charlton Athletic

Reformed in 1984 after a traumatic period in their history that saw them move away from The Valley and play for a while at West Ham. Revitalised and regenerated the club achieved Premiership status for the first time in 1998 having won through the play-offs. Originally formed in 1905 by a number of youths, they joined the Football League in 1921 as members of Division 3 South. Played largely in Division 2 and 3 throughout their years. The Addicks flirted briefly with the old Division 1 at the end of the 1980s, having been runners-up in their first season in the top flight (1936-37). Promoted to Premier League in 1998 but relegated back in 1999.

Ground: The Valley, Floyd Road, Charlton, London SE7 8BL
Phone: 0181-333 4000 **Fax:** 0181-333 4001
Box Office: 0181-334 4010 **News:** 0891 12 11 40
Capacity: 21,500 **Pitch:** 111yds x 73 yds
Colours: Red with White trim, White with Red trim, Red with White.
Nickname: Addicks
Radio: 1548AM Capital Radio
Internet: www.charlton-athletic.co.uk

Chairman: Martin Simons **MD:** Peter Varney
Secretary: Chris Parkes
Manager: Alan Curbishley **Assistant:** Keith Peacock
Physio: Jimmy Hendry

League History: 1921 Elected to Division 3(S); 1929-33 Division 2; 1933-35 Division 3(S); 1935-36 Division 2; 1936-57 Division 1; 1957-72 Division 2; 1972-75 Division 3; 1975-80 Division 2; 1980-81 Division 3; 1981-86 Division 2; 1986-90 Division 1; 1990-92 Division 2; 1992-98 Division 1; 1998-1999 FA Premier League; 1999 – Division 1.

Honours: *Football League: Division 1 Runners-up* 1936-37; *Play-Off winners* 1997-98; *Division 2 Runners-up* 1935-36, 1985-86; *Division 3 South Champions* 1928-29, 1934-35. *FA Cup: Winners* 1946-47. *Full Members' Cup: Runners-up* 1986-87.

European Record: Never qualified.

Managers: Walter Rayner 1920-25; Alex McFarlane 1925-28; Albert Lindon 1928; Alex McFarlane 1928-32; Albert Lindon 1932-33; Jimmy

Seed 1935-56; Jimmy Trotter 1956-61; Frank Hill 1961-65; Bob Stokoe 1965-67; Eddie Firmani 1967-70; Theo Foley 1970-74; Andy Nelson 1974-80; Mike Bailey 1980-81; Alan Mullery 1981-82; Ken Craggs 1982; Lennie Lawrence 1982-91; Alan Curbishley and Steve Gritt 1991-95; Alan Curbishley 1995-.

All-Time Records

Record FAPL Win: 5-0 v Southampton, 22/08/98
Record FAPL Defeat: 1-4 on four occasions, 1998-99
Record FL Win: 8-1 v Middlesbrough, Div 1, 12/9/53
Record FL Defeat: 1-11 v Aston Villa, Div 2, 14/11/59
Record Cup Win: 7-0 v Burton Albion, FAC 3R, 1/1/56
Record Fee Received: £2.8m from Leeds United for Lee Bowyer, 7/96
Record Fee Paid: £1m for Neil Readfearn from Barnsley, 6/98
Most FL Apps: Sam Bartram, 583, 1934-56
Most FAPL Apps: 38 – Mark Kinsella, 1998-99
Most FAPL Goals: 8 – Clive Mendonca, 1998-99
Highest Scorer in FAPL Season: 8 – Clive Mendonca, 1998-99
Record Attendance (all-time): 75,031 v Aston Villa, FAC 5R 12/2/38
Record Attendance (FAPL): 20,046 v Chelsea, 03/04/99
Most FAPL Goals in Season: 41, 1998-99 – 38 games
Most FAPL Points in Season: 36, 1998-99 – 38 games

5-Year Record

	Div.	*P*	*W*	*D*	*L*	*F*	*A*	*Pts*	*Pos*	*FAC*	*FLC*
94-95	1	46	16	11	19	58	66	59	15	3	2
95-96	1	46	17	20	9	57	45	71	6	5	3
96-97	1	46	16	11	19	52	66	59	15	3	3
97-98	1	46	26	10	10	80	49	88	4	4	3
98-99	PL	38	8	12	18	41	56	36	18	3	3

Summary 1998-99

Player	*Tot*	*St*	*Sb*	*Snu*	*PS*	*Gls*	*Y*	*R*	*Fa*	*Fg*	*La*	*Lg*
ALLEN	0	0	0	0	0	0	0	0	0	0	1	0
BALMER	0	0	0	3	0	0	0	0	0	0	0	0
BARNES	12	2	10	2	0	0	0	0	0	0	0	0
BARNESS	3	0	3	10	0	0	0	0	0	0	0	0
BOWEN	6	2	4	3	1	0	0	0	0	0	0	0
BROWN	18	13	5	15	1	0	1	0	0	0	2	0
BRIGHT	5	1	4	6	1	1	0	0	1	0	1	0
HOLMES	0	0	0	1	0	0	0	0	1	0	0	0
HUNT	34	32	2	0	14	6	3	0	1	0	2	0
ILIC	23	23	0	6	2	0	1	0	1	0	2	0
JONES, K.	22	13	9	9	3	1	2	1	0	0	3	0
JONES, S.	26	7	19	0	1	1	4	0	0	0	2	0
KINSELLA	38	38	0	0	8	3	5	0	1	0	1	0
KONCHESKY	2	1	1	6	0	0	0	0	0	0	0	0
LISBIE	1	0	1	0	0	0	0	0	0	0	1	0
MENDONCA	25	19	6	1	8	8	0	0	0	0	3	0
MILLS	36	36	0	0	4	2	9	0	1	0	3	0
MORTIMER	17	10	7	1	8	1	1	0	0	0	3	1
NEWTON	16	13	3	2	8	0	2	0	1	0	2	1
PARKER	4	0	4	4	0	0	0	0	1	0	1	0
PETTERSON	10	7	3	12	0	0	0	1	0	0	1	0
POWELL	38	38	0	0	2	0	2	0	1	0	3	0
PRINGLE	18	15	3	0	5	3	1	0	0	0	0	0
REDFEARN	30	29	1	0	9	3	9	0	1	0	2	1
ROBINSON	30	27	3	0	9	3	8	0	1	0	3	0
ROYCE	8	8	0	11	1	0	0	0	0	0	0	0
RUFUS	27	27	0	0	2	1	1	2	1	0	3	0
SALMON	0	0	0	5	0	0	0	0	0	0	0	0
STUART	9	9	0	0	0	3	2	0	0	0	0	0
TILER	27	27	0	2	2	1	6	1	1	0	0	0
YOUDS	22	21	1	2	0	2	6	0	1	0	3	1
Own Goals						2						
31 Players	507	418	89	101	89	41	63	5	14	0	42	4

Adrenalin Rush Fades

One of the hottest tips for relegation for many years, Charlton Athletic made a sensational start to life in the Premier League. Successive goalless draws at Newcastle and Arsenal came either side of a 5-0 thrashing of Southampton with Clive Mendonca scoring the first Premiership hat-trick of the season as the Valley welcomed top-flight football for the first time in 41 years. For the second consecutive year Mendonca went on to be the club's leading goalscorer.

The good start was shattered by defeats against Manchester United and Derby and, following a 4-2 win over West Ham on 24 October, it was to be a further 14 games before the Addicks again collected maximum league points. Then, a 2-0 win over Wimbledon sparked a run of three straight successes and four consecutive clean sheets – a run of shut-outs only bettered by two other sides throughout the entire season. By the time of Charlton's 0-0 draw with Forest on 27 February the club was a couple of places clear of the relegation zone although just two points separated five sides. But with just one win from nine games – the double over West Ham – Alan Curbishley's side went into the final week of the season staring relegation in the face. A stunning 4-3 win at Villa Park, clinched by Danny Mills' last-minute strike ten minutes after goalkeeper Andy Petterson had been dismissed and replaced by defender Steve Brown, gave a stay of execution but a home defeat by Sheffield Wednesday on the last day of the season terminated Charlton's top-flight existence after just one stint.

Charlton's indifferent cup form of recent years persisted with a 3rd Round FA Cup exit being suffered at Blackburn – indeed Athletic failed to score in three games against Rovers during the season. Their Worthington Cup exploits took them past Southend before they went down at home to eventual finalists Leicester.

Curbishley was restricted in his movements in the transfer market and following Charlton's promotion made just two significant signings in Neil Redfearn and Chris Powell for close on £2m, while during the season a further £2.7m was spent on Carl Tiler, Graham Stuart and Martin Pringle, the latter after a loan spell.

On reflection the Charlton manager may realise that his team won results on adrenalin in those early games – in reality £15 million worth of additional expenditure may have helped but it wouldn't have been a guarantee of ensuring a relegation-free finish. Such is life in the Premier League. ■

Results 1998-99

FA Carling Premiership

Date	Opponents	Ven	Res	Atten	Scorers
15-Aug	Newcastle U.	A	0-0	36,719	
22-Aug	Southampton	H	5-0	16,488	Robinson (3); Redfearn (46); Mendonca (63 pen, 80, 90)
29-Aug	Arsenal	A	0-0	38,014	
09-Sep	Manchester U.	A	1-4	55,147	Kinsella
12-Sep	Derby Co.	H	1-2	19,516	Mendonca (89 pen)
19-Sep	Liverpool	A	3-3	44,526	Rufus (24); Mendonca (61); S.Jones (83)
27-Sep	Coventry C.	H	1-1	20,043	Hunt (74)
03-Oct	N.Forest	A	1-0	22,661	Youds (5)
17-Oct	Chelsea	A	1-2	34,639	Youds (58)
24-Oct	West Ham U.	H	4-2	20,043	Tiler (29); Mills (73); Hunt (87); Redfearn (90 pen)
02-Nov	Tottenham H.	A	2-2	32,202	Hunt (32, 75)
07-Nov	Leicester C.	H	0-0	20,021	
14-Nov	Middlesbrough	H	1-1	20,043	Mendonca (37 pen)
21-Nov	Leeds U.	A	1-4	32,487	Mortimer (65)
28-Nov	Everton	H	1-2	20,043	Kinsella (72)
05-Dec	Blackburn R.	A	0-1	22,568	
12-Dec	Sheffield W.	A	0-3	26,010	
21-Dec	Aston Villa	H	0-1	20,043	
26-Dec	Wimbledon	A	1-2	19,106	Redfearn (29)
28-Dec	Arsenal	H	0-1	20,043	
09-Jan	Southampton	A	1-3	15,222	Hunt (13)
17-Jan	Newcastle U.	H	2-2	20,043	Bright (64); Pringle (90)
31-Jan	Manchester U.	H	0-1	20,043	
08-Feb	Wimbledon	H	2-0	20,002	Pringle (36); OG (69, Blackwell)
13-Feb	Liverpool	H	1-0	20,043	K.Jones (70)
20-Feb	Derby Co.	A	2-0	27,853	Hunt (64); Pringle (86)
27-Feb	N.Forest	H	0-0	20,007	
06-Mar	Coventry C.	A	1-2	20,259	Robinson (55)
13-Mar	Leicester C.	A	1-1	20,220	Mendonca (90)
03-Apr	Chelsea	H	0-1	20,046	
05-Apr	West Ham U.	A	1-0	26,041	Stuart (76)
10-Apr	Middlesbrough	A	0-2	34,529	
17-Apr	Leeds U.	H	1-1	20,043	Stuart (20)
20-Apr	Tottenham H.	H	1-4	20,043	Kinsella (5)
24-Apr	Everton	A	1-4	40,089	Stuart (81 pen)

01-May	Blackburn R.	H	0-0	20,041	
08-May	Aston Villa	A	4-3	37,705	OG (3, Barry); Mendonca (56); Robinson (68); Mills (89)
16-May	Sheffield W.	H	0-1	20,043	

FA Challenge Cup

Sponsored by AXA

Date	*Opponents*	*Vn*	*Rnd*	*Res*	*Atten*	*Scorers*
02-Jan	Blackburn R.	A	3R	0-2	16,631	

Worthington Cup

Date	*Opponents*	*Vn*	*Rnd*	*Res*	*Atten*	*Scorers*
16-Sep	QPR	A	2Rf	2-0	6,497	Newton (15); OG (45, Harper)
22-Sep	QPR	H	2Rs	1-0	11,726	Youds (18)
	Charlton Athletic win 3-0 on aggregate					
27-Oct	Leicester C.	H	3R	1-2	19,671	Mortimer (56)

D1: Nottingham Forest

Founded in 1865 by players of a hockey-like game, shinney, who played at the Forest Recreation Ground. They played their first game in 1866. Had several early homes, including a former Notts County ground, The Meadows, and Trent Bridge Cricket Ground.

Founder members of the Football Alliance in 1889 and champions in 1892 when elected to an extended Football League top division. In 1898 moved from the Town Ground to the City Ground at West Bridgford. Run by a committee until 1982, the last league club to become a limited company. Premier League founder members 1992. Relegated after one season, but promoted back at the first attempt, only to be relegated once again in 1997.

Ground: City Ground, Nottingham NG2 5FJ
Phone: 0115-982 4444 **Fax:** 0115-982 4455
Box Office: 0115-982 4445
News: 0891 12 11 74 **Club Shop:** 0115-952 6026
Capacity: 30,539 **Pitch:** 116 yds x 77 yds
Colours: Red, White, Red **Nickname:** Reds
Radio: 945AM/999AM GEM AM
Internet: www.nottinghamforest.co.uk

CEO: Phil Soar **Secretary:** Paul White
Manager: tba **Coaches:** tba
Physio: John Haselden

League History: 1892 elected to Division 1; 1906-07 Division 2; 1907-11 Division 1; 1911-22 Division 2; 1922-25 Division 1; 1925-49 Division 2; 1949-51 Division 3 (S); 1951-57 Division 2; 1957-72 Division 1; 1972-77 Division 2; 1977-92 Division 1; 1992-93 FAPL; 1993-94 Division 1; 1994-1997 FAPL; 1997-98 Division 1; 1998-99 FAPL; 1999– Division 1.

Honours: *Football League: Division 1 Champions* 1977-78; *Runners-up* 1966-67, 1978-79; *Division 2 Champions* 1906-07, 1921-22; *Runners-up* 1956-57; *Division 3 (S) Champions* 1950-51. *FA Cup: Winners* 1898, 1959; *Runners-up* 1991. *Anglo-Scottish Cup: Winners* 1976-77. *Football League Cup: Winners* 1977-78, 1978-79, 1988-89, 1989-90; *Runners-up* 1979-80, 1991-92. *Simod Cup: Winners* 1989. *Zenith Data Systems Cup: Winners* 1991-92. *Champions' Cup: Winners* 1978-79, 1979-80;

European Super Cup: Winners 1979-80; *Runners-up* 1980-81. *World Club Championship: Runners-up* 1980-81.

European Record: CC (3): 78-79 (W), 79-80 (W), 80-81 (1); CWC (0): –; UEFA (5): 61-62 (1), 67-68 (2), 83-84 (3), 84-85 (1), 95-96 (QF).

Managers: Harry Radford 1889-97; Harry Haslam 1897-09; Fred Earp 1909-12; Bob Masters 1912-25; Jack Baynes 1925-29; Stan Hardy 1930-31; Noel Watson 1931-36; Harold Wightman 1936-39; Billy Walker 1939-60; Andy Beattie 1960-63; John Carey 1963-68; Matt Gillies 1969-72; Dave Mackay 1972-73; Allan Brown 1973-75; *(FAPL)* Brian Clough 1975-93; Frank Clark June 1993-Dec 1996; Stuart Pearce (Player-Manager) Dec 1996-Jun 1997; Dave Bassett June 1997-Jan 1999; Mick Adams (Caretaker Manager) Jan 1999; Ron Atkinson Jan 1999–May 1999.

All-Time Records

Record FAPL Win: 7-1 v Sheffield Wednesday, Away, 01/04/95
Record FAPL Defeat: 1-8 v Manchester United, Home, 06/02/99
Record FL Win: 12-0 v Leicester Fosse, Div 1, 12/4/09
Record FL Defeat: 1-9 v Blackburn R, Div 2, 10/4/37
Record Cup Win: 14-0 v Clapton (away), FAC 1R, 17/1/1891
Record Fee Received: £8.5m from Liverpool for Stan Collymore, 6/95
Record Fee Paid: £3.5m to Celtic for Pierre van Hooijdonk, 3/97
Most FL Apps: Bob McKinlay, 614, 1951-70
Most FAPL Apps: 174 – Steve Chettle, 1992-99
Most FAPL Goals: 24 – Bryan Roy, 1994-97
Highest Scorer in FAPL Season: 23 – Stan Collymore, 1994-95
Record Attendance (all-time): 49,945 v Manchester United, Div 1, 28/10/67
Record Attendance (FAPL): 30,025 v Manchester United, 06/02/99
Most FAPL Goals in Season: 72, 1994-95 – 42 games
Most FAPL Points in Season: 77, 1994-95 – 42 games

5-Year Record

	Div.	*P*	*W*	*D*	*L*	*F*	*A*	*Pts*	*Pos*	*FAC*	*FLC*
94-95	PL	42	22	11	9	72	43	77	3	4	4
95-96	PL	38	15	13	10	50	54	58	9	QF	2
96-97	PL	38	6	16	16	31	59	34	20	5	3
97-98	1	46	28	10	8	82	42	94	1	3	2
98-99	PL	38	7	9	22	35	69	30	20	3	4

Summary 1998-99

Player	*Tot*	*St*	*Sb*	*Snu*	*PS*	*Gls*	*Y*	*R*	*Fa*	*Fg*	*La*	*Lg*
ALLOU	2	0	2	3	0	0	0	0	0	0	0	0
ARMSTRONG	22	20	2	2	4	0	2	0	0	0	4	1
BART -WILLIAMS	23	19	4	1	5	3	4	0	1	0	2	0
BEASANT	26	26	0	11	0	0	1	0	1	0	3	0
BONALAIR	28	24	4	2	3	1	3	0	0	0	3	0
BUROC	0	0	0	0	0	0	0	0	0	0	1	0
CHETTLE	34	32	2	1	2	2	7	1	1	0	3	0
CROSSLEY	12	12	0	26	0	0	0	0	0	0	2	0
DARCHEVILLE	16	14	2	6	12	2	3	0	0	0	3	0
DAWSON	0	0	0	1	0	0	0	0	0	0	1	0
DOIG	2	1	1	0	0	0	0	0	0	0	0	0
EDWARDS	12	7	5	8	1	0	1	0	0	0	0	0
FREEDMAN	31	20	11	2	9	9	1	0	1	0	4	3
GEMMILL	21	19	2	0	6	0	3	0	1	0	2	0
GOODLAD	0	0	0	1	0	0	0	0	0	0	0	0
GOUGH	7	7	0	1	1	0	3	1	0	0	0	0
GRAY	8	3	5	5	2	0	0	0	1	0	3	0
HAREWOOD	23	11	12	3	6	1	5	0	1	0	4	2
HARKES	3	3	0	0	1	0	1	0	0	0	0	0
HJELDE	17	16	1	4	2	1	3	0	1	0	2	0
HODGES	5	3	2	0	1	0	1	0	0	0	0	0
JOHNSON	28	25	3	0	4	0	7	0	1	0	2	1
LOUIS-JEAN	15	14	1	2	1	0	5	1	1	0	3	0
LYTTLE	10	5	5	6	2	0	1	0	1	0	2	0
MATTSON	6	5	1	1	1	0	1	0	0	0	0	0
MELTON	1	1	0	0	0	0	0	0	0	0	0	0
PALMER	13	13	0	0	0	0	4	1	0	0	0	0
PORFIRIO	9	3	6	0	3	1	4	0	0	0	0	0
QUASHIE	16	12	4	1	6	0	5	0	1	0	2	0
ROGERS	34	34	0	1	4	4	8	0	0	0	4	0
SHIPPERLEY	20	12	8	4	3	1	0	0	1	0	0	0
STENSAAS	7	6	1	1	5	0	1	0	0	0	0	0
STONE	26	26	0	0	1	3	6	1	1	0	3	2
THOMAS	5	5	0	0	2	1	1	0	0	0	0	0
VAN HOOIJDONK	21	19	2	1	1	6	5	1	0	0	1	0
WILLIAMS	1	1	0	2	0	0	0	0	0	0	0	0
WOAN	2	0	2	6	0	0	1	0	0	0	0	0
37 Players	506	418	88	102	88	35	87	6	14	0	54	9

Down Again...

The tradition of sides promoted to the Premiership facing relegation 12 months later was easily maintained by Nottingham Forest whose hopes of survival were dashed before a ball had been kicked. Manager Dave Bassett was given limited funds to bolster the side and matters were made worse by the start of the new season as Forest took to the field without their two top scorers from the previous season. Kevin Campbell was sold to Trabzonspor for £2.5m, without the manager's consent, while the egotistical Pierre van Hooijdonk went AWOL. On the plus side, in came Nigel Quashie and Dougie Freedman at a cost of almost £2.5m.

Forest still succeeded in winning two of their first three games but the party ended there. The club set a new Premiership record of 19 matches without a win although the run did include four successive home draws. During the run van Hooijdonk returned to the City Ground and it was his goal on 30 January, at Everton, which earned the players a rare win bonus. But the win was too late for Bassett who was sacked following a home 3rd Round FA Cup defeat by Portsmouth. Forest turned to Ron Atkinson in an effort to stave off the inevitable but even buoyed by the Everton win, Forest could not hold Atkinson's former club Manchester United who created a new Premiership record when winning 8-1 at the City Ground. Atkinson had little scope in the transfer market and made Carlton Palmer his biggest signing at just £1.1m. Ironically, after relegation had already been confirmed, Forest strung together a run of three consecutive wins which did at least save them from the embarrassment of setting new lows for the number of points gained and games won. Once Forest's fate had been decided, Atkinson announced his retirement from management. Another late-season departure was former England midfielder Steve Stone who joined Midlands rivals Aston Villa in a £5.5m deal.

Although Forest made an early exit from the FA Cup, overall in the two knock-out competitions they fared better than a year earlier as Leyton Orient and then Cambridge United, the latter only on penalties, were removed from the Worthington Cup before Forest suffered one of three defeats at the hands of Manchester United. ■

Results 1998-99

FA Carling Premiership

Date	*Opponents*	*Ven*	*Res*	*Atten*	*Scorers*
17-Aug	Arsenal	A	1-2	38,064	Thomas (77)
22-Aug	Coventry C.	H	1-0	22,546	Stone (52)
29-Aug	Southampton	A	2-1	14,942	Darcheville (52); Stone (68)
08-Sep	Everton	H	0-2	25,610	
12-Sep	Chelsea	A	1-2	34,809	Darcheville (89)
19-Sep	West Ham U.	H	0-0	28,463	
27-Sep	Newcastle U.	A	0-2	36,760	
03-Oct	Charlton A.	H	0-1	22,661	
17-Oct	Leeds U.	H	1-1	23,911	Stone (85)
24-Oct	Liverpool	A	1-5	44,595	Freedman (18)
01-Nov	Middlesbrough	A	1-1	34,223	Harewood (88)
07-Nov	Wimbledon	H	0-1	21,362	
16-Nov	Derby Co.	H	2-2	24,014	Freedman (57); Van Hooijdonk (62)
21-Nov	Tottenham H.	A	0-2	35,832	
28-Nov	Aston Villa	H	2-2	25,753	Bart-Williams (32); Freedman (44)
07-Dec	Sheffield W.	A	2-3	19,321	Bonalair (55); Van Hooijdonk (70)
12-Dec	Leicester C.	A	1-3	20,891	Van Hooijdonk (14)
19-Dec	Blackburn R.	H	2-2	22,013	Chettle (22 pen); Freedman (30)
26-Dec	Manchester U.	A	0-3	55,216	
28-Dec	Southampton	H	1-1	23,456	Chettle (54 pen)
09-Jan	Coventry C.	A	0-4	17,172	
16-Jan	Arsenal	H	0-1	26,021	
30-Jan	Everton	A	1-0	34,175	Van Hooijdonk (51)
06-Feb	Manchester U.	H	1-8	30,025	Rogers (6)
13-Feb	West Ham U.	A	1-2	25,458	Hjelde (84)
20-Feb	Chelsea	H	1-3	26,351	Van Hooijdonk (39)
27-Feb	Charlton A.	A	0-0	20,007	
10-Mar	Newcastle U.	H	1-2	22,852	Freedman (45)
13-Mar	Wimbledon	A	3-1	12,149	Rogers (21); Freedman (59); Shipperley (84)
21-Mar	Middlesbrough	H	1-2	21,468	Freedman (37)
03-Apr	Leeds U.	A	1-3	39,645	Rogers (53)
05-Apr	Liverpool	H	2-2	28,374	Freedman (60); Van Hooijdonk (90)
10-Apr	Derby Co.	A	0-1	32,217	
17-Apr	Tottenham H.	H	0-1	25,181	

24-Apr	Aston Villa	A	0-2	34,492	
01-May	Sheffield W.	H	2-0	20,480	Porfirio (14); Rogers (16)
08-May	Blackburn R.	A	2-1	24,565	Freedman (12); Bart-Williams (56)
16-May	Leicester C.	H	1-0	25,353	Bart-Williams (76)

FA Challenge Cup

Sponsored by AXA

Date	*Opponents*	*Vn*	*Rnd*	*Res*	*Atten*	*Scorers*
02-Jan	Portsmouth	A	3R	0-1	10,092	

Worthington Cup

Date	*Opponents*	*Vn*	*Rnd*	*Res*	*Atten*	*Scorers*
15-Sep	Leyton O.	A	2Rf	5-1	5,000	Johnson (4); Freedman (14, 17); Stone (44); Harewood (84)
22-Sep	Leyton O.	H	2Rs	0-0	6,382	
	Nottingham Forest win 5-1 on aggregate					
27-Oct	Cambridge U.	H	3R	3-3	9,192	Freedman (22); Armstrong (45); Harewood (46)
11-Nov	Manchester U.	A	4R	1-2	37,237	Stone (68)

Manchester United

Continued from Page 131

FA Challenge Cup

Sponsored by AXA

Date	*Opponents*	*Vn*	*Rnd*	*Res*	*Atten*	*Scorers*
03-Jan	Middlesbro'	H	3R	3-1	52,232	Cole (68); Irwin (82 pen); Giggs (90);
24-Jan	Liverpool	H	4R	2-1	54,591	Yorke (89); Solskjaer (90)
14-Feb	Fulham	H	5R	1-0	54,798	Cole (26)
7-Mar	Chelsea	H	QF	0-0	54,587	
10-Mar	Chelsea	A	QFR	2-0	33,075	Yorke (4, 59)
12-Apr	Arsenal		SF	0-0	39,217	*aet. At Villa Park*
14-Apr	Arsenal		SFR	2-1	30,223	Beckham (17); Giggs (110) *aet. At Villa Park*
22-May	Newcastle U. *Played at Wembley*		F	2-0	79,101	Sheringham (11); Scholes (53)

Worthington Cup

Date	*Opponents*	*Vn*	*Rnd*	*Res*	*Atten*	*Scorers*
28-Oct	Bury	H	3R	2-0	52,495	Solskjaer (106); Nevland (115)
11-Nov	N.Forest	H	4R	2-1	37,237	Solskjaer (57, 60)
02-Dec	Tottenham H.	A	QF	1-3	35,702	Sheringham (71)

5-Year Record

	Div.	*P*	*W*	*D*	*L*	*F*	*A*	*Pts*	*Pos*	*FAC*	*FLC*
94-95	PL	42	26	10	6	77	28	88	2	F	3
95-96	PL	38	25	7	6	73	35	82	1	W	2
96-97	PL	38	21	12	5	76	44	75	1	4	4
97-98	PL	38	23	8	7	73	26	77	2	5	3
98-99	PL	38	22	13	3	80	37	79	1	W	QF

Stats File

The Stats File supplies the most complete summary of every club's existence, not to be found anywhere else. First comes a complete PWDLFA for every division the club has competed in and then for each of the major cup competitions, including Europe where the totals for Champions' League, Cup-Winners' Cup and UEFA Cup are displayed. The league summaries are given for combined divisions. Thus 'Division 1n/2' relates to the new Division 1 which was also the old Division 2. The values of Yr, B, W are the number of Years (seasons) in that division, and the Best and Worst positions achieved in the division.

This is followed by a list of sequences relating to the Football League. Dates for the start and end of the sequence are given:

Winning Run	The highest number of successive wins
Without Defeat	The highest number of games gone without a defeat
Without Win	The highest number of games gone without a win
Drawn Games	The highest number of successive drawn games
Without Draw	The highest number of games gone without a draw
Losing Run	The highest number of successive defeats
Clean Sheets	The highest games gone without conceding a goal
Goals Scored	The highest number of successive games in which a goal has been scored
No Goals For	The highest number of games gone in which a goal has not been scored by the team
SOS Undefeated	SOS = Start of Season. This is the number of games at the start of a season before a defeat (thus games were either won or drawn)
SOS No Wins	Number of games at the start of the season without a win

There may be several instances of a particular sequence. In such cases the number of times the sequence occurred is listed in brackets and the last two occasions it happened are detailed. Thus:

Clean Sheets (5)

would indicate that the specified number of clean sheets have been maintained on five different occasions.

Arsenal

Division	P	W	D	L	F	A	Pts	Yr	B	W
Premier/1:	3374	1448	881	1045	5403	4406	4116	82	1	20
Division 1n/2:	428	216	73	139	824	550	505	13	2	10
Totals:	3802	1664	954	1184	6228	4956	4621	95	–	–

Cup Records	P	W	D	L	F	A
Europe:	83	40	20	23	147	80
FA Cup:	350	176	84	90	573	383
League Cup:	163	91	39	33	287	150

Sequence	Games	Start		End
Winning Run:	10	12-Sep-87	to	14-Nov-87
	10	11-Mar-98	to	03-May-98
Without Defeat:	26	28-Apr-90	to	19-Jan-91
Without Win:	23	28-Sep-12	to	01-Mar-13
Drawn Games:	6	04-Mar-61	to	01-Apr-61
Without Draw:	28	04-Apr-83	to	26-Dec-83
Losing Run:	7	12-Feb-77	to	12-Mar-77
Clean Sheets:	8	10-Apr-03	to	03-Oct-03
	8	31-Jan-98	to	31-Mar-98
Goals Scored:	31	03-May-30	to	28-Feb-31
No Goals For:	6	25-Feb-87	to	28-Mar-87
SOS Undefeated:	23	1990-91		
SOS No Wins (3):	8	1927-28		
	8	1912-13		

Aston Villa

Division	P	W	D	L	F	A	Pts	Yr	B	W
Premier/1:	3424	1440	768	1216	5844	5200	3904	88	1	22
Division 1n/2:	422	179	111	132	617	487	491	10	1	21
Division 2n/3:	92	51	21	20	139	78	123	2	1	4
Totals:	3938	1670	900	1368	6600	5765	4518	100	–	–

Cup Records	P	W	D	L	F	A
Europe:	55	27	13	15	78	48
FA Cup:	372	195	75	102	773	469
League Cup:	181	102	42	37	347	210
A/F Members:	12	6	0	6	21	17

Sequence	Games	Start		End
Winning Run:	9	15-Oct-10	to	10-Dec-10
Without Defeat (3):	15	18-Dec-09	to	26-Mar-10

	15	12-Mar-49	to	27-Aug-49
Without Win:	12	10-Nov-73	to	2-Feb-74
	12	27-Dec-86	to	25-Mar-87
Drawn Games:	6	12-Sep-81	to	10-Oct-81
Without Draw:	51	01-Jan-1891	to	17-Dec-1892
Losing Run:	11	23-Mar-63	to	4-May-63
Clean Sheets:	7	27-Oct-23	to	8-Dec-23
Goals Scored:	35	10/11/1894	to	12/12/1895
No Goals For (4):	5	11-Jan-92	to	8-Feb-92
	5	29-Feb-92	to	21-Mar-92
SOS Undefeated:	12	15-Aug-98	to	14-Nov-98
SOS No Wins (3):	9	1958-59		
	9	1966-67		

Bradford City

Division	*P*	*W*	*D*	*L*	*F*	*A*	*Pts*	*Yr*	*B*	*W*
Premier/1:	392	138	106	148	516	533	382	10	5	21
Division 1n/2:	1086	380	274	432	1462	1600	1161	26	1	23
Division 2n/3:	736	269	192	275	1022	1059	902	16	1	24
Division 3N:	704	285	169	250	1166	996	739	16	1	22
Division 3n/4:	780	307	205	268	1174	1089	845	17	2	23
Totals:	3698	1379	946	1373	5340	5277	4029	85	–	–

Cup Records	*P*	*W*	*D*	*L*	*F*	*A*
Europe:	0	0	0	0	0	0
FA Cup:	225	94	48	83	371	310
League Cup:	125	47	30	48	190	206
A/F Members:	32	13	6	13	62	56

Sequence	*Games*	*Start*		*End*
Winning Run:	10	26-Nov-83	to	3-Feb-84
Without Defeat:	21	11-Jan-69	to	2-May-69
Without Win:	16	28-Aug-48	to	20-Nov-48
Drawn Games:	6	30-Jan-76	to	13-Mar-76
Without Draw:	24	7-Oct-63	to	7-Mar-64
Losing Run:	8	21-Jan-33	to	11-Mar-33
Clean Sheets (6):	5	29-Aug-53	to	12-Sep-53
	5	16-Jan-54	to	20-Feb-54
Goal Scored:	30	26-Dec-61	to	15-Sep-62
No. Goals For:	7	18-Apr-25	to	5-Sep-25
SOS Undefeated:	8	1979-80		
SOS No Wins:	9	1926-27		

Chelsea

Division	*P*	*W*	*D*	*L*	*F*	*A*	*Pts*	*Yr*	*B*	*W*
Premier/1:	2638	936	703	999	3821	4088	2785	64	1	22
Division 1n/2:	786	383	202	201	1323	887	1048	19	1	18
Totals:	3424	1319	905	1200	5144	4975	3833	83	–	–

Cup Records	*P*	*W*	*D*	*L*	*F*	*A*
Europe:	59	33	15	11	114	52
FA Cup:	299	138	79	82	491	338
League Cup:	135	60	34	41	234	173
A/F Members:	27	18	3	6	55	41

Sequence	*Games*	*Start*		*End*
Winning Run:	8	06-Oct-27	to	19-Nov-27
	8	15-Mar-89	to	08-Apr-89
Without Defeat:	27	29-Oct-88	to	08-Apr-89
Without Win:	21	3-Nov-87	to	02-Apr-88
Drawn Games:	6	20-Aug-69	to	13-Sep-69
Without Draw:	24	10-Sep-32	to	11-Feb-33
Losing Run:	7	01-Nov-52	to	20-Dec-52
Clean Sheets:	9	04-Nov-05	to	25-Dec-05
Goals Scored:	27	31-Aug-85	to	22-Mar-86
	27	29-Oct-88	to	08-Apr-89
No Goals For:	9	14-Mar-81	to	02-May-81
SOS Undefeated:	14	1925-26		
SOS No Wins:	6	1914-15		
	6	1988-89		

Coventry City

Division	*P*	*W*	*D*	*L*	*F*	*A*	*Pts*	*Yr*	*B*	*W*
Premier/1:	1314	410	378	526	1521	1837	1422	32	6	20
Division 1n/2:	756	279	186	291	1050	1099	744	18	1	22
Division 2n/3:	230	93	66	71	403	347	252	5	1	15
Division 3S/3N:	738	298	164	276	1351	1184	760	17	1	20
Division 3n/4:	46	24	12	10	84	47	60	1	2	2
Totals:	3084	1104	806	1174	4409	4514	3238	73	–	–

Cup Records	*P*	*W*	*D*	*L*	*F*	*A*
Europe:	4	3	0	1	9	8
FA Cup:	186	74	39	73	295	276
League Cup:	127	63	21	43	215	185
A/F Members:	10	2	2	6	8	15

Sequence	*Games*	*Start*		*End*
Winning Run:	6	20-Apr-54	to	28-Aug-54
	6	25-Apr-64	to	05-Sep-64
Without Defeat:	25	26-Nov-66	to	13-May-67
Without Win:	19	30-Aug-19	to	20-Dec-19
Drawn Games:	6	28-Sep-96	to	16-Nov-96
Without Draw:	25	06-Sep-26	to	12-Feb-27
Losing Run:	9	30-Aug-19	to	11-Oct-19
Clean Sheets:	6	28-Apr-34	to	03-Sep-34
Goals Scored:	25	10-Sep-66	to	25-Feb-67
No Goals For:	11	11-Oct-19	to	20-Dec-19
SOS Undefeated:	15	1937-38		
SOS No Wins:	19	1919-20		

Derby County

Division	*P*	*W*	*D*	*L*	*F*	*A*	*Pts*	*Yr*	*B*	*W*
Premier/1:	2316	878	548	890	3630	3641	2389	61	1	22
Division 1n/2:	1466	598	357	511	2293	2062	1712	35	1	22
Division 3N:	92	54	18	20	221	108	126	2	1	2
Division 2n/3:	92	42	28	22	145	95	154	2	3	7
Totals:	3966	1572	951	1443	6289	5906	4381	100	–	–

Cup Records	*P*	*W*	*D*	*L*	*F*	*A*
Europe:	22	11	4	7	50	29
FA Cup:	300	141	55	104	563	455
League Cup:	133	52	33	48	209	141
A/F Members:	16	7	2	7	24	24

Sequence	*Games*	*Start*		*End*
Winning Run:	9	15-Mar-69	to	19-Apr-69
Without Defeat:	22	08-Mar-69	to	20-Sep-69
Without Win:	20	15-Dec-90	to	23-Apr-91
Drawn Games:	6	26-Mar-27	to	18-Apr-27
Without Draw:	28	25-Sep-26	to	19-Mar-27
Losing Run (3):	8	17-Apr-65	to	01-Sep-65
	8	12-Dec-87	to	10-Feb-88
Clean Sheets:	6	08-Apr-12	to	22-Apr-12
Goals Scored:	29	03-Dec-60	to	06-Sep-61
No Goals For:	8	30-Oct-20	to	18-Dec-20
SOS Undefeated:	16	1948-49		
SOS No Wins:	9	1990-91		

Everton

Division	*P*	*W*	*D*	*L*	*F*	*A*	*Pts*	*Yr*	*B*	*W*
Premier/1:	3758	1545	917	1296	6000	5317	4299	96	1	22
Division 1n/2:	168	77	45	46	348	257	199	4	1	16
Totals:	3926	1622	962	1342	6348	5574	4498	100	–	–

Cup Records	*P*	*W*	*D*	*L*	*F*	*A*
Europe:	45	23	12	10	71	35
FA Cup:	363	197	71	95	671	405
League Cup:	131	64	32	35	242	142
A/F Members:	15	9	2	4	36	25

Sequence	*Games*	*Start*		*End*
Winning Run:	12	24-Mar-1894	to	13-Oct-1894
Without Defeat:	20	29-Apr-78	to	16-Dec-78
Without Win:	14	06-Mar-37	to	04-Sep-37
Drawn Games (3):	5	05-Oct-74	to	26-Oct-74
	5	04-May-77	to	16-May-77
Without Draw:	26	22-Feb-58	to	18-Oct-58
Losing Run (7):	6	04-Nov-72	to	09-Dec-72
	6	26-Dec-96	to	29-Jan-97
Clean Sheets:	7	01-Nov-94	to	17-Dec-94
Goals Scored:	40	15-Mar-30	to	07-Mar-31
No Goals For:	6	03-Mar-51	to	31-Mar-51
	6	08-Dec-93	to	01-Jan-94
SOS Undefeated:	19	1978-79		
SOS No Wins:	12	1994-95		

Leeds United

Division	*P*	*W*	*D*	*L*	*F*	*A*	*Pts*	*Yr*	*B*	*W*
Premier/1:	1870	765	483	622	2806	2525	2172	45	1	22
Division 1n/2:	1144	483	309	352	1731	1451	1417	27	1	19
Division 1n/2:*	380	140	77	163	575	616	357	10	4	19
Totals:	3394	1388	869	1137	5114	4592	3946	82	–	–

** as Leeds City*

Cup Records	*P*	*W*	*D*	*L*	*F*	*A*
Europe:	104	54	25	25	179	86
FA Cup:	212	89	52	71	338	280
League Cup:	133	61	23	49	218	179
A/F Members:	17	7	3	7	24	29

Sequence	*Games*	*Start*		*End*
Winning Run:	9	26-Sep-31	to	21-Nov-31
Without Defeat:	34	26-Oct-68	to	26-Aug-69
Without Win:	17	01-Feb-47	to	26-May-47
Drawn Games:	5	09-Apr-62	to	24-Apr-62
	5	19-Apr-97	to	09-Aug-97
Without Draw:	24	12-Sep-36	to	13-Feb-37
Losing Run:	6	26-Apr-47	to	26-May-47
	6	06-Apr-96	to	02-May-96
Clean Sheets:	9	03-Mar-28	to	14-Apr-28
Goals Scored:	30	27-Aug-27	to	25-Feb-28
No Goals For:	6	30-Jan-82	to	10-Mar-82
SOS Undefeated:	29	1973-74		
SOS No Wins:	6	1951-52		
	6	1935-36		

Leicester City

Division	*P*	*W*	*D*	*L*	*F*	*A*	*Pts*	*Yr*	*B*	*W*
Premier/1:	1748	562	459	727	2624	3012	1675	42	2	22
Division 1n/2:	2074	854	514	706	3212	2933	2401	52	1	22
Totals:	3822	1416	973	1433	5837	5944	4076	94	–	–

Cup Records	*P*	*W*	*D*	*L*	*F*	*A*
Europe:	6	2	1	3	9	9
FA Cup:	242	102	52	88	363	344
League Cup:	125	57	25	43	195	158
A/F Members:	12	6	2	4	17	14

Sequence	*Games*	*Start*		*End*
Winning Run:	7	15-Feb-08	to	28-Mar-08
	7	24-Jan-25	to	17-Mar-25
Without Defeat:	19	06-Feb-71	to	18-Aug-71
Without Win:	18	12-Apr-75	to	01-Nov-75
Drawn Games:	6	21-Apr-73	to	01-Sep-73
	6	21-Aug-76	to	18-Sep-76
Without Draw:	44	30-Jan-09	to	26-Mar-10
Losing Run:	7	28-Nov-31	to	16-Jan-32
	7	28-Aug-90	to	29-Sep-90
Clean Sheets:	7	14-Feb-20	to	27-Mar-20
Goals Scored:	31	12-Nov-32	to	28-Aug-33
No Goals For:	7	21-Nov-87	to	01-Jan-88
SOS Undefeated:	11	1899-00		
SOS No Wins:	15	1975-76		

Liverpool

Division	*P*	*W*	*D*	*L*	*F*	*A*	*Pts*	*Yr*	*B*	*W*
Premier/1:	3374	1533	842	999	5548	4265	4287	84	1	22
Division 1n/2:	428	243	82	103	977	571	568	11	1	11
Totals:	3802	1776	924	1102	6525	4836	4855	95	–	–

Cup Records	*P*	*W*	*D*	*L*	*F*	*A*
Europe:	174	99	33	42	338	145
FA Cup:	365	189	85	91	588	344
League Cup:	169	97	43	29	332	144

Sequence	*Games*	*Start*		*End*
Winning Run:	12	21-Apr-90	to	06-Oct-90
Without Defeat:	31	4-May-87	to	16-Mar-88
Without Win:	14	12-Dec-53	to	20-Mar-54
Drawn Games:	6	19-Feb-75	to	19-Mar-75
Without Draw:	23	28-Nov-81	to	01-May-82
Losing Run:	9	29-Apr-1899	to	14-Oct-1899
Clean Sheets:	8	30-Dec-22	to	03-Mar-23
Goals Scored:	29	27-Apr-57	to	11-Jan-58
No Goals For (4):	5	18-Dec-71	to	22-Jan-72
	5	01-Sep-93	to	02-Oct-93
SOS Undefeated:	29	1987-88		
SOS No Wins:	9	1894-95		

Manchester United

Division	*P*	*W*	*D*	*L*	*F*	*A*	*Pts*	*Yr*	*B*	*W*
Premier/1:	3018	1330	777	911	5049	4114	3809	74	1	22
Division 1n/2:	816	406	168	242	1433	966	980	22	1	20
Totals:	3834	1736	945	1153	6482	5080	4789	96	–	–

Cup Records	*P*	*W*	*D*	*L*	*F*	*A*
Europe:	143	72	44	27	278	149
FA Cup:	353	187	82	84	632	417
League Cup:	132	72	25	35	227	145

Sequence	*Games*	*Start*		*End*
Winning Run:	14	15-Oct-04	to	03-Jan-05
Without Defeat:	26	04-Feb-56	to	13-Oct-56
Without Win:	16	03-Nov-28	to	09-Feb-29
	16	19-Apr-30	to	25-Oct-30
Drawn Games:	6	30-Oct-88	to	27-Nov-88
Without Draw:	26	23-Nov-1895	to	26-Sep-1896

Losing Run:	14	26-Apr-30	to	25-Oct-30
Clean Sheets (3):	7	20-Sep-24	to	01-Nov-24
	7	08-May-97	to	30-Aug-97
Goals Scored:	27	11-Oct-58	to	04-Apr-59
No Goals For (3):	5	26-Jan-24	to	23-Feb-24
	5	07-Feb-81	to	07-Mar-81
SOS Undefeated:	15	1985-86		
SOS No Wins:	12	1930-31		

Middlesbrough

Division	*P*	*W*	*D*	*L*	*F*	*A*	*Pts*	*Yr*	*B*	*W*
Premier/1:	2020	697	493	830	2966	3211	1945	50	3	22
Division 1n/2:	1556	651	377	528	2466	2094	1870	37	1	21
Division 2n/3:	92	51	19	22	154	94	149	2	2	2
Totals:	3668	1399	889	1380	5586	5399	3964	89	–	–

Cup Records	*P*	*W*	*D*	*L*	*F*	*A*
Europe:	0	0	0	0	0	0
FA Cup:	271	100	73	98	421	377
League Cup:	128	52	32	44	190	151
A/F Members:	22	13	1	8	35	23

Sequence	*Games*	*Start*		*End*
Winning Run:	9	16-Feb-74	to	06-Apr-74
Without Defeat:	24	08-Sep-73	to	19-Jan-74
Without Win:	19	03-Oct-81	to	06-Mar-82
Drawn Games:	8	03-Apr-71	to	01-May-71
Without Draw:	33	02-May-25	to	27-Feb-26
Losing Run:	8	25-Aug-54	to	18-Sep-54
	8	26-Dec-95	to	17-Feb-96
Clean Sheets:	7	07-Nov-87	to	19-Dec-87
Goals Scored:	26	21-Sep-46	to	08-Mar-47
No Goals For (10):	4	05-Dec-81	to	06-Feb-82
	4	02-Nov-93	to	04-Dec-93
SOS Undefeated:	10	1910-11		
SOS No Wins:	9	1954-55		
	9	1982-83		

Newcastle United

Division	P	W	D	L	F	A	Pts	Yr	B	W
Premier/1:	2780	1099	667	1014	4326	4037	3036	69	1	21
Division 1n/2:	1046	481	218	347	1798	1438	1318	26	1	20
Totals:	3826	1580	885	1361	6124	5475	4354	95	–	–

Cup Records	P	W	D	L	F	A
Europe:	50	24	10	16	83	54
FA Cup:	319	152	78	89	563	391
League Cup:	99	42	16	41	152	131
A/F Members:	9	3	1	5	18	21

Sequence	Games	Start		End
Winning Run:	13	25-Apr-92	to	18-Oct-92
Without Defeat:	14	22-Apr-50	to	30-Sep-50
Without Win:	21	14-Jan-78	to	23-Aug-78
Drawn Games (14):	4	21-Dec-85	to	11-Jan-86
	4	20-Jan-90	to	24-Feb-90
Without Draw:	34	16-Nov-1895	to	5-Dec-1896
Losing Run:	10	23-Aug-77	to	15-Oct-77
Clean Sheets:	6	06-Mar-82	to	03-Apr-82
Goals Scored:	25	15-Apr-39	to	26-Dec-46
No Goals For:	6	31-Dec-38	to	15-Feb-39
	6	29-Oct-88	to	03-Dec-88
SOS Undefeated (3):	11	1950-51		
	11	1994-95		
SOS No Wins:	10	1898-99		

Sheffield Wednesday

Division	P	W	D	L	F	A	Pts	Yr	B	W
Premier/1:	2544	972	605	967	3938	3958	2750	65	1	22
Division 1n/2:	1088	460	281	347	1693	1401	1285	26	1	22
Division 2n/3:	230	83	76	71	297	266	242	5	3	20
Totals:	3862	1515	962	1385	5928	5617	4277	96	–	–

Cup Records	P	W	D	L	F	A
Europe:	14	7	1	6	38	25
FA Cup:	357	169	84	104	639	443
League Cup:	127	60	31	36	209	153
A/F Members:	9	3	1	5	12	15

Sequence	Games	Start		End
Winning Run:	9	23-Apr-04	to	15-Oct-04
Without Defeat:	19	10-Dec-60	to	08-Apr-61

Without Win:	20	23-Oct-54	to	12-Mar-55
	20	11-Jan-75	to	30-Aug-75
Drawn Games (3):	5	01-Dec-90	to	26-Dec-90
	5	24-Oct-92	to	28-Nov-92
Without Draw:	22	30-Nov-07	to	18-Apr-08
Losing Run:	7	07-Jan-1893	to	18-Mar-1893
Clean Sheets (4):	5	21-Feb-61	to	18-Mar-61
	5	04-Apr-92	to	20-Apr-92
Goals Scored:	40	14-Nov-59	to	29-Oct-60
No Goals For:	8	08-Mar-75	to	12-Apr-75
SOS Undefeated:	15	1983-84		
SOS No Wins:	17	1974-75		

Southampton

Division	*P*	*W*	*D*	*L*	*F*	*A*	*Pts*	*Yr*	*B*	*W*
Premier/1:	1188	395	326	467	1605	1759	1361	29	2	20
Division 1n/2:	1428	559	353	516	2221	2140	1471	34	2	21
Division 2n/3:	92	43	20	29	194	155	106	2	1	14
Division 3S	314	150	77	87	562	368	377	7	1	14
Totals:	3022	1147	776	1099	4582	4422	3315	72	–	–

Cup Records	*P*	*W*	*D*	*L*	*F*	*A*
Europe:	22	8	8	6	37	26
FA Cup:	284	113	76	95	433	366
League Cup:	145	62	43	40	237	173
A/F Members:	13	8	0	5	24	14

Sequence	*Games*	*Start*		*End*
Winning Run:	6	03-Mar-92	to	04-Apr-92
Without Defeat:	19	05-Sep-21	to	31-Dec-21
Without Win:	20	30-Aug-69	to	27-Dec-69
Drawn Games:	7	28-Dec-94	to	11-Feb-95
Without Draw:	27	24-Jan-31	to	10-Oct-31
Losing Run (10):	5	29-Nov-93	to	18-Dec-93
	5	16-Nov-96	to	07-Dec-96
	5	16-Aug-98	to	12-Sep-98
Clean Sheets:	8	17-Apr-22	to	26-Aug-22
Goals Scored:	24	05-Sep-66	to	11-Feb-67
No Goals For:	5	26-Aug-22	to	09-Sep-22
	5	01-Sep-37	to	15-Sep-37
SOS Undefeated:	7	1950-51		
SOS No Wins (1):	9	1998-99		

Sunderland

Division	*P*	*W*	*D*	*L*	*F*	*A*	*Pts*	*Yr*	*B*	*W*
Premier/1:	2770	1117	631	1022	4566	4270	2927	71	1	21
Division 1n/2:	1128	478	315	335	1683	1348	1469	26	1	21
Division 2n/3:	46	27	12	7	92	48	93	1	1	1
Totals:	3944	1622	958	1364	6341	5666	4489	98	–	–

Cup Records	*P*	*W*	*D*	*L*	*F*	*A*
Europe:	4	3	0	1	5	3
FA Cup:	301	126	73	102	499	410
League Cup:	122	48	31	43	186	175
A/F Members:	14	5	3	6	24	20

Sequence	*Games*	*Start*		*End*
Winning Run:	13	14-Nov-1891	to	2-Apr-1892
Without Defeat:	19	03-May-98	to	14-Nov-98
Without Win:	14	16-Apr-85	to	14-Sep-85
Drawn Games:	6	26-Mar-49	to	19-Apr-49
Without Draw:	46	26-Dec-07	to	13-Mar-09
Losing Run:	9	23-Nov-76	to	15-Jan-77
Clean Sheets (5):	6	18-Dec-82	to	15-Jan-83
	6	6-Apr-96	to	27-Apr-96
Goal Scored:	29	8-Nov-97	to	25-Apr-98
No. Goals For:	10	27-Nov-76	to	5-Feb-77
SOS Undefeated:	18	1998-99		
SOS No Wins:	10	1969-70		
	10	1976-77		

Tottenham Hotspur

Division	*P*	*W*	*D*	*L*	*F*	*A*	*Pts*	*Yr*	*B*	*W*
Premier/1:	2634	1058	645	931	4177	3819	3047	64	1	22
Division 1n/2:	668	311	172	185	1253	851	794	16	1	12
Totals:	3302	1369	817	1116	5430	4670	3841	80	–	–

Cup Records	*P*	*W*	*D*	*L*	*F*	*A*
Europe:	95	57	18	20	215	87
FA Cup:	346	175	88	83	665	409
League Cup:	149	87	26	36	276	158

Sequence	*Games*	*Start*		*End*
Winning Run:	13	23-Apr-60	to	01-Oct-60
Without Defeat:	22	31-Aug-49	to	31-Dec-49
Without Win:	16	29-Dec-34	to	13-Apr-35

Drawn Games:	6	09-Jan-99	to	27-Feb-99
Without Draw:	19	15-Feb-30	to	13-Sep-30
Losing Run:	7	01-Jan-94	to	27-Feb-94
Clean Sheets (4):	5	17-Dec-94	to	02-Jan-95
	5	21-Nov-95	to	16-Dec-95
Goals Scored:	32	09-Apr-49	to	31-Dec-49
	32	24-Feb-62	to	24-Nov-62
No Goals For:	6	28-Dec-85	to	08-Feb-86
SOS Undefeated:	16	1960-61		
SOS No Wins:	12	1912-13		

Watford

Division	*P*	*W*	*D*	*L*	*F*	*A*	*Pts*	*Yr*	*B*	*W*
Premier/1:	250	93	58	99	386	372	337	6	2	20
Division 1n/2:	666	220	190	256	801	863	798	15	2	23
Division 2n/3:	690	281	199	210	998	845	801	15	1	23
Division 3S:	1334	488	333	513	1972	2029	1309	31	4	23
Division 3n/4:	230	110	51	69	387	296	271	5	1	15
Totals:	3170	1192	831	1147	4544	4405	3516	72	–	–

Cup Records	*P*	*W*	*D*	*L*	*F*	*A*
Europe:	22	4	1	17	21	61
FA Cup:	250	111	59	80	401	328
League Cup:	124	47	30	47	200	189
A/F Members:	13	4	2	7	14	20

Sequence	*Games*	*Start*		*End*
Winning Run:	7	17-Nov-34	to	29-Dec-34
Without Defeat:	22	1-Oct-96	to	1-Mar-97
Without Win:	19	27-Nov-71	to	8-Apr-72
Drawn Games:	7	30-Nov-96	to	27-Jan-97
Without Draw:	19	29-Apr-78	to	18-Nov-78
Losing Run:	9	18-Dec-71	to	26-Feb-72
	9	26-Dec-72	to	27-Feb-73
Clean Sheets:	8	24-Sep-49	to	12-Nov-49
Goal Scored:	22	20-Aug-85	to	28-Dec-85
No. Goals For:	7	18-Dec-71	to	12-Feb-72
SOS Undefeated:	7	1923-24		
SOS No Wins:	9	1990-91		
	9	1984-85		

West Ham United

Division	*P*	*W*	*D*	*L*	*F*	*A*	*Pts*	*Yr*	*B*	*W*
Premier/1:	1826	631	450	745	2702	2930	1926	44	3	22
Division 1n/2:	1230	537	300	393	1958	1622	1444	29	1	20
Totals:	3056	1168	750	1138	4660	4552	3370	73	–	–

Cup Records	*P*	*W*	*D*	*L*	*F*	*A*
Europe:	30	15	6	9	58	42
FA Cup:	270	113	76	81	415	357
League Cup:	165	84	36	45	316	200
A/F Members:	10	4	1	5	22	21

Sequence	*Games*	*Start*		*End*
Winning Run:	9	19-Oct-85	to	14-Dec-85
Without Defeat:	27	27-Dec-80	to	10-Oct-81
Without Win:	17	31-Jan-76	to	21-Aug-76
Drawn Games:	5	07-Sep-68	to	05-Oct-68
Without Draw:	29	14-Dec-29	to	13-Sep-30
Losing Run:	9	28-Mar-32	to	29-Aug-32
Clean Sheets (5):	5	23-Nov-85	to	21-Dec-85
	5	26-Dec-90	to	19-Jan-91
Goals Scored:	27	22-Jan-27	to	15-Oct-27
	27	05-Oct-57	to	04-Apr-58
No Goals For:	5	01-May-71	to	23-Aug-71
SOS Undefeated:	21	1990-91		
SOS No Wins:	11	1973-74		

Wimbledon

Division	*P*	*W*	*D*	*L*	*F*	*A*	*Pts*	*Yr*	*B*	*W*
Premier/1:	516	179	159	178	656	680	696	13	6	16
Division 1n/2:	84	37	23	24	129	112	134	2	3	12
Division 2n/3:	138	50	34	54	210	232	174	3	2	24
Division 3n/4:	184	91	47	46	304	204	258	4	1	13
Totals:	922	357	263	302	1299	1228	1262	22	–	–

Cup Records	*P*	*W*	*D*	*L*	*F*	*A*
Europe:	0	0	0	0	0	0
FA Cup:	116	48	30	38	146	147
League Cup:	85	35	22	28	124	107
A/F Members:	10	2	1	7	11	18

Sequence	*Games*	*Start*		*End*
Winning Run:	7	09-Apr-83	to	07-May-83
Without Defeat:	22	15-Jan-83	to	14-May-83
Without Win:	14	23-Feb-80	to	15-Apr-80
	14	16-Sep-95	to	23-Dec-95
Drawn Games (5):	4	29-Apr-95	to	13-May-95
	4	26-Oct-96	to	23-Nov-96
Without Draw:	20	15-Oct-83	to	15-Feb-84
Losing Run:	7	16-Sep-95	to	06-Nov-95
Clean Sheets (6):	4	30-Jan-93	to	20-Feb-93
	4	31-Mar-98	to	13-Apr-98
Goals Scored:	23	18-Feb-84	to	22-Sep-84
No Goals For:	5	13-Apr-95	to	04-May-95
	5	27-Apr-96	to	27-Aug-96
SOS Undefeated:	13	1978-79		
SOS No Wins:	9	1981-82		

FA PREMIER LEAGUE CLUB TRANSFERS 1998-99

August 1998

Player	*From*	*To*	*Fee*
Dwight Yorke	Aston Villa	Manchester U.	£12.6m
Christian Dailly	Derby Co.	Blackburn R.	£5.3m
Dietman Hamann	B.Munich	Newcastle U.	£5.25m
Olivier Dacourt	Strasbourg	Everton	£4m
Colin Hendry	Blackburn R.	Rangers	£4m
Robert Jarni	Coventry C.	Real Madrid	£3.35m
David Unsworth	Aston Villa	Everton	£3m
Robert Jarni	Real Betis	Coventry C.	£2.6m
Kevin Campbell	N.Forest	Trabzonspor	£2.5m
John Collins	Monaco	Everton	£2.5m
Wim Jonk	PSV	Sheffield W.	£2.5m
Nigel Quashie	QPR	N.Forest	£2.5m
Nolberto Solano	Boca Juniors	Newcastle U.	£2.5m
Colin Cooper	N.Forest	Middlesbrough	£2.5m
Jon Dahl Tomasson	Newcastle U.	Feyenoord	£2.5m
Javier Margas	Univ Catolica	West Ham U.	£2m
Frank Sinclair	Chelsea	Leicester C.	£2m
Nelson Vivas	Lugano	Arsenal	£1.6m
Isaiah Rankin	Arsenal	Bradford C.	£1.3m
Gary Rowett	Derby Co.	Birmingham C.	£1m
Dougie Freedman	Wolverhampton W.	N.Forest	£950,000
Per Pedersen	Blackburn R.	Strasbourg	£900,000
Gary Rowett	Derby Co.	Birmingham C.	£900,000
Marc Edworthy	C.Palace	Coventry C.	£800,000
	Rises to £1.2m after 60 appearances		
Spencer Prior	Leicester C.	Derby Co.	£700,000
George Georgiadis	Panathinaikos	Newcastle U.	£420,000
Paul Hall	Portsmouth	Coventry C.	£300,000
Lee Todd	Southampton	Bradford C.	£250,000
Juan Manual Cobian	Boca Juniors	Sheffield W.	£250,000
Stig Johansen	Southampton	Helsingborgs	£250,000
Andy Gray	Leeds U.	N.Forest	£175,000
Ben Thornley	Manchester U.	Huddersfield T.	£175,000

Richard Hughes	Arsenal	Bournemouth	£20,000
Nicky Rizzo	Liverpool	C.Palace	Tribunal
Stephen Bywater	Rochdale	West Ham U.	Undisclosed
Chris Kiwomya	Arsenal	QPR	Free
Martyn McGee	Leicester C.	King's Lynn	Free
Ian Milbourne	Newcastle U.	Scarborough	Free
Ross Millard	Manchester U.	Northwich V.	Free
Jason Moore	West Ham U.	Dover	Free
Dominic Reece	Aston Villa	Hednesford	Free
Ian Rush	Newcastle U.	Wrexham	Free
Pavel Srnicek	Newcastle U.	Banik Ostrava	Free
Edmond Turkington	Liverpool	Stockport Co.	Free
Steve Wilson	Leicester C.	Kettering T.	Free
Michael Watt	Blackburn R.	Norwich C.	Non-contract
Neil Davis	Aston Villa	Walsall	Monthly
Simon Livett	West Ham U.	Southend U.	Monthly

September 1998

Player	*From*	*To*	*Fee*
Paul Merson	Middlesbrough	Aston Villa	£6.75m
Steve Simonsen	Tranmere R.	Everton	£3.3m
Fredrik Ljungberg	Halmstads	Arsenal	£3m
Steve Froggatt	Wolverhampton W.	Coventry C.	£1.9m
Neil Shipperley	C.Palace	N.Forest	£1.5m
Carl Tiler	Everton	Charlton A.	£700,000
Stephen Glass	Aberdeen	Newcastle U.	£650,000
Kevin Harper	Hibernian	Derby Co.	£300,000
Stuart Balmer	Charlton A.	Wigan A.	£200,000
Paul Emblen	Charlton A.	Wycombe W.	£60,000
Lee Stratford	N.Forest	Exeter C.	Non-contract
Graham Allen	Everton	Tranmere R.	Free
Chris Boden	Derby Co.	Hereford U.	Free
Andy Dibble	Middlesbrough	Altrincham	Free
Peter Kidd	West Ham U.	Dorchester T.	Free
Steve Nicol	Sheffield W.	Doncaster R.	Free
Michael O'Neill	Coventry C.	Wigan A.	Free
Gavin O'Toole	Coventry C.	Leek T.	Free
Nando Perna	Arsenal	Brackley	Free
James Evans	Tottenham H.	Bristol C.	Monthly
Mark Wright	Liverpool		Retired

October 1998

Player	*From*	*To*	*Fee*
Ibrahim Bakayako	Montpellier	Everton	£4.5m
Nathan Blake	Bolton W.	Blackburn R.	£4.25m
Steve Watson	Newcastle U.	Aston Villa	£4m
Brian Deane	Benfica	Middlesbrough	£3m
Gareth Ainsworth	Port Vale	Wimbledon	£2m
Garry Brady	Tottenham H.	Newcastle U.	£650,000
Simon Haworth	Coventry C.	Wigan A.	£600,000
Oumar Konde	Basle	Blackburn R.	£500,000
Tore Pedersen	Blackburn R.	E.Frankfurt	£225,000
Gareth Barry	Brighton & HA	Aston Villa	£150,000
Daniel Sonner	Ipswich T.	Sheffield W.	£75,000
Jay Lloyd Samuel	Charlton A.	Aston Villa	£50,000
Malcolm Christie	Nuneaton	Derby Co.	£50,000
Michael Ferrante	Australian IOS	West Ham U.	Unknown
Samuelle Dalla Bona	Atalanta	Chelsea	Unknown
Les Hines	Aston Villa	Kidderminster H.	Free
Hassan Kachloul	St Etienne	Southampton	Free
Tony Browne	West Ham U.	Brighton & HA	NC
Nuno Santos	Vitoria Setubal	Leeds U.	Monthly

November 1998

Player	*From*	*To*	*Fee*
Duncan Ferguson	Everton	Newcastle U.	£8m
Includes £1m payable after 60 appearances			
Dion Dublin	Coventry C.	Aston Villa	£5.75m
Stephane Guivarc'h	Newcastle U.	Rangers	£3.5m
Andy Impey	West Ham U.	Leicester C.	£1.6m
Johan Mjallby	Stockholm	Chelsea	£1.5m
Jean-Michel Ferri	Istanbulspor	Liverpool	£1.5m
Pending international clearance			
Laurent Delorge	Gent	Coventry C.	£1.25m
Brian Laudrup	Chelsea	FC Copenhagen	£1m
Gavin McCann	Everton	Sunderland	£500,000
Bjarni Goldbaek	FC Copenhagen	Chelsea	£350,000
Chris Casper	Manchester U.	Reading	£300,000
Bjarne Gudjonsson	Newcastle U.	Genk	£125,000
Gavin Holligan	Kingstonian	West Ham U.	£100,000
Mark Arber	Tottenham H.	Barnet	£75,000
Stuart Thom	N.Forest	Oldham A.	£45,000

Willie Huck	Monaco	Arsenal	Undisclosed
Tony Dorigo	Torino	Derby Co.	Free
Ben Petty	Aston Villa	Stoke C.	Free
Pavel Srnicek	Banik Ostrava	Sheffield W.	Free
Ross Taylor	Arsenal	Stevenage B.	Free
Daren Twidell	Tottenham H.	Stevenage B.	Free

December 1998

Player	*From*	*To*	*Fee*
David Batty	Newcastle U.	Leeds U.	£4.4m
Ashley Ward	Barnsley	Blackburn R.	£4.25m
Didier Domi	Paris SG	Newcastle U.	£3.25m
Keith Gillespie	Newcastle U.	Blackburn R.	£2.25m
Mauricio Taricco	Ipswich T.	Tottenham	£1.8m
Steffen Freund	B.Dortmund	Tottenham	£750,000
John Aloisi	Portsmouth	Coventry C.	£650,000
Jean-Guy Wallcmme	Coventry C.	Sochaux	£400,000
Patrick Colleter	Marseille	Southampton	£300,000
Jesper Mattsson	Halmstads	N.Forest	£300,000
Morton Hyldgaard	Ikast	Coventry C.	£250,000
Tony Thomas	Everton	Motherwell	£150,000
Ludek Miklosko	West Ham U.	QPR	£50,000
Nicola Berti	Tottenham H.	Alaves	Free
David Lee	Chelsea	Bristol R	Free
Mickael Madar	Everton	Paris SG	Free
Michael Stensgaard	FC Copenhagen	Southampton	Free

January 1999

Player	*From*	*To*	*Fee*
John Hartson	West Ham U.	Wimbledon	£7.5m
Comprised – £3 million down, £3million after a year. A further £1.5 million is payable after various landmarks.			
Nwankwo Kanu	Internazionale	Arsenal	£4.5m
Marc-Vivien Foe	Lens	West Ham	£4.2m
Matt Jansen	C.Palace	Blackburn R.	£4.1m
Jason McAteer	Liverpool	Blackburn R.	£4m
Rigobert Song	Salernitana	Liverpool	£2.72m
Kaba Diawara	Bordeaux	Arsenal	£2.5m
Muhamed Konjic	AS Monaco	Coventry C.	£2m
Paolo Di Canio	Sheffield W.	West Ham	£1.7m
Gary Charles	Aston Villa	Benfica	£1.5m

Jermaine Pennant	Notts County	Arsenal	£1.5m
Carlton Palmer	Southampton	N.Forest	£1.1m
Scott Minto	Benfica	West Ham	£1m
Chris Marsden	Birmingham C.	Southampton	£800,000
Frode Kippe	Lillestrom	Liverpool	£700,000
John Spencer	Everton	Motherwell	£600,000
Peter Enckelman	TPS, Finland	Aston Villa	£200,000
Gareth Roberts	Liverpool	Panionios	£50,000
Willem Korsten	Vitesse	Leeds U.	Nominal
Stefano Gioacchino	Venezia	Coventry C.	Unknown
Anthony Duffy	Manchester U.	Leigh RMI	Free
Nicky Hunt	Tottenham H.	Wembley	Free
Nuno Santos V	Vitoria Setubal	Leeds U.	Free

February 1999

Player	*From*	*To*	*Fee*
Tim Sherwood	Blackburn R.	Tottenham	£3.8m
Silvio Maric	Croatia Zagreb	Newcastle U.	£3.65m
Arnar Gunnlaugsson	Bolton W.	Leicester C.	£2m
Bojan Djordic	B Pojkarna	Manchester U.	£1m
Mariana Pahars	Skonto Riga	Southampton	£800,000
Craig Armstrong	N.Forest	Huddersfield T.	£750,000
Djimi Troare	Laval	Liverpool	£550,000
Burton O'Brien	St Mirren	Blackburn R.	£300,000
	Plus £1m after unspecified appearances		
David McNamee	St Mirren	Blackburn R.	£300,000
	Plus £1m after unspecified appearances		
David Weir	Hearts	Everton	£250,000
Dani Rodrigues	Farense	Southampton	£180,000
Peter Degn	Aarhus	Everton	£200,000
Jimmy Bullard	Gravesend & N.	West Ham	£30,000
Gerard Doherty	Derry Co.	Derby Co.	£30,000
Gary Strodder	Notts County	Hartlepool	£25,000
John Barnes	Newcastle U.	Charlton A.	Free
Clayton Blackmore	Middlesbrough	Barnsley	Free
Tim Breacker	West Ham U.	QPR	Free
Lee Collins	Aston Villa	Stoke C.	Free
Graham Hyde	Sheffield W.	Birmingham C.	Free
Goce Sedloski	Sheffield W.	Croatia Zagreb	Free

March 1999

Player	*From*	*To*	*Fee*
Steve Stone	N.Forest	Aston Villa	£5.5m
Lee Carsley	Derby Co.	Blackburn R.	£3.375m
Graham Stuart	Sheffield U.	Charlton A.	£1.1m
Richard Cresswell	York C.	Sheffield W.	£950,000
Marian Pahars	Skonto Riga	Southampton	£800,000
Martin Pringle	Benfica	Charlton A.	£800,000
Steve Harkness	Liverpool	Benfica	£750,000
Keith O'Neill	Norwich C.	Middlesbrough	£700,000
Jim Magilton	Sheffield W.	Ipswich T.	£682,500
Vassilis Borbokis	Sheffield U.	Derby Co.	£600,000
Mikkel Beck	Middlesbrough	Derby Co.	£500,000
Phil Mulryne	Manchester U.	Norwich C.	£500,000
Paul Boertien	Carlisle U.	Derby Co.	£250,000
Scot Gemmill	N.Forest	Everton	£250,000
Mark Delaney	Cardiff C.	Aston Villa	£250,000
Colin Calderwood	Tottenham H.	Aston Villa	£225,000
Phillip Scott	St Johnstone	Sheffield W.	£75,000
Andy Dawson	N.Forest	Scunthorpe	£50,000
Willie Huck	Arsenal	Bournemouth	£50,000
David Partridge	West Ham U.	Dundee U.	£40,000
Richard Jackson	Scarborough	Derby Co.	£30,000
Jamie Day	Arsenal	Bournemouth	£20,000
Michael Ryan	Manchester U.	Wrexham	Undisclosed
Jonathan Hunt	Derby Co.	Sheffield U.	Swap
Rob Kozluk	Derby Co.	Sheffield U.	Swap
Paul McGregor	N.Forest	Preston NE	Free
Roger Nilson	Sheffield U.	Tottenham	Free
Mark Platts	Sheffield W.	Torquay	Free
Daniel Williams	Liverpool	Wrexham	Free
Paul Gibson	Manchester U.	Notts County	Free
Paul Barrett	Newcastle U.	Wrexham	Free
Chris Allen	N.Forest	Port Vale	Free
Bernard Allou	Grampus 8	N.Forest	Free
Lee Doherty	Charlton A.	Brighton	Free
Richard Gough	San Jose	N.Forest	Free
Ronnie O'Brien	Middlesbrough	Juventus	Free
Paul McGregor	N.Forest	Preston NE	Free
Ross Millard	Manchester U.	Weston-super-Mare	Free
Cosimo Sarli	Southampton	Aalst	Free

May 1999

Player	*From*	*To*	*Fee*
Sami Hyypia	Willem II	Liverpool	£3m
Seth Johnson	Crewe	Derby	£2.5m
Oleg Luzhny	Dynamo Kyiv	Arsenal	£1.8m
Willem Korsten	Vitesse Arnhem	Tottenham Hotspur	£1.5m
Eirik Bakke	Sojndal	Leeds United	£1m
Richard Gough	Nottingham Forest	Everton	Free

June 1999

Player	*From*	*To*	*Fee*
Olivier Dacourt	Everton	RC Lens	£6.5m
Elena Marcelino	Real Mallorca	Newcastle United	£5m
Alain Goma	Paris St Germain	Newcastle United	£4.75m
Sander Westerveld	Vitesse Arnhem	Liverpool	£4m
Danny Mills	Charlton	Leeds United	£4m
I Bakayoko	Everton	Marseille	£4m
Stephane Henchoz	Blackburn Rovers	Liverpool	£3.5m
Didier Deschamps	Juventus	Chelsea	£3m
Titi Camara	Marseille	Liverpool	£2.5m
Brian Laudrup	Chelsea	Ajax	£2m
David James	Liverpool	Aston Villa	£1.8m
Phillipe Clement	Coventry City	Club Brugge	£800,000
Stefan Malz	Munich 1860	Arsenal	£650,000
FRanck Dumas	Monaco	Newcastle United	£500,000
Andy Oakes	Hull City	Derby County	£450,000
Gunnar Halle	Leeds United	Bradford	£200,000
Lee Sharpe	Leeds United	Bradford	£200,000
Barry Prenderville	Coventry City	Ayr	Undisclosed
Kaba Diawara	Arsenal	Marseille	Undisclosed
Silvinho	Corinthians	Arsenal	Undisclosed
Peter Schmeichel	Manchester United	S Lisbon	Free
Mario Malchiot	Ajax	Chelsea	Free
Mark Bosnich	Aston Villa	Manchester United	Free

Note: Where two figures are given, ie, £500,000 > £1.2m, this indicates that the transfer fee was an initial down-payment of £500,000 and could rise to £1.2m. Normally the additional payment is staged and will depend on the number of appearances made by the player (for example, an additional £250,000 might be payable when the player has made 50 appearances for his new club) and other factors, such as if the player goes on to win international recognition etc.

PLAYER DIRECTORY 1999-2000

This section lists players who are likely to feature in Premiership action during the 1999-2000 season. Players are listed alphabetically and where possible major close-season signings are included. Details of the players who featured in the majority of games last season for the three promoted sides are also included.

Previous Club Details includes all Premiership games played to date. Specific appearance details for 1998-99 can be found in the Club Directory section. A club with * next to it in the Previous Club Details list indicates that the figures do not include those for the 1998-99 season. When figures are given for a non-English club they refer to the relevant country's league and cup competitions.

Under Fee, an 'm' indicates million, thus £3.5m should be read as £3,500,000 or £3.5 million; 'k' indicates thousand (kilo) thus £350k should be read as £350,000. If 'Free' is used as an entry under Fee or a fee is given for their first club then this generally indicates that the player came from a non-league club.

Other abbreviations used in this section include: NL=Non-League; App=Apprentice.

ADAMS Tony — Arsenal

Full Name: Anthony Alexander Adams
DOB: 10-Oct-66 Romford, Essex

Previous Club Details			*Apps*					*Goals*		
Club	Signed	Fee	Tot	Start	Sub	FA	FL	Lge	FA	FL
Arsenal	1/84	Amateur	447	443	4	46	59	31	8	5
FAPL Summary by Club										
Arsenal	92/3 to 98/9		198	195	3	28	25	11	7	3
Totals			*198*	*195*	*3*	*28*	*25*	*11*	*7*	*3*

AINSWORTH Gareth — Wimbledon

Full Name: Gareth Ainsworth
DOB: 10-May-73 Blackburn

Previous Club Details			*Apps*					*Goals*		
Club	Signed	Fee	Tot	Start	Sub	FA	FL	Lge	FA	FL
Preston NE	1/92	Free NL	5	2	3	0	0	0	0	0
Cambridge U.	8/92	Free	4	1	3	0	1	1	0	0
Preston NE	12/92	Free	82	76	6	4	5	12	0	0
Lincoln C.	10/95	£25k	83	83	0	2	0	37	0	0
Port Vale	9/97	£500k	40	38	2	2	0	5	0	0
Wimbledon	10/98	£2m	8	5	3	0	0	0	0	0
FAPL Summary by Club										
Wimbledon	1998/9		8	5	3	0	0	0	0	0
Totals			*8*	*5*	*3*	*0*	*0*	*0*	*0*	*0*

ALEXANDERSSON Niclas — Sheffield W.

Full Name: Niclas Alexandersson
DOB: 29-Dec-71 Halmstad, Sweden

Previous Club Details			*Apps*					*Goals*		
Club	Signed	Fee	Tot	Start	Sub	FA	FL	Lge	FA	FL
IFK Gothenburg			50	49	1	–	–	13	–	–
Sheffield W.	12/97	£750k	38	36	2	5	1	3	1	0
FAPL Summary by Club										
Sheffield W.	97/8 to 98/9		38	36	2	5	1	3	1	0
Totals			*38*	*36*	*2*	*5*	*1*	*3*	*1*	*0*

ALOISI John — Coventry City

Full Name: John Aloisi
DOB: 05-Feb-76 Australia

Previous Club Details			*Apps*					*Goals*		
Club	Signed	Fee	Tot	Start	Sub	FA	FL	Lge	FA	FL
Cremonese										
Portsmouth	8/97	£300k	60	55	5	1	6	26	0	3
Coventry C.	12/98	£650k	16	7	9	2	0	5	0	0
FAPL Summary by Club										
Coventry C.	1998/9		16	7	9	2	0	5	0	0
Totals			*16*	*7*	*9*	*2*	*0*	*5*	*0*	*0*

ANDERSSON Andreas — Newcastle United

Full Name: Andreas Claus Andersson
DOB: 10-Apr-76 Stockholm

Previous Club Details			*Apps*					*Goals*		
Club	Signed	Fee	Tot	Start	Sub	FA	FL	Lge	FA	FL
Milan			13	1	12	–	–	1	–	–
Newcastle U.	1/98	£3.6m	27	21	6	4	0	4	0	0
FAPL Summary by Club										
Newcastle U.	97/8 to 98/9		27	21	6	4	0	4	0	0
Totals			*27*	*21*	*6*	*4*	*0*	*4*	*0*	*0*

ANDERTON Darren — Tottenham Hotspur

Full Name: Darren Robert Anderton
DOB: 03-Mar-72 Southampton

Previous Club Details			*Apps*					*Goals*		
Club	Signed	Fee	Tot	Start	Sub	FA	FL	Lge	FA	FL
Portsmouth	2/90	Trainee	62	53	9	8	5	7	5	1
Tottenham H.	6/92	£1.75m	179	162	17	21	19	25	4	4
FAPL Summary by Club										
Tottenham H.	92/3 to 98/9		179	162	17	21	19	25	4	4
Totals			*179*	*162*	*17*	*21*	*19*	*25*	*4*	*4*

ARDLEY Neal — Wimbledon

Full Name: Neal Christopher Ardley
DOB: 01-Sep-72 Epsom

Previous Club Details			*Apps*					*Goals*		
Club	Signed	Fee	Tot	Start	Sub	FA	FL	Lge	FA	FL
Wimbledon	7/91	Trainee	152	139	13	23	21	10	1	5
FAPL Summary by Club										
Wimbledon	92/3 to 98/9		153	131	22	23	21	10	1	5
Totals			*153*	*131*	*22*	*23*	*21*	*10*	*1*	*5*

ARMSTRONG Chris — Tottenham Hotspur

Full Name: Christopher Peter Armstrong
DOB: 19-Jun-71 Newcastle

Previous Club Details			*Apps*					*Goals*		
Club	Signed	Fee	Tot	Start	Sub	FA	FL	Lge	FA	FL
Wrexham	3/89		60	40	20	1	3	13	0	0
Millwall	8/91	£50k	28	11	17	1	4	5	0	2
Crystal Palace	9/92	£1m	118	118	0	8	8	46	5	6
Tottenham H.	7/94	£4.5m	101	85	16	12	13	32	4	10
FAPL Summary by Club										
Crystal Palace	92/3 to 94/5		75	75	0	6	5	23	5	5
Tottenham H.	95/6 to 98/9		101	85	16	12	13	32	4	10
Totals			*176*	*160*	*16*	*18*	*18*	*55*	*9*	*15*

ARPHEXAD Pegguy — Leicester City

Full Name: Pegguy Michel Arphexad
DOB: 18-May-73 Guadeloupe

Previous Club Details			*Apps*					*Goals*		
Club	Signed	Fee	Tot	Start	Sub	FA	FL	Lge	FA	FL
Racing Club Paris										
Leicester C.	8/97	Free	9	7	2	0	1	0	0	0
FAPL Summary by Club										
Leicester C.	97/8 to 98/9		9	7	2	0	1	0	0	0
Totals			*9*	*7*	*2*	*0*	*1*	*0*	*0*	*0*

BAARDSEN Espen — Tottenham Hotspur

Full Name: Espen Baardsen
DOB: 07-Dec-77 San Rafael, California

Previous Club Details			*Apps*					*Goals*		
Club	Signed	Fee	Tot	Start	Sub	FA	FL	Lge	FA	FL
San Francisco All Blacks										
Tottenham H.	7/96	Free	23	22	1	3	3	0	0	0
FAPL Summary by Club										
Tottenham H.	96/7 to 98/9		23	22	1	3	3	0	0	0
Totals			*23*	*22*	*1*	*3*	*3*	*0*	*0*	*0*

BABAYARO Celestine — Chelsea

Full Name: Celestine Babayaro
DOB: 29-Aug-78 Nigeria

Previous Club Details			*Apps*					*Goals*		
Club	Signed	Fee	Tot	Start	Sub	FA	FL	Lge	FA	FL
Anderlecht										
Chelsea	4/97	£2.25m	36	34	2	5	5	3	0	0
FAPL Summary by Club										
Chelsea	97/8 to 98/9		36	34	2	5	5	3	0	0
Totals			*36*	*34*	*2*	*5*	*5*	*3*	*0*	*0*

BABB Phil — Liverpool

Full Name: Phillip Andrew Babb
DOB: 30-Nov-70 London

Previous Club Details			*Apps*					*Goals*		
Club	Signed	Fee	Tot	Start	Sub	FA	FL	Lge	FA	FL
Bradford C.	8/90		80	73	7	3	6	14	0	0
Coventry C.	7/92	£500k	77	70	7	2	5	3	0	1
Liverpool	9/94	£3.6m	128	124	4	12	16	1	0	0
FAPL Summary by Club										
Coventry C.	92/3 to 94/5		77	70	7	2	5	3	0	1
Liverpool	94/5 to 98/9		128	124	4	12	16	1	0	0
Totals			*205*	*194*	*11*	*14*	*21*	*4*	*0*	*1*

BAIANO Francesco — Derby County

Full Name: Francesco Baiano
DOB: 24-Feb-68 Napoli

Previous Club Details			*Apps*					*Goals*		
Club	Signed	Fee	Tot	Start	Sub	FA	FL	Lge	FA	FL
Napoli	85-86		4					0		
Empoli	86-87		26					2		
Napoli	87-88		1					0		
Parma	87	Loan	25					4		
Empoli	88-89		38					14		
Avellino	89-90		32					6		
Foggia	90-92		69					38		
Fiorentina	92-97		119	105	14			29		
Derby Co.	8/97	£650k	55	47	8	3	4	16	4	0
FAPL Summary by Club										
Derby Co.	97/8 to 98/9		55	47	8	3	4	16	4	0
Totals			*55*	*47*	*8*	*3*	*4*	*16*	*4*	*0*

BALL Kevin — Sunderland

Full Name: Kevin Anthony Ball
DOB: 12-Nov-64 Hastings

Previous Club Details			*Apps*					*Goals*		
Club	Signed	Fee	Tot	Start	Sub	FA	FL	Lge	FA	FL
Coventry C.		Juniors								
Portsmouth	10/82	Free	105	96	9	8	9	4	0	0
Sunderland	7/90	£350k	328	323	5	17	25	21	0	3
FAPL Summary by Club										
Sunderland	1996/7		32	32	0	0	3	3	0	1
Totals			*32*	*32*	*0*	*0*	*3*	*3*	*0*	*1*

BALL Michael — Everton

Full Name: Michael Ball
DOB: 02-Oct-77 Liverpool

Previous Club Details			*Apps*					*Goals*		
Club	Signed	Fee	Tot	Start	Sub	FA	FL	Lge	FA	FL
Everton	10/96	Trainee	65	57	8	4	6	4	0	0
FAPL Summary by Club										
Everton	96/7 to 98/9		67	59	8	4	6	4	0	0
Totals			*67*	*59*	*8*	*4*	*6*	*4*	*0*	*0*

BARMBY Nicky — Everton

Full Name: Nicholas Jonathan Barmby
DOB: 11-Feb-74 Hull

Previous Club Details			*Apps*					*Goals*		
Club	Signed	Fee	Tot	Start	Sub	FA	FL	Lge	FA	FL
Tottenham H.	4/91	Trainee	87	81	6	13	8	20	5	1
Middlesbrough	8/95	£5.25m	50	43	7	3	4	8	1	1
Everton	10/96	£5.75m	79	68	11	7	4	9	2	2
FAPL Summary by Club										
Tottenham H.	92/3 to 94/5		87	81	6	13	8	20	5	1
Middlesbrough	95/6 to 96/7		42	42	0	3	4	8	1	1
Everton	96/7 to 98/9		79	68	11	7	4	9	2	2
Totals			*208*	*191*	*17*	*23*	*16*	*37*	*8*	*4*

BARRY Gareth — Aston Villa

Full Name: Gareth Barry
DOB: 23-Feb-81 Hastings

Previous Club Details			*Apps*					*Goals*		
Club	Signed	Fee	Tot	Start	Sub	FA	FL	Lge	FA	FL
Brighton HA		Trainee	0	0	0	0	0	0	0	0
Aston Villa	2/98		34	28	6	2	0	0	0	0
FAPL Summary by Club										
Aston Villa	97/8 to 98/9		34	28	6	2	0	2	0	0
Totals			*34*	*28*	*6*	*2*	*0*	*2*	*0*	*0*

BARTON Warren — Newcastle United

Full Name: Warren Dean Barton
DOB: 19-Mar-69 Stoke Newington

Previous Club Details			*Apps*					*Goals*		
Club	Signed	Fee	Tot	Start	Sub	FA	FL	Lge	FA	FL
Maidstone U.	7/87	£10k	42	41	1	3	2	0	1	0
Wimbledon	6/90	£300k	180	178	2	11	16	10	0	1
Newcastle U.	6/95	£4m+	98	78	18	14	9	3	0	0
FAPL Summary by Club										
Wimbledon	92/3 to 94/5		101	99	2	6	12	6	0	1
Newcastle U.	95/6 to 98/9		96	78	18	14	9	4	0	1
Totals			*197*	*177*	*20*	*20*	*21*	*10*	*0*	*2*

BASHAM Steve — Southampton

Full Name: Steve Basham
DOB: 02-Dec-77 Southampton

Previous Club Details			*Apps*					*Goals*		
Club	Signed	Fee	Tot	Start	Sub	FA	FL	Lge	FA	FL
Southampton	5/96	Trainee	19	1	18	0	1	1	0	0
Wrexham	2/98	Loan	5	4	1	0	0	0	0	0
FAPL Summary by Club										
Southampton	96/7 to 98/9		19	1	18	0	1	1	0	0
Totals			*19*	*1*	*18*	*0*	*1*	*1*	*0*	*0*

BATTY David — Leeds United

Full Name: David Batty
DOB: 02-Dec-68 Leeds

Previous Club Details			*Apps*					*Goals*		
Club	Signed	Fee	Tot	Start	Sub	FA	FL	Lge	FA	FL
Leeds U.	7/87	Trainee	211	201	10	12	17	4	0	0
Blackburn R.	10/93	£2.75m	54	53	1	5	6	1	0	0
Newcastle U.	2/96	£3.75m	83	81	2	9	6	3	0	0
Leeds U.	12/98	£4.4m	10	10	0	0	0	0	0	0
FAPL Summary by Club										
Leeds U.	92/3 to 93/4		39	38	1	3	2	1	0	0
Blackburn R.	93/4 to 95/6		54	53	1	5	6	1	0	0
Newcastle U.	95/6 to 97/8		83	81	2	9	6	3	0	0

Club	Signed	Fee	Tot	Start	Sub	FA	FL	Lge	FA	FL
Leeds U.	98/9		10	10	0	0	0	0	0	0
Totals			*176*	*172*	*4*	*17*	*14*	*5*	*0*	*0*

BAZELEY Darren — Watford

Full Name: Darren Shaun Bazeley
DOB: 05-Oct-72 Northampton

Previous Club Details			*Apps*					*Goals*		
Club	Signed	Fee	Tot	Start	Sub	FA	FL	Lge	FA	FL
Watford	5/91	Trainee	240	187	53	13	18	21	3	2

BEATTIE James — Southampton

Full Name: Southampton
DOB: 27-Feb-78 Lancaster

Previous Club Details			*Apps*					*Goals*		
Club	Signed	Fee	Tot	Start	Sub	FA	FL	Lge	FA	FL
Blackburn R.	9/95	Trainee	3	0	3	1	1	0	0	0
Southampton	7/98	£1m	35	22	13	2	2	5	0	1
FAPL Summary by Club										
Blackburn R.	1997/8		3	0	3	1	1	0	0	0
Southampton	1998/9		35	22	13	2	2	5	0	1
Totals			*38*	*22*	*16*	*3*	*3*	*5*	*0*	*1*

BECK Mikkel — Derby County

Full Name: Mikkel Beck
DOB: 12-May-73 Denmark

Previous Club Details			*Apps*					*Goals*		
Club	Signed	Fee	Tot	Start	Sub	FA	FL	Lge	FA	FL
Fortuna Koln										
Middlesbrough	8/96	Free	65	54	11	7	14	19	2	5
Derby Co.	3/98	£500k	7	6	1	0	0	0	0	0
FAPL Summary by Club										
Middlesbrough	96/7 to 98/9		62	45	17	7	9	10	2	4
Derby Co.	1998/9		7	6	1	0	0	1	0	0
Totals			*69*	*51*	*18*	*7*	*9*	*11*	*2*	*4*

BECKHAM David — Manchester United

Full Name: David Beckham
DOB: 02-May-75 Leytonstone

Previous Club Details			*Apps*					*Goals*		
Club	Signed	Fee	Tot	Start	Sub	FA	FL	Lge	FA	FL
Manchester U.	1/93	Trainee	144	128	16	18	6	31	5	0
Preston NE	2/95	Loan	5	4	1			2		
FAPL Summary by Club										
Manchester U.	94/5 to 98/9		144	128	16	18	6	29	5	0
Totals			*144*	*128*	*16*	*18*	*6*	*29*	*5*	*0*

BENALI Franny — Southampton

Full Name: Francis Vincent Benali
DOB: 30-Dec-68 Southampton

Previous Club Details			*Apps*					*Goals*		
Club	Signed	Fee	Tot	Start	Sub	FA	FL	Lge	FA	FL
Southampton	1/87	App	276	244	32	20	28	1	0	0
FAPL Summary by Club										
Southampton	92/3 to 98/9		209	191	18	9	17	1	0	0
Totals			*209*	*191*	*18*	*9*	*17*	*1*	*0*	*0*

BERESFORD Marlon — Middlesbrough

Full Name: Marlon Beresford
DOB: 02-Sep-69 Lincoln

Previous Club Details			Apps					Goals		
Club	Signed	Fee	Tot	Start	Sub	FA	FL	Lge	FA	FL
Sheffield W.	9/87	Trainee								
Bury	8/89	Loan	1	1	0	0	0	0	0	0
Northampton T.	9/90	Loan	13	13	0	0	0	0	0	0
Crewe Alex.	2/91	Loan	2	2	0	0	0	0	0	0
Northampton T.	8/91	Loan	15	15	0	0	0	0	0	0
Burnley	8/92	£95k	240	240	0	20	18	0	0	0
Middlesbrough	3/98	£500k	3	7	0	0	3	0	0	0
FAPL Summary by Club										
Middlesbrough	1998/9		4	4	0	0	3	0	0	0
Totals			*4*	*4*	*0*	*0*	*3*	*0*	*0*	*0*

BERG Henning — Manchester United

Full Name: Henning Berg
DOB: 01-Sep-69 Eidsvell

Previous Club Details			Apps					Goals		
Club	Signed	Fee	Tot	Start	Sub	FA	FL	Lge	FA	FL
Lillestrom										
Blackburn R.	1/93	£400k	159	154	5	10	16	4	0	0
Manchester U.	8/97	£5.0m	43	33	10	7	3	0	0	0
FAPL Summary by Club										
Blackburn R.	92/3 to 96/7		159	154	5	10	16	4	0	0
Manchester U.	97/8 to 98/9		43	33	10	7	3	2	0	0
Totals			*202*	*187*	*15*	*17*	*19*	*6*	*0*	*0*

BERGER Patrik — Liverpool

Full Name: Patrik Berger
DOB: 10-Nov-73 Prague

Previous Club Details			Apps					Goals		
Club	Signed	Fee	Tot	Start	Sub	FA	FL	Lge	FA	FL
Slavia Pargue	1991		89	83	6			24		
B.Dortmund	1995		25	13	12			4		
Liverpool	8/96	£3.25m	77	49	28	5	7	16	0	1
FAPL Summary by Club										
Liverpool	96/7 to 98/9		77	49	28	5	7	16	0	2
Totals			*77*	*49*	*28*	*5*	*7*	*16*	*0*	*2*

BERGKAMP Dennis — Arsenal

Full Name: Dennis Nicolaas Bergkamp
DOB: 18-May-69 Amsterdam

Previous Club Details			Apps					Goals		
Club	Signed	Fee	Tot	Start	Sub	FA	FL	Lge	FA	FL
Ajax	7/86		185	185	0			103		
Internazionale	7/93	£12m	52	50	2			11		
Arsenal	7/95	£7.5m	119	117	2	16	14	51	7	8
FAPL Summary by Club										
Arsenal	95/6 to 98/9		119	117	2	16	14	51	7	8
Totals			*119*	*117*	*2*	*16*	*14*	*51*	*7*	*8*

BERKOVIC Eyal — West Ham United

Full Name: Eyal Berkovic
DOB: 02-Apr-72 Haifa

Previous Club Details			Apps					Goals		
Club	Signed	Fee	Tot	Start	Sub	FA	FL	Lge	FA	FL
Maccabi Haifa	(1992)		128	126	2			25		
Southampton	9/96	£1m	28	26	2	1	6	4	0	2
West Ham U.	6/97	£1.75m	65	62	3	8	6	10	2	0

FAPL Summary by Club

Club	Signed	Fee	Tot	Start	Sub	FA	FL	Lge	FA	FL
Southampton	1996/7		28	26	2	1	6	4	0	2
West Ham U.	97/8 to 98/9		65	62	3	8	6	10	2	0
Totals			*93*	*88*	*5*	*9*	*12*	*14*	*2*	*2*

BJORNEBYE Stig Inge — Liverpool

Full Name: Stig Inge Bjornebye
DOB: 11-Dec-69 Norway

Previous Club Details			*Apps*					*Goals*		
Club	Signed	Fee	Tot	Start	Sub	FA	FL	Lge	FA	FL
Rosenborg										
Liverpool	12/92	£600k	139	132	7	13	18	2	0	0
FAPL Summary by Club										
Liverpool	92/3 to 98/9		139	132	7	12	17	2	0	0
Totals			*139*	*132*	*7*	*12*	*17*	*2*	*0*	*0*

BLACKWELL Dean — Wimbledon

Full Name: Dean Robert Blackwell
DOB: 05-Dec-69 Camden

Previous Club Details			*Apps*					*Goals*		
Club	Signed	Fee	Tot	Start	Sub	FA	FL	Lge	FA	FL
Wimbledon	7/88	Trainee	182	159	23	23	15	1	0	0
Plymouth Ar.	3/90	Loan	7	5	2	0	0	0	0	0
FAPL Summary by Club										
Wimbledon	92/3 to 98/9		140	127	13	19	13	0	0	0
Totals			*140*	*127*	*13*	*19*	*13*	*0*	*0*	*0*

BLAKE Robbie — Bradford City

Full Name: Robert James Blake
DOB: 04-Mar-76 Middlesbrough

Previous Club Details			*Apps*					*Goals*		
Club	Signed	Fee	Tot	Start	Sub	FA	FL	Lge	FA	FL
Darlington	7/94	Trainee	68	54	14	4	6	21	0	1
Bradford C.	3/97	£300k	78	61	17	3	5	37	0	1

BLOMQVIST Jesper — Manchester United

Full Name: Jesper Blomqvist
DOB: 05-Feb-74 Sweden

Previous Club Details			*Apps*					*Goals*		
Club	Signed	Fee	Tot	Start	Sub	FA	FL	Lge	FA	FL
FC Umea										
IFK Gothenburg	92		73	69	4	–	–	13	–	–
Milan	97		1	0	1	–	–	0	–	–
Parma	97		28	24	4	–	–	1	–	–
Manchester U.	8/98	£4.4m	25	20	5	5	1	1	0	0
FAPL Summary by Club										
Manchester U.	1998/9		25	20	5	5	1	1	0	0
Totals			*25*	*20*	*5*	*5*	*1*	*1*	*0*	*0*

BOATENG George — Coventry City

Full Name: George Boateng
DOB: 05-Sep-75 Accra, Ghana

Previous Club Details			*Apps*					*Goals*		
Club	Signed	Fee	Tot	Start	Sub	FA	FL	Lge	FA	FL
Feyenoord			68	61	7	–	–	1	–	–
Coventry C.	12/97	£250k	47	43	4	8	3	5	1	1
FAPL Summary by Club										
Coventry C.	97/8 to 98/9		47	43	4	8	3	5	1	1
Totals			*47*	*43*	*4*	*8*	*3*	*5*	*1*	*1*

BOHINEN Lars — Derby County

Full Name: Lars Bohinen
DOB: 08-Sep-69 Vadso, Norway

Previous Club Details			*Apps*					*Goals*		
Club	Signed	Fee	Tot	Start	Sub	FA	FL	Lge	FA	FL
Young Boys Berne										
N.Forest	11/93	£450k	64	59	5	2	8	6	1	2
Blackburn R.	10/95	£700k	59	41	18	3	5	7	1	1
Derby Co.	3/98	£1.45m	41	38	3	5	0	1	0	0
FAPL Summary by Club										
N.Forest	94/5 to 95/6		41	37	4	1	5	6	0	2
Blackburn R.	95/6 to 97/8		59	41	18	3	5	7	1	1
Derby Co.	97/8 to 98/9		41	38	3	5	0	1	0	0
Totals			*141*	*116*	*25*	*9*	*10*	*14*	*1*	*3*

BOOTH Andy — Sheffield Wednesday

Full Name: Andrew David Booth
DOB: 06-Dec-73 Huddersfield

Previous Club Details			*Apps*					*Goals*		
Club	Signed	Fee	Tot	Start	Sub	FA	FL	Lge	FA	FL
Huddersfield T.	7/92	Trainee	123	109	14	6	7	54	3	3
Sheffield W.	7/96	£2.7m	92	87	5	8	4	23	3	0
FAPL Summary by Club										
Sheffield W.	96/7 to 98/9		92	87	5	8	4	23	3	0
Totals			*92*	*87*	*5*	*8*	*4*	*23*	*3*	*0*

BOSNICH Mark — Manchester United

Full Name: Mark John Bosnich
DOB: 13-Jan-72 Sydney

Previous Club Details			*Apps*					*Goals*		
Club	Signed	Fee	Tot	Start	Sub	FA	FL	Lge	FA	FL
Manchester U.	6/89		3	3	0	0	0	0	0	0
Croatia Sydney	8/91									
Aston Villa	2/92	Free	179	179	0	17	21	0	0	0
Manchester U.	6/99	Free								
FAPL Summary by Club										
Aston Villa	92/3 to 98/9		178	178	0	17	21	0	0	0
Totals			*178*	*178*	*0*	*17*	*21*	*0*	*0*	*0*

BOULD Steve — Sunderland

Full Name: Stephen Andrew Bould
DOB: 16-Nov-62 Stoke

Previous Club Details			*Apps*					*Goals*		
Club	Signed	Fee	Tot	Start	Sub	FA	FL	Lge	FA	FL
Stoke C.	11/80		183	179	4	10	13	6	0	1
Torquay U.	10/82	Loan	9	9	0	2	0	0	0	0
Arsenal	6/89	£390k	287	271	16	29	34	5	0	1
FAPL Summary by Club										
Arsenal	92/3 to 98/9		175	164	11	17	24	2	0	1
Totals			*175*	*164*	*11*	*17*	*24*	*2*	*0*	*1*

BOWYER Lee — Leeds United

Full Name: Lee David Bowyer
DOB: 03-Jan-77 London

Previous Club Details			*Apps*					*Goals*		
Club	Signed	Fee	Tot	Start	Sub	FA	FL	Lge	FA	FL
Charlton A.	4/94	Trainee	46	46	0	3	7	8	1	5
Leeds U.	7/96	£3m	96	88	8	11	5	16	2	1

FAPL Summary by Club

Club	Seasons	Tot	Start	Sub	FA	FL	Lge	FA	FL
Leeds U.	96/7 to 98/9	92	88	4	11	5	16	2	1
Totals		*92*	*88*	*4*	*11*	*5*	*16*	*2*	*1*

BRADY Garry — Newcastle United

Full Name: Garry Brady
DOB: 07-Sep-76 Glasgow

Previous Club Details — *Apps* — *Goals*

Club	Signed	Fee	Tot	Start	Sub	FA	FL	Lge	FA	FL
Tottenham H.		Trainee	9	0	9	2	0	0	0	0
Newcastle U.		£600k	0	3	6	3	0	0	0	0

FAPL Summary by Club

Club	Seasons	Tot	Start	Sub	FA	FL	Lge	FA	FL
Newcastle U.	97/8 to 98/9	18	3	15	5	0	0	0	0
Totals		*18*	*3*	*15*	*5*	*0*	*0*	*0*	*0*

BRANCH Michael — Everton

Full Name: Michael Paul Branch
DOB: 18-Oct-72 Liverpool

Previous Club Details — *Apps* — *Goals*

Club	Signed	Fee	Tot	Start	Sub	FA	FL	Lge	FA	FL
Everton	10/95	Trainee	41	16	25	3	1	3	0	0

FAPL Summary by Club

Club	Seasons	Tot	Start	Sub	FA	FL	Lge	FA	FL
Everton	95/6 to 98/9	41	16	25	3	1	3	0	0
Totals		*41*	*16*	*25*	*3*	*1*	*3*	*0*	*0*

BREEN Gary — Coventry City

Full Name: Gary Patrick Breen
DOB: 12-Dec-73 Hendon

Previous Club Details — *Apps* — *Goals*

Club	Signed	Fee	Tot	Start	Sub	FA	FL	Lge	FA	FL
Maidstone U.	3/91	Free	19	19	0	0	0	0	0	0
Gillingham	7/92	Free	51	45	6	5	4	0	0	0
Peterborough	8/94	£70k	69	68	1	6	6	1	0	0
Birmingham C.	2/96	£400k	40	37	3	1	4	2	0	0
Coventry C.	1/97	£2.5m	64	59	5	6	6	1	0	0

FAPL Summary by Club

Club	Seasons	Tot	Start	Sub	FA	FL	Lge	FA	FL
Coventry C.	96/7 to 98/9	64	59	5	6	6	1	0	0
Totals		*64*	*59*	*5*	*6*	*6*	*1*	*0*	*0*

BRIDGE Wayne — Southampton

Full Name: Wayne Bridge
DOB: 05-Aug-80 Southampton

Previous Club Details — *Apps* — *Goals*

Club	Signed	Fee	Tot	Start	Sub	FA	FL	Lge	FA	FL
Southampton		Trainee	23	15	8	0	1	0	0	0

FAPL Summary by Club

Club	Seasons	Tot	Start	Sub	FA	FL	Lge	FA	FL
Southampton	1998/9	23	15	8	0	1	0	0	0
Totals		*23*	*15*	*8*	*0*	*1*	*0*	*0*	*0*

BRIDGES Michael — Sunderland

Full Name: Michael Bridges
DOB: 05-Aug-78 North Shields

Previous Club Details — *Apps* — *Goals*

Club	Signed	Fee	Tot	Start	Sub	FA	FL	Lge	FA	FL
Sunderland	11/95	Trainee	76	31	45	2	11	16	0	5

FAPL Summary by Club

Club	Seasons	Tot	Start	Sub	FA	FL	Lge	FA	FL
Sunderland	1996/7	24	10	14	2	2	3	0	0
Totals		*24*	*10*	*14*	*2*	*2*	*3*	*0*	*0*

BRISCOE Lee — Sheffield Wednesday

Full Name: Lee Stephen Briscoe
DOB: 30-Sep-75 Pontefract

Previous Club Details

Club	Signed	Fee	Apps Tot	Start	Sub	FA	FL	Goals Lge	FA	FL
Sheffield W.	5/94	Trainee	62	41	21	2	4	1	0	0
Manchester C.	2/98	Loan	5	5	0	0	0	1	0	0
FAPL Summary by Club										
Sheffield W.	93/4 to 98/9		61	41	20	2	4	1	0	0
Totals			*61*	*41*	*20*	*2*	*4*	*1*	*0*	*0*

BROWN Wes — Manchester United

Full Name: Wesley Brown
DOB: 16-Mar-79 Manchester

Previous Club Details

Club	Signed	Fee	Apps Tot	Start	Sub	FA	FL	Goals Lge	FA	FL
Manchester U.		Trainee	16	12	4	2	1	0	0	0
FAPL Summary by Club										
Manchester U.	97/8 to 98/9		16	12	4	2	1	0	0	0
Totals			*16*	*12*	*4*	*2*	*1*	*0*	*0*	*0*

BURROWS David — Coventry City

Full Name: David Burrows
DOB: 25-Oct-68 Dudley

Previous Club Details

Club	Signed	Fee	Apps Tot	Start	Sub	FA	FL	Goals Lge	FA	FL
WBA	10/86	App	46	37	9	2	4	1	0	0
Liverpool	10/88	£550k	146	135	11	17	16	3	0	0
West Ham U.	9/93	Swap	29	29	0	3	3	1	0	1
Everton	9/94	Swap	19	19	0	2	2	0	0	0
Coventry C.	3/95	£1.1m	96	95	1	5	8	0	0	0
FAPL Summary by Club										
Liverpool	92/3 to 93/4		34	32	2	0	5	2	0	0
West Ham U.	93/4 to 94/5		29	29	0	3	3	1	0	1
Everton	1994-94		19	19	0	2	2	0	0	0
Coventry C.	94/5 to 98/9		96	95	1	5	8	0	0	0
Totals			*178*	*175*	*3*	*10*	*18*	*3*	*0*	*1*

BURTON Deon — Derby County

Full Name: Deon John Burton
DOB: 25-Oct-76 Ashford

Previous Club Details

Club	Signed	Fee	Apps Tot	Start	Sub	FA	FL	Goals Lge	FA	FL
Portsmouth	2/94	Trainee	62	42	20	2	5	10	1	2
Cardiff C.	12/96	Loan	5	5	0	0	0	2	0	0
Derby Co.	8/97	£1.0m	50	26	24	7	2	12	3	0
FAPL Summary by Club										
Derby Co.	97/8 to 98/9		50	26	24	7	2	12	3	0
Totals			*50*	*26*	*24*	*7*	*2*	*12*	*3*	*0*

BUTT Nicky — Manchester United

Full Name: Nicholas Butt
DOB: 21-Jan-75 Manchester

Previous Club Details

Club	Signed	Fee	Apps Tot	Start	Sub	FA	FL	Goals Lge	FA	FL
Manchester U.	1/93	Trainee	146	119	27	18	5	12	1	0
FAPL Summary by Club										
Manchester U.	92/3 to 97/8		146	119	27	18	5	12	1	0
Totals			*146*	*119*	*27*	*18*	*5*	*12*	*1*	*0*

CADAMARTERI Danny — Everton

Full Name: Daniel Cadamarteri
DOB: 12-Oct-79 Bradford

Previous Club Details			*Apps*					*Goals*		
Club	Signed	Fee	Tot	Start	Sub	FA	FL	Lge	FA	FL
Everton	10/96	Trainee	57	26	31	5	7	8	0	1
FAPL Summary by Club										
Everton	96/7 to 98/9		57	26	31	5	7	8	0	1
Totals			*57*	*26*	*31*	*5*	*7*	*8*	*0*	*1*

CALDERWOOD Colin — Aston Villa

Full Name: Colin Calderwood

DOB: 20-Jan-65 Stranraer

Previous Club Details			*Apps*					*Goals*		
Club	Signed	Fee	Tot	Start	Sub	FA	FL	Lge	FA	FL
Mansfield T.	3/82		100	97	3	6	4	1	1	0
Swindon T.	7/85	£30k	330	328	2	17	35	20	1	0
Tottenham H.	7/93	£1.25m	163	152	11	16	20	7	1	0
Aston Villa	3/99	£225k	8	8	0	0	0	0	0	0
FAPL Summary by Club										
Tottenham H.	93/4 to 98/9		163	152	11	16	20	7	1	0
Aston Villa	1998/9		8	8	0	0	0	0	0	0
Totals			*171*	*160*	*11*	*16*	*20*	*7*	*1*	*0*

CAMPBELL Kevin — Everton

Full Name: Kevin Joseph Campbell

DOB: 04-Feb-70 Lambeth

Previous Club Details			*Apps*					*Goals*		
Club	Signed	Fee	Tot	Start	Sub	FA	FL	Lge	FA	FL
Arsenal	2/88	Trainee	166	124	42	19	24	46	2	6
Leyton Orient	1/89	Loan	16	16	0	0	0	9	0	0
Leicester C.	11/89	Loan	11	11	0	0	0	5	0	0
N.Forest	6/95	£2.5m	80	79	1	11	2	32	3	0
Trabzonspor	8/98	£2.5m								
Everton	3/98	Loan	8	8	0	0	0	9	0	0
FAPL Summary by Club										
Arsenal	92/3 to 94/5		97	79	18	12	18	22	1	6
N.Forest	95/6 to 96/7		38	37	1	10	0	9	3	0
Everton	1998/9		8	8	0	0	0	9	0	0
Totals			*143*	*124*	*19*	*22*	*18*	*40*	*4*	*6*

CAMPBELL Sol — Tottenham Hotspur

Full Name: Sulzeer Jeremiah Campbell

DOB: 18-Sep-74 Newham, London

Previous Club Details			*Apps*					*Goals*		
Club	Signed	Fee	Tot	Start	Sub	FA	FL	Lge	FA	FL
Tottenham H.	9/92	Trainee	205	196	9	23	24	2	1	4
FAPL Summary by Club										
Tottenham H.	92/3 to 98/9		205	196	9	23	24	2	1	4
Totals			*205*	*196*	*9*	*23*	*24*	*2*	*1*	*4*

CAMPBELL Stuart — Leicester City

Full Name: Stuart Pearson Campbell

DOB: 09-Dec-77 Corby

Previous Club Details			*Apps*					*Goals*		
Club	Signed	Fee	Tot	Start	Sub	FA	FL	Lge	FA	FL
Leicester C.	7/96	Trainee	33	11	22	3	5	0	0	0
FAPL Summary by Club										
Leicester C.	96/7 to 98/9		33	11	22	3	5	0	0	0
Totals			*33*	*11*	*22*	*3*	*5*	*0*	*0*	*0*

CARBONARI Horacio — Derby County

Full Name: Horacio Angel Carbonari

DOB: Argentina

Previous Club Details			*Apps*					*Goals*		
Club	Signed	Fee	Tot	Start	Sub	FA	FL	Lge	FA	FL
Rosario Central										
Derby Co.	5/98	£2.7m	29	28	1	4	0	5	0	0
FAPL Summary by Club										
Derby Co.	1998/9		29	28	1	4	0	5	0	0
Totals			*29*	*28*	*1*	*4*	*0*	*5*	*0*	*0*

CARBONE Benito — Sheffield Wednesday

Full Name: Benito Carbone
DOB: 14-Aug-71 Bagnara Calabra, Italy

Previous Club Details			*Apps*					*Goals*		
Club	Signed	Fee	Tot	Start	Sub	FA	FL	Lge	FA	FL
Torino	1988		8					0		
Reggina	1990		31					5		
Casertana	1991		31					4		
Ascoli	1992		28					6		
Torino	1993		28	25	3			6		
Napoli	1994		29	27	2			4		
Internazionale	1995		31	25	6			2		
Sheffield W.	10/96	£3m	89	83	6	7	3	23	1	0
FAPL Summary by Club										
Sheffield W.	96/7 to 98/9		89	83	6	7	3	23	1	0
Totals			*89*	*83*	*6*	*7*	*3*	*23*	*1*	*0*

CARR Stephen — Tottenham Hotspur

Full Name: Stephen Carr
DOB: 29-Aug-76 Dublin

Previous Club Details			*Apps*					*Goals*		
Club	Signed	Fee	Tot	Start	Sub	FA	FL	Lge	FA	FL
Tottenham H.	8/93		102	99	3	11	14	0	0	1
FAPL Summary by Club										
Tottenham H.	93/4 to 98/9		102	99	3	11	14	0	0	1
Totals			*102*	*99*	*3*	*11*	*14*	*0*	*0*	*1*

CARRAGHER Jamie — Liverpool

Full Name: James Carragher
DOB: 28-Jan-78 Bootle

Previous Club Details			*Apps*					*Goals*		
Club	Signed	Fee	Tot	Start	Sub	FA	FL	Lge	FA	FL
Liverpool		Trainee	56	52	4	2	5	2	0	0
FAPL Summary by Club										
Liverpool	96/7 to 98/9		56	52	4	2	5	2	0	0
Totals			*56*	*52*	*4*	*2*	*5*	*2*	*0*	*0*

CASIRAGHI Pier Luigi — Chelsea

Full Name: Pier Luigi Casiraghi
DOB: 04-Mar-69 Monza, Italy

Previous Club Details			*Apps*					*Goals*		
Club	Signed	Fee	Tot	Start	Sub	FA	FL	Lge	FA	FL
Monza	1985		92					28		
Juventus	1989		98					20		
Lazio	1993		140	105	35			41		
Chelsea	6/98	£5.4m	10	10	0	0	0	1	0	0
FAPL Summary by Club										
Chelsea	1998/9		10	10	0	0	0	1	0	0
Totals			*10*	*10*	*0*	*0*	*0*	*1*	*0*	*0*

CHAMBERLAIN Alec — Watford

Full Name: Alec Francis Roy Chamberlain
DOB: 20-Jun-64 March

Previous Club Details

Club	Signed	Fee	Apps Tot	Start	Sub	FA	FL	Goals Lge	FA	FL
Ipswich T.	7/81	Free	0	0	0	0	0	0	0	0
Colchester U.	8/82	Free	188	188	0	10	11	0	0	0
Everton	7/87	£80k	0	0	0	0	0	0	0	0
Tranmere R.	11/87	Loan	15	15	0	0	0	0	0	0
Luton T.	7/88	£150k	138	138	0	7	7	0	0	0
Sunderland	7/93	Free	90	89	1	8	9	0	0	0
Watford	7/96	£40k	96	96	0	5	5	0	0	0

CHARLES Gary — Aston Villa

Full Name: Gary Andrew Charles
DOB: 13-Apr-70 Newham

Previous Club Details

Club	Signed	Fee	Apps Tot	Start	Sub	FA	FL	Goals Lge	FA	FL
N.Forest	11/87		56	54	2	10	9	1	1	0
Leicester C.	3/89	Loan	8	5	3	0	0	0	0	0
Derby Co.	7/93	£750k	61	61	0	1	3	3	0	0
Aston Villa	1/95	£2.9m +	79	72	7	7	10	2	0	0
FAPL Summary by Club										
N.Forest	1992/3		14	14	0	0	0	0	0	0
Aston Villa	94/5 to 98/9		79	72	7	7	10	3	0	0
Totals			*93*	*86*	*7*	*7*	*10*	*3*	*0*	*0*

CLARK Lee — Sunderland

Full Name: Lee Robert Clark
DOB: 27-Oct-72 Wallsend

Previous Club Details

Club	Signed	Fee	Apps Tot	Start	Sub	FA	FL	Goals Lge	FA	FL
Newcastle U.	12/89	Trainee	195	153	42	16	17	23	3	0
Sunderland	6/97	£2.5m	73	72	1	4	5	16	0	0

FAPL Summary by Club

Club	Seasons	Tot	Start	Sub	FA	FL	Lge	FA	FL
Newcastle U.	93/4 to 96/7	101	69	32	10	9	7	2	0
Totals		*101*	*69*	*32*	*10*	*9*	*7*	*2*	*0*

CLELAND Alec — Everton

Full Name: Alec Cleland
DOB: 10-Dec-70 Glasgow

Previous Club Details

Club	Signed	Fee	Apps Tot	Start	Sub	FA	FL	Goals Lge	FA	FL
Dundee U.										
Rangers			96	90	6			4		
Everton	7/98	Free	18	16	2	1	3	0	0	0
FAPL Summary by Club										
Everton	1998/9		18	16	2	1	3	0	0	0
Totals			*18*	*16*	*2*	*1*	*3*	*0*	*0*	*0*

CLEMENCE Stephen — Tottenham Hotspur

Full Name: Stephen Clemence
DOB: 31-Mar-78 Liverpool

Previous Club Details

Club	Signed	Fee	Apps Tot	Start	Sub	FA	FL	Goals Lge	FA	FL
Tottenham H.	4/95	Trainee	35	21	14	3	5	0	1	0
FAPL Summary by Club										
Tottenham H.	97/8 to 98/9		35	21	14	3	5	0	1	0
Totals			*35*	*21*	*14*	*3*	*5*	*0*	*1*	*0*

CLEMENT Philippe — Coventry City

Full Name: Philippe Clement
DOB: 22-Mar-74 Antwerp

Previous Club Details

Club	Signed	Fee	Apps Tot	Start	Sub	FA	FL	Goals Lge	FA	FL
St. Anneke Sport, Beerschot, Racing Genk										
Coventry C.	3/98	£500k	12	6	6	2	2	0	0	0
FAPL Summary by Club										
Coventry C.	1998/9		12	6	6	2	2	0	0	0
Totals			*12*	*6*	*6*	*2*	*2*	*0*	*0*	*0*

COBIAN Juan Manuel — Sheffield Wednesday

Full Name: Juan Manuel Cobian
DOB:

Previous Club Details

Club	Signed	Fee	Apps Tot	Start	Sub	FA	FL	Goals Lge	FA	FL
Boca Juniors										
Sheffield W.	8/98	£250k	9	7	2	0	1	0	0	0
FAPL Summary by Club										
Sheffield W.	1998/9		9	7	2	0	1	0	0	0
Totals			*9*	*7*	*2*	*0*	*1*	*0*	*0*	*0*

COLE Andy — Manchester United

Full Name: Andrew Alexander Cole
DOB: 15-Oct-71 Nottingham

Previous Club Details

Club	Signed	Fee	Apps Tot	Start	Sub	FA	FL	Goals Lge	FA	FL
Arsenal	10/89	Trainee	1	0	1	0	0	0	0	0
Fulham	9/91	Loan	13	13	0	0	0	3	0	0
Bristol C.	3/92	£500k	41	41	0	1	3	20	4	0
Newcastle U.	3/93	£1.75m	70	69	1	4	7	55	1	8
Manchester U.	1/95	£7m +	137	116	21	20	2	62	9	0
FAPL Summary by Club										
Newcastle U.	93/4 to 94/5		58	58	0	4	7	43	1	8
Manchester U.	94/5 to 98/9		137	116	21	20	2	62	9	0
Totals			*195*	*174*	*21*	*24*	*9*	*105*	*10*	*8*

COLLETER Patrik — Southampton

Full Name: Patrik Colleter
DOB: 06-Nov-65

Previous Club Details

Club	Signed	Fee	Apps Tot	Start	Sub	FA	FL	Goals Lge	FA	FL
Marseille										
Southampton	3/12	£300k	16	16	0	2	0	0	0	0
FAPL Summary by Club										
Southampton	1998/9		16	16	0	2		1	0	
Totals			*16*	*16*	*0*	*2*	*0*	*1*	*0*	*0*

COLLINS John — Everton

Full Name: John Angus Paul Collins
DOB: 31-Jan-68 Gallashiels

Previous Club Details

Club	Signed	Fee	Apps Tot	Start	Sub	FA	FL	Goals Lge	FA	FL
Hibernain	1/84		163					16		
Celtic	7/90	£1m	216	211	5			47		
Monaco	96		53	45	8			7		
Everton	8/98	£2.5m	20	19	1	0	4	1	0	1
FAPL Summary by Club										
Everton	1998/9		20	19	1	0	4	1	0	1
Totals			*20*	*19*	*1*	*0*	*4*	*1*	*0*	*1*

COLLYMORE Stan — Aston Villa

Full Name: Stanley Victor Collymore
DOB: 22-Jan-71 Stone

Previous Club Details

Club	Signed	Fee	Apps Tot	Start	Sub	FA	FL	Goals Lge	FA	FL
Crystal Palace	1/91	£100k	20	4	16	0	5	1	0	1
Southend U.	11/92	£100k	30	30	0	3	0	15	3	0
N.Forest	7/93	£2.0m	65	64	1	2	9	41	1	2
Liverpool	7/95	£8.5m	59	54	5	9	4	26	7	0
Aston Villa	5/97	£7m	45	34	11	5	1	7	3	0
FAPL Summary by Club										
Crystal Palace	1992/3		2	0	2	0	2	0	0	0
N.Forest	1994/5		37	37	0	2	4	23	1	2
Liverpool	95/6 to 96/7		60	54	6	9	4	26	7	0
Aston Villa	97/8 to 98/9		45	34	11	5	1	7	3	0
Totals			*144*	*125*	*19*	*16*	*11*	*56*	*11*	*2*

COOPER Colin — Middlesbrough

Full Name: Colin Terence Cooper
DOB: 28-Feb-67 Durham

Previous Club Details

Club	Signed	Fee	Apps Tot	Start	Sub	FA	FL	Goals Lge	FA	FL
Middlesbrough	7/84		188	183	5	13	18	6	0	0
Millwall	7/91	£300k	77	77	0	2	6	6	0	0
N.Forest	6/93	£1.7m	177	176	1	12	14	20	1	2
Middlesbrough	8/98	£2.5m	32	31	1	1	1	1	0	0
FAPL Summary by Club										
N.Forest	94/5 to 96/7		108	108	0	9	9	8	0	1
Middlesbrough	1998/9		32	31	1	1	1	1	0	0
Totals			*140*	*139*	*1*	*10*	*10*	*9*	*0*	*1*

CORT Carl — Wimbledon

Full Name: Carl Edward Richard Cort
DOB: 01-Nov-77 London

Previous Club Details

Club	Signed	Fee	Apps Tot	Start	Sub	FA	FL	Goals Lge	FA	FL
Wimbledon	6/96	Trainee	39	22	17	8	5	7	0	2
Lincoln C.	2/97	Loan	6	5	1	0	0	1	0	0
FAPL Summary by Club										
Wimbledon	96/7 to 98/9		39	22	17	8	5	7	1	2
Totals			*39*	*22*	*17*	*8*	*5*	*7*	*1*	*2*

COTTEE Tony — Leicester City

Full Name: Anthony Richard Cottee
DOB: 11-Jul-65 West Ham

Previous Club Details

Club	Signed	Fee	Apps Tot	Start	Sub	FA	FL	Goals Lge	FA	FL
West Ham U.	9/82		212	203	9	24	19	92	11	14
Everton	8/88	£2.3m	184	161	23	21	23	72	11	4
West Ham U.	9/94	£300k+	67	63	4	5	8	23	1	4
Selangor	10/96	£750k								
Leicester C.	8/97	£500k	50	36	14	3	6	14	2	5
FAPL Summary by Club										
Everton	92/3 to 94/5		68	64	4	2	8	28	3	0
West Ham U.	94/5 to 96/7		67	63	4	5	8	23	1	4
Leicester C.	97/8 to 98/9		50	36	14	3	6	14	2	5
Totals			*185*	*163*	*22*	*10*	*22*	*65*	*6*	*9*

CRADDOCK Jody — Sunderland

Full Name: Jody Darryl Craddock
DOB: 25-Jul-75 Bromsgrove

Previous Club Details

Club	Signed	Fee	Apps Tot	Start	Sub	FA	FL	Goals Lge	FA	FL
Cambridge U.	8/93	From NL	145	142	3	6	3	4	0	1
Sunderland	8/97	£300k	38	34	4	2	8	0	0	0

CRESSWELL Richard — Sheffield Wednesday

Full Name: Richard Paul Wesley Cresswell
DOB: 20-Sep-77 Bridlington

Previous Club Details

Club	Signed	Fee	Apps Tot	Start	Sub	FA	FL	Goals Lge	FA	FL
York C.	11/95	Trainee	95	72	23	6	6	21	1	0
Mansfield T.	3/97	Loan	5	5	0	0	0	1	0	0
Sheffield W.	3/99	£950k	7	1	6	0	0	1	0	0
FAPL Summary by Club										
Sheffield W.	1998/9		7	1	6	0	0	1	0	0
Totals			*7*	*1*	*6*	*0*	*0*	*1*	*0*	*0*

CRUYFF Jordi — Manchester United

Full Name: Johan Jordi Cruyff
DOB: 09-Feb-74 Amsterdam

Previous Club Details

Club	Signed	Fee	Apps Tot	Start	Sub	FA	FL	Goals Lge	FA	FL
Barcelona	1994		41	32	9			11		
Manchester U.	8/96	£1.4m	27	14	13	1	4	5	0	0
Celta Vigo	1999	Loan								
FAPL Summary by Club										
Manchester U.	96/7 to 98/9		26	14	12	1	4	5	0	0
Totals			*26*	*14*	*12*	*1*	*4*	*5*	*0*	*0*

CUNNINGHAM Kenny — Wimbledon

Full Name: Kenneth Edward Cunningham
DOB: 28-Jun-71 Dublin

Previous Club Details

Club	Signed	Fee	Apps Tot	Start	Sub	FA	FL	Goals Lge	FA	FL
Millwall	9/89		136	132	4	1	10	1	0	0
Wimbledon	11/94	£1.3m +	164	163	1	24	19	0	0	0
FAPL Summary by Club										
Wimbledon	94/5 to 98/9		164	163	1	23	19	0	0	0
Totals			*164*	*163*	*1*	*23*	*19*	*0*	*0*	*0*

DABIZAS Nikos — Newcastle United

Full Name: Nikolaos Dabizas
DOB: 03-Aug-73 Amyndaeo, Greece

Previous Club Details

Club	Signed	Fee	Apps Tot	Start	Sub	FA	FL	Goals Lge	FA	FL
Olympiakos										
Newcastle U.	3/98	£2.0m	11	10	1	2	0	1	0	0
FAPL Summary by Club										
Newcastle U.	97/8 to 98/9		41	35	6	8	2	4	0	0
Totals			*41*	*35*	*6*	*8*	*2*	*4*	*0*	*0*

DALGLISH Paul — Newcastle United

Full Name: Paul Dalglish
DOB: 18-Feb-77 Glasgow

Previous Club Details

Club	Signed	Fee	Apps Tot	Start	Sub	FA	FL	Goals Lge	FA	FL
Celtic	7/95	Juniors	0	0	0	0	0	0	0	0
Liverpool	8/96	Free	0	0	0	0	0	0	0	0
Newcastle U.	11/97	Free	11	6	5	0	2	1	0	1

Bury	11/97	Loan	12	1	11	1	0	0	0	0
FAPL Summary by Club										
Newcastle U.	1998/9		11	6	5	0	2	1	0	1
Totals			*11*	*6*	*5*	*0*	*2*	*1*	*0*	*1*

DAY Chris — Watford

Full Name: Christopher Day
DOB: 28-Jul-75 Whipps Cross

Previous Club Details			*Apps*					*Goals*		
Club	Signed	Fee	Tot	Start	Sub	FA	FL	Lge	FA	FL
Tottenham	1992	Trainee	0	0	0	0	0	0	0	0
Crystal Palace	8/96	£225k	24	24	0	2	2	0	0	0
Watford	7/97		0	0	0	0	0	0	0	0

DE GOEY Ed — Chelsea

Full Name: Edward De Goey
DOB: 20-Dec-66 Gouda

Previous Club Details			*Apps*					*Goals*		
Club	Signed	Fee	Tot	Start	Sub	FA	FL	Lge	FA	FL
Sparta Rotterdam, Feyenoord										
Chelsea	7/97	£2.5m	63	63	0	7	4	0	0	0
FAPL Summary by Club										
Chelsea	97/8 to 98/9		63	63	0	7	4	0	0	0
Totals			*63*	*63*	*0*	*7*	*4*	*0*	*0*	*0*

DEANE Brian — Middlesbrough

Full Name: Brian Christopher Deane
DOB: 07-Feb-68 Leeds

Previous Club Details			*Apps*					*Goals*		
Club	Signed	Fee	Tot	Start	Sub	FA	FL	Lge	FA	FL
Doncaster R.	12/85	Juniors	66	59	7	3	3	12	1	0
Sheffield U.	7/88	£30k	197	197	0	24	16	82	11	11
Leeds U.	7/93	£2.9m	138	131	7	16	11	32	4	2
Sheffield U.	7/97	£1.5m	24	24	0	1	4	11	0	2
Benfica	1/98									
Middlesbrough	10/98	£3m	26	24	2	1	1	6	0	0
FAPL Summary by Club										
Sheffield U.	1992/3		41	41	0	6	4	15	3	2
Leeds U.	93/4 to 96/7		138	131	7	16	10	32	4	2
Middlesbrough	1998/9		26	24	2	1	1	6	0	0
Totals			*205*	*196*	*9*	*23*	*15*	*53*	*7*	*4*

DELAP Rory — Derby County

Full Name: Rory John Delap
DOB: 06-Jul-76 Sutton Coalfield

Previous Club Details			*Apps*					*Goals*		
Club	Signed	Fee	Tot	Start	Sub	FA	FL	Lge	FA	FL
Carlisle U.	7/94	Trainee	56	32	24	3	4	7	0	0
Derby Co.	2/98	£500k>	13	10	3	0	0	0	0	0
FAPL Summary by Club										
Derby Co.	97/8 to 98/9		36	31	5	1	3	0	0	1
Totals			*36*	*31*	*5*	*1*	*3*	*0*	*0*	*1*

DESAILLY Marcel — Chelsea

Full Name: Marcel Desailly
DOB: 07-Sep-68 Accra, Ghana

Previous Club Details			*Apps*					*Goals*		
Club	Signed	Fee	Tot	Start	Sub	FA	FL	Lge	FA	FL
Nantes	1986		164					5		
Marseille	1992		46					1		
Milan	1993		104	104	0			5		
Chelsea	6/97	£4.6m	31	30	1	6	0	0	0	0

FAPL Summary by Club										
Chelsea	1998/9		31	30	1	6	0	0	0	0
Totals			*31*	*30*	*1*	*6*	*0*	*0*	*0*	*0*

DI CANIO Paulo — West Ham United

Full Name: Paulo Di Canio
DOB: 09-Jul-68 Rome

Previous Club Details			*Apps*					*Goals*		
Club	Signed	Fee	Tot	Start	Sub	FA	FL	Lge	FA	FL
Milan										
Celtic	7/96		26	25	1	6	2	12	3	0
Sheffield W.	8/97	£3m	41	39	2	3	4	15	0	2
West Ham U.	1/99	£1.7m	13	12	1	0	0	4	0	0
FAPL Summary by Club										
Sheffield W.	97/8 to 98/9		41	39	2	3	4	15	0	2
West Ham U.	1998/9		13	12	1	0	0	4	0	0
Totals			*54*	*51*	*3*	*3*	*4*	*19*	*0*	*2*

DI MATTEO Robert — Chelsea

Full Name: Robert Di Matteo
DOB: 29-May-70 Sciaffusa, Switzerland

Previous Club Details			*Apps*					*Goals*		
Club	Signed	Fee	Tot	Start	Sub	FA	FL	Lge	FA	FL
Schaffhausen	1988		50					2		
FC Zurich	1991		34					6		
Aarau	1992		31					1		
Lazio	1993		88					7		
Chelsea	7/96	£4.9m	94	87	7	14	9	12	3	3
FAPL Summary by Club										
Chelsea	96/7 to 98/9		94	87	7	14	9	12	3	3
Totals			*94*	*87*	*7*	*14*	*9*	*12*	*3*	*3*

DICKS Julian — West Ham United

Full Name: Julian Andrew Dicks
DOB: 08-Aug-68 Bristol

Previous Club Details			*Apps*					*Goals*		
Club	Signed	Fee	Tot	Start	Sub	FA	FL	Lge	FA	FL
Birmingham C.	4/86	App	89	83	6	5	6	1	0	0
West Ham U.	3/88	£300k	159	159	0	14	19	29	2	5
Liverpool	9/93	£1.5m	24	24	0	1	3	3	0	0
West Ham U.	10/94	£500k+	103	103	0	9	11	21	1	3
FAPL Summary by Club										
West Ham U.	1993/4		7	7	0	0	0	0	0	0
Liverpool	1993/4		24	24	0	1	3	3	0	0
West Ham U.	94/5 to 98/9		103	103	0	9	11	21	1	3
Totals			*134*	*134*	*0*	*10*	*14*	*24*	*1*	*3*

DIXON Lee — Arsenal

Full Name: Lee Michael Dixon
DOB: 17-Mar-64 Manchester

Previous Club Details			*Apps*					*Goals*		
Club	Signed	Fee	Tot	Start	Sub	FA	FL	Lge	FA	FL
Burnley	7/82	Juniors	4	4	0	0	1	0	0	0
Chester C.	2/84	Free	57	56	1	1	2	1	0	0
Bury	7/85	Free	45	45	0	8	4	5	1	0
Stoke C.	7/86	£40k	71	71	0	7	6	5	0	0
Arsenal	1/88	£400k	388	382	6	41	45	20	1	0
FAPL Summary by Club										
Arsenal	92/3 to 98/9		235	231	4	28	29	5	0	0
Totals			*235*	*231*	*4*	*28*	*29*	*5*	*0*	*0*

DODD Jason — Southampton

Full Name: Jason Robert Dodd
DOB: 02-Nov-70 Bath

Previous Club Details			*Apps*					*Goals*		
Club	Signed	Fee	Tot	Start	Sub	FA	FL	Lge	FA	FL
Southampton	3/89	£50k	259	242	17	24	31	8	1	0
FAPL Summary by Club										
Southampton	92/3 to 98/9		189	178	11	14	16	8	1	0
Totals			*189*	*178*	*11*	*14*	*16*	*8*	*1*	*0*

DOMI Didi — Newcastle United

Full Name: Didier Domi
DOB: 02-May-78 Sarcelles

Previous Club Details			*Apps*					*Goals*		
Club	Signed	Fee	Tot	Start	Sub	FA	FL	Lge	FA	FL
PSG										
Newcastle U.	12/98	£3.25m	14	14	0	4	0	0	0	0
FAPL Summary by Club										
Newcastle U.	1998/9		14	14	0	4	0	0	0	0
Totals			*14*	*14*	*0*	*4*	*0*	*0*	*0*	*0*

DRAPER Mark — Aston Villa

Full Name: Mark Draper
DOB: 11-Nov-70 Long Eaton

Previous Club Details			*Apps*					*Goals*		
Club	Signed	Fee	Tot	Start	Sub	FA	FL	Lge	FA	FL
Notts Co.	12/88	Trainee	222	206	16	10	15	40	2	2
Leicester C.	7/94	£1.25m	39	39	0	2	2	5	0	0
Aston Villa	7/95	£3.25m	119	108	11	10	12	7	2	2
FAPL Summary by Club										
Leicester C.	1994/5		39	39	0	2	2	5	0	0
Aston Villa	95/6 to 98/9		119	108	11	10	12	7	2	2
Totals			*158*	*147*	*11*	*12*	*14*	*12*	*2*	*2*

DREYER John — Bradford City

Full Name: John Brian Dreyer
DOB: 11-Jun-63 Alnwick

Previous Club Details			*Apps*					*Goals*		
Club	Signed	Fee	Tot	Start	Sub	FA	FL	Lge	FA	FL
Oxford U.	1/85		60	57	3	2	11	2	0	0
Torquay U.	2/85	Loan	5	5	0	0	0	0	0	0
Fulham	3/86	Loan	14	12	0	0	0	2	0	0
Luton T.	6/88	£140k	214	212	2	14	14	13	0	1
Stoke C.	7/94	Free	49	32	17	1	5	3	0	0
Bolton W.	3/95	Loan	2	1	1	0	0	0	0	0
Bradford C.	11/96	£25k	66	61	5	3	9	1	3	0

DUBERRY Michael — Chelsea

Full Name: Michael Wayne Duberry
DOB: 14-Oct-75 London

Previous Club Details			*Apps*					*Goals*		
Club	Signed	Fee	Tot	Start	Sub	FA	FL	Lge	FA	FL
Chelsea	6/93	Trainee	86	77	9	12	8	1	2	0
Bournemouth	9/95	Loan	7	7						
FAPL Summary by Club										
Chelsea	93/4 to 98/9		86	77	9	12	8	1	2	0
Totals			*86*	*77*	*9*	*12*	*8*	*1*	*2*	*0*

DUBLIN Dion — Aston Villa

Full Name: Dion Dublin
DOB: 22-Apr-69 Leicester

Previous Club Details			*Apps*					*Goals*		
Club	Signed	Fee	Tot	Start	Sub	FA	FL	Lge	FA	FL
Norwich C.	3/88	Trainee	0	0	0	0	0	0	0	0
Cambridge U.	8/88	Free	156	133	23	21	10	52	11	5
Manchester U.	8/92	£1m	12	4	8	2	2	2	0	1
Coventry C.	9/94	£2m	145	144	1	13	13	62	7	4
Aston Villa	11/98	£5.75m	24	24	0	0	0	11	0	0
FAPL Summary by Club										
Manchester U.	92/3 to 93/4		12	4	8	2	2	2	0	1
Coventry C.	94/5 to 98/9		145	144	1	13	13	62	7	4
Aston Villa	1998/9		24	24	0	0	0	11	0	0
Totals			*181*	*172*	*9*	*15*	*15*	*75*	*7*	*5*

DUNNE Richard — Everton

Full Name: Richard Patrick Dunne
DOB: 21-Sep-79 Dublin

Previous Club Details			*Apps*					*Goals*		
Club	Signed	Fee	Tot	Start	Sub	FA	FL	Lge	FA	FL
Everton	10/96	Trainee	25	23	2	4	2	0	0	0
FAPL Summary by Club										
Everton	96/7 to 98/9		25	23	2	4	2	0	0	0
Totals			*25*	*23*	*2*	*4*	*2*	*0*	*0*	*0*

EARLE Robbie — Wimbledon

Full Name: Robert Gerald Earle
DOB: 27-Jan-65 Newcastle-under-Lyme

Previous Club Details			*Apps*					*Goals*		
Club	Signed	Fee	Tot	Start	Sub	FA	FL	Lge	FA	FL
Port Vale	7/82	Juniors	294	284	10	21	23	77	4	4
Wimbledon	7/91	£775k	257	255	2	33	26	56	8	6
FAPL Summary by Club										
Wimbledon	92/3 to 98/9		219	217	2	32	24	42	8	6
Totals			*219*	*217*	*2*	*32*	*24*	*42*	*8*	*6*

EASTON Clint — Watford

Full Name: Clint Jude Easton
DOB: 01-Oct-77 Barking

Previous Club Details			*Apps*					*Goals*		
Club	Signed	Fee	Tot	Start	Sub	FA	FL	Lge	FA	FL
Watford	7/96	Watford	36	32	4	4	1	1	0	0

EDINBURGH Justin — Tottenham Hotspur

Full Name: Justin Charles Edinburgh
DOB: 18-Dec-69 Brentwood

Previous Club Details			*Apps*					*Goals*		
Club	Signed	Fee	Tot	Start	Sub	FA	FL	Lge	FA	FL
Southend U.	7/88	Trainee	37	36	1	2	3	0	0	0
Tottenham H.	7/90	£150k	206	184	22	26	28	1	0	0
FAPL Summary by Club										
Tottenham H.	92/3 to 98/9		167	148	19	21	20	0	0	0
Totals			*167*	*148*	*19*	*21*	*20*	*0*	*0*	*0*

EDWORTHY Marc — Coventry City

Full Name: Marc Edworthy
DOB: 24-Dec-74 Barnstaple

Club	Signed	Fee	Apps Tot	Start	Sub	FA	FL	Goals Lge	FA	FL
Previous Club Details										
Plymouth Arg	3/91	Trainee	69	52	17	7	7	1	0	0
Crystal Palace	6/95	£350k	126	120	6	8	8	0	0	1
Coventry C.	8/98	£800k	22	16	6	1	0	0	0	0
FAPL Summary by Club										
Crystal Palace	1997/8		34	33	1	4	1	0	0	0
Coventry C.	1998/9		22	16	6	1	0	0	0	0
Totals			*56*	*49*	*7*	*5*	*1*	*0*	*0*	*0*

EHIOGU Ugo — Aston Villa

Full Name: Ugochuku Ehiogu
DOB: 03-Nov-72 Hackney

Club	Signed	Fee	Apps Tot	Start	Sub	FA	FL	Goals Lge	FA	FL
Previous Club Details										
WBA	7/89		2	0	2	0	0	0	0	0
Aston Villa	7/91	£40k	204	191	13	18	17	11	1	1
FAPL Summary by Club										
Aston Villa	92/3 to 98/9		196	187	9	17	17	8	1	1
Totals			*196*	*187*	*9*	*17*	*17*	*8*	*1*	*1*

EKOKU Efan — Wimbledon

Full Name: Efangwu Goziem Ekoku
DOB: 08-Jun-67 Manchester

Club	Signed	Fee	Apps Tot	Start	Sub	FA	FL	Goals Lge	FA	FL
Previous Club Details										
Bournemouth	5/90	£100k	62	43	19	7	2	21	2	0
Norwich C.	3/93	£500k	37	26	11	2	3	15	0	1
Wimbledon	10/94	£900k	123	102	21	17	13	37	3	4
FAPL Summary by Club										
Norwich C.	92/3 to 94/5		37	26	11	1	3	15	0	2
Wimbledon	94/5 to 98/9		123	102	21	17	13	37	3	4
Totals			*160*	*128*	*32*	*18*	*16*	*52*	*3*	*6*

ELLIOTT Matt — Leicester City

Full Name: Matthew Stephen Elliot
DOB: 01-Nov-68 Wandsworth

Club	Signed	Fee	Apps Tot	Start	Sub	FA	FL	Goals Lge	FA	FL
Previous Club Details										
Charlton A.	9/88	£5k	0	0	0	0	1	0	0	0
Torquay U.	3/89	£10k	124	123	1	9	9	15	2	2
Scunthorpe U.	3/92	£50k	61	61	0	2	6	8	0	0
Oxford U.	11/93	£150k	148	148	0	11	16	21	2	1
Leicester C.	1/97	£1.6m	90	90	0	6	9	14	0	0
FAPL Summary by Club										
Leicester C.	96/7 to 98/9		90	90	0	6	9	14	0	0
Totals			*90*	*90*	*0*	*6*	*9*	*14*	*0*	*0*

ERANIO Stefano — Derby County

Full Name: Stefano Eranio
DOB: 29-Dec-66 Genova

Club	Signed	Fee	Apps Tot	Start	Sub	FA	FL	Goals Lge	FA	FL
Previous Club Details										
Genoa	1985		213					13		
Milan	1990		77					4		
Derby Co.	5/97	Free	48	41	7	5	3	5	0	0
(Milan not inc 96-7)										
FAPL Summary by Club										
Derby Co.	97/8 to 98/9		48	41	7	5	3	5	0	0
Totals			*48*	*41*	*7*	*5*	*3*	*5*	*0*	*0*

EUELL Jason — Wimbledon

Full Name: Jason Euell
DOB: 06-Feb-77 South London

Previous Club Details			*Apps*					*Goals*		
Club	Signed	Fee	Tot	Start	Sub	FA	FL	Lge	FA	FL
Wimbledon	6/95	Trainee	68	53	15	11	11	18	1	3
FAPL Summary by Club										
Wimbledon	95/6 to 98/9		68	53	15	11	11	18	1	3
Totals			*68*	*53*	*15*	*11*	*11*	*18*	*1*	*3*

FENTON Graham — Leicester City

Full Name: Graham Anthony Fenton
DOB: 22-May-74 Wallsend

Previous Club Details			*Apps*					*Goals*		
Club	Signed	Fee	Tot	Start	Sub	FA	FL	Lge	FA	FL
Aston Villa	2/92		32	16	16	0	7	3	0	0
WBA	1/94	Loan	7	7	0	0	0	3	0	0
Blackburn R.	12/95	£1.5m	27	9	18	1	2	7	0	0
Leicester C.	8/97	£1.1m	32	12	20	1	3	3	0	2
FAPL Summary by Club										
Aston Villa	93/4 to 95/6		32	16	16	0	7	3	0	0
Blackburn R.	95/6 to 96/7		27	9	18	1	2	7	0	0
Leicester C.	97/8 to 98/9		32	12	20	1	3	3	0	1
Totals			*91*	*37*	*54*	*2*	*12*	*13*	*0*	*1*

FERDINAND Les — Tottenham Hotspur

Full Name: Leslie Ferdinand
DOB: 18-Dec-66 Acton

Previous Club Details			*Apps*					*Goals*		
Club	Signed	Fee	Tot	Start	Sub	FA	FL	Lge	FA	FL
QPR	4/87	£15k	163	152	11	8	13	80	3	7
Brentford	3/88	Loan	3	3	0	0	0	0	0	0
Besiktas	6/88	Loan								
Newcastle U.	6/95	£6m	68	67	1	5	6	41	2	3
Tottenham H.	7/97	£6m	45	41	4	9	5	10	0	0
FAPL Summary by Club										
QPR	92/3 to 94/5		110	109	1	7	8	60	3	5
Newcastle U.	95/6 to 96/7		68	67	1	5	6	41	2	3
Tottenham H.	97/8 to 98/9		45	41	4	9	5	10	0	0
Totals			*223*	*217*	*6*	*21*	*19*	*111*	*5*	*8*

FERDINAND Rio — West Ham United

Full Name: Rio Gavin Ferdinand
DOB: 07-Nov-78 London

Previous Club Details			*Apps*					*Goals*		
Club	Signed	Fee	Tot	Start	Sub	FA	FL	Lge	FA	FL
West Ham U.	11/95	Trainee	82	77	5	8	7	2	0	0
Bournemouth	11/96	Loan	10	10	0	0	0	0	0	0
FAPL Summary by Club										
West Ham U.	95/6 to 98/9		82	77	5	8	7	2	0	0
Totals			*82*	*77*	*5*	*8*	*7*	*2*	*0*	*0*

FERGUSON Duncan — Newcastle United

Full Name: Duncan Ferguson
DOB: 27-Dec-71 Stirling

Previous Club Details			*Apps*					*Goals*		
Club	Signed	Fee	Tot	Start	Sub	FA	FL	Lge	FA	FL
Dundee	2/90	Free NL	79	75	2	3	6	27	4	2
Rangers	7/93	£4m	14	8	6	3	4	2	0	3
Everton	10/94	£4.4m	116	110	6	9	8	37	4	1
Newcastle U.	11/98	£7m	7	7	0	2	0	2	0	0

FAPL Summary by Club

Club	Signed	Fee	Tot	Start	Sub	FA	FL	Lge	FA	FL
Everton	94/5 to 98/9		116	110	6	9	8	37	4	1
Newcastle U.	1998/9		7	7	0	2	0	2	0	0
Totals			*123*	*117*	*6*	*11*	*8*	*39*	*4*	*1*

FERRER Albert — Chelsea

Full Name: Albert Ferrer
DOB: 06-Jun-70 Spain

Previous Club Details			*Apps*					*Goals*		
Club	Signed	Fee	Tot	Start	Sub	FA	FL	Lge	FA	FL
Barcelona										
Chelsea	7/98	£2.2m	30	30	0	2	1	0	0	0
FAPL Summary by Club										
Chelsea	1998/9		30	30	0	2	1	0	0	0
Totals			*30*	*30*	*0*	*2*	*1*	*0*	*0*	*0*

FERRI Jean-Michel — Liverpool

Full Name: Jean-Michel Ferri
DOB: 09-Sep-69 France

Previous Club Details			*Apps*					*Goals*		
Club	Signed	Fee	Tot	Start	Sub	FA	FL	Lge	FA	FL
Nantes, Istanbulspor										
Liverpool	11/98	£1.5m	2	0	2	0	0	0	0	0
FAPL Summary by Club										
Liverpool	1998/9		2	0	2	0	0	0	0	0
Totals			*2*	*0*	*2*	*0*	*0*	*0*	*0*	*0*

FESTA Gianluca — Middlesbrough

Full Name: Gianluca Festa
DOB: 12-Mar-69 Cagliari

Previous Club Details			*Apps*					*Goals*		
Club	Signed	Fee	Tot	Start	Sub	FA	FL	Lge	FA	FL
Cagliari	1986		3					0		
Fersulcis	1987		26					2		
Cagliari	1988		153					0		
Roma	1993		21	20	1			1		
Internazionale	1993		66	63	3			3		
Middlesbrough	1/97	£2.2m	76	74	2	7	13	5	1	1
FAPL Summary by Club										
Middlesbrough	96/7 to 98/9		38	38	0	5	6	3	1	1
Totals			*38*	*38*	*0*	*5*	*6*	*3*	*1*	*1*

FLO Tore Andre — Chelsea

Full Name: Tore Andre Flo
DOB: 15-Jun-73 Norway

Previous Club Details			*Apps*					*Goals*		
Club	Signed	Fee	Tot	Start	Sub	FA	FL	Lge	FA	FL
Tromso	1995		26					18		
SK Brann	1996		24					19		
Chelsea			64	34	30	4	7	21	0	3
FAPL Summary by Club										
Chelsea	97/8 to 98/9		64	34	30	4	7	21	0	3
Totals			*64*	*34*	*30*	*4*	*7*	*21*	*0*	*3*

FLOWERS Tim — Blackburn Rovers

Full Name: Timothy David Flowers
DOB: 03-Feb-67 Kenilworth

Previous Club Details			*Apps*					*Goals*		
Club	Signed	Fee	Tot	Start	Sub	FA	FL	Lge	FA	FL
Wolves	8/84		63	63	0	2	5	0	0	0

			Apps					Goals		
Southampton	6/86	£70k	192	192	0	16	26	0	0	0
Swindon T.	3/87	Loan	2	2	0	0	0	0	0	0
Swindon T.	11/87	Loan	5	5	0	0	0	0	0	0
Blackburn R.	11/93	£2.4m	177	175	2	14	14	0	0	0
FAPL Summary by Club										
Southampton	92/3 to 93/4		54	54	0	1	5	0	0	0
Blackburn R.	93/4 to 98/9		177	175	2	10	18	0	0	0
Totals			*231*	*229*	*2*	*11*	*23*	*0*	*0*	*0*

FOE Mark-Vivien — West Ham United

Full Name: Mark-Vivien Foe
DOB:

Previous Club Details			*Apps*					*Goals*		
Club	Signed	Fee	Tot	Start	Sub	FA	FL	Lge	FA	FL
RC Lens										
West Ham U.	1/99	£4.2m	13	13	0	0	0	0	0	0
FAPL Summary by Club										
West Ham U.	1998/9		13	13	0	0	0	0	0	0
Totals			*13*	*13*	*0*	*0*	*0*	*0*	*0*	*0*

FORSSELL Mikael — Chelsea

Full Name: Mikael Forssell
DOB: 15-Mar-81 Steinfurt, Germany

Previous Club Details			*Apps*					*Goals*		
Club	Signed	Fee	Tot	Start	Sub	FA	FL	Lge	FA	FL
HJK Helsinki										
Chelsea	11/98	Free	10	4	6	3	0	1	2	0
FAPL Summary by Club										
Chelsea	1998/9		10	4	6	3	0	1	2	0
Totals			*10*	*4*	*6*	*3*	*0*	*1*	*2*	*0*

FOWLER Robbie — Liverpool

Full Name: Robert Bernard Fowler
DOB: 09-Apr-75 Liverpool

Previous Club Details			*Apps*					*Goals*		
Club	Signed	Fee	Tot	Start	Sub	FA	FL	Lge	FA	FL
Liverpool	4/92	Trainee	185	179	6	19	27	106	10	21
FAPL Summary by Club										
Liverpool	93/4 to 98/9		185	179	6	19	27	106	8	20
Totals			*185*	*179*	*6*	*19*	*27*	*106*	*8*	*20*

FOX Ruel — Tottenham Hotspur

Full Name: Ruel Adrian Fox
DOB: 14-Jan-68 Ipswich

Previous Club Details			*Apps*					*Goals*		
Club	Signed	Fee	Tot	Start	Sub	FA	FL	Lge	FA	FL
Norwich C.	1/86	App	172	148	24	15	16	22	0	3
Newcastle U.	2/94	£2.25m	58	56	2	5	3	12	0	1
Tottenham H.	10/95	£4.2m	103	94	9	10	10	13	1	1
FAPL Summary by Club										
Norwich C.	92/3 to 93/4		59	57	2	4	5	11	0	2
Newcastle U.	93/4 to 95/6		58	56	2	5	3	12	0	1
Tottenham H.	95/6 to 98/9		103	94	9	10	10	13	1	1
Totals			*220*	*207*	*13*	*19*	*18*	*36*	*1*	*4*

FREUND Steffen — Tottenham Hotspur

Full Name: Steffen Freund
DOB: 19-Jan-70 Germany

Previous Club Details			*Apps*					*Goals*		
Club	Signed	Fee	Tot	Start	Sub	FA	FL	Lge	FA	FL

Motor Sud Brandenburg, Stahl Brandenburg, Schalke 04

Club	Signed	Fee	Tot	Start	Sub	FA	FL	Lge	FA	FL
B.Dortmund										
Tottenham H.	12/98	£750k	17	17	0	6	3	0	0	0
FAPL Summary by Club										
Tottenham H.	1998/9		17	17	0	6	3	0	0	0
Totals			*17*	*17*	*0*	*6*	*3*	*0*	*0*	*0*

FRIEDEL Brad — Liverpool

Full Name: Bradley Howard Friedel
DOB: 18-May-71 USA

Previous Club Details			*Apps*					*Goals*		
Club	Signed	Fee	Tot	Start	Sub	FA	FL	Lge	FA	FL
Colombus Crew										
Liverpool	12/97	£1.0m	23	23	0	0	2	0	0	0
FAPL Summary by Club										
Liverpool	97/8 to 98/9		23	23	0	0	2	0	0	0
Totals			*23*	*23*	*0*	*0*	*2*	*0*	*0*	*0*

FROGGATT Stephen — Coventry City

Full Name: Stephen Junior Froggatt
DOB: 09-Mar-73 Lincoln

Previous Club Details			*Apps*					*Goals*		
Club	Signed	Fee	Tot	Start	Sub	FA	FL	Lge	FA	FL
Aston Villa	1/91	Trainee	35	30	5	7	2	2	1	0
Wolverh.. W.	7/94	£1m	107	99	8	3	8	7	0	2
Coventry C.	9/98	£1.9m	0	23	0	3	0	1	2	0
FAPL Summary by Club										
Aston Villa	92/3 to 93/4		26	24	2	4	2	2	0	0
Coventry C.	1998/9		23	23	0	3	0	1	2	0
Totals			*49*	*47*	2	*7*	2	*3*	2	*0*

GASCOIGNE Paul — Middlesbrough

Full Name: Paul John Gascoigne
DOB: 27-May-67 Gateshead

Previous Club Details			*Apps*					*Goals*		
Club	Signed	Fee	Tot	Start	Sub	FA	FL	Lge	FA	FL
Newcastle U.	1984	Trainee	92	83	9	4	8	21	3	1
Tottenham H.	7/88	£2m	92	91	1	6	15	19	6	8
Lazio	5/92	£5.5m	41					6		
Rangers	7/95	£4.3m	74	64	10	8	7	30	3	4
Middlesbrough	3/98	£3.45m	33	32	1	1	3	3	0	0
FAPL Summary by Club										
Middlesbrough	1998/9		26	25	1	1	2	3	0	0
Totals			*26*	*25*	*1*	*1*	*2*	*3*	*0*	*0*

GAYLE Marcus — Wimbledon

Full Name: Marcus Anthony Gayle
DOB: 27-Sep-70 Hammersmith

Previous Club Details			*Apps*					*Goals*		
Club	Signed	Fee	Tot	Start	Sub	FA	FL	Lge	FA	FL
Brentford	7/89		156	118	38	8	9	22	2	0
Wimbledon	3/94	£250k	168	139	29	19	18	27	3	6
FAPL Summary by Club										
Wimbledon	93/4 to 98/9		168	139	29	19	18	27	3	6
Totals			*168*	*139*	29	*19*	*18*	27	*3*	*6*

GEMMILL Scot — Everton

Full Name: Scot Gemmill
DOB: 02-Jan-71 Paisley

Previous Club Details			*Apps*					*Goals*		
Club	Signed	Fee	Tot	Start	Sub	FA	FL	Lge	FA	FL
N.Forest	1/90	Trainee	245	228	17	21	31	21	1	3

Club	Signed	Fee	Tot	Start	Sub	FA	FL	Lge	FA	FL
Everton	3/99	£250k	7	7	0	0	0	1	0	0
FAPL Summary by Club										
N.Forest	92/3 to 98/9		128	115	13	16	12	3	1	0
Everton	1998/9		7	7	0	0	0	1	0	0
Totals			*135*	*122*	*13*	*16*	*12*	*4*	*1*	*0*

GEORGIADIS George — Newcastle United

Full Name: George Georgiadis
DOB: 08-Mar-72 Kavala, Greece

Previous Club Details			*Apps*					*Goals*		
Club	Signed	Fee	Tot	Start	Sub	FA	FL	Lge	FA	FL
Panathinaikos										
Newcastle U.	7/98	£500k	10	7	3	2	1	0	1	0
FAPL Summary by Club										
Newcastle U.	1998/9		10	7	3	2	1	0	1	0
Totals			*10*	*7*	*3*	*2*	*1*	*0*	*1*	*0*

GERRARD Steven — Liverpool

Full Name: Steven Gerrad
DOB: 30-May-80 Whiston

Previous Club Details			*Apps*					*Goals*		
Club	Signed	Fee	Tot	Start	Sub	FA	FL	Lge	FA	FL
Liverpool		Trainee	12	4	8	0	0	0	0	0
FAPL Summary by Club										
Liverpool	1998/9		12	4	8	0	0	0	0	0
Totals			*12*	*4*	*8*	*0*	*0*	*0*	*0*	*0*

GIBBS Nigel — Watford

Full Name: Nigel James Gibbs
DOB: 20-Nov-65 St Albans

Previous Club Details			*Apps*					*Goals*		
Club	Signed	Fee	Tot	Start	Sub	FA	FL	Lge	FA	FL
Watford	11/83	Watford	384	371	13	40	22	5	0	2

GIGGS Ryan — Manchester United

Full Name: Ryan Joseph Giggs
DOB: 29-Nov-73 Cardiff

Previous Club Details			*Apps*					*Goals*		
Club	Signed	Fee	Tot	Start	Sub	FA	FL	Lge	FA	FL
Manchester U.	12/90		260	237	23	37	21	53	7	6
FAPL Summary by Club										
Manchester U.	92/3 to 98/9		220	204	16	34	13	48	7	3
Totals			*220*	*204*	*16*	*34*	*13*	*48*	*7*	*3*

GILLESPIE Keith — Newcastle United

Full Name: Keith Robert Gillespie
DOB: 18-Feb-75 Bangor

Previous Club Details			*Apps*					*Goals*		
Club	Signed	Fee	Tot	Start	Sub	FA	FL	Lge	FA	FL
Manchester U.	2/93	Trainee	9	6	3	3	1	2	1	0
Wigan A.	9/93	Loan	8	8	0	0	0	4	0	0
Newcastle U.	1/95	£1m +	113	94	19	10	8	9	2	1
Blackburn R.	12/98	£2.25m	16	13	3	4	0	1	1	0
FAPL Summary by Club										
Manchester U.	1994/5		9	3	6	2	3	1	1	0
Newcastle U.	94/5 to 98/9		113	94	19	10	8	11	2	1
Blackburn R.	1998/9		16	13	3	4	0	1	1	0
Totals			*138*	*110*	*28*	*16*	*11*	*13*	*4*	*1*

GINOLA David — Tottenham Hotspur

Full Name: David Ginola
DOB: 25-Jan-67 Gassin, nr St. Tropez

Previous Club Details			*Apps*					*Goals*		
Club	Signed	Fee	Tot	Start	Sub	FA	FL	Lge	FA	FL
PSG										
Newcastle U.	7/95	£2.5m	58	54	4	4	6	6	0	0
Tottenham H.	7/97	£2m	64	64	0	9	11	9	4	3
FAPL Summary by Club										
Newcastle U.	95/6 to 96/7		58	54	4	4	6	6	0	0
Tottenham H.	97/8 to 98/9		64	64	0	9	11	9	4	3
Totals			*122*	*118*	*4*	*13*	*17*	*15*	*4*	*3*

GIOACCHINI Stefano — Coventry City

Full Name: Stefano Gioacchini
DOB: 25-Nov-76 Rome

Previous Club Details			*Apps*					*Goals*		
Club	Signed	Fee	Tot	Start	Sub	FA	FL	Lge	FA	FL
Perugia, Cosenza, Venezia										
Coventry C.	1/99		3	0	3	0	0	0	0	0
FAPL Summary by Club										
Coventry C.	1998/9		3	0	3	0	0	0	0	0
Totals			*3*	*0*	*3*	*0*	*0*	*0*	*0*	*0*

GIVEN Shay — Newcastle United

Full Name: Seamus John Given
DOB: 20-Apr-76 Lifford

Previous Club Details			*Apps*					*Goals*		
Club	Signed	Fee	Tot	Start	Sub	FA	FL	Lge	FA	FL
Blackburn R.	8/94	From Celtic	2	2	0	0	1	0	0	0
Swindon	8/95	Loan	5	5	0	0	0	0	0	0
Sunderland	1/96	Loan	17	17	0	0	0	0	0	0
Newcastle U.	7/97	£1.5m	55	55	0	10	2	0	0	0
FAPL Summary by Club										
Blackburn R.	1996/7		2	2	0	0	1	0	0	0
Newcastle U.	97/8 to 98/9		55	55	0	10	2	0	0	0
Totals			*57*	*57*	*0*	*10*	*3*	*0*	*0*	*0*

GLASS Stephen — Newcastle United

Full Name: Stephen Glass
DOB: 25-May-76 Dundee

Previous Club Details			*Apps*					*Goals*		
Club	Signed	Fee	Tot	Start	Sub	FA	FL	Lge	FA	FL
Aberdeen										
Newcastle U.	9/98	£650k	22	18	4	4	2	3	0	0
FAPL Summary by Club										
Newcastle U.	1998/9		22	18	4	4	2	3	0	0
Totals			*22*	*18*	*4*	*4*	*2*	*3*	*0*	*0*

GOLDBAEK Bjarne — Chelsea

Full Name: Bjarne Goldbaek
DOB: 16-Aug-68 Denmark

Previous Club Details			*Apps*					*Goals*		
Club	Signed	Fee	Tot	Start	Sub	FA	FL	Lge	FA	FL
Schalke 04, Kaiserslautern, 1.FC Koln										
FC Copenhagen										
Chelsea	11/98	£350k	23	13	10	6	2	5	0	0
FAPL Summary by Club										
Chelsea	1998/9		23	13	10	6	2	5	0	0
Totals			*23*	*13*	*10*	*6*	*2*	*5*	*0*	*0*

GORDON Dean — Middlesbrough

Full Name: Dean Dwight Gordon
DOB: 10-Feb-73 Croydon

Previous Club Details			Apps					Goals		
Club	Signed	Fee	Tot	Start	Sub	FA	FL	Lge	FA	FL
Crystal Palace	7/91	Trainee	201	181	20	15	19	20	1	2
Middlesbrough	7/98	£600k	38	38	0	1	2	3	0	0
FAPL Summary by Club										
Crystal Palace	92/3 to 97/8		88	80	8	10	11	4	1	1
Middlesbrough	1998/9		38	38	0	1	2	3	0	0
Totals			*126*	*118*	*8*	*11*	*13*	*7*	*1*	*1*

GRANT Tony — Everton

Full Name: Anthony James Grant
DOB: 14-Nov-74 Liverpool

Previous Club Details			Apps					Goals		
Club	Signed	Fee	Tot	Start	Sub	FA	FL	Lge	FA	FL
Everton	7/93	Trainee	59	43	16	8	6	2	0	0
Swindon T.	1/96	Loan	3	3	0	0	0	1	0	0
FAPL Summary by Club										
Everton	94/5 to 98/9		59	43	16	8	6	2	0	0
Totals			*59*	*43*	*16*	*8*	*6*	*2*	*0*	*0*

GRANVILLE Danny — Leeds United

Full Name: Daniel Patrick Granville
DOB: 19-Jan-75 Islington

Previous Club Details			Apps					Goals		
Club	Signed	Fee	Tot	Start	Sub	FA	FL	Lge	FA	FL
Cambridge U.	19/5/93	Trainee	99	89	10	4	5	7	0	0
Chelsea	3/97	£300k	18	12	6	0	3	0	0	0
Leeds U.	6/98	£1.6m	9	7	2	3	1	0	0	0
FAPL Summary by Club										
Leeds U.	96/7 to 98/9		27	19	8	3	4	0	0	0
Totals			*27*	*19*	*8*	*3*	*4*	*0*	*0*	*0*

GRAY Michael — Sunderland

Full Name: Michael Gray
DOB: 03-Aug-74 Sunderland

Previous Club Details			Apps					Goals		
Club	Signed	Fee	Tot	Start	Sub	FA	FL	Lge	FA	FL
Sunderland	7/92	Trainee	225	205	20	10	16	14	1	0
FAPL Summary by Club										
Sunderland	1996/7		35	32	3	2	2	3	1	0
Totals			*35*	*32*	*3*	*2*	*2*	*3*	*1*	*0*

GRAYSON Simon — Aston Villa

Full Name: Simon Nicholas Grayson
DOB: 16-Dec-69 Ripon

Previous Club Details			Apps					Goals		
Club	Signed	Fee	Tot	Start	Sub	FA	FL	Lge	FA	FL
Leeds U.	6/88	Trainee	2	2	0	0	0	0	0	0
Leicester C.	3/92	£50k	188	175	13	9	18	4	0	2
Aston Villa			48	32	16	5	2	0	2	0
FAPL Summary by Club										
Leicester C.	94/5 to 96/7		70	70	0	6	9	0	0	2
Aston Villa	97/8 to 98/9		48	32	16	5	2	0	2	0
Totals			*118*	*102*	*16*	*11*	*11*	*0*	*2*	*2*

GRIFFIN Andy — Newcastle United

Full Name: Andrew Griffin
DOB: 07-Mar-79 Billinge

Previous Club Details

Club	Signed	Fee	Apps Tot	Start	Sub	FA	FL	Goals Lge	FA	FL
Stoke C.	9/96	Trainee	34	29	5	1	1	1	0	0
Newcastle U.	1/98	£1.5m >	22	18	0	3	1	0	0	0
FAPL Summary by Club										
Newcastle U.	97/8 to 98/9		18	18	0	3	1	0	0	0
Totals			*18*	*18*	*0*	*3*	*1*	*0*	*0*	*0*

GUDMUNDSSON Johann — Watford

Full Name: Johann Gudmundsson
DOB: 05-Dec-77 Iceland

Previous Club Details

Club	Signed	Fee	Apps Tot	Start	Sub	FA	FL	Goals Lge	FA	FL
Keflavik										
Watford			13	6	7	0	0	2	0	0

GUNNLAUGSSON Arnar — Leicester City

Full Name: Arnar Bergmann Gunnlaugsson
DOB: 06-Mar-73 Iceland

Previous Club Details

Club	Signed	Fee	Apps Tot	Start	Sub	FA	FL	Goals Lge	FA	FL
IA Akranes										
Bolton W.	7/97	£100k	44	25	19	2	9	12	0	2
Leicester C.	2/99	£2m	9	5	4	0	0	0	0	0
FAPL Summary by Club										
Bolton Wanderers	1997/8		15	2	13	1	3	0	0	1
Leicester C.	1998/9		9	5	4	0	0	0	0	0
Totals			*24*	*7*	*17*	*1*	*3*	*0*	*0*	*1*

GUPPY Steve — Leicester City

Full Name: Stephen Guppy
DOB: 29-Mar-69 Winchester

Previous Club Details

Club	Signed	Fee	Apps Tot	Start	Sub	FA	FL	Goals Lge	FA	FL
Wycombe W.	1989		41	41	0	8	4	8	2	0
Newcastle U.	8/94	£150k	0	0	0	0	1	0	0	0
Port Vale	11/94	£225k	105	102	3	8	7	12	0	0
Leicester C.	2/97	£850k	88	87	1	4	9	6	1	0
FAPL Summary by Club										
Leicester C.	96/7 to 98/9		88	87	1	4	9	6	1	0
Totals			*88*	*87*	*1*	*4*	*9*	*6*	*1*	*0*

HAALAND Alf-Inge — Leeds United

Full Name: Alf-Inge Rasdal Haaland
DOB: 23-Nov-72 Stavanger, Norway

Previous Club Details

Club	Signed	Fee	Apps Tot	Start	Sub	FA	FL	Goals Lge	FA	FL
Young Boys										
N.Forest	1/94		75	66	9	6	7	7	0	0
Leeds U.	6/97	£1.6m	61	50	11	6	3	8	0	0
FAPL Summary by Club										
N.Forest	94/5 to 96/7		71	63	8	6	4	7	0	0
Leeds U.	97/8 to 98/9		61	50	11	6	3	8	0	0
Totals			*132*	*113*	*19*	*12*	*7*	*15*	*0*	*0*

HALL Marcus — Coventry City

Full Name: Marcus Hall
DOB: 24-Mar-76 Coventry

Previous Club Details

Club	Signed	Fee	Apps Tot	Start	Sub	FA	FL	Goals Lge	FA	FL
Coventry C.	7/94	Trainee	73	58	15	9	11	1	0	1
FAPL Summary by Club										
Coventry C.	94/5 to 98/9		73	58	15	9	11	1	0	1
Totals			*73*	*58*	*15*	*9*	*11*	*1*	*0*	*1*

HALL Paul — Coventry City

Full Name: Paul Anthony Hall
DOB: 03-Jul-72 Manchester

Previous Club Details

Club	Signed	Fee	Apps Tot	Start	Sub	FA	FL	Goals Lge	FA	FL
Torquay U.	7/90	Trainee	93	77	16	5	7	1	2	0
Portsmouth	3/93	£70k	188	148	40	8	13	37	2	1
Coventry C.	8/98	£300k	9	2	7	0	2	0	0	1
FAPL Summary by Club										
Coventry C.	1998/9		9	2	7	0	2	0	0	1
Totals			*9*	*2*	*7*	*0*	*2*	*0*	*0*	*1*

HALLE Gunnar — Bradford City

Full Name: Gunnar Halle
DOB: 11-Aug-65 Oslo

Previous Club Details

Club	Signed	Fee	Apps Tot	Start	Sub	FA	FL	Goals Lge	FA	FL
Lillestrom										
Oldham A.	2/91	£280k	188	185	3	8	16	17	2	2
Leeds U.	12/96	£400k	70	65	5	9	4	4	0	0
Bradford C.	7/99	£200k								
FAPL Summary by Club										
Oldham A.	92/3 to 93/4		64	63	1	3	4	6	0	1
Leeds U.	96/7 to 98/9		70	65	5	9	4	4	0	0
Totals			*134*	*128*	*6*	*12*	*8*	*10*	*0*	*1*

HAMANN Dietman — Newcastle United

Full Name: Dietman Hamann
DOB: 27-Aug-93 Waldsasson, Germany

Previous Club Details

Club	Signed	Fee	Apps Tot	Start	Sub	FA	FL	Goals Lge	FA	FL
Bayern Munich										
Newcastle U.	8/98	£5.25m	23	22	1	7	1	4	1	0
FAPL Summary by Club										
Newcastle U.	1998/9		23	22	1	7	1	4	1	0
Totals			*23*	*22*	*1*	*7*	*1*	*4*	*1*	*0*

HARPER Kevin — Derby County

Full Name: Kevin Harper
DOB: 15-Jan-76 Oldham

Previous Club Details

Club	Signed	Fee	Apps Tot	Start	Sub	FA	FL	Goals Lge	FA	FL
Hibernian										
Derby Co.	9/98	£300k								
FAPL Summary by Club										
Derby Co.	1998/9		27	6	21	3	3	1	1	0
Totals			*27*	*6*	*21*	*3*	*3*	*1*	*1*	*0*

HARPER Steve — Newcastle United

Full Name: Stephen Alan Harper
DOB: 14-Mar-75 Easington

Previous Club Details

Club	Signed	Fee	Apps Tot	Start	Sub	FA	FL	Goals Lge	FA	FL
Newcastle U.	7/93	Free NL	8	7	1	2	0	0	0	0

Club	Signed	Fee	Tot	Start	Sub	FA	FL	Lge	FA	FL
Bradford C.	9/95	Loan	1	1	0	0	0	0	0	0
Hartlepool U.	8/97	Loan	15	15	0	0	0	0	0	0
Huddersfield	12/97	Loan	24	24	0	2	0	0	0	0
FAPL Summary by Club										
Newcastle U.	1998/9		8	7	1	2	0	0	0	0
Totals			*8*	*7*	*1*	*2*	*0*	*0*	*0*	*0*

HARTE Ian — Leeds United

Full Name: Ian Harte
DOB: 31-Aug-77 Drogheda

Previous Club Details			*Apps*					*Goals*		
Club	Signed	Fee	Tot	Start	Sub	FA	FL	Lge	FA	FL
Leeds U.	12/95	Trainee	65	58	7	9	4	6	2	1
FAPL Summary by Club										
Leeds U.	95/6 to 98/9		65	58	7	9	5	6	2	1
Totals			*65*	*58*	*7*	*9*	*5*	*6*	*2*	*1*

HARTSON John — West Ham United

Full Name: John Hartson
DOB: 05-Apr-75 Swansea

Previous Club Details			*Apps*					*Goals*		
Club	Signed	Fee	Tot	Start	Sub	FA	FL	Lge	FA	FL
Luton T.	12/92	Trainee	34	21	13	5	1	6	0	1
Arsenal	1/95	£2.5m	53	43	10	3	6	14	1	1
West Ham U.	2/97	>£7.5m	60	59	1	7	6	24	3	6
Wimbledon	1/99	£6m	14	12	2	0	0	2	0	0
FAPL Summary by Club										
Arsenal	94/5 to 96/7		53	44	9	3	6	14	1	1
West Ham U.	96/7 to 98/9		60	59	1	7	6	24	3	6
Wimbledon	1998/9		14	12	2	0	0	2	0	0
Totals			*127*	*115*	*12*	*10*	*12*	*40*	*4*	*7*

HASSELBAINK Jimmy — Leeds United

Full Name: Jerrel Hasselbaink
DOB: 27-Mar-72 Surinam

Previous Club Details			*Apps*					*Goals*		
Club	Signed	Fee	Tot	Start	Sub	FA	FL	Lge	FA	FL
Boavista										
Leeds U.	6/97	£2m	69	66	3	9	5	34	5	2
FAPL Summary by Club										
Leeds U.	97/8 to 98/9		69	66	3	9	5	34	5	2
Totals			*69*	*66*	*3*	*9*	*5*	*34*	*5*	*2*

HAZAN Alon — Watford

Full Name: Alon Hazan
DOB: 14-Sep-67 Ashdod, Israel

Previous Club Details			*Apps*					*Goals*		
Club	Signed	Fee	Tot	Start	Sub	FA	FL	Lge	FA	FL
Ironi Ashdod										
Watford	1/98	£200k	33	15	18	0	2	2	0	0

HEDMAN Magnus — Coventry City

Full Name: Magnus Hedman
DOB: 19-Mar-77 Sweden

Previous Club Details			*Apps*					*Goals*		
Club	Signed	Fee	Tot	Start	Sub	FA	FL	Lge	FA	FL
AIK Stockholm										
Coventry C.	7/97	£500k	50	50	0	3	0	0	0	0
FAPL Summary by Club										
Coventry C.	97/8 to 98/9		50	50	0	3	0	0	0	0
Totals			*50*	*50*	*0*	*3*	*0*	*0*	*0*	*0*

HEGGEM Vegard — Liverpool

Full Name: Vegard Heggem
DOB: 13-Jul-75 Norway

Previous Club Details

Club	Signed	Fee	Apps Tot	Start	Sub	FA	FL	Goals Lge	FA	FL
Rennebu, Orkdal										
Rosenborg										
Liverpool	7/98		29	27	2	1	1	2	9	0
FAPL Summary by Club										
Liverpool	1998/9		29	27	2	1	1	2	0	0
Totals			*29*	*27*	*2*	*1*	*1*	*2*	*0*	*0*

HENCHOZ Stephane — Liverpool

Full Name: Stephane Henchoz
DOB: 07-Sep-74 Billens, Switzerland

Previous Club Details

Club	Signed	Fee	Apps Tot	Start	Sub	FA	FL	Goals Lge	FA	FL
Stade Payern, Bulle, Neuchatel Xamax										
Hamburg SV	7/95									
Blackburn R.	7/97	£3m	70	70	0	6	4	0	0	0
Liverpool	7/97	Undisclosed								
FAPL Summary by Club										
Blackburn R.	97/8 to 98/9		70	70	0	6	4	0	0	0
Totals			*70*	*70*	*0*	*6*	*4*	*0*	*0*	*0*

HENDRIE Lee — Aston Villa

Full Name: Lee Hendrie
DOB: 18-May-77 Birmingham

Previous Club Details

Club	Signed	Fee	Apps Tot	Start	Sub	FA	FL	Goals Lge	FA	FL
Aston Villa		Trainee	58	46	12	9	0	6	0	0
FAPL Summary by Club										
Aston Villa	95/6 to 98/9		58	46	12	9	0	6	0	0
Totals			*58*	*46*	*12*	*9*	*0*	*6*	*0*	*0*

HESKEY Emile — Leicester City

Full Name: Emile Heskey
DOB: 11-Jan-78 Leicester

Previous Club Details

Club	Signed	Fee	Apps Tot	Start	Sub	FA	FL	Goals Lge	FA	FL
Leicester C.	10/95	Trainee	131	120	11	7	19	33	0	5
FAPL Summary by Club										
Leicester C.	94/5 to 98/9		101	100	1	7	17	26	0	5
Totals			*101*	*100*	*1*	*7*	*17*	*26*	*0*	*5*

HIDEN Martin — Leeds United

Full Name: Martin Hiden
DOB: 11-Mar-73 Stainz, Austria

Previous Club Details

Club	Signed	Fee	Apps Tot	Start	Sub	FA	FL	Goals Lge	FA	FL
Rapid Vienna										
Leeds U.	2/98	£1.3m	25	25	0	1	1	0	0	0
FAPL Summary by Club										
Leeds U.	97/8 to 98/9		25	25	0	1	1	0	0	0
Totals			*25*	*25*	*0*	*1*	*1*	*0*	*0*	*0*

HILEY Scott — Southampton

Full Name: Scott Hiley
DOB: 27-Sep-68 Plymouth

Previous Club Details

Club	Signed	Fee	Apps Tot	Start	Sub	FA	FL	Goals Lge	FA	FL
Exeter C.	8/86	Train	210	205	5	14	17	12	0	0

Club	Signed	Fee	Tot	Start	Sub	FA	FL	Lge	FA	FL
Birmingham C.	3/93	£100k	49	49	0	1	7	0	0	0
Manchester C.	2/96	£250k	9			0	0	0	0	0
Southampton	8/98	Free	29	27	2	1	0	0	0	0
FAPL Summary by Club										
Manchester C.	1995/6		5	2	3	0	0	0	0	0
Southampton	1998/9		29	27	2	1	0	0	0	0
Totals			*29*	*27*	*2*	*1*	*0*	*0*	*0*	*0*

HINCHCLIFFE Andy — Sheffield Wednesday

Full Name: Andrew George Hinchcliffe
DOB: 05-Feb-69 Manchester

Previous Club Details			*Apps*					*Goals*		
Club	Signed	Fee	Tot	Start	Sub	FA	FL	Lge	FA	FL
Manchester C.	2/86		112	107	5	12	11	8	1	1
Everton	7/90	£800k	182	170	12	14	23	6	1	1
Sheffield W.	1/98	£3.0m	47	47	0	2	2	4	0	0
FAPL Summary by Club										
Everton	92/3 to 97/8		143	134	9	9	18	6	1	1
Sheffield W.	97/8 to 98/9		47	47	0	2	2	4	0	0
Totals			*190*	*181*	*9*	*11*	*20*	*10*	*1*	*1*

HISLOP Shaka — West Ham United

Full Name: Neil Hislop
DOB: 22-Feb-69 London

Previous Club Details			*Apps*					*Goals*		
Club	Signed	Fee	Tot	Start	Sub	FA	FL	Lge	FA	FL
Reading	9/92		104	104	0	3	10	0	0	0
Newcastle U.	8/95	£1.575m	53	53	0	6	8	0	0	0
West Ham U.	7/97	Free	37	37	0	2	2	0	0	0
FAPL Summary by Club										
Newcastle U.	95/6 to 97/8		53	53	0	6	8	0	0	0
West Ham U.	1998/9		37	37	0	2	2	0	0	0
Totals			*90*	*90*	*0*	*8*	*10*	*0*	*0*	*0*

HOPKIN David — Leeds United

Full Name: David Hopkin
DOB: 21-Aug-70 Greenock

Previous Club Details			*Apps*					*Goals*		
Club	Signed	Fee	Tot	Start	Sub	FA	FL	Lge	FA	FL
Morton	1989	NL	48	33	15	2	2	4	1	2
Chelsea	9/92	£300k	40	21	19	5	1	1	0	0
Crystal Palace	7/95	£850k	83	79	4	3	6	21	0	6
Leeds U.	7/97	£3.25m	59	54	5	6	6	5	0	0
FAPL Summary by Club										
Chelsea	92/3 to 94/5		40	21	19	5	1	1	0	0
Leeds U.	97/8 to 98/9		59	54	5	6	6	5	0	0
Totals			*99*	*75*	*24*	*11*	*7*	*6*	*0*	*0*

HOULT Russell — Derby County

Full Name: Russell Hoult
DOB: 22-Nov-72 Leicester

Previous Club Details			*Apps*					*Goals*		
Club	Signed	Fee	Tot	Start	Sub	FA	FL	Lge	FA	FL
Leicester C.	3/91		10	10	0	0	3	0	0	0
Lincoln C.	8/91	Loan	2	2	0	0	1	0	0	0
Bolton W.	11/93	Loan	4	3	1	0	0	0	0	0
Lincoln C.	8/94		15	15	1	0	0	0	0	0
Derby Co.	2/95	£300k	113	111	2	4	3	0	0	0

FAPL Summary by Club										
Derby Co.	96/7 to 98/9		57	56	1	3	1	0	0	0
Totals			*57*	*56*	*1*	*3*	*1*	*0*	*0*	*0*

HOWELLS David — Southampton

Full Name: David Howells
DOB: 15-Dec-67 Guildford

Previous Club Details			*Apps*					*Goals*		
Club	Signed	Fee	Tot	Start	Sub	FA	FL	Lge	FA	FL
Tottenham H.	1/85	App	276	237	39	22	31	22	1	4
Southampton	7/98	Free	9	8	1	1	1	1	0	0
FAPL Summary by Club										
Tottenham H.	92/3 to 97/8		142	131	11	13	12	8	0	2
Southampton	1998/9		9	8	1	1	1	1	0	0
Totals			*151*	*139*	*12*	*14*	*13*	*9*	*0*	*2*

HOWEY Steve — Newcastle United

Full Name: Stephen Norman Howey
DOB: 26-Oct-71 Sunderland

Previous Club Details			*Apps*					*Goals*		
Club	Signed	Fee	Tot	Start	Sub	FA	FL	Lge	FA	FL
Newcastle U.	12/89	Trainee	182	160	22	22	16	6	0	1
FAPL Summary by Club										
Newcastle U.	93/4 to 98/9		108	103	5	14	10	3	0	0
Totals			*108*	*103*	*5*	*14*	*10*	*3*	*0*	*0*

HUCKERBY Darren — Coventry City

Full Name: Darren Carl Huckerby
DOB: 27-Apr-76 Nottingham

Previous Club Details			*Apps*					*Goals*		
Club	Signed	Fee	Tot	Start	Sub	FA	FL	Lge	FA	FL
Lincoln C.	7/93	Trainee	30	20	10	0	2	3	0	0
Newcastle U.	11/95	£400k	1	0	1	1	0	0	0	0
Millwall	9/96	Loan	6	6	0	0	0	3	0	0
Coventry C.	11/96	£1m	93	84	9	12	3	26	6	0
FAPL Summary by Club										
Newcastle U.	1995/6		1	0	1	1	0	0	0	0
Coventry C.	96/7 to 98/9		93	84	9	12	3	28	6	0
Totals			*94*	*84*	*10*	*13*	*3*	*28*	*6*	*0*

HUGHES Aaron — Newcastle United

Full Name: Aaron Hughes
DOB: 08-Nov-79 Magherafelt

Previous Club Details			*Apps*					*Goals*		
Club	Signed	Fee	Tot	Start	Sub	FA	FL	Lge	FA	FL
Newcastle U.	3/97	Trainee	18	16	2	3	2	0	0	0
FAPL Summary by Club										
Newcastle U.	97/8 to 98/9		18	16	2	3	2	0	0	0
Totals			*18*	*16*	*2*	*3*	*2*	*0*	*0*	*0*

HUGHES Ceri — Wimbledon

Full Name: Ceri Morgan Hughes
DOB: 26-Feb-71 Pontypridd

Previous Club Details			*Apps*					*Goals*		
Club	Signed	Fee	Tot	Start	Sub	FA	FL	Lge	FA	FL
Luton T.	7/89	Trainee	175	157	18	11	13	17	2	1
Wimbledon	7/97	£400k	31	21	10	8	3	1	0	0
FAPL Summary by Club										
Wimbledon	97/8 to 98/9		31	21	10	5	3	1	0	0
Totals			*31*	*21*	*10*	*5*	*3*	*1*	*0*	*0*

HUGHES David — Southampton

Full Name: David Robert Hughes
DOB: 30-Dec-72 St Albans

Previous Club Details			*Apps*					*Goals*		
Club	Signed	Fee	Tot	Start	Sub	FA	FL	Lge	FA	FL
Southampton	7/91	Juniors	53	21	32	6	4	3	1	0
FAPL Summary by Club										
Southampton	93/4 to 98/9		53	21	32	6	4	3	1	0
Totals			*53*	*21*	*32*	*6*	*4*	*3*	*1*	*0*

HUGHES Mark — Southampton

Full Name: Leslie Mark Hughes
DOB: 01-Nov-63 Wrexham

Previous Club Details			*Apps*					*Goals*		
Club	Signed	Fee	Tot	Start	Sub	FA	FL	Lge	FA	FL
Manchester U.	11/80	App	89	85	4	10	6	37	4	4
Barcelona	7/86	£2.5m	0	0	0	0	0	0	0	0
Bayern Munich	10/87	Loan	0	0	0	0	0	0	0	0
Manchester U.	7/88	£1.5m	256	251	5	35	32	82	13	12
Chelsea	7/95	£1.5m	95	88	7	14	10	25	9	3
Southampton	7/98	£650k	32	32	0	2	2	1	0	0
FAPL Summary by Club										
Manchester U.	92/3 to 94/5		111	110	1	15	11	35	6	6
Chelsea	95/6 to 97/8		95	88	7	14	10	25	9	3
Southampton	1998/9		32	32	0	2	2	1	0	0
Totals			*238*	*230*	*8*	*31*	*23*	*61*	*15*	*9*

HUGHES Michael — Wimbledon

Full Name: Michael Eamonn Hughes
DOB: 02-Aug-71 Larne

Previous Club Details			*Apps*					*Goals*		
Club	Signed	Fee	Tot	Start	Sub	FA	FL	Lge	FA	FL
Manchester C.	8/88	Trainee	26	25	1	1	0	1	0	0
Strasbourg	7/92	£450k	83	78	5	0	0	7	0	0
West Ham U.	11/94	Free	83	76	7	7	7	5	1	0
Wimbledon	9/97	£800k>	59	57	2	6	4	6	2	1
FAPL Summary by Club										
West Ham U.	94/5 to 97/8		83	76	7	7	7	5	1	0
Wimbledon	97/8 to 98/9		59	57	2	6	4	6	2	1
Totals			*142*	*133*	*9*	*13*	*11*	*11*	*3*	*1*

HUGHES Steve — Arsenal

Full Name: Stephen John Hughes
DOB: 18-Sep-76 Reading

Previous Club Details			*Apps*					*Goals*		
Club	Signed	Fee	Tot	Start	Sub	FA	FL	Lge	FA	FL
Arsenal	7/95	Trainee	46	21	25	12	7	4	1	1
FAPL Summary by Club										
Arsenal	94/5 to 98/9		46	21	25	12	7	4	1	1
Totals			*46*	*21*	*25*	*12*	*7*	*4*	*1*	*1*

HUMPHREYS Richie — Sheffield Wednesday

Full Name: Richard John Humphreys
DOB: 30-Nov-77 Sheffield

Previous Club Details			*Apps*					*Goals*		
Club	Signed	Fee	Tot	Start	Sub	FA	FL	Lge	FA	FL
Sheffield W.	2/96	Trainee	60	27	33	9	2	4	4	0
FAPL Summary by Club										
Sheffield W.	95/6 to 98/9		60	27	33	9	2	4	4	0
Totals			*60*	*27*	*33*	*9*	*2*	*4*	*4*	*0*

HUNT Jon — Derby County

Full Name: Jonathan Richard Hunt
DOB: 02-Nov-71 Camden

Previous Club Details			*Apps*					*Goals*		
Club	Signed	Fee	Tot	Start	Sub	FA	FL	Lge	FA	FL
Barnet	1989	Juniors	33	12	21	1	1	0	0	0
Southend U.	7/93	Free	49	41	8	1	4	6	0	0
Birmingham C.	9/94	£50k	77	67	10	4	15	18	1	2
Derby Co.	7/97	£500k	25	7	18	3	4	1	0	0
FAPL Summary by Club										
Derby Co.	97/8 to 98/9		25	7	18	3	4	1	0	0
Totals			*25*	*7*	*18*	*3*	*4*	*1*	*0*	*0*

HUTCHISON Don — Everton

Full Name: Donald Hutchison
DOB: 09-May-71 Gateshead

Previous Club Details			*Apps*					*Goals*		
Club	Signed	Fee	Tot	Start	Sub	FA	FL	Lge	FA	FL
Hartlepool U.	3/90		24	19	5	2	2	3	0	0
Liverpool	11/90	£175k	45	33	12	3	8	7	0	2
West Ham U.	8/94	£1.5m	35	30	5	1	3	11	0	2
Sheffield U.	1/96	£1.2m	78	70	8	5	5	5	1	0
Everton	2/98	£1.0m	44	40	4	4	4	4	0	1
FAPL Summary by Club										
Liverpool	92/3 to 93/4		42	33	9	3	8	7	0	2
West Ham U.	94/5 to 95/6		28	23	5	1	3	9	0	2
Everton	97/8 to 98/9		44	40	4	4	4	4	0	1
Totals			*114*	*96*	*18*	*8*	*15*	*20*	*0*	*5*

HYDE Micah — Watford

Full Name: Micah Anthony Hyde
DOB: 10-Nov-74 Newham

Previous Club Details			*Apps*					*Goals*		
Club	Signed	Fee	Tot	Start	Sub	FA	FL	Lge	FA	FL
Cambridge U.	5/93	Trainee	107	89	18	9	3	13	0	0
Watford	7/97	£225k	84	83	1	5	4	6	0	0

IMPEY Andy — Leicester City

Full Name: Andrew Rodney Impey
DOB: 30-Sep-71 Hammersmith

Previous Club Details			*Apps*					*Goals*		
Club	Signed	Fee	Tot	Start	Sub	FA	FL	Lge	FA	FL
QPR	6/90	£35k NL	187	177	10	10	16	13	1	3
West Ham U.	9/97	£1.3m	27	25	2	3	4	0	0	0
Leicester C.	11/98	£1.6m	18	17	1	1	0	0	0	0
FAPL Summary by Club										
QPR	92/3 to 95/6		142	138	4	7	13	11	1	2
West Ham U.	97/8 to 98/9		27	25	2	3	4	0	0	0
Leicester C.	1998/9		18	17	1	1	0	0	0	0
Totals			*187*	*180*	7	*11*	*17*	*11*	*1*	2

INCE Paul — Liverpool

Full Name: Paul Emerson Carlyle Ince
DOB: 21-Oct-67 Ilford

Previous Club Details			*Apps*					*Goals*		
Club	Signed	Fee	Tot	Start	Sub	FA	FL	Lge	FA	FL
West Ham U.	7/85		72	66	6	10	9	7	1	3
Manchester U.	8/89	£125k	170	167	3	21	24	20	1	2
Internazionale	6/95	£7.5m								
Liverpool	7/97	£4.2m	65	65	0	3	6	14	1	1

FAPL Summary by Club										
Manchester U.	92/3 to 94/5		116	116	0	15	8	19	1	0
Liverpool	97/8 to 98/9		65	65	0	3	6	14	1	1
Totals			*181*	*181*	*0*	*18*	*14*	*33*	*2*	*1*

IRWIN Denis — Manchester United

Full Name: Joseph Denis Irwin
DOB: 31-Oct-65 Cork

Previous Club Details			*Apps*					*Goals*		
Club	Signed	Fee	Tot	Start	Sub	FA	FL	Lge	FA	FL
Leeds U.	11/83	App	72	72	0	3	5	1	0	0
Oldham A.	5/86	Free	167	166	1	13	19	4	0	3
Manchester U.	6/90	£625k	310	301	9	42	31	19	7	0
FAPL Summary by Club										
Manchester U.	92/3 to 98/9		238	231	7	36	16	15	7	0
Totals			*238*	*231*	*7*	*36*	*16*	*15*	*7*	*0*

IVERSEN Steffen — Tottenham Hotspur

Full Name: Steffen Iversen
DOB: 10-Nov-76 Oslo

Previous Club Details			*Apps*					*Goals*		
Club	Signed	Fee	Tot	Start	Sub	FA	FL	Lge	FA	FL
Rosenborg	1995		25	8	17	0	0	8	0	0
Tottenham H.	11/96	£2.7m	56	46	10	7	6	15	2	2
FAPL Summary by Club										
Tottenham H.	96/7 to 98/9		56	46	10	7	6	15	2	2
Totals			*56*	*46*	*10*	*7*	*6*	*15*	*2*	*2*

IZZET Muzzy — Leicester City

Full Name: Mustafa Izzet
DOB: 31-Oct-74 Mile End, London

Previous Club Details			*Apps*					*Goals*		
Club	Signed	Fee	Tot	Start	Sub	FA	FL	Lge	FA	FL
Chelsea	5/93	Trainee								
Leicester C.	3/96	£800k	111	109	2	7	13	13	0	2
FAPL Summary by Club										
Leicester C.	96/7 to 98/9		102	101	1	7	13	12	0	2
Totals			*102*	*101*	*1*	*7*	*13*	*12*	*0*	*2*

JACOBS Wayne — Bradford City

Full Name: Wayne Graham Jacobs
DOB: 03-Feb-69 Sheffield

Previous Club Details			*Apps*					*Goals*		
Club	Signed	Fee	Tot	Start	Sub	FA	FL	Lge	FA	FL
Sheffield W.	1/87	Apprentice	6	5	1	0	3	0	0	0
Hull C.	3/88	£27k	129	127	2	8	7	4	0	0
Rotherham U.	8/93	Free	42	40	2	1	4	2	0	0
Bradford C.	8/94	Free	185	181	4	10	14	9	2	0

JAMES David — Aston Villa

Full Name: David Benjamin James
DOB: 01-Aug-70 Welwyn Garden City

Previous Club Details			*Apps*					*Goals*		
Club	Signed	Fee	Tot	Start	Sub	FA	FL	Lge	FA	FL
Watford	7/88	Trainee	89	89	0	2	6	0	0	0
Liverpool	7/92	£1m	214	213	1	20	22	0	0	0
Aston Villa	6/99	£1.7m								
FAPL Summary by Club										
Liverpool	92/3 to 98/9		214	213	1	20	21	0	0	0
Totals			*214*	*213*	*1*	*20*	*21*	*0*	*0*	*0*

JEFFERS Francis — Everton

Full Name: Francis Jeffers
DOB: 25-Jan-81 Merseyside

Previous Club Details			*Apps*					*Goals*		
Club	Signed	Fee	Tot	Start	Sub	FA	FL	Lge	FA	FL
Everton		Trainee	16	11	5	2	0	6	1	0
FAPL Summary by Club										
Everton	97/8 to 98/9		16	11	5	2	0	6	1	0
Totals			*16*	*11*	*5*	*2*	*0*	*6*	*1*	*0*

JOACHIM Julian — Aston Villa

Full Name: Julian Kevin Joachim
DOB: 12-Sep-74 Peterborough

Previous Club Details			*Apps*					*Goals*		
Club	Signed	Fee	Tot	Start	Sub	FA	FL	Lge	FA	FL
Leicester C.	9/92	Trainee	99	77	22	5	9	25	1	3
Aston Villa	2/96	£1.5m	88	52	36	5	2	26	1	0
FAPL Summary by Club										
Leicester C.	1994/5		15	11	4	0	2	3	0	0
Aston Villa	95/6 to 98/9		88	52	36	5	2	26	1	0
Totals			*103*	*63*	*40*	*5*	*4*	*29*	*1*	*0*

JOHNSEN Ronny — Manchester United

Full Name: Ronny Jean Johnsen
DOB: 10-Jun-69 Norway

Previous Club Details			*Apps*					*Goals*		
Club	Signed	Fee	Tot	Start	Sub	FA	FL	Lge	FA	FL
Lillestrom	(1995)		23	23	0	0	0	4	0	0
Besiktas	1996		22	22	1	0	0	1	0	0
Manchester U.	7/96	£1.2m	75	63	12	10	2	5	1	0
FAPL Summary by Club										
Manchester U.	96/7 to 98/9		75	63	12	10	2	5	1	0
Totals			*75*	*63*	*12*	*10*	*2*	*5*	*1*	*0*

JOHNSON Richard — Watford

Full Name: Richard Mark Johnson
DOB: 27-Apr-74 Kurri Kurri, Australia

Previous Club Details			*Apps*					*Goals*		
Club	Signed	Fee	Tot	Start	Sub	FA	FL	Lge	FA	FL
Watford	5/92	Trainee	204	184	20	13	13	17	1	1

JOHNSTON Alan — Sunderland

Full Name: Alan Johnston
DOB: 14-Dec-73 Glasgow

Previous Club Details			*Apps*					*Goals*		
Club	Signed	Fee	Tot	Start	Sub	FA	FL	Lge	FA	FL
Hearts	1992	NL	84	46	38	5	5	12	0	2
Rennes	7/96		23	23	0	0	0	2	0	0
Sunderland	3/97	£550k	6	4	2	0	0	1	0	0
FAPL Summary by Club										
Sunderland	1996/7		6	4	2	0	0	1	0	0
Totals			*6*	*4*	*2*	*0*	*0*	*1*	*0*	*0*

JONES Paul — Southampton

Full Name: Paul Steven Jones
DOB: 18-Apr-67 Chick

Previous Club Details			*Apps*					*Goals*		
Club	Signed	Fee	Tot	Start	Sub	FA	FL	Lge	FA	FL
Wolverhampton	7/91	£40k nl	33	33	0	5	2	0	0	0
Stockport Co.	7/96	£60k	46	46	0	4	11	0	0	0
Southampton	7/97	£900k	69	69	0	3	6	0	0	0

FAPL Summary by Club

Club	Signed	Fee	Tot	Start	Sub	FA	FL	Lge	FA	FL
Southampton	97/8 to 98/9		69	69	0	3	6	0	0	0
Totals			*69*	*69*	*0*	*3*	*6*	*0*	*0*	*0*

JONK Wim — Sheffield Wednesday

Full Name: Wim Jonk
DOB: 12-Oct-66 Holland

Previous Club Details			*Apps*					*Goals*		
Club	Signed	Fee	Tot	Start	Sub	FA	FL	Lge	FA	FL
PSV										
Sheffield W.	8/98	£2.5m	38	38	0	3	2	2	0	0
FAPL Summary by Club										
Sheffield W.	1998/9		38	38	0	3	2	2	0	0
Totals			*38*	*38*	*0*	*3*	*2*	*2*	*0*	*0*

JUPP Duncan — Wimbledon

Full Name: Duncan Alan Jupp
DOB: 25-Jan-75 Guildford

Previous Club Details			*Apps*					*Goals*		
Club	Signed	Fee	Tot	Start	Sub	FA	FL	Lge	FA	FL
Fulham	7/93	Trainee	105	101	4	10	12	2	1	2
Wimbledon	6/96	£125k	15	12	3	5	5	0	0	0
FAPL Summary by Club										
Wimbledon	96/7 to 98/9		15	12	3	5	4	0	0	0
Totals			*15*	*12*	*3*	*5*	*4*	*0*	*0*	*0*

KAAMARK Pontus — Leicester City

Full Name: Pontus Sven Kaamark
DOB: 05-Apr-69 Vasteras, Sweden

Previous Club Details			*Apps*					*Goals*		
Club	Signed	Fee	Tot	Start	Sub	FA	FL	Lge	FA	FL
IFK Gothenburg			126	114	12			1		
Leicester C.	11/95	£840k	65	60	5	4	5	0	0	0
FAPL Summary by Club										
Leicester C.	96/7 to 98/9		64	59	5	4	5	0	0	0
Totals			*64*	*59*	*5*	*4*	*5*	*0*	*0*	*0*

KACHLOUL Hassan — Southampton

Full Name: Hassan Kachloul
DOB:

Previous Club Details			*Apps*					*Goals*		
Club	Signed	Fee	Tot	Start	Sub	FA	FL	Lge	FA	FL
St Etienne										
Southampton	10/98	Free	22	18	4	2	0	5	0	0
FAPL Summary by Club										
Southampton	1998/9		22	18	4	2	0	5	0	0
Totals			*22*	*18*	*4*	*2*	*0*	*5*	*0*	*0*

KANU Nwankwo — Arsenal

Full Name: Nwankwo Kanu
DOB: 01-Aug-76 Owerri, Nireria

Previous Club Details			*Apps*					*Goals*		
Club	Signed	Fee	Tot	Start	Sub	FA	FL	Lge	FA	FL
Fed Works, Iwanyanwu										
Ajax	1993		54					25		
Internazionale	1996									
Arsenal	1/99	£4.5m	12	5	7	5	0	6	1	0
FAPL Summary by Club										
Arsenal	1998/9		12	5	7	5	0	6	1	0
Totals			*12*	*5*	*7*	*5*	*0*	*6*	*1*	*0*

KEANE Roy — Manchester United

Full Name: Roy Maurice Keane
DOB: 10-Aug-71 Cork

Previous Club Details

Club	Signed	Fee	Apps Tot	Start	Sub	FA	FL	Goals Lge	FA	FL
Cobh Ramblers										
N.Forest	6/90	£10k	114	114	0	18	17	22	3	6
Manchester U.	7/93	£3.75m	156	149	7	30	11	19	1	0

FAPL Summary by Club

Club	Seasons		Tot	Start	Sub	FA	FL	Lge	FA	FL
N.Forest	1992/3		40	40	0	4	5	6	1	1
Manchester U.	93/4 to 98/9		156	149	7	30	11	19	1	0
Totals			*196*	*189*	*7*	*34*	*16*	*25*	*2*	*1*

KELLER Kasey — Leicester City

Full Name: Kasey Keller
DOB: 27-Nov-69 Washington, USA

Previous Club Details

Club	Signed	Fee	Apps Tot	Start	Sub	FA	FL	Goals Lge	FA	FL
Millwall	02/92	Free	176	176	0	8	14	0	0	0
Leicester C.	08/96	£900k	100	100	0	8	16	0	0	0

FAPL Summary by Club

Club	Seasons		Tot	Start	Sub	FA	FL	Lge	FA	FL
Leicester C.	1996/7 to 98/9		100	100	0	8	16	0	0	0
Totals			*100*	*100*	*0*	*8*	*16*	*0*	*0*	*0*

KELLER Marc — West Ham United

Full Name: Marc Keller
DOB: 14-Jan-68 France

Previous Club Details

Club	Signed	Fee	Apps Tot	Start	Sub	FA	FL	Goals Lge	FA	FL
Racing Strasbourg, Karlsruhe										
West Ham U.	4/98		21	17	4	0	1	5	0	0

FAPL Summary by Club

Club	Seasons		Tot	Start	Sub	FA	FL	Lge	FA	FL
West Ham U.	1998/9		21	17	4	0	1	5	0	0
Totals			*21*	*17*	*4*	*0*	*1*	*5*	*0*	*0*

KENNEDY Mark — Wimbledon

Full Name: Mark Kennedy
DOB: 15-May-76 Dublin

Previous Club Details

Club	Signed	Fee	Apps Tot	Start	Sub	FA	FL	Goals Lge	FA	FL
Millwall	5/92	Trainee	43	37	6	4	7	9	1	2
Liverpool	3/95	£1.5m +	16	5	11	1	2	0	0	0
Wimbledon	3/98	£1.75m	21	11	10	2	5	0	0	1

FAPL Summary by Club

Club	Seasons		Tot	Start	Sub	FA	FL	Lge	FA	FL
Liverpool	94/5 to 97/8		16	5	11	1	2	0	0	0
Wimbledon	97/8 to 98/9		21	11	10	2	5	0	0	1
Totals			*37*	*16*	*21*	*3*	*7*	*0*	*0*	*1*

KENNEDY Peter — Watford

Full Name: Peter Henry James Kennedy
DOB: 13-Sep-73 Lurhan, N.Ireland

Previous Club Details

Club	Signed	Fee	Apps Tot	Start	Sub	FA	FL	Goals Lge	FA	FL
Portadown										
Notts Co.	8/96	£100k	22	20	2	3	0	0	1	0
Watford	7/97	£130k	80	80	0	6	6	17	2	1

KEOWN Martin — Arsenal

Full Name: Martin Raymond Keown
DOB: 24-Jul-66 Oxford

Previous Club Details

Club	Signed	Fee	Tot	Start	Sub	FA	FL	Lge	FA	FL
			Apps					*Goals*		
Arsenal	1/84	App	22	22	0	5	0	0	0	0
Brighton HA	2/85	Loan	23	21	2	0	2	1	0	1
Aston Villa	6/86	£200k	112	109	3	6	13	3	0	0
Everton	8/89	£750k	96	92	4	13	11	0	0	0
Arsenal	2/93	£2m	199	181	18	21	18	3	0	1
FAPL Summary by Club										
Everton	1992/3		13	13	0	2	4	0	0	0
Arsenal	92/3 to 98/9		199	181	18	21	18	3	0	1
Totals			*212*	*194*	*18*	*23*	*22*	*3*	*0*	*1*

KETSBAIA Temuri — Newcastle United

Full Name: Temuri Ketsbaia
DOB: 18-Mar-68 Gale, Georgia

Previous Club Details

Club	Signed	Fee	Tot	Start	Sub	FA	FL	Lge	FA	FL
			Apps					*Goals*		
AEK Athens										
Newcastle U.	7/97	Free	57	30	27	11	2	8	3	0
FAPL Summary by Club										
Newcastle U.	97/8 to 98/9		57	30	27	11	2	8	3	0
Totals			*57*	*30*	*27*	*11*	*2*	*8*	*3*	*0*

KEWELL Harry — Leeds United

Full Name: Harold Kewell
DOB: 22-Sep-78 Australia

Previous Club Details

Club	Signed	Fee	Tot	Start	Sub	FA	FL	Lge	FA	FL
			Apps					*Goals*		
Aus. Academy Sport										
Leeds U.	12/95		70	64	6	9	4	11	3	3
FAPL Summary by Club										
Leeds U.	95/6 to 98/9		70	64	6	9	4	11	3	3
Totals			*70*	*64*	*6*	*9*	*4*	*11*	*3*	*3*

KIMBLE Alan — Wimbledon

Full Name: Alan Frank Kimble
DOB: 06-Aug-66 Dagenham

Previous Club Details

Club	Signed	Fee	Tot	Start	Sub	FA	FL	Lge	FA	FL
			Apps					*Goals*		
Charlton A.	8/84		6	6	0	0	0	0	0	0
Exeter C.	8/85	Loan	1	1	0	0	1	0	0	0
Cambridge U.	8/86	Free	299	295	4	29	24	24	1	0
Wimbledon	7/93	£175k	152	144	8	22	18	0	0	0
FAPL Summary by Club										
Wimbledon	93/4 to 98/9		153	144	9	22	18	0	0	0
Totals			*153*	*144*	*9*	*22*	*18*	*0*	*0*	*0*

KINDER Vladimir — Middlesbrough

Full Name: Vladimir Kinder
DOB: 04-Mar-69 Bratislava

Previous Club Details

Club	Signed	Fee	Tot	Start	Sub	FA	FL	Lge	FA	FL
			Apps					*Goals*		
Slovan Bratislava	1990		148	140	8	0	0	19	0	0
Middlesbrough	1/97	£1m	37	29	8	4	7	5	0	0
FAPL Summary by Club										
Middlesbrough	96/7 to 98/9		11	4	7	3	2	3	0	0
Totals			*11*	*4*	*7*	*3*	*2*	*3*	*0*	*0*

KITSON Paul — West Ham United

Full Name: Paul Kitson
DOB: 09-Jan-71 Peterlee

Previous Club Details			*Apps*					*Goals*		
Club	Signed	Fee	Tot	Start	Sub	FA	FL	Lge	FA	FL
Leicester C.	12/88		50	39	11	2	5	6	1	3
Derby Co.	3/92	£1.3m	105	105	0	5	7	36	1	3
Newcastle U.	9/94	£2.25m	36	26	10	9	5	10	3	1
West Ham U.	2/97	£2.3m	44	39	5	2	2	15	1	0
FAPL Summary by Club										
Newcastle U.	94/5 to 96/7		36	26	10	9	5	10	3	1
West Ham U.	96/7 to 98/9		44	39	5	2	2	15	1	0
Totals			*80*	*65*	*15*	*11*	*7*	*25*	*4*	*1*

KONJIC Mohamed — Coventry City

Full Name: Mohamed Konjic
DOB: 14-May-70 Bosnia-Herzegovina

Previous Club Details			*Apps*					*Goals*		
Club	Signed	Fee	Tot	Start	Sub	FA	FL	Lge	FA	FL
Sloboda-Tuzia, Croatia Belisce, Croatia Zagreb, FC Zurich, AS Monaco										
Coventry C.	1/99	£2m	4	3	1	0	0	0	0	0
FAPL Summary by Club										
Coventry C.	1998/9		4	3	1	0	0	0	0	0
Totals			*4*	*3*	*1*	*0*	*0*	*0*	*0*	*0*

KORSTEN Willem — Tottenham Hotspur

Full Name: Willem Korsten
DOB: 21-Jan-75 Boxtel, Holland

Previous Club Details			*Apps*					*Goals*		
Club	Signed	Fee	Tot	Start	Sub	FA	FL	Lge	FA	FL
NEC Nijmegen, Vitesse										
Leeds U.	2/99	Loan	7	4	3	3	0	2	0	0
Tottenham H.	7/99									
FAPL Summary by Club										
Leeds U.	1998/9		7	4	3	3	0	2	0	0
Totals			*7*	*4*	*3*	*3*	*0*	*2*	*0*	*0*

KOZLUK Rob — Derby County

Full Name: Robert Kozluk
DOB: 05-Aug-77 Mansfield

Previous Club Details			*Apps*					*Goals*		
Club	Signed	Fee	Tot	Start	Sub	FA	FL	Lge	FA	FL
Derby Co.		Trainee	16	9	7	3	3	0	0	0
FAPL Summary by Club										
Derby Co.	97/8 to 98/9		16	9	7	3	3	0	0	0
Totals			*16*	*9*	*7*	*3*	*3*	*0*	*0*	*0*

KVARME Bjorn Tore — Liverpool

Full Name: Bjorn Tore Kvarme
DOB: 17-Jul-72 Trondheim

Previous Club Details			*Apps*					*Goals*		
Club	Signed	Fee	Tot	Start	Sub	FA	FL	Lge	FA	FL
Rosenborg			67	59	8			1		
Liverpool	1/97	Free	45	39	6	3	2	0	0	0
FAPL Summary by Club										
Liverpool	96/7 to 98/9		45	39	6	2	2	0	0	0
Totals			*45*	*39*	*6*	*2*	*2*	*0*	*0*	*0*

LAMBOURDE Bernard — Chelsea

Full Name: Bernard Lambourde
DOB: 11-May-71 Guadeloupe

Previous Club Details

Club	Signed	Fee	Apps Tot	Start	Sub	FA	FL	Goals Lge	FA	FL
Cannes, Bordeaux										
Chelsea	6/97	£1.5m	24	17	7	2	6	0	0	0

FAPL Summary by Club

Club	Seasons	Tot	Start	Sub	FA	FL	Lge	FA	FL
Chelsea	97/8 to 98/9	24	17	7	2	6	0	0	0
Totals		*24*	*17*	*7*	*2*	*6*	*0*	*0*	*0*

LAMPARD Frank — West Ham United

Full Name: Frank Lampard Jnr
DOB: 21-Jun-78 Romford

Previous Club Details

Club	Signed	Fee	Apps Tot	Start	Sub	FA	FL	Goals Lge	FA	FL
West Ham U.		Trainee	84	68	16	8	9	9	1	5
Swansea C.	10/95	Loan	9	8	1	0	0	1	0	0

FAPL Summary by Club

Club	Seasons	Tot	Start	Sub	FA	FL	Lge	FA	FL
West Ham U.	95/6 to 98/9	84	68	16	8	9	9	1	5
Totals		*84*	*68*	*16*	*8*	*9*	*9*	*1*	*5*

LAURSEN Jacob — Derby County

Full Name: Jacob Laursen
DOB: 06-Oct-71 Denmark

Previous Club Details

Club	Signed	Fee	Apps Tot	Start	Sub	FA	FL	Goals Lge	FA	FL
Silkeborg			128					8		
Derby Co.	7/96	£500k	101	99	2	7	7	2	0	0

FAPL Summary by Club

Club	Seasons	Tot	Start	Sub	FA	FL	Lge	FA	FL
Derby Co.	96/7 to 98/9	101	99	2	7	7	2	0	0
Totals		*101*	*99*	*2*	*7*	*7*	*2*	*0*	*0*

LAWRENCE Jamie — Bradford City

Full Name: James Hubert Lawrence
DOB: 08-Mar-70 Balham

Previous Club Details

Club	Signed	Fee	Apps Tot	Start	Sub	FA	FL	Goals Lge	FA	FL
Sunderland	10/93	NL	4	2	2	0	1	0	0	0
Doncaster R.	3/94	£20k	25	16	9	1	2	3	0	0
Leicester C.	1/95	£125k	47	21	26	2	7	1	0	2
Bradford C.	6/97	£50k	78	71	7	3	5	5	0	0

FAPL Summary by Club

Club	Seasons	Tot	Start	Sub	FA	FL	Lge	FA	FL
Leicester C.	94/5 to 96/7	32	11	21	2	7	1	0	2
Totals		*32*	*11*	*21*	*2*	*7*	*1*	*0*	*2*

LAZARIDIS Stan — West Ham United

Full Name: Stanley Lazaridis
DOB: 16-Aug-72 Perth, W.Australia

Previous Club Details

Club	Signed	Fee	Apps Tot	Start	Sub	FA	FL	Goals Lge	FA	FL
West Adelaide (Aus)										
West Ham U.	8/95	£300k	79	53	26	10	7	3	0	0

FAPL Summary by Club

Club	Seasons	Tot	Start	Sub	FA	FL	Lge	FA	FL
West Ham U.	95/6 to 98/9	79	53	26	10	7	3	0	0
Totals		*79*	*53*	*26*	*10*	*7*	*3*	*0*	*0*

LE SAUX Graeme — Chelsea

Full Name: Graeme Pierre Le Saux
DOB: 17-Oct-68 Jersey

Previous Club Details			*Apps*					*Goals*		
Club	Signed	Fee	Tot	Start	Sub	FA	FL	Lge	FA	FL
Chelsea	12/87	Free	90	77	13	8	13	8	0	1
Blackburn R.	3/93	Swap	130	128	2	8	10	7	0	0
Chelsea	8/97	£5.0m	57	56	1	7	4	1	1	1
FAPL Summary by Club										
Chelsea	1992/3		14	10	4	1	4	0	0	0
Blackburn R.	92/3 to 96/7		130	128	2	8	10	7	0	0
Chelsea	97/8 to 98/9		57	56	1	7	4	1	1	1
Totals			*201*	*194*	*7*	*16*	*18*	*8*	*1*	*1*

LE TISSIER Matthew — Southampton

Full Name: Matthew Paul Le Tissier
DOB: 14-Oct-68 Guernsey

Previous Club Details			*Apps*					*Goals*		
Club	Signed	Fee	Tot	Start	Sub	FA	FL	Lge	FA	FL
Southampton	10/86	App	413	366	47	32	47	158	12	26
FAPL Summary by Club										
Southampton	92/3 to 98/9		240	223	17	16	21	98	7	15
Totals			*240*	*223*	*17*	*16*	*21*	*98*	*7*	*15*

LEABURN Carl — Wimbledon

Full Name: Carl Winston Leaburn
DOB: 30-Mar-69 Lewisham

Previous Club Details			*Apps*					*Goals*		
Club	Signed	Fee	Tot	Start	Sub	FA	FL	Lge	FA	FL
Charlton A.	4/87	App	322	276	46	21	19	53	4	5
Wimbledon	1/98	£300k	38	29	9	3	7	4	0	1
FAPL Summary by Club										
Wimbledon	97/8 to 98/9		38	29	9	3	7	4	0	1
Totals			*38*	*29*	*9*	*3*	*7*	*4*	*0*	*1*

LEBOEUF Franck — Chelsea

Full Name: Franck Leboeuf
DOB: 22-Jan-68 Marseille

Previous Club Details			*Apps*					*Goals*		
Club	Signed	Fee	Tot	Start	Sub	FA	FL	Lge	FA	FL
Hyeres	1986		14					1		
Meaux	1987		39					3		
Laval	1988		69					10		
Strasbourg	1991		189					49		
Chelsea	7/96	£2.5m	91	91	0	12	8	15	1	2
FAPL Summary by Club										
Chelsea	96/7 to 98/9		91	91	0	12	8	15	2	2
Totals			*91*	*91*	*0*	*12*	*8*	*15*	*2*	*2*

LEE Robert — Newcastle United

Full Name: Robert Martin Lee
DOB: 01-Feb-66 West Ham

Previous Club Details			*Apps*					*Goals*		
Club	Signed	Fee	Tot	Start	Sub	FA	FL	Lge	FA	FL
Charlton A.	7/83		298	274	24	14	19	59	2	1
Newcastle U.	9/92	£700k	235	226	9	23	15	43	4	3
FAPL Summary by Club										
Newcastle U.	93/4 to 98/9		199	190	9	19	12	32	2	2
Totals			*199*	*190*	*9*	*19*	*12*	*32*	*2*	*2*

LENNON Neil — Leicester City

Full Name: Neil Francis Lennon
DOB: 25-Jun-71 Lurgan

Previous Club Details			*Apps*					*Goals*		
Club	Signed	Fee	Tot	Start	Sub	FA	FL	Lge	FA	FL
Manchester C.	8/89	Trainee	1	1	0	0	0	0	0	0

Club	Signed	Fee	Tot	Start	Sub	FA	FL	Lge	FA	FL
Crewe Alex.	9/90	Free	147	142	5	12	9	15	1	1
Leicester C.	2/96	£750k	124	123	1	6	16	5	0	2
FAPL Summary by Club										
Leicester C.	96/7 to 98/9		109	109	0	6	16	4	0	2
Totals			*109*	*109*	*0*	*6*	*16*	*4*	*0*	*2*

LEONHARDSEN Oyvind — Liverpool

Full Name: Oyvind Leonhardsen
DOB: 17-Aug-70 Norway

Previous Club Details			*Apps*					*Goals*		
Club	Signed	Fee	Tot	Start	Sub	FA	FL	Lge	FA	FL
Rosenborg	(1992)		63	63	0			20		
Wimbledon	1/95	£660k	76	73	3	17	9	13	2	1
Liverpool	6/97	£3.5m	37	34	3	1	6	7	0	0
FAPL Summary by Club										
Wimbledon	94/5 to 96/7		76	73	3	17	9	13	2	1
Liverpool	97/8 to 98/9		37	34	3	1	6	7	0	0
Totals			*113*	*107*	*6*	*18*	*15*	*20*	*2*	*1*

LOMAS Stephen — West Ham United

Full Name: Stephen Martin Lomas
DOB: 18-Jan-74 Hanover

Previous Club Details			*Apps*					*Goals*		
Club	Signed	Fee	Tot	Start	Sub	FA	FL	Lge	FA	FL
Manchester C.	1/91	Trainee	111	102	9	11	15	8	1	2
West Ham U.	3/97	£1.6m +	70	70	0	7	4	3	1	0
FAPL Summary by Club										
Manchester C.	93/4 to 95/6		76	67	9	8	13	5	1	2
West Ham U.	96/7 to 98/9		70	70	0	7	4	3	1	0
Totals			*146*	*137*	*9*	*15*	*17*	*8*	*2*	*2*

LUNDEKVAM Claus — Southampton

Full Name: Claus Lundekvam
DOB: 22-Feb-73 Norway

Previous Club Details			*Apps*					*Goals*		
Club	Signed	Fee	Tot	Start	Sub	FA	FL	Lge	FA	FL
SK Brann	1993		37	33	4			0		
Southampton	9/96	£400k	93	89	4	3	14	0	0	0
FAPL Summary by Club										
Southampton	96/7 to 98/9		93	89	4	3	14	0	0	0
Totals			*93*	*89*	*4*	*3*	*14*	*0*	*0*	*0*

MADAR Michael — Everton

Full Name: Michael Madar
DOB: 08-May-68 Paris

Previous Club Details			*Apps*					*Goals*		
Club	Signed	Fee	Tot	Start	Sub	FA	FL	Lge	FA	FL
Cannes, Monaco										
Deportivo La Coruna										
Everton	12/97	Free	19	17	2	0	1	6	0	0
FAPL Summary by Club										
Everton	97/8 to 98/9		19	17	2	0	1	6	0	0
Totals			*19*	*17*	*2*	*0*	*1*	*6*	*0*	*0*

MADDISON Neil — Middlesbrough

Full Name: Neil Stanley Maddison
DOB: 02-Oct-69 Darlington

Previous Club Details			*Apps*					*Goals*		
Club	Signed	Fee	Tot	Start	Sub	FA	FL	Lge	FA	FL
Southampton	4/88	Trainee	168	149	19	13	14	19	0	0
Middlesbrough	10/97	£250k	36	20	16	4	5	4	0	0

FAPL Summary by Club

Club	Signed	Fee	Tot	Start	Sub	FA	FL	Lge	FA	FL
Southampton	92/3 to 97/8		151	141	10	10	12	17	0	0
Middlesbrough	1998/9		20	10	10	1	1	0	0	0
Totals			*171*	*151*	*20*	*11*	*13*	*17*	*0*	*0*

MAGILTON Jim — Sheffield Wednesday

Full Name: James Magilton
DOB: 06-May-69 Belfast

Previous Club Details			*Apps*					*Goals*		
Club	Signed	Fee	Tot	Start	Sub	FA	FL	Lge	FA	FL
Liverpool	5/86	App	0	0	0	0	0	0	0	0
Oxford U.	10/90	£100k	150	150	0	8	9	34	4	1
Southampton	2/94	£600k	130	124	6	12	14	13	3	2
Sheffield W.	9/97	£1.6m	27	14	13	1	2	1	0	0
FAPL Summary by Club										
Southampton	93/4 to 97/8		130	124	6	12	14	13	3	2
Sheffield W.	97/8 to 98/9		26	14	12	1	2	1	0	0
Totals			*156*	*138*	*18*	*13*	*16*	*14*	*3*	*2*

MAKIN Chris — Sunderland

Full Name: Christopher Makin
DOB: 08-May-73 Manchester

Previous Club Details			*Apps*					*Goals*		
Club	Signed	Fee	Tot	Start	Sub	FA	FL	Lge	FA	FL
Oldham A.	11/91	Trainee	94	93	1	11	7	4	0	0
Marseille	96		29					0		
Wigan A.	8/92	Loan	15	14	1	0	0	2	0	0
Sunderland	8/97	£500k	63	60	3	3	10	1	0	0
FAPL Summary by Club										
Oldham A.	1993/4		27	26	1	0	0	1	0	0
Totals			*27*	*26*	*1*	*0*	*0*	*1*	*0*	*0*

MANNINGER Alex — Arsenal

Full Name: Alex Manninger
DOB: 04-Jun-77 Salzburg

Previous Club Details			*Apps*					*Goals*		
Club	Signed	Fee	Tot	Start	Sub	FA	FL	Lge	FA	FL
Vorwarts Seyr	1995		5	5	0			0		
Salzburg	1995		1	0	1			0		
Grazer AK	1996		23	23	0			0		
Arsenal	3/97	£500k	13	13	0	7	7	0	0	0
FAPL Summary by Club										
Arsenal	97/8 to 98/9		13	13	0	7	7	0	0	0
Totals			*13*	*13*	*0*	*7*	*7*	*0*	*0*	*0*

MARIC Silvio — Newcastle United

Full Name: Silvio Maric
DOB: 20-Mar-79 Croatia

Previous Club Details			*Apps*					*Goals*		
Club	Signed	Fee	Tot	Start	Sub	FA	FL	Lge	FA	FL
Croatia Zagreb										
Newcastle U.	3/99	£3.3m	10	9	1	3	0	0	0	0
FAPL Summary by Club										
Newcastle U.	1998/9		10	9	1	3	0	0	0	0
Totals			*10*	*9*	*1*	*3*	*0*	*0*	*0*	*0*

MARSDEN Chris — Southampton

Full Name: Christopher Marsden
DOB: 03-Jan-69 Sheffield

Previous Club Details			*Apps*					*Goals*		
Club	Signed	Fee	Tot	Start	Sub	FA	FL	Lge	FA	FL
Sheffield U.	1/87	App	16	13	3	0	1	1	0	0
Huddersfield T.	7/88	Free	121	113	8	8	16	9	0	0

Club	Signed	Fee	Tot	Start	Sub	FA	FL	Lge	FA	FL
Coventry C.	11/93	Loan	7	5	2	0	0	0	0	0
Wolverhampton	1/94	£250k	8	8	0	3	0	0	0	0
Notts Co.	11/94	£250k	10	10	0	0	1	0	0	0
Stockport Co.	1/96	£70k	65	63	2	4	13	3	0	0
Birmingham C.	10/97	£500k	52	51	1	2	5	4	0	2
Southampton	1/99	£800k	14	14	0	0	0	2	0	0
FAPL Summary by Club										
Coventry C.	1993/4		7	5	2	0	0	0	0	0
Southampton	1998/9		14	14	0	0	0	2	0	0
Totals			*21*	*19*	2	*0*	*0*	2	*0*	*0*

MARSHALL Ian — Leicester City

Full Name: Ian Paul Marshall
DOB: 20-Mar-66 Liverpool

Previous Club Details			*Apps*					*Goals*		
Club	Signed	Fee	Tot	Start	Sub	FA	FL	Lge	FA	FL
Everton	3/84	App	15	9	6	0	2	1	0	1
Oldham A.	3/88	£100k	170	165	5	14	17	36	3	0
Ipswich T.	8/93	£750k	82	77	5	9	3	32	3	2
Leicester C.	8/96	£800k	62	47	15	7	2	18	3	1
FAPL Summary by Club										
Oldham A.	1992/3		27	26	1	1	3	2	0	0
Ipswich T.	93/4 to 94/5		47	42	5	5	3	13	3	2
Leicester C.	96/7 to 98/9		62	47	15	7	2	18	3	1
Totals			*136*	*115*	*21*	*13*	*8*	*33*	*6*	*3*

MARTYN Nigel — Leeds United

Full Name: Nigel Anthony Martyn
DOB: 11-Aug-66 St Austell

Previous Club Details			*Apps*					*Goals*		
Club	Signed	Fee	Tot	Start	Sub	FA	FL	Lge	FA	FL
Bristol R.	8/87	From NL	101	101	0	6	6	0	0	0
Crystal Palace	11/89	£1m	189	189	0	13	25	0	0	0
Leeds U.	7/96	£2.25m	108	108	0	13	8	0	0	0
FAPL Summary by Club										
Crystal Palace	92/3 to 94/5		79	79	0	8	15	0	0	0
Leeds U.	96/7 to 98/9		108	108	0	13	8	0	0	0
Totals			*187*	*187*	*0*	*21*	*23*	*0*	*0*	*0*

MATERAZZI Marco — Everton

Full Name: Marco Materazzi
DOB: 18-Aug-73 Lecce, Italy

Previous Club Details			*Apps*					*Goals*		
Club	Signed	Fee	Tot	Start	Sub	FA	FL	Lge	FA	FL
Perugia										
Everton	7/98	£2.8m	27	26	1	2	4	1	0	1
FAPL Summary by Club										
Everton	1998/9		27	26	1	2	4	1	0	1
Totals			*27*	*26*	*1*	*2*	*4*	*1*	*0*	*1*

MATTEO Dominic — Liverpool

Full Name: Dominic Matteo
DOB: 28-Apr-74 Dumfries

Previous Club Details			*Apps*					*Goals*		
Club	Signed	Fee	Tot	Start	Sub	FA	FL	Lge	FA	FL
Liverpool	5/92	Trainee	94	80	14	6	9	1	0	0
Sunderland	3/95	Loan	1	1	0	0	0	0	0	0
FAPL Summary by Club										
Liverpool	93/4 to 98/9		94	80	14	5	9	1	0	0
Totals			*94*	*80*	*14*	*5*	*9*	*1*	*0*	*0*

MAY David — Manchester United

Full Name: David May
DOB: 24-Jun-70 Oldham

Previous Club Details			*Apps*					*Goals*		
Club	Signed	Fee	Tot	Start	Sub	FA	FL	Lge	FA	FL
Blackburn R.	6/88	Trainee	123	123	0	10	13	3	1	2
Manchester U.	7/94	£1.4m	79	65	14	6	7	6	0	1
FAPL Summary by Club										
Blackburn R.	92/3 to 93/4		74	74	0	7	10	2	1	2
Manchester U.	94/5 to 98/9		79	65	14	6	7	6	0	1
Totals			*153*	*139*	*14*	*13*	*17*	*8*	*1*	*3*

McALLISTER Gary — Coventry City

Full Name: Gary McAllister
DOB: 25-Dec-64 Motherwell

Previous Club Details			*Apps*					*Goals*		
Club	Signed	Fee	Tot	Start	Sub	FA	FL	Lge	FA	FL
Leicester C.	8/85	£125k	201	199	2	5	15	46	2	3
Leeds U.	6/90	£1m	231	230	1	24	26	32	6	4
Coventry C.			81	81	0	7	9	9	1	3
FAPL Summary by Club										
Leeds U.	92/3 to 95/6		151	151	0	17	15	24	5	2
Coventry C.	96/7 to 98/9		81	81	0	7	9	9	1	3
Totals			*232*	*232*	*0*	*24*	*24*	*33*	*6*	*5*

McCALL Stuart — Bradford City

Full Name: Stuart Murray McCall
DOB: 10-Jun-64 Leeds

Previous Club Details			*Apps*					*Goals*		
Club	Signed	Fee	Tot	Start	Sub	FA	FL	Lge	FA	FL
Bradford C.	6/82	App	238	235	3			37		
Everton	6/88		103	99	4			6		
Rangers			194					14		
Bradford C.			43	43	0	2	3	3	0	0

McCANN Gavin — Sunderland

Full Name: Gavin McCann
DOB: 10-Jan-78 Blackpool

Previous Club Details			*Apps*					*Goals*		
Club	Signed	Fee	Tot	Start	Sub	FA	FL	Lge	FA	FL
Everton		Trainee	11	5	6	0	0	0	0	0
Sunderland			11	5	6	2	1	0	1	1
FAPL Summary by Club										
Everton	1997/8		11	5	6	0	0	0	0	0
Totals			*11*	*5*	*6*	*0*	*0*	*0*	*0*	*0*

McPHAIL Stephen — Leeds United

Full Name: Stephen McPhail
DOB: 09-Dec-79 London

Previous Club Details			*Apps*					*Goals*		
Club	Signed	Fee	Tot	Start	Sub	FA	FL	Lge	FA	FL
Leeds U.		Trainee	21	11	10	2	1	0	0	0
FAPL Summary by Club										
Leeds U.	97/8 to 98/9		21	11	10	2	1	0	0	0
Totals			*21*	*11*	*10*	*2*	*1*	*0*	*0*	*0*

MELVILLE Andy — Sunderland

Full Name: Andrew Roger Melville
DOB: 29-Nov-68 Swansea

Previous Club Details			*Apps*					*Goals*		
Club	Signed	Fee	Tot	Start	Sub	FA	FL	Lge	FA	FL
Swansea C.	7/86	Trainee	175	165	10	15	10	22	5	0

Club	Signed	Fee	Tot	Start	Sub	FA	FL	Lge	FA	FL
Oxford U.	7/90	£275k	135	135	0	6	12	13	0	1
Sunderland	8/93		204	204	0	11	19	14	0	1
Bradford C.	2/98	Loan	6	6	0	0	0	1	0	0
FAPL Summary by Club										
Sunderland	1996/7		30	30	0	2	3	1	0	0
Totals			*30*	*30*	*0*	*2*	*3*	*1*	*0*	*0*

MERSON Paul — Aston Villa

Full Name: Paul Charles Merson
DOB: 20-Mar-68 Harlesden

Previous Club Details			*Apps*					*Goals*		
Club	Signed	Fee	Tot	Start	Sub	FA	FL	Lge	FA	FL
Arsenal	12/85	Apprentice	327	289	38	31	38	78	4	9
Brentford	1/87	Loan	7	6	1	0	0	0	0	0
Middlesbrough	7/97	£5m	48	48	0	3	7	12	1	3
Aston Villa	9/98	£6.75m	26	21	5	1	0	5	0	0
FAPL Summary by Club										
Arsenal	92/3 to 96/7		160	150	10	16	25	28	1	4
Middlesbrough	1998/9		3	3	0	0	0	0	0	0
Aston Villa	1998/9		26	21	5	1	0	5	0	0
Totals			*189*	*174*	*15*	*17*	*25*	*33*	*1*	*4*

MILLEN Keith — Watford

Full Name: Keith Derek Millen
DOB: 26-Sep-66 Croydon

Previous Club Details			*Apps*					*Goals*		
Club	Signed	Fee	Tot	Start	Sub	FA	FL	Lge	FA	FL
Brentford	8/84	Juniors	305	301	4	18	26	17	1	2
Watford	3/94		165	163	2	14	11	6	0	0

MILLS Danny — Leeds United

Full Name: Daniel John Mills
DOB: 18-May-77 Norwich

Previous Club Details			*Apps*					*Goals*		
Club	Signed	Fee	Tot	Start	Sub	FA	FL	Lge	FA	FL
Norwich C.	11/94	Trainee	66	46	20	2	5	0	0	1
Charlton A.	3/98	£350k	45	45	0	1	3	3	0	0
Leeds U.	6/99	£4m								
FAPL Summary by Club										
Charlton A.	1998/9		36	36	0	1	3	2	0	0
Totals			*36*	*36*	*0*	*1*	*3*	*2*	*0*	*0*

MILLS Lee — Bradford City

Full Name: Rowan Lee Mills
DOB: 10-Jul-70 Mexborough

Previous Club Details			*Apps*					*Goals*		
Club	Signed	Fee	Tot	Start	Sub	FA	FL	Lge	FA	FL
Wolverhampton	12/92		25	12	13	4	1	2	1	0
Derby Co.	2/95	£400k	16	16	0	0	0	7	0	0
Port Vale	8/95	£200k	109	81	28	3	10	35	0	5
Bradford C.	1998		44	44	0	2	4	24	1	0

MONCUR John — West Ham United

Full Name: John Frederick Moncur
DOB: 22-Sep-66 Stepney

Previous Club Details			*Apps*					*Goals*		
Club	Signed	Fee	Tot	Start	Sub	FA	FL	Lge	FA	FL
Tottenham H.	8/84	App	21	10	11	0	3	1	0	0
Doncaster R.	9/86	Loan	4	4	0	0	0	0	0	0
Cambridge U.	3/87	Loan	4	3	1	0	0	0	0	0

Club	Signed	Fee	Tot	Start	Sub	FA	FL	Lge	FA	FL
Portsmouth	3/89	Loan	7	7	0	0	0	0	0	0
Brentford	10/89	Loan	5	5	0	0	0	1	0	0
Ipswich T.	10/91	Loan	6	5	1	0	0	0	0	0
N.Forest	2/92	Loan	0	0	0	0	0	0	0	0
Swindon T.	3/92	£80k	58	53	5	1	4	5	0	0
West Ham U.	6/94	£900k	111	98	13	7	12	5	1	2
FAPL Summary by Club										
Swindon T.	1993/4		41	41	0	1	3	4	0	0
West Ham U.	94/5 to 98/9		111	98	13	7	12	5	1	2
Totals			*152*	*139*	*13*	*8*	*15*	*9*	*1*	*2*

MONKOU Ken — Southampton

Full Name: Kenneth John Monkou

DOB: 29-Nov-64 Necare, Surinam

Previous Club Details			*Apps*					*Goals*		
Club	Signed	Fee	Tot	Start	Sub	FA	FL	Lge	FA	FL
Chelsea	3/89	£100k	94	92	2	3	12	2	0	0
Southampton	8/92	£750k	198	190	8	16	19	10	1	2
FAPL Summary by Club										
Southampton	92/3 to 98/9		198	190	8	16	19	10	0	2
Totals			*198*	*190*	*8*	*16*	*19*	*10*	*0*	*2*

MOONEY Tommy — Watford

Full Name: Thomas John Mooney

DOB: 11-Aug-71 Middlesbrough

Previous Club Details			*Apps*					*Goals*		
Club	Signed	Fee	Tot	Start	Sub	FA	FL	Lge	FA	FL
Aston Villa	11/89	Trainee	0	0	0	0	0	0	0	0
Scarborough	7/90	Free	107	96	11	3	13	5	0	8
Southend U.	7//93	£100k	14	9	5	11	14	5	1	5
Watford	3/94		199	175	24	11	16	39	1	1

MOORE Darren — Bradford City

Full Name: Darren Mark Moore

DOB: 22-Apr-74 Birmingham

Previous Club Details			*Apps*					*Goals*		
Club	Signed	Fee	Tot	Start	Sub	FA	FL	Lge	FA	FL
Torquay U.	11/92	Trainee	103	102	1	7	6	8	2	0
Doncaster R.	7/95	£62,500	76	76	0	1	4	7	0	0
Bradford C.	6/97	£310k	62	62	0	2	5	3	0	1

MORRIS Jody — Chelsea

Full Name: Jody Morris

DOB: 22-Dec-78 London

Previous Club Details			*Apps*					*Goals*		
Club	Signed	Fee	Tot	Start	Sub	FA	FL	Lge	FA	FL
Chelsea	1/96	Trainee	43	29	14	5	5	1	0	2
FAPL Summary by Club										
Chelsea	95/6 to 98/9		43	29	14	5	5	2	0	2
Totals			*43*	*29*	*14*	*5*	*5*	*2*	*0*	*2*

MOSS Neil — Southampton

Full Name: Neil Graham Moss

DOB: 10-May-75 New Milton

Previous Club Details			*Apps*					*Goals*		
Club	Signed	Fee	Tot	Start	Sub	FA	FL	Lge	FA	FL
Bournemouth	1/93	Trainee	22	21	1	4	1	0	0	0
Southampton	12/95	£250k	10	10	0	0	2	0	0	0
Gillingham	8/97	Loan	10	10	0	0	2	0	0	0
FAPL Summary by Club										
Southampton	96/7 to 98/9		10	10	0	0	2	3	0	0
Totals			*10*	*10*	*0*	*0*	*2*	*3*	*0*	*0*

MUSTOE Robbie — Middlesbrough

Full Name: Robin Mustoe
DOB: 28-Aug-68 Witney

Previous Club Details			*Apps*					*Goals*		
Club	Signed	Fee	Tot	Start	Sub	FA	FL	Lge	FA	FL
Oxford U.	7/86	Junior	91	78	13	2	2	10	0	0
Middlesbrough	7/90	£375k	276	265	11	21	41	22	2	7
FAPL Summary by Club										
Middlesbrough	92/3 to 98/9		108	105	3	8	12	8	0	1
Totals			*108*	*105*	*3*	*8*	*12*	*8*	*0*	*1*

MYHRE Thomas — Everton

Full Name: Thomas Myhre
DOB: 16-Oct-73 Norway

Previous Club Details			*Apps*					*Goals*		
Club	Signed	Fee	Tot	Start	Sub	FA	FL	Lge	FA	FL
Viking Stavanger										
Everton	11/97		60	60	0	5	3	0	0	0
FAPL Summary by Club										
Everton	97/8 to 98/9		60	60	0	5	3	0	0	0
Totals			*60*	*60*	*0*	*5*	*3*	*0*	*0*	*0*

NEVILLE Gary — Manchester United

Full Name: Gary Alexander Neville
DOB: 18-Feb-75 Bury

Previous Club Details			*Apps*					*Goals*		
Club	Signed	Fee	Tot	Start	Sub	FA	FL	Lge	FA	FL
Manchester U.	1/93	Trainee	149	145	4	23	5	2	0	0
FAPL Summary by Club										
Manchester U.	93/4 to 98/9		149	145	4	23	5	2	0	0
Totals			*149*	*145*	*4*	*23*	*5*	*2*	*0*	*0*

NEVILLE Phil — Manchester United

Full Name: Philip John Neville
DOB: 21-Jan-77 Bury

Previous Club Details			*Apps*					*Goals*		
Club	Signed	Fee	Tot	Start	Sub	FA	FL	Lge	FA	FL
Manchester U.	06/94	Trainee	102	80	22	18	6	1	0	0
FAPL Summary by Club										
Manchester U.	94/5 to 98/9		102	80	22	18	6	1	0	0
Totals			*102*	*80*	*22*	*18*	*6*	*1*	*0*	*0*

NEWTON Eddie — Chelsea

Full Name: Edward John Ikem Newton
DOB: 13-Dec-71 Hammersmith

Previous Club Details			*Apps*					*Goals*		
Club	Signed	Fee	Tot	Start	Sub	FA	FL	Lge	FA	FL
Chelsea	5/90	Trainee	165	139	26	19	17	8	1	1
Cardiff C.	1/92	Loan	18	18	0	0	0	4	0	0
FAPL Summary by Club										
Chelsea	92/3 to 98/9		164	139	25	19	17	7	1	0
Totals			*164*	*139*	*25*	*19*	*17*	*7*	*1*	*0*

NGONGE Michel — Watford

Full Name: Michel Ngonge

Previous Club Details			*Apps*					*Goals*		
Club	Signed	Fee	Tot	Start	Sub	FA	FL	Lge	FA	FL
Samsunspor (Turkey)										
Watford	8/98	Free	22	13	9	0	1	4	0	1

NICHOLLS Mark — Chelsea

Full Name: Mark Nicholls
DOB: 30-May-77 Hillingdon

Previous Club Details

Club	Signed	Fee	Tot	Start	Sub	FA	FL	Lge	FA	FL
Chelsea		Trainee	36	11	25	4	4	3	0	0
FAPL Summary by Club										
Chelsea	96/7 to 98/9		36	11	25	4	4	3	0	0
Totals			*36*	*11*	*25*	*4*	*4*	*3*	*0*	*0*

NIELSEN Allan — Tottenham Hotspur

Full Name: Allan Nielsen
DOB: 13-Mar-71 Esbjerg

Previous Club Details

Club	Signed	Fee	Tot	Start	Sub	FA	FL	Lge	FA	FL
Bayern Munich			3					0		
Esbjerg										
OB Odense	1992		55	53	2			9		
FC Copenhagen	1995		26	25	1			3		
Brondby	1996	£100k	38	38	0			9		
Tottenham H.	9/96	£1.6m	82	73	9	5	11	12	3	3
FAPL Summary by Club										
Tottenham H.	96/7 to 98/9		82	73	9	5	11	12	3	3
Totals			*82*	*73*	*9*	*5*	*11*	*12*	*3*	*3*

NILSSON Roland — Coventry City

Full Name: Nils Lennart Roland Nilsson
DOB: 27-Nov-63 Helsingborg, Sweden

Previous Club Details

Club	Signed	Fee	Tot	Start	Sub	FA	FL	Lge	FA	FL
IFK Gothenburg										
Sheffield W.	11/89	£375k	151	151	0	15	16	2	0	1
Helsingborg	5/94									
Coventry C.	7/97	£200k	60	60	0	6	3	0	0	0
FAPL Summary by Club										
Sheffield W.	92/3 to 93/4		70	70	0	11	11	1	0	1
Coventry C.	97/8 to 98/9		60	60	0	6	3	0	0	0
Totals			*130*	*130*	*0*	*17*	*14*	*1*	*0*	*1*

NOEL-WILLIAMS Gifton — Watford

Full Name: Gifton Ruben Elisha Noel-Williams
DOB: 21-Jan-80 Islington

Previous Club Details

Club	Signed	Fee	Tot	Start	Sub	FA	FL	Lge	FA	FL
Watford	2/97	Trainee	89	55	34	7	4	19	4	1

O'BRIEN Andy — Bradford City

Full Name: Andrew James O'Brien
DOB: 29-Jun-79 Harrogate

Previous Club Details

Club	Signed	Fee	Tot	Start	Sub	FA	FL	Lge	FA	FL
Bradford C.	10/96	Trainee	79	60	19	5	3	2	0	0

O'KANE John — Everton

Full Name: John Andrew O'Kane
DOB: 15-Nov-74 Nottingham

Previous Club Details

Club	Signed	Fee	Tot	Start	Sub	FA	FL	Lge	FA	FL
Manchester U.	1/93	Trainee	2	2	0	1	4	0	0	0
Bury	10/96	Loan (x2)	13	11	2	0	0	3	0	0
Everton	1/98	£250k>	12	14	0	3	0	0	0	0
FAPL Summary by Club										
Manchester U.	95/6 to 96/7		2	1	1	0	2	0	0	0
Everton	97/8 to 98/9		14	14	0	3	0	0	0	0
Totals			*16*	*15*	*1*	*3*	*2*	*0*	*0*	*0*

O'NEILL Keith — Middlesbrough

Full Name: Keith O'Neill
DOB: 16-Feb-76 Dublin

Previous Club Details			*Apps*					*Goals*		
Club	Signed	Fee	Tot	Start	Sub	FA	FL	Lge	FA	FL
Norwich C.	7/94	Trainee	55	40	15	3	8	8	0	0
Middlesbrough	3/99	£700k	6	4	2	0	0	0	0	0
FAPL Summary by Club										
Norwich C.	1994/5		1	0	1	0	0	0	0	0
Middlesbrough	1998/9		6	4	2	0	0	0	0	0
Totals			*7*	*4*	*3*	*0*	*0*	*0*	*0*	*0*

OAKES Michael — Aston Villa

Full Name: Michael Oakes
DOB: 30-Oct-73 Northwich

Previous Club Details			*Apps*					*Goals*		
Club	Signed	Fee	Tot	Start	Sub	FA	FL	Lge	FA	FL
Aston Villa	07/91		51	49	2	2	2	0	0	0
Scarborough	11/93	Loan	1	1	0	0	0	0	0	0
FAPL Summary by Club										
Aston Villa	96/7 to 98/9		51	49	2	2	2	0	0	0
Totals			*51*	*49*	2	2	2	*0*	*0*	*0*

OAKES Stefan — Leicester City

Full Name: Stefan Oakes
DOB: 06-Sep-78 Leicester

Previous Club Details			*Apps*					*Goals*		
Club	Signed	Fee	Tot	Start	Sub	FA	FL	Lge	FA	FL
Leicester C.		Trainee	3	2	1	0	0	0	0	0
FAPL Summary by Club										
Leicester C.	1998/9		3	2	1	0	0	0	0	0
Totals			*3*	*2*	*1*	*0*	*0*	*0*	*0*	*0*

OAKLEY Matthew — Southampton

Full Name: Matthew Oakley
DOB: 17-Aug-77 Peterborough

Previous Club Details			*Apps*					*Goals*		
Club	Signed	Fee	Tot	Start	Sub	FA	FL	Lge	FA	FL
Southampton	7/95	Trainee	94	81	13	7	11	6	1	0
FAPL Summary by Club										
Southampton	94/5 to 98/9		94	81	13	7	11	6	1	0
Totals			*94*	*81*	*13*	*7*	*11*	*6*	*1*	*0*

OSTENSTAD Egil — Southampton

Full Name: Egil Ostenstadt
DOB: 02-Jan-72 Haugesund

Previous Club Details			*Apps*					*Goals*		
Club	Signed	Fee	Tot	Start	Sub	FA	FL	Lge	FA	FL
Viking FK	1990		104	81	23			31		
Southampton	10/96	£800k	93	77	16	4	9	28	2	3
FAPL Summary by Club										
Southampton	96/7 to 98/9		93	77	16	4	9	28	2	3
Totals			*93*	*77*	*16*	*4*	*9*	*28*	*2*	*3*

OSTER John — Everton

Full Name: John Morgan Oster
DOB: 08-Dec-78 Boston

Previous Club Details			*Apps*					*Goals*		
Club	Signed	Fee	Tot	Start	Sub	FA	FL	Lge	FA	FL
Grimsby T.	7/96	Trainee	24	21	3	1	0	3	1	0

Club	Signed	Fee	Tot	Start	Sub	FA	FL	Lge	FA	FL
Everton	7/97	£1.5m	40	22	18	5	5	1	1	2
FAPL Summary by Club										
Everton	97/8 to 98/9		40	22	18	5	5	1	1	2
Totals			*40*	*22*	*18*	*5*	*5*	*1*	*1*	*2*

OVERMARS Marc — Arsenal

Full Name: Marc Overmars
DOB: 29-Mar-73 Emst, Holland

Previous Club Details			*Apps*					*Goals*		
Club	Signed	Fee	Tot	Start	Sub	FA	FL	Lge	FA	FL
Willem II		Trainee	31	31	0			1		
Ajax	7/92		135	130	5			36		
Arsenal	7/97	£7.0m	69	69	0	16	3	18	6	2
FAPL Summary by Club										
Arsenal	97/8 to 98/9		69	69	0	16	3	18	6	2
Totals			*69*	*69*	*0*	*16*	*3*	*18*	*6*	*2*

OWEN Michael — Liverpool

Full Name: Michael James Owen
DOB: 14-Dec-79 Chester

Previous Club Details			*Apps*					*Goals*		
Club	Signed	Fee	Tot	Start	Sub	FA	FL	Lge	FA	FL
Liverpool	12/96	Juniors	68	65	3	2	6	37	2	5
FAPL Summary by Club										
Liverpool	96/7 to 98/9		68	65	3	2	6	37	2	5
Totals			*68*	*65*	*3*	*2*	*6*	*37*	*2*	*5*

PAGE Robert — Watford

Full Name: Robert John Page
DOB: 03-Jul-74 Rhondda

Previous Club Details			*Apps*					*Goals*		
Club	Signed	Fee	Tot	Start	Sub	FA	FL	Lge	FA	FL
Watford	4/93	Trainee	144	137	7	11	9	0	0	0

PAHARS Marian — Southampton

Full Name: Marians Pahars
DOB: 1976, Latvia

Previous Club Details			*Apps*					*Goals*		
Club	Signed	Fee	Tot	Start	Sub	FA	FL	Lge	FA	FL
Skonto Riga										
Southampton	2/99	£800k	6	4	2	0	0	3	0	0
FAPL Summary by Club										
Southampton	1998/9		6	4	2	0	0	3	0	0
Totals			*6*	*4*	*2*	*0*	*0*	*3*	*0*	*0*

PALLISTER Gary — Middlesbrough

Full Name: Gary Andrew Pallister
DOB: 30-Jun-65 Ramsgate

Previous Club Details			*Apps*					*Goals*		
Club	Signed	Fee	Tot	Start	Sub	FA	FL	Lge	FA	FL
Middlesbrough	11/84	Free	156	156	0	10	10	5	1	0
Darlington	10/85	Loan	7	7	0	0	0	0	0	0
Manchester U.	8/89	£2.3m	317	314	3	38	36	12	1	0
Middlesbrough	7/98	£2.5m	26	26	0	1	0	0	0	0
FAPL Summary by Club										
Manchester U.	92/3 to 97/8		206	206	0	23	16	8	2	0
Middlesbrough	1998/9		26	26	0	1	0	0	0	0
Totals			*232*	*232*	*0*	*24*	*16*	*8*	*2*	*0*

PALMER Steve — Watford

Full Name: Stephen Leonard Palmer
DOB: 31-Mar-68 Brighton

Previous Club Details			*Apps*					*Goals*		
Club	Signed	Fee	Tot	Start	Sub	FA	FL	Lge	FA	FL
Ipswich T.	8/89		111	87	24	11	3	2	1	0
Watford	9/97	£130k	158	147	11	9	11	4	0	0
FAPL Summary by Club										
Ipswich T.	92/3 to 94/5		55	45	10	5	2	1	1	0
Totals			*55*	*45*	*10*	*5*	*2*	*1*	*1*	*0*

PARKER Garry — Leicester City

Full Name: Garry Stuart Parker
DOB: 07-Sep-65 Oxford

Previous Club Details			*Apps*					*Goals*		
Club	Signed	Fee	Tot	Start	Sub	FA	FL	Lge	FA	FL
Luton T.	5/83	App	42	31	11	8	4	3	0	1
Hull C.	2/86	£72k	84	82	2	4	5	8	0	0
N.Forest	3/88	£260k	103	99	4	16	23	17	5	4
Aston Villa	11/91	£650k	95	91	4	3	4	13	1	0
Leicester C.	2/95	£300k +	114	89	25	11	17	10	2	2
FAPL Summary by Club										
Aston Villa	92/3 to 94/5		70	66	4	5	12	12	0	0
Leicester C.	94/5 to 98/9		74	53	21	9	13	7	2	2
Totals			*144*	*119*	*25*	*14*	*25*	*19*	*2*	*2*

PARLOUR Ray — Arsenal

Full Name: Raymond Parlour
DOB: 07-Mar-73 Romford

Previous Club Details			*Apps*					*Goals*		
Club	Signed	Fee	Tot	Start	Sub	FA	FL	Lge	FA	FL
Arsenal	3/91	Trainee	205	170	35	36	20	16	2	0
FAPL Summary by Club										
Arsenal	92/3 to 98/9		199	168	31	26	20	16	2	0
Totals			*199*	*168*	*31*	*26*	*20*	*16*	*2*	*0*

PEARCE Ian — West Ham United

Full Name: Ian Anthony Pearce
DOB: 07-May-74 Bury St Edmunds

Previous Club Details			*Apps*					*Goals*		
Club	Signed	Fee	Tot	Start	Sub	FA	FL	Lge	FA	FL
Chelsea	8/91	Juniors	4	0	4	0	0	0	0	0
Blackburn R.	10/93	£300k	62	43	19	3	8	2	0	1
West Ham U.	9/97	£1.6m>	63	63	0	7	5	3	1	0
FAPL Summary by Club										
Chelsea	1992/3		1	0	1	0	0	0	0	0
Blackburn R.	93/4 to 97/8		62	43	19	3	8	2	0	1
West Ham U.	97/8 to 98/9		63	63	0	7	5	3	1	0
Totals			*126*	*106*	*20*	*10*	*13*	*5*	*1*	*1*

PEARCE Stuart — Newcastle United

Full Name: Stuart Pearce
DOB: 24-Apr-62 Shepherds Bush

Previous Club Details			*Apps*					*Goals*		
Club	Signed	Fee	Tot	Start	Sub	FA	FL	Lge	FA	FL
Coventry C.	10/83	£25k	52	52	0	2	0	4	0	0
N.Forest	6/85	£200k	401	401	0	37	60	63	9	10
Newcastle U.	7/97	Free	37	37	0	7	2	0	0	0

FAPL Summary by Club

Club	Seasons	Tot	Start	Sub	FA	FL	Lge	FA	FL
N.Forest	92/3 to 96/7	123	123	0	10	11	18	2	3
Newcastle U.	97/8 to 98/9	37	37	0	7	2	0	0	0
Totals		*160*	*160*	*0*	*17*	*13*	*18*	*2*	*3*

PERRY Chris — Wimbledon

Full Name: Christopher John Perry
DOB: 26-Apr-73 Surrey

Previous Club Details			*Apps*					*Goals*		
Club	Signed	Fee	Tot	Start	Sub	FA	FL	Lge	FA	FL
Wimbledon	7/91	Trainee	167	159	8	24	21	2	0	1
FAPL Summary by Club										
Wimbledon	93/4 to 98/9		167	159	8	24	20	2	1	0
Totals			*167*	*159*	*8*	*24*	*20*	*2*	*1*	*0*

PETIT Manu — Arsenal

Full Name: Emmanuel Petit
DOB: 22-Sep-70 Dieppe

Previous Club Details			*Apps*					*Goals*		
Club	Signed	Fee	Tot	Start	Sub	FA	FL	Lge	FA	FL
ES Argues										
AS Monaco			185	184	1			4		
Arsenal	6/97	£3.5m	59	58	1	10	3	6	0	0
FAPL Summary by Club										
Arsenal	97/8 to 98/9		59	58	1	10	3	6	2	0
Totals			*59*	*58*	*1*	*10*	*3*	*6*	*2*	*0*

PETRESCU Dan — Chelsea

Full Name: Dan Vasile Petrescu
DOB: 22-Dec-67 Bucharest

Previous Club Details			*Apps*					*Goals*		
Club	Signed	Fee	Tot	Start	Sub	FA	FL	Lge	FA	FL
Steaua Bucharest	6/86		2	2	0	0	0	0	0	0
Olt Scornicesti	7/86		24	24	0	1	0	0	0	0
Steaua Bucharest	7/87		93	93	0	14	0	27	3	0
Foggia	7/91		55	55	0	6	0	7	0	0
Genoa	7/93		24	24	0	1	0	1	0	0
Sheffield W.	8/94	£1.25m	37	28	9	2	2	3	0	0
Chelsea	11/95	£2.3m	121	110	11	18	8	14	1	2
FAPL Summary by Club										
Sheffield W.	94/5 to 95/6		37	28	9	2	2	3	0	0
Chelsea	95/6 to 98/9		121	110	11	18	8	14	1	2
Totals			*158*	*138*	*20*	*20*	*10*	*17*	*1*	*2*

PHILLIPS Kevin — Sunderland

Full Name: Kevin Phillips
DOB: 25-Jul-73 Hitchin

Previous Club Details			*Apps*					*Goals*		
Club	Signed	Fee	Tot	Start	Sub	FA	FL	Lge	FA	FL
Watford	19/94	£10k	59	54	5	2	2	24	0	1
Sunderland	7/97	£325k	69	68	1	3	5	52	4	2

PISTONE Alessandro — Newcastle United

Full Name: Alessandro Pistone
DOB: 27-Jul-75 Milan

Previous Club Details			*Apps*					*Goals*		
Club	Signed	Fee	Tot	Start	Sub	FA	FL	Lge	FA	FL
Internazionale										
Newcastle U.	7/97	£4.3m	31	30	1	5	1	0	0	0

FAPL Summary by Club

Club	Seasons	Tot	Start	Sub	FA	FL	Lge	FA	FL
Newcastle U.	97/8 to 98/9	31	30	1	5	1	0	0	0
Totals		*31*	*30*	*1*	*5*	*1*	*0*	*0*	*0*

POOM Mart — Derby County

Full Name: Mart Poom
DOB: 03-Feb-72 Tallinn

Previous Club Details			*Apps*					*Goals*		
Club	Signed	Fee	Tot	Start	Sub	FA	FL	Lge	FA	FL
FC Will										
Portsmouth	8/94	£200k	4	4	0	0	4	0	0	0
Flora Tallinn			7	7	0	0	0	0	0	0
Derby Co.	3/97	£500k	40	40	0	2	3	0	0	0
FAPL Summary by Club										
Derby Co.	96/7 to 98/9		57	55	2	4	6	0	0	0
Totals			*57*	*55*	*2*	*4*	*6*	*0*	*0*	*0*

POTTS Steve — West Ham United

Full Name: Steven John Potts
DOB: 07-May-67 Hartford, USA

Previous Club Details			*Apps*					*Goals*		
Club	Signed	Fee	Tot	Start	Sub	FA	FL	Lge	FA	FL
West Ham U.	7/83	Trainee	379	344	35	41	38	1	0	0
FAPL Summary by Club										
West Ham U.	93/4 to 98/9		179	159	20	18	17	0	0	0
Totals			*179*	*159*	*20*	*18*	*17*	*0*	*0*	*0*

POWELL Darryl — Derby County

Full Name: Darryl Anthony Powell
DOB: 15-Nov-71 Lambeth

Previous Club Details			*Apps*					*Goals*		
Club	Signed	Fee	Tot	Start	Sub	FA	FL	Lge	FA	FL
Portsmouth	12/88	Trainee	132	83	49	10	14	16	0	3
Derby Co.	7/95	£750k	127	107	20	11	13	6	0	0
FAPL Summary by Club										
Derby Co.	96/7 to 98/9		90	70	20	11	11	1	0	0
Totals			*90*	*70*	*20*	*11*	*11*	*1*	*0*	*0*

POYET Gustavo — Chelsea

Full Name: Gustavo Poyet
DOB: 15-Nov-67 Montevideo

Previous Club Details			*Apps*					*Goals*		
Club	Signed	Fee	Tot	Start	Sub	FA	FL	Lge	FA	FL
River Plate, Grenoble, Bellavista										
Real Zaragoza			240					60		
Chelsea			42	32	10	0	2	15	0	2
FAPL Summary by Club										
Chelsea	97/8 to 98/9		42	32	10	0	2	15	0	2
Totals			*42*	*32*	*10*	*0*	*2*	*15*	*0*	*2*

PRESSMAN Kevin — Sheffield Wednesday

Full Name: Kevin Paul Pressman
DOB: 06-Nov-67 Fareham

Previous Club Details			*Apps*					*Goals*		
Club	Signed	Fee	Tot	Start	Sub	FA	FL	Lge	FA	FL
Sheffield W.	11/85		247	246	1	16	31	0	0	0
Stoke C.	3/92	Loan	4	4	0	0	0	0	0	0
FAPL Summary by Club										
Sheffield W.	92/3 to 98/9		188	187	1	16	22	0	0	0
Totals			*188*	*187*	*1*	*16*	*22*	*0*	*0*	*0*

PRIOR Spencer — Derby County

Full Name: Spencer Justin Prior
DOB: 22-Apr-71 Hockley

Previous Club Details			*Apps*					*Goals*		
Club	Signed	Fee	Tot	Start	Sub	FA	FL	Lge	FA	FL
Southend U.	5/89		135	135	0	5	9	3	0	0
Norwich C.	6/93	£200k	73	67	6	2	11	1	0	1
Leicester C.	8/96	£600k	64	61	3	5	7	0	0	0
Derby Co.	8/98	£700k	34	33	1	4	2	1	0	0
FAPL Summary by Club										
Norwich C.	93/4 to 94/5		30	25	5	1	4	0	0	0
Leicester C.	96/7 to 97/8		64	61	3	5	7	0	0	0
Derby Co.	1998/9		34	33	1	4	2	1	0	0
Totals			*128*	*119*	*9*	*10*	*13*	*1*	*0*	*0*

QUINN Niall — Sunderland

Full Name: Niall John Quinn
DOB: 06-Oct-66 Dublin

Previous Club Details			*Apps*					*Goals*		
Club	Signed	Fee	Tot	Start	Sub	FA	FL	Lge	FA	FL
Arsenal	11/83	Jnrs	67	59	8	10	16	14	2	4
Manchester C.	3/90	£800k	202	183	20	16	22	66	4	7
Sunderland	8/96	£1.3m	86	77	9	4	6	34	1	4
FAPL Summary by Club										
Manchester C.	92/3 to 95/6		120	100	20	13	15	30	3	4
Sunderland	1996/7		12	8	4	0	1	3	0	1
Totals			*132*	*108*	*24*	*13*	*16*	*33*	*3*	*5*

RADEBE Lucas — Leeds United

Full Name: Lucas Radebe
DOB: 12-Apr-69 Johannesburg

Previous Club Details			*Apps*					*Goals*		
Club	Signed	Fee	Tot	Start	Sub	FA	FL	Lge	FA	FL
Kaiser Chiefs										
Leeds U.	9/94	£250k	113	102	11	14	9	0	1	0
FAPL Summary by Club										
Leeds U.	94/5 to 98/9		113	102	11	14	9	0	1	0
Totals			*113*	*102*	*11*	*14*	*9*	*0*	*1*	*0*

RAE Alex — Sunderland

Full Name: Alexander Scott Rae
DOB: 30-Sep-69 Glasgow

Previous Club Details			*Apps*					*Goals*		
Club	Signed	Fee	Tot	Start	Sub	FA	FL	Lge	FA	FL
Falkirk	1987	NL	83	71	12	3	5	20	0	1
Millwall	8/90	£100k	218	205	13	13	15	63	6	1
Sunderland	7/96	£750k	68	50	18	3	6	5	0	2
FAPL Summary by Club										
Sunderland	1996/7		22	12	10	0	2	3	0	1
Totals			*22*	*12*	*10*	*0*	*2*	*3*	*0*	*1*

RANKIN Izzy — Bradford City

Full Name: Isaiah Rankin
DOB: 22-May-78 London

Previous Club Details			*Apps*					*Goals*		
Club	Signed	Fee	Tot	Start	Sub	FA	FL	Lge	FA	FL
Arsenal	9/95	Trainee	1	0	1	0	0	0	0	0
Colchester U.	9/97	Loan	11	10	1	0	0	5	0	0

Club	Signed	Fee	Tot	Start	Sub	FA	FL	Lge	FA	FL
Bradford C.	8/98	£1.3m	27	15	12	1	2	5	0	1
FAPL Summary by Club										
Arsenal	1997/8		1	0	1	0	0	0	0	0
Totals			*1*	*0*	*1*	*0*	*0*	*0*	*0*	*0*

REDKNAPP Jamie — Liverpool

Full Name: Jamie Frank Redknapp
DOB: 25-Jun-73 Barton on Sea

Previous Club Details			*Apps*					*Goals*		
Club	Signed	Fee	Tot	Start	Sub	FA	FL	Lge	FA	FL
Bournemouth	6/90	Trainee	13	6	7	3	3	0	0	0
Liverpool	1/91	£350k	211	187	24	18	25	27	2	5
FAPL Summary by Club										
Liverpool	92/3 to 98/9		204	182	22	15	25	26	1	6
Totals			*204*	*182*	22	*15*	*25*	*26*	*1*	*6*

RIBEIRO Bruino — Leeds United

Full Name: Bruino Ribeiro
DOB: 22-Oct-75 Setubal, Portugal

Previous Club Details			*Apps*					*Goals*		
Club	Signed	Fee	Tot	Start	Sub	FA	FL	Lge	FA	FL
Vitoria Setubal										
Leeds U.	6/97	£500,00	42	35	7	4	4	4	1	1
FAPL Summary by Club										
Leeds U.	97/8 to 98/9		42	35	7	4	4	4	1	1
Totals			*42*	*35*	7	*4*	*4*	*4*	*1*	*1*

RICARD Hamilton — Middlesbrough

Full Name: Hamilton Cuesta Ricard
DOB: 12-Jan-74 Colombia

Previous Club Details			*Apps*					*Goals*		
Club	Signed	Fee	Tot	Start	Sub	FA	FL	Lge	FA	FL
Deportivo Cali										
Middlesbrough	2/98	£2m	45	36	9	1	4	17	0	3
FAPL Summary by Club										
Middlesbrough	1998/9		36	32	4	1	3	15	0	3
Totals			*36*	*32*	*4*	*1*	*3*	*15*	*0*	*3*

RIEDLE Karlheinz — Liverpool

Full Name: Karlheinz Riedle
DOB: 16-Sep-65 Weiler, Germany

Previous Club Details			*Apps*					*Goals*		
Club	Signed	Fee	Tot	Start	Sub	FA	FL	Lge	FA	FL
TSV Eilhofen, SV Weiler, Augsburg, Blau-Weiss Berlin, Werder Bremen, Lazio, Borussia Dortmund										
Liverpool	7/98	£1.75m	59	34	25	2	6	11	0	0
FAPL Summary by Club										
Liverpool	97/8 to 98/9		59	34	25	2	6	11	0	0
Totals			*59*	*34*	*25*	2	*6*	*11*	*0*	*0*

RIPLEY Stuart — Southampton

Full Name: Stuart Edward Ripley
DOB: 20-Nov-67 Middlesbrough

Previous Club Details			*Apps*					*Goals*		
Club	Signed	Fee	Tot	Start	Sub	FA	FL	Lge	FA	FL
Middlesbrough	11/85	App	249	210	39	18	23	26	1	3
Bolton W.	2/86	Loan	5	5	0	0	0	0	1	0
Blackburn R.	7/92	£1.3m	187	172	15	14	18	13	3	0
Southampton	7/98	£1.5m	22	16	6	1	1	0	0	0

FAPL Summary by Club

Club	Seasons	Tot	Start	Sub	FA	FL	Lge	FA	FL
Blackburn R.	92/3 to 97/8	187	172	15	14	18	13	3	0
Southampton	1998/9	22	16	6	1	1	0	0	0
Totals		*209*	*188*	*21*	*15*	*19*	*13*	*3*	*0*

ROBERTS Andy — Wimbledon

Full Name: Andrew James Roberts
DOB: 20-Mar-74 Dartford

Previous Club Details			*Apps*					*Goals*		
Club	Signed	Fee	Tot	Start	Sub	FA	FL	Lge	FA	FL
Millwall	10/91	Trainee	138	132	6	7	12	5	0	2
Crystal Palace	7/95	£2.52m	108	106	2	8	8	2	0	0
Wimbledon	3/98	£1.2m>	40	35	5	3	4	3	0	0
FAPL Summary by Club										
Crystal Palace	1997/8		25	25	0	4	1	0	0	0
Wimbledon	97/8 to 98/9		40	35	5	3	4	3	0	0
Totals			*65*	*60*	*5*	*7*	*5*	*3*	*0*	*0*

ROBINSON Paul — Watford

Full Name: Paul Peter Robinson
DOB: 14-Dec-78 Watford

Previous Club Details			*Apps*					*Goals*		
Club	Signed	Fee	Tot	Start	Sub	FA	FL	Lge	FA	FL
Watford	2/97	Trainee	63	48	15	6	4	2	0	0

RUDI Petter — Sheffield Wednesday

Full Name: Petter Rudi
DOB: 17-Sep-73 Norway

Previous Club Details			*Apps*					*Goals*		
Club	Signed	Fee	Tot	Start	Sub	FA	FL	Lge	FA	FL
Molde										
Sheffield W.	10/97	£800k	56	52	4	6	1	6	1	0
FAPL Summary by Club										
Sheffield W.	97/8 to 98/9		56	52	4	6	1	6	1	0
Totals			*56*	*52*	*4*	*6*	*1*	*6*	*1*	*0*

SANETTI Francesco — Sheffield Wednesday

Full Name: Francesco Sanetti
DOB: 11-Jan-79 Rome

Previous Club Details			*Apps*					*Goals*		
Club	Signed	Fee	Tot	Start	Sub	FA	FL	Lge	FA	FL
Genoa										
Sheffield W.	4/98	Free	5	1	4	0	2	0	0	0
FAPL Summary by Club										
Sheffield W.	97/8 to 98/9		5	1	4	0	2	0	0	0
Totals			*5*	*1*	*4*	*0*	*2*	*0*	*0*	*0*

SAVAGE Rob — Leicester City

Full Name: Robert William Savage
DOB: 18-Oct-74 Wrexham

Previous Club Details			*Apps*					*Goals*		
Club	Signed	Fee	Tot	Start	Sub	FA	FL	Lge	FA	FL
Manchester U.	7/93	Trainee	0	0	0	0	0	0	0	0
Crewe Alex.	7/94	Free	77	74	3	5	5	10	0	0
Leicester C.	7/97	£400k	69	57	12	2	8	3	1	0
FAPL Summary by Club										
Leicester C.	97/8 to 98/9		69	57	12	2	8	3	1	0
Totals			*69*	*57*	*12*	*2*	*8*	*3*	*1*	*0*

SCALES John — Tottenham Hotspur

Full Name: John Robert Scales
DOB: 04-Jul-66 Harrogate

Previous Club Details			Apps					Goals		
Club	Signed	Fee	Tot	Start	Sub	FA	FL	Lge	FA	FL
Bristol R.	7/85		72	68	4	6	3	2	0	0
Wimbledon	7/87	£70k	240	235	5	21	19	11	1	0
Liverpool	9/94	£3.5m	65	65	0	14	10	2	0	2
Tottenham H.	12/96	£2.6m	29	26	3	0	4	0	0	1
FAPL Summary by Club										
Wimbledon	92/3 to 94/5		72	72	0	8	7	1	1	0
Liverpool	94/5 to 96/7		65	65	0	14	10	2	0	2
Tottenham H.	96/7 to 98/9		29	26	3	0	4	0	0	1
Totals			*166*	*163*	*3*	*22*	*21*	*3*	*1*	*3*

SCHNOOR Stefan — Derby County

Full Name: Stefan Schnoor
DOB: 18-Apr-71 Germany

Previous Club Details			*Apps*					*Goals*		
Club	Signed	Fee	Tot	Start	Sub	FA	FL	Lge	FA	FL
Hamburg										
Derby Co.	6/97	Free	23	20	3	3	2	6	0	0
FAPL Summary by Club										
Derby Co.	1998/9		23	20	3	3	2	2	0	0
Totals			*23*	*20*	*3*	*3*	*2*	*2*	*0*	*0*

SCHOLES Paul — Manchester United

Full Name: Paul Scholes
DOB: 16-Nov-74 Salford

Previous Club Details			*Apps*					*Goals*		
Club	Signed	Fee	Tot	Start	Sub	FA	FL	Lge	FA	FL
Manchester U.	1/93	Trainee	119	80	39	14	8	32	4	5
FAPL Summary by Club										
Manchester U.	94/5 to 98/9		129	90	39	15	8	32	4	5
Totals			*129*	*90*	*39*	*15*	*8*	*32*	*4*	*5*

SCHWARZER Mark — Middlesbrough

Full Name: Mark Schwarzer
DOB: 06-Oct-72 Australia

Previous Club Details			*Apps*					*Goals*		
Club	Signed	Fee	Tot	Start	Sub	FA	FL	Lge	FA	FL
1.FC Kaiserslautern			4	4	0	0	0	0	0	0
Bradford C.	11/96	£350k	13	13	0	3	0	0	0	0
Middlesbrough	2/97	£1.5m	76	76	0	4	10	0	0	0
FAPL Summary by Club										
Middlesbrough	96/7 to 98/9		41	41	0	1	3	0	0	0
Totals			*41*	*41*	*0*	*1*	*3*	*0*	*0*	*0*

SCIMECA Ricky — Aston Villa

Full Name: Riccardo Scimeca
DOB: 13-Aug-75 Leamington

Previous Club Details			*Apps*					*Goals*		
Club	Signed	Fee	Tot	Start	Sub	FA	FL	Lge	FA	FL
Aston Villa	7/93		83	50	23	10	7	2	0	0
FAPL Summary by Club										
Aston Villa	95/6 to 98/9		73	50	23	10	7	2	0	0
Totals			*73*	*50*	*23*	*10*	*7*	*2*	*0*	*0*

SCOTT Martin — Sunderland

Full Name: Martin Scott
DOB: 07-Jan-68 Sheffield

Previous Club Details — *Apps* / *Goals*

Club	Signed	Fee	Tot	Start	Sub	FA	FL	Lge	FA	FL
Rotherham U.	1/86	App	94	93	1	9	11	3	0	2
Bristol C.	12/90	£200k	171	171	0	10	10	14	0	1
Sunderland	12/94	£750k	105	104	1	6	14	9	0	2
FAPL Summary by Club										
Sunderland	1996/7		15	15	0	0	2	1	0	1
Totals			*15*	*15*	*0*	*0*	*2*	*1*	*0*	*1*

SEAMAN David — Arsenal

Full Name: David Andrew Seaman
DOB: 19-Sep-63 Rotherham

Previous Club Details — *Apps* / *Goals*

Club	Signed	Fee	Tot	Start	Sub	FA	FL	Lge	FA	FL
Leeds U.	9/81	App	0	0	0	0	0	0	0	0
Peterborough	8/82	£4k	91	91	0	5	10	0	0	0
Birmingham C.	10/84	£100k	75	75	0	5	4	0	0	0
QPR	8/86	£225k	141	141	0	17	13	0	0	0
Arsenal	5/90	£1.3m	312	312	0	41	31	0	0	0
FAPL Summary by Club										
Arsenal	92/3 to 98/9		232	232	0	26	30	0	0	0
Totals			*232*	*232*	*0*	*26*	*30*	*0*	*0*	*0*

SERRANT Carl — Newcastle United

Full Name: Carl Serrant
DOB: 12-Sep-75 Bradford

Previous Club Details — *Apps* / *Goals*

Club	Signed	Fee	Tot	Start	Sub	FA	FL	Lge	FA	FL
Oldham A.	7/94	Trainee	94	88	6	3	5	1	0	0
Newcastle U.	7/98	£500k	4	3	1	0	0	0	0	0
FAPL Summary by Club										
Newcastle U.	1998/9		4	3	1	0	0	0	0	0
Totals			*4*	*3*	*1*	*0*	*0*	*0*	*0*	*0*

SHARPE Lee — Bradford City

Full Name: Lee Stuart Sharpe
DOB: 27-May-71 Halesowen

Previous Club Details — *Apps* / *Goals*

Club	Signed	Fee	Tot	Start	Sub	FA	FL	Lge	FA	FL
Torquay U.	5/88	Trainee	14	9	5	0	0	3	0	0
Manchester U.	5/88	£185k	193	160	33	29	23	21	3	9
Leeds U.	7/96	£4.5m	34	30	4	1	4	5	0	1
Bradford C.	3/98		9	6	3	0	0	2	0	0
FAPL Summary by Club										
Manchester U.	92/3 to 95/6		116	100	16	19	8	17	3	2
Leeds U.	96/7 to 98/9		30	28	2	1	4	5	0	1
Totals			*146*	*128*	*18*	*20*	*12*	*22*	*3*	*3*

SHAW Richard — Coventry City

Full Name: Richard Edward Shaw
DOB: 11-Sep-68 Brentford

Previous Club Details — *Apps* / *Goals*

Club	Signed	Fee	Tot	Start	Sub	FA	FL	Lge	FA	FL
Crystal Palace	9/86	App	207	193	14	18	30	3	0	0
Hull C.	12/89	Loan	4	4	0	0	0	0	0	0
Coventry C.	11/95	£1m	126	125	1	13	10	0	0	0
FAPL Summary by Club										
Crystal Palace	92/3 to 94/5		74	73	1	9	11	0	0	0
Coventry C.	95/6 to 98/9		126	125	1	13	10	0	0	0
Totals			*200*	*198*	*2*	*22*	*21*	*0*	*0*	*0*

SHEARER Alan — Newcastle United

Full Name: Alan Shearer
DOB: 13-Aug-70 Newcastle

Previous Club Details			*Apps*					*Goals*		
Club	Signed	Fee	Tot	Start	Sub	FA	FL	Lge	FA	FL
Southampton	4/88		118	105	13	14	18	23	4	11
Blackburn R.	7/92	£3.6m	138	132	6	8	16	112	2	14
Newcastle U.	7/96	£15m	78	75	3	15	3	41	6	2
FAPL Summary by Club										
Blackburn R.	92/3 to 95/6		138	132	6	8	16	112	2	12
Newcastle U.	96/7 to 98/9		78	75	3	15	3	41	6	2
Totals			*216*	*207*	*9*	*23*	*19*	*153*	*8*	*14*

SHERINGHAM Teddy — Manchester United

Full Name: Edward Paul Sheringham
DOB: 02-Apr-66 Walthamstow

Previous Club Details			*Apps*					*Goals*		
Club	Signed	Fee	Tot	Start	Sub	FA	FL	Lge	FA	FL
Millwall	1/84	App	220	205	15	12	17	93	5	8
Aldershot	2/85	Loan	5	4	1	0	0	0	0	0
N.Forest	7/91	£2m	42	42	0	4	10	14	2	5
Tottenham H.	8/92	£2.1m	166	163	3	17	14	76	13	7
Manchester U.	6/97	£3.5m	48	35	13	7	1	11	6	1
FAPL Summary by Club										
N.Forest	1992/3		3	3	0	0	0	1	0	0
Tottenham H.	92/3 to 96/7		166	163	3	22	18	74	17	12
Manchester U.	97/8 to 98/9		48	35	13	7	1	11	6	1
Totals			*217*	*201*	*16*	*29*	*19*	*86*	*23*	*13*

SHERWOOD Tim — Tottenham Hotspur

Full Name: Timothy Alan Sherwood
DOB: 06-Feb-69 St Albans

Previous Club Details			*Apps*					*Goals*		
Club	Signed	Fee	Tot	Start	Sub	FA	FL	Lge	FA	FL
Watford	2/87	Trainee	32	23	9	9	5	2	0	0
Norwich C.	7/89	£175k	71	66	5	4	7	10	0	1
Blackburn R.	2/92	£500k	246	239	7	17	26	25	4	2
Tottenham H.	3/99	£3.8m	14	12	2	4	0	2	1	0
FAPL Summary by Club										
Blackburn R.	92/3 to 98/9		235	232	3	17	25	25	4	2
Tottenham H.	1998/9		14	12	2	4	0	2	1	0
Totals			*249*	*244*	*5*	*21*	*25*	*27*	*5*	*2*

SHILTON Sam — Coventry City

Full Name: Sam Shilton
DOB: 21-Jul-78 Nottingham

Previous Club Details			*Apps*					*Goals*		
Club	Signed	Fee	Tot	Start	Sub	FA	FL	Lge	FA	FL
Plymouth Ar.		Trainee	3	1	2	1	0	0	0	0
Coventry C.	10/95	£12,500	2	2	0	0	0	0	0	0
FAPL Summary by Club										
Coventry C.	97/8 to 98/9		7	3	4	1	2	0	0	0
Totals			*7*	*3*	*4*	*1*	*2*	*0*	*0*	*0*

SHORT Craig — Everton

Full Name: Craig Short
DOB: 25-Jun-68 Bridlington

Previous Club Details			*Apps*					*Goals*		
Club	Signed	Fee	Tot	Start	Sub	FA	FL	Lge	FA	FL
Scarborough	10/87	free NL	63	63				7		
Notts Co	7/89	£100k		128		8	6	6	1	1
Derby Co.	9/92	£2.5m	118	118		7	11	9	4	0
Everton	7/95	£2.7m	99	90	9	4	7	4	0	0
FAPL Summary by Club										
Everton	95/6 to 98/9		99	90	9	4	7	4	0	0
Totals			*99*	*90*	*9*	*4*	*7*	*4*	*0*	*0*

SINCLAIR Frank — Leicester City

Full Name: Frank Mohammed Sinclair
DOB: 03-Dec-71 Lambeth

Previous Club Details			*Apps*					*Goals*		
Club	Signed	Fee	Tot	Start	Sub	FA	FL	Lge	FA	FL
Chelsea	5/90	Trainee	169	163	6	18	18	7	1	2
WBA	12/91	Loan	6	6	0	0	0	1	0	0
Leicester C.	8/98	£2m	31	30	1	2	6	1	1	0
FAPL Summary by Club										
Chelsea	92/3 to 97/8		157	151	6	17	18	6	1	2
Leicester C.	1998/9		31	30	1	2	6	1	1	0
Totals			*188*	*181*	*7*	*19*	*24*	*7*	*2*	*2*

SINCLAIR Trevor — West Ham United

Full Name: Trevor Sinclair
DOB: 02-Mar-73 Dulwich

Previous Club Details			*Apps*					*Goals*		
Club	Signed	Fee	Tot	Start	Sub	FA	FL	Lge	FA	FL
Blackpool	8/90	Trainee	112	84	28	7	8	15	0	0
QPR	8/93	£750k	167	162	5	10	13	16	2	3
West Ham U.	1/98	£2.3m	50	50	0	2	2	14	0	0
FAPL Summary by Club										
QPR	93/4 to 95/6		102	99	3	4	9	6	1	2
West Ham U.	97/8 to 98/9		50	50	0	2	2	14	0	0
Totals			*152*	*149*	*3*	*6*	*11*	*20*	*1*	*2*

SINTON Andy — Tottenham Hotspur

Full Name: Andrew Sinton
DOB: 19-Mar-66 Newcastle

Previous Club Details			*Apps*					*Goals*		
Club	Signed	Fee	Tot	Start	Sub	FA	FL	Lge	FA	FL
Cambridge U.	4/83	App	93	90	3	3	6	13	0	1
Brentford	12/85	£25k	149	149	0	11	8	28	1	3
QPR	3/89	£350k	160	160	0	13	14	22	2	0
Sheffield W.	8/93	£2.75m	60	54	6	13	5	3	0	0
Tottenham H.	1/96	£1.5m	83	66	17	8	9	6	1	0
FAPL Summary by Club										
QPR	1992/3		36	36	0	2	4	7	0	0
Sheffield W.	93/4 to 95/6		60	54	6	4	10	3	0	0
Tottenham H.	95/6 to 98/9		83	66	17	8	9	6	1	0
Totals			*179*	*156*	*23*	*14*	*23*	*16*	*1*	*0*

SLATER Stuart — Watford

Full Name: Stuart Ian Slater
DOB: 27-Mar-69 Sudbury

Previous Club Details			*Apps*					*Goals*		
Club	Signed	Fee	Tot	Start	Sub	FA	FL	Lge	FA	FL
West Ham U.	4/87	App	141	134	7	16	17	11	3	2
Celtic	8/92	£1.5m	43	40	3	3	2	3	0	2
Ipswich T.	9/93	£750k	72	61	11	6	6	4	0	0
Leicester C.	10/96	NC	0	0	0	0	0	0	0	0
Watford	11/96	Free	30	22	8	3	3	1	0	0

FAPL Summary by Club

Club	Seasons	Tot	Start	Sub	FA	FL	Lge	FA	FL
Ipswich T.	93/4 to 94/5	55	50	5	6	3	2	0	0
Totals		*55*	*50*	*5*	*6*	*3*	*2*	*0*	*0*

SMART Allan — Watford

Full Name: Allan Andrew Colin Smart
DOB: 08-Jul-74 Perth

Previous Club Details

Club	Signed	Fee	Apps Tot	Start	Sub	FA	FL	Goals Lge	FA	FL
Preston NE	11/94	£15k	21	17	4	2	21	6	1	6
Carlisle U.	11/95	Loan	4	3	1	0	0	0	0	0
Northampton	09/96	Loan	0	1	0	0	0	0	0	0
Carlisle U.	10/96		44	41	3	4	1	17	0	1
Watford			35	34	1	1	1	7	0	0

SMITH Alan — Leeds United

Full Name: Alan Smith
DOB: 28-Oct-80 Wakefield

Previous Club Details

Club	Signed	Fee	Apps Tot	Start	Sub	FA	FL	Goals Lge	FA	FL
Leeds U.		Trainee	22	15	7	4	0	7	2	0

FAPL Summary by Club

Club	Seasons	Tot	Start	Sub	FA	FL	Lge	FA	FL
Leeds U.	1998/9	22	15	7	4	0	7	2	0
Totals		*22*	*15*	*7*	*4*	*0*	*7*	*2*	*0*

SMITH Martin — Sunderland

Full Name: Martin Geoffrey Smith
DOB: 13-Nov-74 Sunderland

Previous Club Details

Club	Signed	Fee	Apps Tot	Start	Sub	FA	FL	Goals Lge	FA	FL
Sunderland	9/92	Trainee	119	90	29	10	17	25	1	2

FAPL Summary by Club

Club	Seasons	Tot	Start	Sub	FA	FL	Lge	FA	FL
Sunderland	1996/7	10	6	4	1	1	0	0	0
Totals		*10*	*6*	*4*	*1*	*1*	*0*	*0*	*0*

SOLANO Norberto — Newcastle United

Full Name: Norberto Salano
DOB: 12-Dec-74 Lima, Peru

Previous Club Details

Club	Signed	Fee	Apps Tot	Start	Sub	FA	FL	Goals Lge	FA	FL
Boca Juniors										
Newcastle U.	8/98	£2.5m	29	24	5	7	1	6	0	0

FAPL Summary by Club

Club	Seasons	Tot	Start	Sub	FA	FL	Lge	FA	FL
Newcastle U.	1998/9	29	24	5	7	1	6	0	0
Totals		*29*	*24*	*5*	*7*	*1*	*6*	*0*	*0*

SOLSKJAER Ole — Manchester United

Full Name: Ole Gunnar Solskjaer
DOB: 26-Feb-73 Kristiansund, Norway

Previous Club Details

Club	Signed	Fee	Apps Tot	Start	Sub	FA	FL	Goals Lge	FA	FL
Molde	(1995)		26	26	0	0	0	20	0	0
Manchester U.	7/96	£1.5m	74	49	25	13	3	36	1	3

FAPL Summary by Club

Club	Seasons	Tot	Start	Sub	FA	FL	Lge	FA	FL
Manchester U.	96/7 to 98/9	74	49	25	13	3	36	1	3
Totals		*74*	*49*	*25*	*13*	*3*	*36*	*1*	*3*

SOLTVEDT Trond — Coventry City

Full Name: Trond Egil Soltvedt
DOB: 15-Feb-67 Norway

Previous Club Details			*Apps*					*Goals*		
Club	Signed	Fee	Tot	Start	Sub	FA	FL	Lge	FA	FL
Rosenborg										
Coventry C.	7/97	£500k	57	47	10	7	5	3	0	1
FAPL Summary by Club										
Coventry C.	97/8 to 98/9		57	47	10	7	5	3	0	1
Totals			*57*	*47*	*10*	*7*	*5*	*3*	*0*	*1*

SONG Rigobert — Liverpool

Full Name: Rigobert Song
DOB: 01-Jul-76 Cameroon

Previous Club Details			*Apps*					*Goals*		
Club	Signed	Fee	Tot	Start	Sub	FA	FL	Lge	FA	FL
Metz, Salernitana										
Liverpool	1/99	£2.72m	13	10	3	0	0	0	0	0
FAPL Summary by Club										
Liverpool	1998/9		13	10	3	0	0	0	0	0
Totals			*13*	*10*	*3*	*0*	*0*	*0*	*0*	*0*

SONNER Danny — Sheffield Wednesday

Full Name: Daniel Sonner
DOB: 09-Jan-72 Wigan

Previous Club Details			*Apps*					*Goals*		
Club	Signed	Fee	Tot	Start	Sub	FA	FL	Lge	FA	FL
Wigan A.		Youth	0	0	0	0	0	0	0	0
Burnley	8/90	Free	6	1	5	0	1	0	0	1
Preussen Koln		Loan								
Bury	11/92	Loan	5	5	0	3	0	3	0	0
Ipswich T.	6/96	Free	56	28	28	2	8	3	0	1
Sheffield W.	10/98	£75k	26	24	2	3	0	3	0	0
FAPL Summary by Club										
Sheffield W.	1998/9		26	24	2	3	0	3	0	0
Totals			*26*	*24*	*2*	*3*	*0*	*3*	*0*	*0*

SORENSEN Thomas — Sunderland

Full Name: Thomas Sorensen
DOB: Denmark

Previous Club Details			*Apps*					*Goals*		
Club	Signed	Fee	Tot	Start	Sub	FA	FL	Lge	FA	FL
OB Odense										
Sunderland	7/98	£1m	45	45	0	2	9	0	0	0

SOUTHGATE Gareth — Aston Villa

Full Name: Gareth Southgate
DOB: 03-Sep-70 Watford

Previous Club Details			*Apps*					*Goals*		
Club	Signed	Fee	Tot	Start	Sub	FA	FL	Lge	FA	FL
Crystal Palace	1/89	Trainee	152	148	4	9	24	15	0	7
Aston Villa	7/95	£2.5m	129	129	0	12	10	3	0	1
FAPL Summary by Club										
Crystal Palace	92/3 to 94/5		75	75	0	8	13	6	0	4
Aston Villa	95/6 to 98/9		129	129	0	12	10	3	0	1
Totals			*204*	*204*	*0*	*20*	*23*	*9*	*0*	*5*

SPEED Gary — Newcastle United

Full Name: Gary Andrew Speed
DOB: 08-Sep-69 Hawarden

Previous Club Details			*Apps*					*Goals*		
Club	Signed	Fee	Tot	Start	Sub	FA	FL	Lge	FA	FL
Leeds U.	6/88	Trainee	248	231	17	21	26	39	5	11
Everton	7/96	£3.5m	58	58	0	2	5	16	1	1

Club	Signed	Fee	Tot	Start	Sub	FA	FL	Lge	FA	FL
Newcastle U.	2/98	£5.5m	51	47	4	10	2	5	1	0
FAPL Summary by Club										
Leeds U.	92/3 to 95/6		143	142	1	11	14	22	5	5
Everton	96/7 to 97/8		58	58	0	2	5	16	1	1
Newcastle U.	97/8 to 98/9		51	47	4	10	2	5	1	0
Totals			*252*	*247*	*5*	*23*	*21*	*43*	*7*	*6*

SRNICEK Pavel — Sheffield Wednesday

Full Name: Pavel Srnicek
DOB: 10-Mar-68 Ostrava, Czechoslovakia

Previous Club Details			*Apps*					*Goals*		
Club	Signed	Fee	Tot	Start	Sub	FA	FL	Lge	FA	FL
Banik Ostrava										
Newcastle U.	2/91	£350k	149	148	1	11	11	0	0	0
Banik Ostrava	7/98	Free								
Sheffield W.	8/98	Free	24	24	0	2	0	0	0	0
FAPL Summary by Club										
Newcastle U.	93/4 to 97/8		97	96	1	7	9	0	0	0
Sheffield W.	1998/9		24	24	0	2	0	0	0	0
Totals			*121*	*120*	*1*	*9*	*9*	*0*	*0*	*0*

STAM Japp — Manchester United

Full Name: Japp Stam
DOB: 17-Jul-72 Kampen, Holland

Previous Club Details			*Apps*					*Goals*		
Club	Signed	Fee	Tot	Start	Sub	FA	FL	Lge	FA	FL
Cambuur Leeuwarden, Willem II										
PSV Eindhoven										
Manchester U.	6/98	£10.5m	30	30	0	7	0	1	0	0
FAPL Summary by Club										
Manchester U.	1998/9		30	30	0	7		1	0	0
Totals			*30*	*30*	*0*	*7*	*0*	*1*	*0*	*0*

STAMP Phillip — Middlesbrough

Full Name: Phillip Lawrence Stamp
DOB: 12-Dec-75 Middlesbrough

Previous Club Details			*Apps*					*Goals*		
Club	Signed	Fee	Tot	Start	Sub	FA	FL	Lge	FA	FL
Middlesbrough	2/93	Trainee	75	48	27	9	14	5	1	1
FAPL Summary by Club										
Middlesbrough	95/6 to 98/9		51	31	20	7	12	5	1	1
Totals			*51*	*31*	*20*	*7*	*12*	*5*	*1*	*1*

STAUNTON Steve — Liverpool

Full Name: Stephen Staunton
DOB: 19-Jan-69 Drogheda

Previous Club Details			*Apps*					*Goals*		
Club	Signed	Fee	Tot	Start	Sub	FA	FL	Lge	FA	FL
Liverpool	9/86	£20k	65	55	10	16	8	0	1	4
Bradford C.	11/87	Loan	8	7	1	0	2	0	0	0
Aston Villa	8/91	£1.1m	208	205	3	20	19	16	1	1
Liverpool	7/98	Free	31	31	0	1	2	0	0	0
FAPL Summary by Club										
Aston Villa	92/3 to 97/8		171	168	3	16	17	13	1	1
Liverpool	1998/9		31	31	0	1	2	0	0	0
Totals			*202*	*199*	*3*	*17*	*19*	*13*	*1*	*1*

STEFANOVIC Dejan — Sheffield Wednesday

Full Name: Dejan Stefanovic
DOB: 28-Oct-74 Yugoslavia

Previous Club Details

Club	Signed	Fee	Tot	Start	Sub	FA	FL	Lge	FA	FL
			Apps					*Goals*		
Red Star Belgrade										
Sheffield W.	12/95	£2m	66	59	7	4	2	4	1	0
FAPL Summary by Club										
Sheffield W.	95/6 to 98/9		66	59	7	4	2	4	1	0
Totals			*66*	*59*	*7*	*4*	*2*	*4*	*1*	*0*

STIMAC Igor — Derby County

Full Name: Igor Stimac
DOB: 06-Sep-67 Croatia

Previous Club Details

Club	Signed	Fee	Tot	Start	Sub	FA	FL	Lge	FA	FL
			Apps					*Goals*		
Hadjuk Split, Cadiz										
Hadjuk Split										
Derby Co.	10/95	£1.5m	84	84	0	15	10	3	0	0
FAPL Summary by Club										
Derby Co.	96/7 to 98/9		57	57	0	14	10	2	0	0
Totals			*57*	*57*	*0*	*14*	*10*	*2*	*0*	*0*

STOCKDALE Robbie — Middlesbrough

Full Name: Robert Keith Stockdale
DOB: 30-Nov-79 Middlesbrough

Previous Club Details

Club	Signed	Fee	Tot	Start	Sub	FA	FL	Lge	FA	FL
			Apps					*Goals*		
Middlesbrough		Trainee	19	18	2	1	3	0	0	0
FAPL Summary by Club										
Middlesbrough	1998/9		19	17	2	0	3	0	0	0
Totals			*19*	*17*	*2*	*0*	*3*	*0*	*0*	*0*

STONE Steve — Aston Villa

Full Name: Steven Brian Stone
DOB: 20-Aug-71 Gateshead

Previous Club Details

Club	Signed	Fee	Tot	Start	Sub	FA	FL	Lge	FA	FL
			Apps					*Goals*		
N.Forest	5/89	Trainee	193	191	2	11	17	23	0	2
Aston Villa	3/99	£5.5m	10	9	1	0	0	0	0	0
FAPL Summary by Club										
N.Forest	92/3 to 98/9		118	117	1	9	10	16	0	2
Aston Villa	1998/9		10	9	1	0	0	0	0	0
Totals			*128*	*126*	*2*	*9*	*10*	*16*	*0*	*2*

STURRIDGE Dean — Derby County

Full Name: Dean Constantine Sturridge
DOB: 27-Jul-73 Birmingham

Previous Club Details

Club	Signed	Fee	Tot	Start	Sub	FA	FL	Lge	FA	FL
			Apps					*Goals*		
Derby Co.	7/91	Trainee	151	125	26	13	16	46	2	3
Torquay U.	12/94	Loan	10	10	0	0	0	5	0	0
FAPL Summary by Club										
Derby Co.	96/7 to 98/9		89	76	13	13	16	25	2	3
Totals			*89*	*76*	*13*	*13*	*16*	*25*	*2*	*3*

SULLIVAN Neil — Wimbledon

Full Name: Neil Sullivan
DOB: 24-Feb-70 Sutton

Previous Club Details

Club	Signed	Fee	Tot	Start	Sub	FA	FL	Lge	FA	FL
			Apps					*Goals*		
Wimbledon	7/88	Trainee	144	143	1	23	13	0	0	0
Crystal Palace	5/92	Loan	1	1	0	0	0	0	0	0

FAPL Summary by Club

Club	Signed	Fee	Tot	Start	Sub	FA	FL	Lge	FA	FL
Wimbledon	92/3 to 98/9		142	141	1	23	13	0	0	0
Totals			*142*	*141*	*1*	*23*	*13*	*0*	*0*	*0*

SUMMERBEE Nicky — Sunderland

Full Name: Nicholas John Summerbee
DOB: 26-Aug-71 Altrincham

Previous Club Details — *Apps* — *Goals*

Club	Signed	Fee	Tot	Start	Sub	FA	FL	Lge	FA	FL
Swindon T.	7/89	Trainee	112	89	23	6	10	6	0	3
Manchester C.	6/94	£1.5m	131	119	12	12	13	6	2	2
Sunderland	11/97	£1m	61	58	3	2	6	6	0	0
FAPL Summary by Club										
Manchester C.	93/4 to 95/6		116	108	8	11	12	5	0	4
Totals			*116*	*108*	*8*	*11*	*12*	*5*	*0*	*4*

SUTTON Chris — Blackburn Rovers

Full Name: Christopher Roy Sutton
DOB: 10-Mar-73 Nottingham

Previous Club Details — *Apps* — *Goals*

Club	Signed	Fee	Tot	Start	Sub	FA	FL	Lge	FA	FL
Norwich C.	7/91	Trainee	102	89	13	10	9	35	5	3
Blackburn R.	7/94	£5m	130	125	5	9	12	47	4	6
FAPL Summary by Club										
Norwich C.	92/3 to 93/4		79	73	6	4	7	33	2	3
Blackburn R.	94/5 to 98/9		130	125	5	9	12	47	4	4
Totals			*209*	*198*	*11*	*13*	*19*	*80*	*6*	*7*

TARICCO Mauricio — Tottenham Hotspur

Full Name: Mauricia Taricco
DOB: 10-Mar-73 Buenos Aires

Previous Club Details — *Apps* — *Goals*

Club	Signed	Fee	Tot	Start	Sub	FA	FL	Lge	FA	FL
Argentina Juniors										
Ipswich T.	9/94	£175k	137	134	3	8	18	4	0	3
Tottenham H.	12/98	£1.8m	13	12	1	3	0	0	0	0
FAPL Summary by Club										
Tottenham H.	1998/9		13	12	1	3	0	0	0	0
Totals			*13*	*12*	*1*	*3*	*0*	*0*	*0*	*0*

TAYLOR Ian — Aston Villa

Full Name: Ian Kenneth Taylor
DOB: 04-Jun-68 Birmingham

Previous Club Details — *Apps* — *Goals*

Club	Signed	Fee	Tot	Start	Sub	FA	FL	Lge	FA	FL
Port Vale	7/92	£15k NL	83	83	0	6	4	28	1	2
Sheffield W.	7/94	£1m	14	9	5	0	4	1	0	1
Aston Villa	12/94	£1m	146	136	10	9	10	16	1	1
FAPL Summary by Club										
Sheffield W.	1994/5		14	9	5	0	4	1	0	1
Aston Villa	94/5 to 98/9		146	136	10	9	10	16	1	2
Totals			*160*	*145*	*15*	*9*	*14*	*17*	*1*	*3*

TELFER Paul — Coventry City

Full Name: Paul Norman Telfer
DOB: 21-Oct-71 Edinburgh

Previous Club Details — *Apps* — *Goals*

Club	Signed	Fee	Tot	Start	Sub	FA	FL	Lge	FA	FL
Luton T.	11/88	Trainee	144	136	8	14	5	19	2	0
Coventry C.	7/95	£1.5m	130	125	5	14	12	6	4	2

FAPL Summary by Club

Club	Seasons	Tot	Start	Sub	FA	FL	Lge	FA	FL
Coventry C.	95/6 to 98/9	130	125	5	14	12	6	4	2
Totals		*130*	*125*	*5*	*14*	*12*	*6*	*4*	*2*

THATCHER Ben — Wimbledon

Full Name: Benjamin David Thatcher
DOB: 30-Nov-75 Swindon

Previous Club Details			*Apps*					*Goals*		
Club	Signed	Fee	Tot	Start	Sub	FA	FL	Lge	FA	FL
Millwall	6/96	Trainee	90	87	3	7	6	1	0	0
Wimbledon	7/96	£1.8m	66	63	3	5	10	0	0	0
FAPL Summary by Club										
Wimbledon	96/7 to 98/9		66	63	3	5	10	0	0	0
Totals			*66*	*63*	*3*	*5*	*10*	*0*	*0*	*0*

THOME Emerson — Sheffield Wednesday

Full Name: Emerson August Thome
DOB: 30-Mar-72 Porto Alegra, Brazil

Previous Club Details			*Apps*					*Goals*		
Club	Signed	Fee	Tot	Start	Sub	FA	FL	Lge	FA	FL
Benfica										
Sheffield W.	3/98	Free	44	44	0	3	2	1	1	0
FAPL Summary by Club										
Sheffield W.	97/8 to 98/9		44	44	0	3	2	1	1	0
Totals			*44*	*44*	*0*	*3*	*2*	*1*	*1*	*0*

THOMPSON Alan — Aston Villa

Full Name: Alan Thompson
DOB: 22-Dec-73 Newcastle

Previous Club Details			*Apps*					*Goals*		
Club	Signed	Fee	Tot	Start	Sub	FA	FL	Lge	FA	FL
Newcastle U.	3/91	Trainee	16	13	3	1	0	0	0	0
Bolton W.	7/93	£250k	157	143	14	8	25	34	2	5
Aston Villa	6/98	£4.5m	25	20	5	0	1	2	0	0
FAPL Summary by Club										
Bolton W.	95/6 to 97/8		59	56	3	2	9	10	0	2
Aston Villa	1998/9		25	20	5	0	1	2	0	0
Totals			*84*	*76*	*8*	*2*	*10*	*12*	*0*	*2*

THOMPSON David — Liverpool

Full Name: David Thompson
DOB: 12-Sep-77 Birkenhead

Previous Club Details			*Apps*					*Goals*		
Club	Signed	Fee	Tot	Start	Sub	FA	FL	Lge	FA	FL
Liverpool		Trainee	22	6	16	0	2	2	0	0
FAPL Summary by Club										
Liverpool	96/7 to 98/9		22	6	16	0	2	2	0	0
Totals			*22*	*6*	*16*	*0*	*2*	*2*	*0*	*0*

TODD Lee — Bradford City

Full Name: Lee Todd
DOB: 07-Mar-72 Hartlepool

Previous Club Details			*Apps*					*Goals*		
Club	Signed	Fee	Tot	Start	Sub	FA	FL	Lge	FA	FL
Stockport Co.	7/90	Free	225	214	11	17	26	2	2	0
Southampton	7/97	£500k	10	9	1	0	1	0	0	0
Bradford C.	8/98	£250k	14	13	1	0	2	0	0	0
FAPL Summary by Club										
Southampton	1997/8		10	9	1	0	1	0	0	0
Totals			*10*	*9*	*1*	*0*	*1*	*0*	*0*	*0*

TRAMEZZANI Paolo — Tottenham Hotspur

Full Name: Paolo Tramezzani
DOB: 20-Jul-70 Castelnovo ne Monti, Italy

Previous Club Details			Apps					Goals		
Club	Signed	Fee	Tot	Start	Sub	FA	FL	Lge	FA	FL
Internazionale, Prato, Cosenza, Lucchese, Internazionale, Venezia, Cesena, Piacenza										
Tottenham H.	7/98		6	6	0	0	1	0	0	0
FAPL Summary by Club										
Tottenham H.	1998/9		6	6	0	0	1	0	0	0
Totals			*6*	*6*	*0*	*0*	*1*	*0*	*0*	*0*

ULLATHORNE Robert — Leicester City

Full Name: Robert Ullathorne
DOB: 11-Oct-71 Wakefield

Previous Club Details			Apps					Goals		
Club	Signed	Fee	Tot	Start	Sub	FA	FL	Lge	FA	FL
Norwich C.	7/90	Trainee	94	86	8	8	12	7	0	1
Osasuna										
Leicester C.	2/97	£600k	31	28	3	2	9	1	1	0
FAPL Summary by Club										
Leicester C.	93/4 to 98/9		74	66	8	7	11	5	1	0
Totals			*74*	*66*	*8*	*7*	*11*	*5*	*1*	*0*

UNSWORTH David — Everton

Full Name: David Gerald Unsworth
DOB: 16-Oct-73 Chorley

Previous Club Details			Apps					Goals		
Club	Signed	Fee	Tot	Start	Sub	FA	FL	Lge	FA	FL
Everton	6/92	Trainee	116	108	8	7	7	11	0	0
West Ham U.	8/97	£1m	32	32	0	4	5	2	0	0
Aston Villa	7/98		0	0	0	0	0	0	0	0
Everton	8/98	£3m	34	33	1	3	3	1	1	0
FAPL Summary by Club										
Everton	92/3 to 96/7		114	107	7	7	7	10	0	0
West Ham U.	1997/8		32	32	0	4	5	2	0	0
Everton	1998/9		34	33	1	3	3	1	1	0
Totals			*180*	*172*	*8*	*14*	*15*	*13*	*1*	*0*

VAN DER GOUW Rai — Manchester United

Full Name: Raimond Van der Gouw
DOB: 24-Mar-63 Oldenzaal, Holland

Previous Club Details			Apps					Goals		
Club	Signed	Fee	Tot	Start	Sub	FA	FL	Lge	FA	FL
Vitesse	(1990)		188	188	0	0	0	0	0	0
Manchester U.	7/96	undis	12	10	2	0	6	0	0	0
FAPL Summary by Club										
Manchester U.	96/7 to 98/9		12	10	2	0	6	0	0	0
Totals			*12*	*10*	*2*	*0*	*6*	*0*	*0*	*0*

VEGA Ramon — Tottenham Hotspur

Full Name: Ramon Vega
DOB: 14-Jun-71 Zurich

Previous Club Details			Apps					Goals		
Club	Signed	Fee	Tot	Start	Sub	FA	FL	Lge	FA	FL
Grasshopper	1990		156	154	2	0	0	13	0	0
Cagliari	8/96									
Tottenham H.	1/97	£3.75m	49	43	6	7	7	6	0	1
FAPL Summary by Club										
Tottenham H.	96/7 to 98/9		49	43	6	7	7	6	0	1
Totals			*49*	*43*	*6*	*7*	*7*	*6*	*0*	*1*

VIALLI Gianluca — Chelsea

Full Name: Gianluca Vialli
DOB: 09-Jul-64 Cremona, Italy

Previous Club Details			Apps					Goals		
Club	Signed	Fee	Tot	Start	Sub	FA	FL	Lge	FA	FL
Cremonese	1980		105					23		
Sampdoria	1984		223					82		
Juventus	1992		102					38		
Chelsea	6/96	Free	58	46	12	9	6	21	6	5
FAPL Summary by Club										
Chelsea	96/7 to 98/9		58	46	12	9	6	21	6	5
Totals			*58*	*46*	*12*	*9*	*6*	*21*	*6*	*5*

VICKERS Steve — Middlesbrough

Full Name: Stephen Vickers
DOB: 13-Oct-67 Bishop Auckland

Previous Club Details			Apps					Goals		
Club	Signed	Fee	Tot	Start	Sub	FA	FL	Lge	FA	FL
Tranmere R.	9/85		311	310	1	19	21	11	3	5
Middlesbrough	12/93	£700k	195	187	6	16	24	8	0	2
FAPL Summary by Club										
Middlesbrough	95/6 to 98/9		92	88	4	9	15	2	0	2
Totals			*92*	*88*	*4*	*9*	*15*	*2*	*0*	*2*

VIEIRA Patrick — Arsenal

Full Name: Patrick Vieira
DOB: 23-Jun-76 Dakar, Senegal

Previous Club Details			Apps					Goals		
Club	Signed	Fee	Tot	Start	Sub	FA	FL	Lge	FA	FL
AS Cannes	1993		36	32	4			2		
Milan	1995		2	1	1			0		
Arsenal	8/96	£3.5m	98	95	3	17	5	7	1	0
FAPL Summary by Club										
Arsenal	96/7 to 98/9		98	95	3	17	5	7	1	0
Totals			*98*	*95*	*3*	*17*	*5*	*7*	*1*	*0*

VIVAS Nelson — Arsenal

Full Name: Nelson Vivas
DOB: 18-Oct-69 San Nicolas, Argentina

Previous Club Details			Apps					Goals		
Club	Signed	Fee	Tot	Start	Sub	FA	FL	Lge	FA	FL
Quilmes, Boca Juniors, Lugano										
Arsenal	8/98	£1.6m	22	10	12	6	2	0	0	1
FAPL Summary by Club										
Arsenal	1998/9		22	10	12	6	2	0	0	1
Totals			22	*10*	*12*	*6*	*2*	*0*	*0*	*1*

WALKER Des — Sheffield Wednesday

Full Name: Desmond Sinclair Walker
DOB: 26-Nov-65 Hackney

Previous Club Details			Apps					Goals		
Club	Signed	Fee	Tot	Start	Sub	FA	FL	Lge	FA	FL
N.Forest	11/83	App	264	259	5	27	40	1	0	0
Sampdoria	8/92	£1.5m								
Sheffield W.	7/93	£2.70m	227	227	0	18	19	0	0	0
FAPL Summary by Club										
Sheffield W.	93/4 to 98/9		227	227	0	18	19	0	0	0
Totals			227	227	*0*	*18*	*19*	*0*	*0*	*0*

WALKER Ian — Tottenham Hotspur

Full Name: Ian Michael Walker
DOB: 31-Oct-71 Watford

Previous Club Details

Club	Signed	Fee	Tot	Start	Sub	FA	FL	Lge	FA	FL
			Apps					*Goals*		
Tottenham H.	12/89	Trainee	217	216	1	23	20	0	0	0
Oxford U.	8/90	Loan	2	2	0	0	1	0	0	0
FAPL Summary by Club										
Tottenham H.	92/3 to 98/9		198	197	1	23	19	0	0	0
Totals			*198*	*197*	*1*	*23*	*19*	*0*	*0*	*0*

WALLEMME Jean-Guy — Coventry City

Full Name: Jean-Guy Wallemme
DOB: 10-Aug-67 Maubeuge, France

Previous Club Details

Club	Signed	Fee	Tot	Start	Sub	FA	FL	Lge	FA	FL
			Apps					*Goals*		
RC Lens										
Coventry C.	6/97	£700k	6	4	2	0	2	0	0	0
FAPL Summary by Club										
Coventry C.	1998/9		6	4	2	0	2	0	0	0
Totals			*6*	*4*	*2*	*0*	*2*	*0*	*0*	*0*

WALSH Gary — Bradford City

Full Name: Gary Walsh
DOB: 21-Mar-68 Wigan

Previous Club Details

Club	Signed	Fee	Tot	Start	Sub	FA	FL	Lge	FA	FL
			Apps					*Goals*		
Manchester U.	4/85	Junior	50	49	1	0	7	0	0	0
Airdrieonians	8/88	Loan	3	3	0	0	3	0	0	0
Oldham A.	11/93	Loan	6	6	0	0	0	0	0	0
Middlesbrough	8/95	£250k	44	44	0	4	9	0	0	0
Bradford C.	9/97	£500k	81	81	0	3	3	0	0	0
FAPL Summary by Club										
Oldham A.	1993/4		6	6	0	0	0	0	0	0
Manchester U.	1994/5		10	10	0	0	3	0	0	0
Middlesbrough	95/6 to 96/7		43	43	0	4	9	0	0	0
Totals			*59*	*59*	*0*	*4*	*12*	*0*	*0*	*0*

WALSH Steve — Leicester City

Full Name: Steven Walsh
DOB: 03-Nov-64 Preston

Previous Club Details

Club	Signed	Fee	Tot	Start	Sub	FA	FL	Lge	FA	FL
			Apps					*Goals*		
Wigan A.	9/82	Jnrs	125	123	2	6	7	4	0	0
Leicester C.	6/86	£100k	357	347	10	13	37	53	1	3
FAPL Summary by Club										
Leicester C.	94/5 to 98/9		75	67	8	4	14	8	1	0
Totals			*75*	*67*	*8*	*4*	*14*	*8*	*1*	*0*

WANCHOPE Paulo — Derby County

Full Name: Pablo Cesar Wanchope
DOB: 31-Jul-76 Costa Rica

Previous Club Details

Club	Signed	Fee	Tot	Start	Sub	FA	FL	Lge	FA	FL
			Apps					*Goals*		
CS Heridiano										
Derby Co.	3/97	£600k	72	65	7	4	7	23	0	5
FAPL Summary by Club										
Derby Co.	96/7 to 98/9		72	65	7	4	7	23	0	5
Totals			*72*	*65*	*7*	*4*	*7*	*23*	*0*	*5*

WATSON Dave — Everton

Full Name: David Watson
DOB: 20-Nov-61 Liverpool

Previous Club Details — *Apps* / *Goals*

Club	Signed	Fee	Tot	Start	Sub	FA	FL	Lge	FA	FL
Liverpool	5/79	Juniors	0	0	0	0	0	0	0	0
Norwich C.	11/80	£100k	212	212	0	18	21	11	1	3
Everton	8/86	£900k	417	414	3	49	39	23	5	7

FAPL Summary by Club

Club	Seasons	Tot	Start	Sub	FA	FL	Lge	FA	FL
Everton	92/3 to 98/9	217	215	2	17	16	6	2	2
Totals		*217*	*215*	*2*	*17*	*16*	*6*	*2*	*2*

WATSON Gordon — Bradford City

Full Name: Gordon William George Watson

DOB: 20-Mar-71 Sidcup

Previous Club Details — *Apps* / *Goals*

Club	Signed	Fee	Tot	Start	Sub	FA	FL	Lge	FA	FL
Charlton A.	4/89	Trainee	31	20	11	1	2	7	0	1
Sheffield W.	2/91	£250k	66	29	37	7	11	15	2	3
Southampton	3/95	£1.2m	52	37	15	5	3	8	1	2
Bradford C.	1/97	£550k	21	8	13	0	4	5	0	0

FAPL Summary by Club

Club	Seasons	Tot	Start	Sub	FA	FL	Lge	FA	FL
Sheffield W.	92/3 to 94/5	57	24	33	6	10	15	2	3
Southampton	94/5 to 95/6	37	30	7	5	3	6	1	2
Totals		*94*	*54*	*40*	*11*	*13*	*21*	*3*	*5*

WATSON Steve — Aston Villa

Full Name: Stephen Craig Watson

DOB: 01-Apr-74 North Shields

Previous Club Details — *Apps* / *Goals*

Club	Signed	Fee	Tot	Start	Sub	FA	FL	Lge	FA	FL
Newcastle U.	4/91	Trainee	208	179	29	17	16	12	0	1
Aston Villa	10/98	£4m	27	26	1	2	1	0	0	0

FAPL Summary by Club

Club	Seasons	Tot	Start	Sub	FA	FL	Lge	FA	FL
Newcastle U.	93/4 to 98/9	154	133	21	10	16	11	0	1
Aston Villa	1998/9	27	26	1	2	1	0	0	0
Totals		*181*	*159*	*22*	*12*	*17*	*11*	*0*	*1*

WEIR David — Everton

Full Name: David Wier

DOB: 10-May-70 Falkirk

Previous Club Details — *Apps* / *Goals*

Club	Signed	Fee	Tot	Start	Sub	FA	FL	Lge	FA	FL
Falkirk, Hearts										
Everton	2/99	£250k	14	11	3	1	0	0	0	0

FAPL Summary by Club

Club	Seasons	Tot	Start	Sub	FA	FL	Lge	FA	FL
Everton	1998/9	14	11	3	1	0	0	0	0
Totals		*14*	*11*	*3*	*1*	*0*	*0*	*0*	*0*

WETHERALL David — Leeds United

Full Name: David Wetherall

DOB: 14-Mar-71 Sheffield

Previous Club Details — *Apps* / *Goals*

Club	Signed	Fee	Tot	Start	Sub	FA	FL	Lge	FA	FL
Sheffield W.	7/89	Trainee	0	0	0	0	0	0	0	0
Leeds U.	7/91	£125k	202	188	14	24	20	12	4	2

FAPL Summary by Club

Club	Seasons	Tot	Start	Sub	FA	FL	Lge	FA	FL
Leeds U.	92/3 to 98/9	201	188	13	24	20	12	4	2
Totals		*201*	*188*	*13*	*24*	*20*	*12*	*4*	*2*

WHALLEY Gareth — Bradford City

Full Name: Gareth Whalley

DOB: 19-Dec-73 Manchester

Previous Club Details			*Apps*					*Goals*		
Club	Signed	Fee	Tot	Start	Sub	FA	FL	Lge	FA	FL
Crewe Alex.	7/92	Trainee	180	174	6	16	11	9	4	1
Bradford C.	98		45	45	0	2	5	2	0	0

WHELAN Noel — Coventry City

Full Name: Noel Whelan
DOB: 30-Dec-74 Leeds

Previous Club Details			*Apps*					*Goals*		
Club	Signed	Fee	Tot	Start	Sub	FA	FL	Lge	FA	FL
Leeds U.	3/93	Trainee	48	28	20	2	5	7	0	1
Coventry C.	12/95	£2m	108	107	1	14	6	30	5	1
FAPL Summary by Club										
Leeds U.	92/3 to 95/6		48	28	20	2	5	7	0	1
Coventry C.	95/6 to 98/9		108	107	1	14	6	30	5	1
Totals			*156*	*135*	*21*	*16*	*11*	*37*	*5*	*2*

WIJNARD Clive — Leeds United

Full Name: Clive Wijnard
DOB: 09-Nov-73 Surinam

Previous Club Details			*Apps*					*Goals*		
Club	Signed	Fee	Tot	Start	Sub	FA	FL	Lge	FA	FL
Ajax, FC Gronigen, RKC Waalwijk, Willem II										
Leeds U.	5/98		18	11	7	2	1	3	1	0
FAPL Summary by Club										
Leeds U.	1998/9		18	11	7	2	1	3	1	0
Totals			*18*	*11*	*7*	*2*	*1*	*3*	*1*	*0*

WILLIAMS Andy — Southampton

Full Name: Andrew Williams
DOB: 06-Oct-77 Bristol

Previous Club Details			*Apps*					*Goals*		
Club	Signed	Fee	Tot	Start	Sub	FA	FL	Lge	FA	FL
Southampton	Jul-94	Trainee	21	3	18	2	0	1	3	0
FAPL Summary by Club										
Southampton	97/8 to 99-98		21	3	18	1	3	0	0	0
Totals			*21*	*3*	*18*	*1*	*3*	*0*	*0*	*0*

WILLIAMS Darren — Sunderland

Full Name: Darren Williams
DOB: 28-Apr-77 Middlesbrough

Previous Club Details			*Apps*					*Goals*		
Club	Signed	Fee	Tot	Start	Sub	FA	FL	Lge	FA	FL
York C.	6/95	Trainee	20	16	4	1	5	0	0	0
Sunderland	10/96	£50k	73	61	12	4	7	4	0	1
FAPL Summary by Club										
Sunderland	1996/7		11	10	1	2	0	2	0	0
Totals			*11*	*10*	*1*	*2*	*0*	*2*	*0*	*0*

WILLIAMS Paul — Coventry City

Full Name: Paul Darren Williams
DOB: 26-Mar-71 Burton

Previous Club Details			*Apps*					*Goals*		
Club	Signed	Fee	Tot	Start	Sub	FA	FL	Lge	FA	FL
Derby Co.	7/89	Trainee	160	153	7	8	12	25	3	2
Lincoln C.	11/89	Loan	3	3	0	2	0	0	0	0
Coventry C.	8/95	£975k	106	96	10	8	12	4	0	1
FAPL Summary by Club										
Coventry C.	95/6 to 98/9		106	96	10	8	12	4	0	1
Totals			*106*	*96*	*10*	*8*	*12*	*4*	*0*	*1*

WILSON Stuart — **Leicester City**

Full Name: Stuart Kevin Wilson
DOB: 16-Sep-77 Leicester

Previous Club Details			*Apps*					*Goals*		
Club	Signed	Fee	Tot	Start	Sub	FA	FL	Lge	FA	FL
Leicester C.	7/96	Trainee	22	1	21	3	6	3	0	1
FAPL Summary by Club										
Leicester C.	96/7 to 98/9		22	1	21	3	6	3	0	1
Totals			*22*	*1*	*21*	*3*	*6*	*3*	*0*	*1*

WINTERBURN Nigel — **Arsenal**

Full Name: Nigel Winterburn
DOB: 11-Dec-63 Nuneaton

Previous Club Details			*Apps*					*Goals*		
Club	Signed	Fee	Tot	Start	Sub	FA	FL	Lge	FA	FL
Wimbledon	9/83	Free	165	164	1	12	13	8	0	0
Arsenal	5/87	£407k	412	411	1	47	48	8	0	3
FAPL Summary by Club										
Arsenal	92/3 to 98/9		242	241	1	30	29	4	0	1
Totals			*242*	*241*	*1*	*30*	*29*	*4*	*0*	*1*

WISE Dennis — **Chelsea**

Full Name: Dennis Frank Wise
DOB: 15-Dec-66 Kensington

Previous Club Details			*Apps*					*Goals*		
Club	Signed	Fee	Tot	Start	Sub	FA	FL	Lge	FA	FL
Wimbledon	3/85		135	127	8	11	14	27	3	0
Chelsea	7/90	£1.6m	266	258	8	30	30	47	7	6
FAPL Summary by Club										
Chelsea	92/3 to 98/9		195	188	7	25	21	27	5	3
Totals			*195*	*188*	*7*	*25*	*21*	*27*	*5*	*3*

WOODGATE Jonathan — **Leeds United**

Full Name: Jonathan Woodgate
DOB: 22-Jan-80 Middlesbrough

Previous Club Details			*Apps*					*Goals*		
Club	Signed	Fee	Tot	Start	Sub	FA	FL	Lge	FA	FL
Leeds U.		Trainee	25	25	0	5	2	2	0	0
FAPL Summary by Club										
Leeds U.	1998/9		25	25	0	5	2	2	0	0
Totals			*25*	*25*	*0*	*5*	*2*	*2*	*0*	*0*

WRIGHT Alan — **Aston Villa**

Full Name: Alan Geoffrey Wright
DOB: 28-Sep-71 Ashton-under-Lyme

Previous Club Details			*Apps*					*Goals*		
Club	Signed	Fee	Tot	Start	Sub	FA	FL	Lge	FA	FL
Blackpool	4/89	Juniors	98	91	7	8	12	0	0	0
Blackburn R.	10/91	£400k	74	67	7	5	8	1	0	0
Aston Villa	3/95	£1m	159	157	2	14	12	3	0	0
FAPL Summary by Club										
Blackburn R.	92/3 to 94/5		41	35	6	4	8	0	0	0
Aston Villa	94/5 to 98/9		159	157	2	14	12	3	0	0
Totals			*200*	*192*	*8*	*18*	*20*	*3*	*0*	*0*

WRIGHT Ian — **West Ham United**

Full Name: Ian Edward Wright
DOB: 03-Nov-63 Woolwich

Previous Club Details			*Apps*					*Goals*		
Club	Signed	Fee	Tot	Start	Sub	FA	FL	Lge	FA	FL
Crystal Palace	8/85	Free	225	206	19	11	19	89	3	9
Arsenal	9/91	£2.5m	221	212	9	16	29	128	12	29
West Ham U.	7/98	undis	22	20	2	1	2	9	0	0

FAPL Summary by Club

Club	Signed	Fee	Tot	Start	Sub	FA	FL	Lge	FA	FL
Arsenal	92/3 to 97/8		191	182	9	16	26	104	12	27
West Ham U.	1998/9		22	20	2	1	2	9	0	0
Totals			*213*	*202*	*11*	*17*	*28*	*113*	*12*	*27*

WRIGHT Nick — Watford

Full Name: Nicholas John Wright
DOB: 15-Oct-75 Derby

Previous Club Details			*Apps*					*Goals*		
Club	Signed	Fee	Tot	Start	Sub	FA	FL	Lge	FA	FL
Derby Co.	7/94	Trainee	0	0	0	0	0	0	0	0
Carlisle U.*	11/97		25	25	0	0	0	5	0	0
Watford			33	31	2	1	0	6	0	0

YORKE Dwight — Manchester United

Full Name: Dwight Yorke
DOB: 03-Nov-71 Tobago, West Indies

Previous Club Details			*Apps*					*Goals*		
Club	Signed	Fee	Tot	Start	Sub	FA	FL	Lge	FA	FL
Aston Villa	12/89	£120k	231	195	36	24	22	73	13	8
Manchester U.	8/98	£12.6m	32	32	0	8	0	18	3	0
FAPL Summary by Club										
Aston Villa	92/3 to 98/9		179	160	19	17	19	60	9	8
Manchester U.	1998/9		32	32	0	8	0	18	3	0
Totals			*211*	*192*	*19*	*25*	*19*	*78*	*12*	*8*

YOUNG Luke — Tottenham Hotspur

Full Name: Luke Young
DOB: 19-Jul-79 Harlow

Previous Club Details			*Apps*					*Goals*		
Club	Signed	Fee	Tot	Start	Sub	FA	FL	Lge	FA	FL
Tottenham H.		Trainee	14	13	1	5	2	0	0	0
FAPL Summary by Club										
Tottenham H.	1998/9		14	13	1	5	2	0	0	0
Totals			*14*	*13*	*1*	*5*	*2*	*0*	*0*	*0*

ZAGORAKIS Theo — Leicester City

Full Name: Theodoros Zagorakis
DOB: 27-Oct-71 Kavala, Greece

Previous Club Details			*Apps*					*Goals*		
Club	Signed	Fee	Tot	Start	Sub	FA	FL	Lge	FA	FL
PAOK Salonika										
Leicester C.	2/98	£750k	31	28	5	2	5	2	0	0
FAPL Summary by Club										
Leicester C.	97/8 to 98/9		33	28	5	2	5	2	0	0
Totals			*33*	*28*	*5*	*2*	*5*	*2*	*0*	*0*

ZOLA Gianfranco — Chelsea

Full Name: Gianfranco Zola
DOB: 05-Jul-66 Oliena, Sardinia

Previous Club Details			*Apps*					*Goals*		
Club	Signed	Fee	Tot	Start	Sub	FA	FL	Lge	FA	FL
Nuorse	1984		31					10		
Torres	1986		88					21		
Napoli	1989		105	102	3			32		
Parma	1993		94	93	1			47		
Chelsea	11/96	£4.5m	87	80	7	14	4	29	5	0
FAPL Summary by Club										
Chelsea	96/7 to 98/9		87	80	7	14	4	29	5	0
Totals			*87*	*80*	*7*	*14*	*4*	*29*	*5*	*0*

Form 'n' Encounter Guide

Our unique *Form 'n' Encounter Guide* will allow you to plan your season's FA Carling Premiership schedule by providing you with a form guide which helps you to predict what are likely to be the most exciting games to attend on a day-by-day basis. The next few pages provide the home records for each of this season's Premiership sides in a simple PWDLFA format. From page 310 you will find the individual results from the previous six years' Premiership encounters for the corresponding fixtures. Please do check that the game you are looking to attend is on before you set out. Match dates and kick-off times are all *subject to change* to cope with TV schedules and the like.

Cup matches and international dates are shown in *italic*. Dates given for the UEFA European club competitions are for the three days of events. Champions' League games will generally be played on Tuesdays and Wednesdays with UEFA Cup games generally being on Thursdays. Some UEFA Cup games may well be switched to Tuesdays or Wednesdays to accommodate TV.

Matches selected for live transmission on Sky Sports at the time of going to press are indicated – check kick-off times as appropriate.

Opponents	*P*	*W*	*D*	*L*	*F*	*A*	*Pt*
Arsenal v							
Aston Villa	7	2	3	2	6	5	9
Bradford C.	0	0	0	0	0	0	0
Chelsea	7	5	2	0	13	6	17
Coventry C.	7	4	2	1	10	5	14
Derby Co.	3	2	1	0	4	2	7
Everton	7	5	1	1	14	4	16
Leeds United	7	5	1	1	13	7	16
Leicester C.	4	3	1	0	10	2	10
Liverpool	7	1	2	4	2	5	5
Manchester U.	7	3	2	2	10	7	11
Middlesbrough	4	1	3	0	5	3	6
Newcastle U.	6	4	0	2	12	6	12
Sheffield W.	7	6	1	0	15	4	19
Southampton	7	5	2	0	17	8	17
Sunderland	1	1	0	0	2	0	3
Tottenham H.	7	1	5	1	6	6	8
Watford	0	0	0	0	0	0	0
West Ham U.	6	4	0	2	8	3	12
Wimbledon	7	2	2	3	12	7	8

Opponents	*P*	*W*	*D*	*L*	*F*	*A*	*Pt*
Aston Villa v							
Arsenal	7	3	2	2	9	11	11
Bradford C.	0	0	0	0	0	0	0
Chelsea	7	2	0	5	5	11	6
Coventry C.	7	3	3	1	10	6	12
Derby	3	3	0	0	5	1	9
Everton	7	5	2	0	11	3	17
Leeds U.	7	4	2	1	9	3	14
Leicester C.	4	0	3	1	7	9	3
Liverpool	7	5	0	2	13	10	15
Manchester U.	7	2	2	3	7	8	8
Middlesbrough	4	3	1	0	9	2	10
Newcastle U.	6	1	2	3	4	8	5
Sheffield W.	7	3	3	1	12	9	12
Southampton	7	3	3	1	10	5	12
Sunderland	1	1	0	0	1	0	3
Tottenham H.	7	5	2	0	12	5	17
Watford	0	0	0	0	0	0	0
West Ham U.	6	2	3	1	6	4	9
Wimbledon	7	5	0	2	18	4	15

Bradford City v

Bradford City have not played any games in the Premiership prior to 1999-2000.

Chelsea v

Opponents	P	W	D	L	F	A	Pt
Arsenal	7	3	1	3	6	9	10
Aston Villa	7	2	2	3	6	7	8
Bradford C.	0	0	0	0	0	0	0
Coventry C.	7	4	2	1	14	9	14
Derby Co.	3	3	0	0	9	2	9
Everton	7	4	2	1	13	7	14
Leeds U.	7	3	3	1	7	5	12
Leicester C.	4	3	1	0	9	3	10
Liverpool	7	4	3	0	10	4	15
Manchester U.	7	1	3	3	6	10	6
Middlesbrough	4	4	0	0	12	0	12
Newcastle U.	6	3	3	0	6	3	12
Sheffield W.	7	1	5	1	6	7	8
Southampton	7	5	1	1	12	5	16
Sunderland	1	1	0	0	6	2	3
Tottenham H.	7	4	3	0	13	6	15
Watford	0	0	0	0	0	0	0
West Ham U.	6	3	0	3	9	7	9
Wimbledon	7	3	2	2	14	10	11

Coventry City v

Opponents	P	W	D	L	F	A	Pt
Arsenal	7	1	3	3	4	7	6
Aston Villa	7	1	0	6	6	11	3
Bradford C.	0	0	0	0	0	0	0
Chelsea	7	4	2	1	13	9	14
Derby Co.	3	1	1	1	3	3	4
Everton	7	3	3	1	7	3	12
Leeds U.	7	2	4	1	9	9	10
Leicester C.	4	1	2	1	5	5	5
Liverpool	7	4	2	1	11	5	14
Manchester U.	7	1	0	6	5	14	3
Middlesbrough	4	2	1	1	6	3	7
Newcastle U.	6	2	2	2	7	10	8
Sheffield W.	7	4	2	1	6	2	14
Southampton	7	3	3	1	8	6	12
Sunderland	1	0	1	0	2	2	1
Tottenham H.	7	3	1	3	10	10	10
Watford	0	0	0	0	0	0	0
West Ham U.	6	1	4	1	7	7	7
Wimbledon	7	1	4	2	8	10	7

Derby County v

Opponents	P	W	D	L	F	A	Pt
Arsenal	3	1	1	1	4	3	4
Aston Villa	3	2	0	1	4	3	6
Bradford C.	0	0	0	0	0	0	0
Chelsea	3	1	1	1	5	5	4
Coventry C.	3	2	1	0	5	2	7
Everton	3	2	0	1	5	3	6
Leeds U.	3	0	2	1	5	10	2
Leicester C.	3	2	0	1	4	4	6
Liverpool	3	2	0	1	4	3	6
Manchester U.	3	0	3	0	4	4	3
Middlesbrough	2	2	0	0	4	2	6
Newcastle U.	3	1	0	2	4	5	3
Sheffield W.	3	2	1	0	6	2	7
Southampton	3	1	2	0	5	1	5
Sunderland	1	1	0	0	1	0	3
Tottenham H.	3	2	0	1	6	4	6
Watford	0	0	0	0	0	0	0
West Ham U.	3	2	0	1	3	2	6
Wimbledon	3	0	2	1	1	3	2

Everton v

Opponents	P	W	D	L	F	A	Pt
Arsenal	7	0	4	3	4	10	4
Aston Villa	7	2	2	3	5	8	8
Bradford C.	0	0	0	0	0	0	0
Chelsea	7	2	3	2	12	10	9
Coventry C.	7	1	5	1	7	7	8
Derby Co.	3	1	1	1	2	2	4
Leeds U.	7	4	3	0	10	1	15
Leicester C.	4	0	4	0	3	3	4
Liverpool	7	4	3	0	10	3	15
Manchester U.	7	1	0	6	4	14	3
Middlesbrough	4	2	1	1	12	4	7
Newcastle U.	6	3	1	2	6	5	10
Sheffield W.	7	1	2	4	8	14	5
Southampton	7	5	1	1	13	4	16
Sunderland	1	0	0	1	1	3	0
Tottenham H.	7	1	2	4	3	7	5
Watford	0	0	0	0	0	0	0
West Ham U.	6	5	0	1	14	3	15
Wimbledon	7	1	4	2	7	10	7

Leeds United v

Opponents	*P*	*W*	*D*	*L*	*F*	*A*	*Pt*
Arsenal	7	4	2	1	8	5	14
Aston Villa	7	3	4	0	7	2	13
Bradford C.	0	0	0	0	0	0	0
Chelsea	7	4	2	1	13	6	14
Coventry C.	7	4	2	1	15	9	14
Derby Co.	3	2	1	0	8	4	7
Everton	7	5	2	0	10	2	17
Leicester C.	4	2	0	2	5	3	6
Liverpool	7	2	2	3	5	8	8
Manchester U.	7	3	2	2	7	9	11
Middlesbrough	4	2	1	1	6	2	7
Newcastle U.	6	1	2	3	5	5	5
Sheffield W.	7	3	1	3	10	9	10
Southampton	7	3	3	1	6	2	12
Sunderland	1	1	0	0	3	0	3
Tottenham H.	7	4	2	1	12	4	14
Watford	0	0	0	0	0	0	0
West Ham U.	6	5	1	0	13	3	16
Wimbledon	7	4	3	0	14	6	15

Liverpool v

Opponents	*P*	*W*	*D*	*L*	*F*	*A*	*Pt*
Arsenal	7	4	2	1	12	3	14
Aston Villa	7	5	0	2	15	6	15
Bradford C.	0	0	0	0	0	0	0
Chelsea	7	6	1	0	19	7	19
Coventry C.	7	4	1	2	11	5	13
Derby Co.	3	2	0	1	7	3	6
Everton	7	3	3	1	9	7	12
Leeds U.	7	5	0	2	17	5	15
Leicester C.	4	1	1	2	4	4	4
Manchester U.	7	2	2	3	12	13	8
Middlesbrough	4	4	0	0	13	3	12
Newcastle U.	6	5	0	1	15	10	15
Sheffield W.	7	6	0	1	12	3	18
Southampton	7	4	2	1	20	10	14
Sunderland	1	0	1	0	0	0	1
Tottenham H.	7	4	2	1	17	8	14
Watford	0	0	0	0	0	0	0
West Ham U.	6	3	3	0	11	2	12
Wimbledon	7	3	3	1	14	7	12

Leicester City v

Opponents	*P*	*W*	*D*	*L*	*F*	*A*	*Pt*
Arsenal	4	1	2	1	6	7	5
Aston Villa	4	2	2	0	5	3	8
Bradford C.	0	0	0	0	0	0	0
Chelsea	4	1	1	2	6	8	4
Coventry C.	4	1	2	1	4	5	5
Derby Co.	3	1	0	2	6	6	3
Everton	4	1	1	2	5	5	4
Leeds	4	2	0	2	4	5	6
Liverpool	4	1	1	2	2	5	4
Manchester U.	4	0	2	2	4	12	2
Middlesbrough	2	0	0	2	1	4	0
Newcastle U.	4	2	1	1	5	3	7
Sheffield W.	4	1	1	2	2	4	4
Southampton	4	3	1	0	11	7	10
Sunderland	1	0	1	0	1	1	1
Tottenham H.	4	3	1	0	9	3	10
Watford	0	0	0	0	0	0	0
West Ham U.	4	1	1	2	3	4	4
Wimbledon	4	1	1	2	5	6	4

Manchester U. v

Opponents	*P*	*W*	*D*	*L*	*F*	*A*	*Pt*
Arsenal	7	4	2	1	7	2	14
Aston Villa	7	4	3	0	8	3	15
Bradford C.	0	0	0	0	0	0	0
Chelsea	7	1	4	2	8	7	7
Coventry C.	7	6	1	0	16	1	19
Derby Co.	3	2	0	1	5	3	6
Everton	7	5	1	1	12	6	16
Leeds U.	7	5	2	0	10	2	17
Leicester C.	4	1	2	1	6	5	5
Liverpool	7	4	3	0	11	5	15
Middlesbrough	4	2	1	1	10	6	7
Newcastle U.	6	2	4	0	6	2	10
Sheffield W.	7	6	1	0	21	4	19
Southampton	7	7	0	0	15	5	21
Sunderland	1	1	0	0	5	0	3
Tottenham H.	7	6	1	0	13	3	19
Watford	0	0	0	0	0	0	0
West Ham U.	6	6	0	0	14	3	18
Wimbledon	7	6	0	1	18	5	18

Middlesbrough v

Opponents	*P*	*W*	*D*	*L*	*F*	*A*	*Pt*
Arsenal	4	1	0	3	4	11	3
Aston Villa	4	1	1	2	5	7	4
Bradford C.	0	0	0	0	0	0	0
Chelsea	4	2	2	0	3	0	8
Coventry C.	4	3	0	1	8	3	9
Derby Co.	2	1	1	0	7	2	4
Everton	4	1	1	2	7	8	4
Leeds U.	4	1	3	0	5	2	6
Leicester C.	2	0	1	1	0	2	1
Liverpool	4	1	1	2	7	9	4
Manchester U.	4	0	2	2	3	7	2
Newcastle U.	3	0	2	1	4	5	2
Sheffield W.	4	3	1	0	12	4	10
Southampton	4	2	1	1	5	2	7
Sunderland	1	0	0	1	0	1	0
Tottenham H.	4	1	1	2	3	4	4
Watford	0	0	0	0	0	0	0
West Ham U.	3	3	0	0	9	3	9
Wimbledon	4	2	1	1	6	3	7

Newcastle U. v

Opponents	*P*	*W*	*D*	*L*	*F*	*A*	*Pt*
Arsenal	6	3	1	2	7	4	10
Aston Villa	6	6	0	0	16	6	18
Bradford C.	0	0	0	0	0	0	0
Chelsea	6	4	1	1	12	5	13
Coventry C.	6	5	1	0	19	1	16
Derby Co.	3	2	1	0	5	2	7
Everton	6	5	0	1	10	4	15
Leeds U.	6	2	2	2	8	8	8
Leicester C.	4	3	1	0	11	7	10
Liverpool	6	2	2	2	9	9	8
Manchester U.	6	1	2	3	8	6	5
Middlesbrough	3	2	1	0	5	2	7
Sheffield W.	6	4	1	1	12	7	13
Southampton	6	4	0	2	13	5	12
Sunderland	1	0	1	0	1	1	1
Tottenham H.	6	2	3	1	13	7	9
Watford	0	0	0	0	0	0	0
West Ham U.	6	3	1	2	8	5	10
Wimbledon	6	5	0	1	18	6	15

Sheffield W. v

Opponents	*P*	*W*	*D*	*L*	*F*	*A*	*Pt*
Arsenal	7	5	1	1	8	2	16
Aston Villa	7	2	1	4	7	9	7
Bradford C.	0	0	0	0	0	0	0
Chelsea	7	1	4	2	8	11	7
Coventry C.	7	2	3	2	11	8	9
Derby	3	0	1	2	2	6	1
Everton	7	4	2	1	15	9	14
Leeds U.	7	1	4	2	14	14	7
Leicester C.	4	3	0	1	4	2	9
Liverpool	7	2	4	1	11	9	10
Manchester U.	7	3	3	1	12	8	12
Middlesbrough	4	2	0	2	8	6	6
Newcastle U.	6	1	3	2	4	6	6
Southampton	7	3	4	0	12	6	13
Sunderland	1	1	0	0	2	1	3
Tottenham H.	7	4	1	2	10	8	13
Watford	0	0	0	0	0	0	0
West Ham U.	6	2	2	2	7	3	8
Wimbledon	7	2	3	2	10	9	9

Southampton v

Opponents	*P*	*W*	*D*	*L*	*F*	*A*	*Pt*
Arsenal	7	2	2	3	4	9	8
Aston Villa	7	3	0	4	10	10	9
Bradford C.	0	0	0	0	0	0	0
Chelsea	7	3	1	3	7	7	10
Coventry C.	7	3	3	1	9	7	12
Derby Co.	3	1	0	2	3	4	3
Everton	7	3	3	1	10	7	12
Leeds U.	7	1	2	4	6	11	5
Leicester C.	4	2	2	0	8	6	8
Liverpool	7	2	1	4	9	12	7
Manchester U.	7	3	1	3	13	13	10
Middlesbrough	4	3	1	0	11	5	10
Newcastle U.	6	5	1	0	12	6	16
Sheffield W.	7	1	2	4	7	10	5
Sunderland	1	1	0	0	3	0	3
Tottenham H.	7	3	3	1	9	7	12
Watford	0	0	0	0	0	0	0
West Ham U.	6	3	2	1	7	3	11
Wimbledon	7	2	3	2	8	7	9

Sunderland v

Opponents	*P*	*W*	*D*	*L*	*F*	*A*	*Pt*
Arsenal	1	1	0	0	1	0	3
Aston Villa	1	1	0	0	1	0	3
Bradford C.	0	0	0	0	0	0	0
Chelsea	1	1	0	0	3	0	3
Coventry C.	1	1	0	0	1	0	3
Derby Co.	1	1	0	0	2	0	3
Everton	1	1	0	0	2	0	3
Leeds U.	1	0	0	1	0	1	0
Leicester C.	1	0	1	0	0	0	1
Liverpool	1	0	0	1	1	2	0
Manchester U.	1	1	0	0	2	1	3
Middlesbrough	1	0	1	0	2	2	1
Newcastle U.	1	0	0	1	1	2	0
Sheffield W.	1	0	1	0	1	1	1
Southampton	1	0	0	1	0	1	0
Tottenham	1	0	0	1	0	4	0
Watford	0	0	0	0	0	0	0
West Ham U.	1	0	1	0	0	0	1
Wimbledon	1	0	0	1	1	3	0

Tottenham Hotspur v

Opponents	*P*	*W*	*D*	*L*	*F*	*A*	*Pt*
Arsenal	7	3	2	2	6	6	11
Aston Villa	7	3	2	2	9	8	11
Bradford C.	0	0	0	0	0	0	0
Chelsea	7	0	4	3	7	14	4
Coventry C.	7	1	2	4	7	11	5
Derby	3	1	2	0	3	2	5
Everton	7	4	3	0	12	6	15
Leeds U.	7	3	3	1	12	7	12
Leicester C.	4	1	1	2	3	5	4
Liverpool	7	2	3	2	11	12	9
Manchester U.	7	1	2	4	8	10	5
Middlesbrough	4	1	2	1	4	6	5
Newcastle U.	6	3	1	2	11	7	10
Sheffield W.	7	3	1	3	9	12	10
Southampton	7	5	1	1	16	6	16
Sunderland	1	1	0	0	2	0	3
Watford	0	0	0	0	0	0	0
West Ham U.	6	3	0	3	7	8	9
Wimbledon	7	2	4	1	7	5	10

Watford v

Watford have not played any games in the Premiership prior to 1999-00.

West Ham United v

Opponents	*P*	*W*	*D*	*L*	*F*	*A*	*Pt*
Arsenal	6	0	2	4	1	9	2
Aston Villa	6	2	2	2	4	7	8
Bradford C.	0	0	0	0	0	0	0
Chelsea	6	3	1	2	9	9	10
Coventry C.	6	4	1	1	10	6	13
Derby Co.	3	1	2	0	6	2	5
Everton	6	2	3	1	10	9	9
Leeds U.	6	1	1	4	5	10	4
Leicester C.	4	4	0	0	9	5	12
Liverpool	6	3	1	2	9	6	10
Manchester U.	6	0	5	1	6	7	5
Middlesbrough	3	2	1	0	6	0	7
Newcastle U.	6	2	1	3	7	8	7
Sheffield W.	6	3	1	2	9	8	10
Southampton	6	5	1	0	12	6	16
Sunderland	1	1	0	0	2	0	3
Tottenham H.	6	3	1	2	11	11	10
Watford	0	0	0	0	0	0	0
Wimbledon	6	2	1	3	10	10	7

Wimbledon v

Opponents	*P*	*W*	*D*	*L*	*F*	*A*	*Pt*
Arsenal	7	2	1	4	7	14	7
Aston Villa	7	2	3	2	13	14	9
Bradford C.	0	0	0	0	0	0	0
Chelsea	7	0	4	3	4	8	4
Coventry C.	7	2	1	4	9	11	7
Derby Co.	3	1	2	0	3	2	5
Everton	7	2	2	3	11	10	8
Leeds U.	7	4	2	1	8	5	14
Leicester C.	4	2	0	2	5	6	6
Liverpool	7	4	3	0	8	3	15
Manchester U.	7	1	1	5	7	16	4
Middlesbrough	4	1	3	0	5	3	6
Newcastle U.	6	2	4	0	12	9	10
Sheffield W.	7	3	3	1	12	9	12
Southampton	7	3	0	4	7	9	9
Sunderland	1	1	0	0	1	0	3
Tottenham H.	7	3	1	3	10	12	10
Watford	0	0	0	0	0	0	0
West Ham U.	6	1	2	3	4	6	5

Date	*Match/Event*	*93-94*	*94-95*	*95-96*	*96-97*	*97-98*	*98-99*
07-Aug	Arsenal v Leicester C.	–	1-1	–	2-0	2-1	5-0
07-Aug	Chelsea v Sunderland	–	–	–	6-2	–	–
07-Aug	Coventry C. v Southampton	1-1	1-3	1-1	1-1	1-0	1-0
07-Aug	Leeds U. v Derby Co.	–	–	–	0-0	4-3	4-1
07-Aug	Middlesbrough v Bradford C.	–	–	–	–	–	–
07-Aug	Newcastle U. v Aston Villa	5-1	3-1	1-0	4-3	1-0	2-1
07-Aug	Sheffield W. v Liverpool	3-1	1-2	1-1	1-1	3-3	1-0
07-Aug	Watford v Wimbledon	–	–	–	–	–	–
07-Aug	West Ham U. v Tottenham H.	1-3	1-2	1-1	4-3	2-1	2-1
08-Aug	Everton v Manchester U. (Sky)	0-1	1-0	2-3	0-2	0-2	1-4
09-Aug	Tottenham H. v Newcastle U. (Sky)	1-2	4-2	1-1	1-2	2-0	2-0
10-Aug	Bradford C. v Chelsea	–	–	–	–	–	–
10-Aug	Derby Co. v Arsenal (Sky)	–	–	–	1-3	3-0	0-0
10-Aug	Sunderland v Watford	–	–	–	–	–	–
10-Aug	Wimbledon v Middlesbrough	–	–	0-0	1-1		2-2
11-Aug	Aston Villa v Everton	0-0	0-0	1-0	3-1	2-1	3-0
11-Aug	Leicester C. v Coventry C.	–	2-2	–	0-2	1-1	1-0
11-Aug	Liverpool v West Ham U.	2-0	0-0	2-0	0-0	5-0	2-2
11-Aug	Manchester U. v Sheffield W.	5-0	1-0	2-2	2-0	6-1	3-0
11-Aug	Southampton v Leeds U.	0-2	1-3	1-1	0-2	0-2	3-0
14-Aug	Bradford C. v Sheffield W.	–	–	–	–	–	–
14-Aug	Derby Co. v Middlesbrough	–	–	–	2-1		2-1
14-Aug	Leicester C. v Chelsea	–	1-1	–	1-3	2-0	2-4
14-Aug	Liverpool v Watford	–	–	–	–	–	–
14-Aug	Manchester U. v Leeds U.	0-0	0-0	1-0	1-0	3-0	3-2
14-Aug	Sunderland v Arsenal	–	–	–	1-0	–	–
14-Aug	Tottenham H. v Everton	3-2	2-1	0-0	0-0	1-1	4-1
14-Aug	Wimbledon v Coventry C.	1-2	2-0	0-2	2-2	1-2	2-1
15-Aug	Southampton v Newcastle U. (Sky)	2-1	3-1	1-0	2-2	2-1	2-1
16-Aug	Aston Villa v West Ham U. (Sky)	3-1	0-2	1-1	0-0	2-0	0-0
21-Aug	Chelsea v Aston Villa	1-1	1-0	1-2	1-1	0-1	2-1
21-Aug	Coventry C. v Derby Co.	–	–	–	1-2	1-0	1-1
21-Aug	Everton v Southampton	1-0	0-0	2-0	7-1	0-2	1-0
21-Aug	Leeds U. v Sunderland	–	–	–	3-0	–	–
21-Aug	Middlesbrough v Liverpool	–	–	2-1	3-3	–	1-3
21-Aug	Newcastle U. v Wimbledon	4-0	2-1	6-1	2-0	1-3	3-1
21-Aug	Sheffield W. v Tottenham H.	1-0	3-4	1-3	2-1	1-0	0-0
21-Aug	Watford v Bradford C.	–	–	–	–	–	–
21-Aug	West Ham U. v Leicester C.	–	1-0	–	1-0	4-3	3-2
22-Aug	Arsenal v Manchester U. (Sky)	2-2	0-0	1-0	1-2	3-2	3-0
23-Aug	Leeds U. v Liverpool (Sky)	2-0	0-2	1-0	0-2	0-2	0-0

Date	*Match/Event*	*93-94*	*94-95*	*95-96*	*96-97*	*97-98*	*98-99*
24-Aug	Arsenal v Bradford C.	–	–	–	–	–	–
24-Aug	Middlesbrough v Leicester C.	–	–	–	0-2	–	0-0
24-Aug	Watford v Aston Villa	–	–	–	–	–	–
25-Aug	Chelsea v Tottenham H.	4-3	1-1	0-0	3-1	2-0	2-0
25-Aug	Coventry C. v Manchester U.	0-1	2-3	0-4	0-2	3-2	0-1
25-Aug	Everton v Wimbledon	3-2	0-0	2-4	1-3	0-0	1-1
25-Aug	Newcastle U. v Sunderland	–	–	–	1-1	–	–
25-Aug	Sheffield W. v Derby	–	–	–	0-0	2-5	0-1
25-Aug	West Ham U. v Southampton	3-3	2-0	2-1	2-1	2-1	1-0
27-Aug	*Super Cup Final – Manchester U. v Lazio – Monaco*						
28-Aug	Aston Villa v Middlesbrough	–	–	0-0	1-0		3-1
28-Aug	Bradford C. v West Ham U.	–	–	–	–	–	–
28-Aug	Derby Co. v Everton	–	–	–	0-1	3-1	2-1
28-Aug	Liverpool v Arsenal	0-0	3-0	3-1	2-0	4-0	0-0
28-Aug	Manchester U. v Newcastle U.	1-1	2-0	2-0	0-0	1-1	0-0
28-Aug	Southampton v Sheffield W.	1-1	0-0	0-1	2-3	2-3	1-0
28-Aug	Tottenham H. v Leeds U.	1-1	1-1	2-1	1-0	0-1	3-3
28-Aug	Wimbledon v Chelsea	1-1	1-1	1-1	0-1	0-2	1-2
29-Aug	Sunderland v Coventry C. (Sky)	–	–	–	1-0	–	–
30-Aug	Leicester C. v Watford (Sky)	–	–	–	–	–	–
04-Sep	*England v Luxembourg – UEFA European Championship*						
07-Sep	*Poland v England – UEFA European Championship*						
11-Sep	Arsenal v Aston Villa	1-2	0-0	2-0	2-2	0-0	1-0
11-Sep	Chelsea v Newcastle U.	1-0	1-1	1-0	1-1	1-0	1-1
11-Sep	Coventry C. v Leeds U.	0-2	2-1	0-0	2-1	0-0	2-2
11-Sep	Liverpool v Manchester U. (Sky)	3-3	2-0	2-0	1-3	1-3	2-2
11-Sep	Middlesbrough v Southampton	–	–	0-0	0-1	–	3-0
11-Sep	Sheffield W. v Everton	5-1	0-0	2-5	2-1	3-1	0-0
11-Sep	Sunderland v Leicester C.	–	–	–	0-0	–	–
11-Sep	West Ham U. v Watford	–	–	–	–	–	–
11-Sep	Wimbledon v Derby Co.	–	–	–	1-1	0-0	2-1
12-Sep	Bradford C. v Tottenham H. (Sky)	–	–	–	–	–	–
14-Sep	*Champions' League 1st Group Phase – Matchday 1*						
15-Sep	*Champions' League 1st Group Phase – Matchday 1*						
16-Sep	*UEFA Cup 1st Round, 1st Leg*						
18-Sep	Aston Villa v Bradford C.	–	–	–	–	–	
18-Sep	Derby Co. v Sunderland	–	–	–	1-0	–	–
18-Sep	Everton v West Ham U.	0-1	1-0	3-0	2-1	2-1	6-0
18-Sep	Leeds U. v Middlesbrough	–	–	0-1	1-1		2-0
18-Sep	Leicester C. v Liverpool	–	1-2	–	0-3	0-0	1-0
18-Sep	Manchester U. v Wimbledon	3-1	3-0	3-1	2-1	2-0	5-1

Date	*Match/Event*	*93-94*	*94-95*	*95-96*	*96-97*	*97-98*	*98-99*
18-Sep	Newcastle U. v Sheffield W.	4-2	2-1	2-0	1-2	2-1	1-1
18-Sep	Southampton v Arsenal	0-4	1-0	0-0	0-2	1-3	0-0
18-Sep	Tottenham H. v Coventry C.	1-2	1-3	3-1	1-2	1-1	0-0
18-Sep	Watford v Chelsea	–	–	–	–	–	–
21-Sep	*Champions' League 1st Group Phase – Matchday 2*						
22-Sep	*Champions' League 1st Group Phase – Matchday 2*						
25-Sep	Arsenal v Watford	–	–	–	–	–	–
25-Sep	Coventry C. v West Ham U.	1-1	2-0	2-2	1-3	1-1	0-0
25-Sep	Derby Co. v Bradford C.	–	–	–	–	–	–
25-Sep	Leeds U. v Newcastle U.	1-1	0-0	0-1	0-1	4-1	0-1
25-Sep	Leicester C. v Aston Villa	–	1-1	–	1-0	1-0	2-2
25-Sep	Manchester U. v Southampton	2-0	2-1	4-1	2-1	1-0	2-1
25-Sep	Middlesbrough v Chelsea	–	–	2-0	1-0	–	0-0
25-Sep	Sunderland v Sheffield W.	–	–	–	1-1	–	–
26-Sep	Wimbledon v Tottenham H. (Sky)	2-1	1-2	0-1	1-0	2-6	3-1
27-Sep	Liverpool v Everton (Sky)	2-1	0-0	1-2	1-1	1-1	3-2
28-Sep	*Champions' League 1st Group Phase – Matchday 3*						
29-Sep	*Champions' League 1st Group Phase – Matchday 3*						
30-Sep	*UEFA Cup 1st Round, 2nd Leg*						
02-Oct	Bradford C. v Sunderland	–	–	–	–	–	–
02-Oct	Everton v Coventry C.	0-0	0-2	2-2	1-1	1-1	2-0
02-Oct	Newcastle U. v Middlesbrough	–	–	1-0	3-1		1-1
02-Oct	Sheffield W. v Wimbledon	2-2	0-1	2-1	3-1	1-1	1-2
02-Oct	Tottenham H. v Leicester C.	–	1-0	–	1-2	1-1	0-2
02-Oct	Watford v Leeds U.	–	–	–	–	–	–
02-Oct	West Ham U. v Arsenal	0-0	0-2	0-1	1-2	0-0	0-4
03-Oct	Chelsea v Manchester U. (Sky)	1-0	2-3	1-4	1-1	0-1	0-0
04-Oct	Southampton v Derby Co. (Sky)	–	–	–	3-1	0-2	0-1
09-Oct	*England – Possible Friendly International*						
16-Oct	Arsenal v Everton	2-0	1-1	1-2	3-1	4-0	1-0
16-Oct	Coventry C. v Newcastle U.	2-1	0-0	0-1	2-1	2-2	1-5
16-Oct	Derby Co. v Tottenham H.	–	–	–	4-2	2-1	0-1
16-Oct	Leeds U. v Sheffield W.	2-2	0-1	2-0	0-2	1-2	2-1
16-Oct	Leicester C. v Southampton	–	4-3	–	2-1	3-3	2-0
16-Oct	Liverpool v Chelsea	2-1	3-1	2-0	5-1	4-2	1-1
16-Oct	Manchester U. v Watford	–	–	–	–	–	–
16-Oct	Wimbledon v Bradford C.	–	–	–	–	–	–
17-Oct	Middlesbrough v West Ham U. (Sky)	–	–	4-2	4-1	–	1-0
18-Oct	Sunderland v Aston Villa (Sky)	–	–	–	1-0	–	–
19-Oct	*Champions' League 1st Group Phase – Matchday 4*						

Date	*Match/Event*	*93-94*	*94-95*	*95-96*	*96-97*	*97-98*	*98-99*
20-Oct	*Champions' League 1st Group Phase – Matchday 4*						
21-Oct	*UEFA Cup 2nd Round, 1st Leg*						
21-Oct	Aston Villa v Liverpool	2-1	2-0	0-2	1-0	2-1	2-4
23-Oct	Aston Villa v Wimbledon	0-1	7-1	2-0	5-0	1-2	2-0
23-Oct	Bradford C. v Leicester C.	–	–	–	–	–	–
23-Oct	Chelsea v Arsenal	0-2	2-1	1-0	0-3	2-3	0-0
23-Oct	Everton v Leeds U.	1-1	3-0	2-0	0-0	2-0	0-0
23-Oct	Sheffield W. v Coventry C.	0-0	5-1	4-3	0-0	0-0	1-2
23-Oct	Southampton v Liverpool	4-2	0-2	1-3	0-1	1-1	1-2
23-Oct	Tottenham H. v Manchester U.	0-1	0-1	4-1	1-2	0-2	2-2
23-Oct	West Ham U. v Sunderland	–	–	–	2-0	–	–
24-Oct	Watford v Middlesbrough (Sky)	–	–	–	–	–	–
25-Oct	Newcastle U. v Derby Co. (Sky)	–	–	–	3-1	0-0	2-1
26-Oct	*Champions' League 1st Group Phase – Matchday 5*						
27-Oct	*Champions' League 1st Group Phase – Matchday 5*						
30-Oct	Arsenal v Newcastle U.	2-1	2-3	2-0	0-1	3-1	3-0
30-Oct	Derby Co. v Chelsea	–	–	–	3-2	0-1	2-2
30-Oct	Leeds U. v West Ham U.	1-0	2-2	2-0	1-0	3-1	4-0
30-Oct	Leicester C. v Sheffield W.	–	0-1	–	1-0	1-1	0-2
30-Oct	Manchester U. v Aston Villa	3-1	1-0	0-0	0-0	1-0	2-1
30-Oct	Middlesbrough v Everton	–	–	0-2	4-2	–	2-2
30-Oct	Sunderland v Tottenham	–	–	–	0-4	–	–
30-Oct	Wimbledon v Southampton	1-0	0-2	1-2	3-1	1-0	0-2
31-Oct	Coventry C. v Watford (Sky)	–	–	–	–	–	–
01-Nov	Liverpool v Bradford C. (Sky)	–	–	–	–	–	–
02-Nov	*Champions' League 1st Group Phase – Matchday 6*						
03-Nov	*Champions' League 1st Group Phase – Matchday 6*						
04-Nov	*UEFA Cup 2nd Round, 2nd Leg*						
06-Nov	Aston Villa v Southampton	0-2	1-1	3-0	1-0	1-1	3-0
06-Nov	Bradford C. v Coventry C.	–	–	–	–	–	–
06-Nov	Chelsea v West Ham U.	2-0	1-2	1-2	3-1	2-1	0-1
06-Nov	Liverpool v Derby Co.	–	–	–	2-1	4-0	1-2
06-Nov	Manchester U. v Leicester C.	–	1-1	–	3-1	0-1	2-2
06-Nov	Middlesbrough v Sunderland	–	–	–	0-1	–	–
06-Nov	Sheffield W. v Watford	–	–	–	–	–	–
06-Nov	Tottenham H. v Arsenal	0-1	1-0	2-1	0-0	1-1	1-3
07-Nov	Wimbledon v Leeds U. (Sky)	1-0	0-0	2-4	2-0	1-0	1-1
08-Nov	Newcastle U. v Everton (Sky)	1-0	2-0	1-0	4-1	1-0	1-3
13-Nov	*England – Possible UEFA European Championship Play-off 1st Leg*						
17-Nov	*England – Possible UEFA European Championship Play-off 2nd Leg*						

Date	*Match/Event*	*93-94*	*94-95*	*95-96*	*96-97*	*97-98*	*98-99*
20-Nov	Arsenal v Middlesbrough	–	–	1-1	2-0		1-1
20-Nov	Derby Co. v Manchester U.	–	–	–	1-1	2-2	1-1
20-Nov	Everton v Chelsea	4-2	3-3	1-1	1-2	3-1	0-0
20-Nov	Leeds U. v Bradford C.	–	–	–	–	–	–
20-Nov	Leicester C. v Wimbledon	–	3-4	–	1-0	0-1	1-1
20-Nov	Southampton v Tottenham H.	1-0	4-3	0-0	0-1	3-2	1-1
20-Nov	Sunderland v Liverpool	–	–	–	1-2	–	–
20-Nov	Watford v Newcastle U.	–	–	–	–	–	–
21-Nov	West Ham U. v Sheffield W. (Sky)	2-0	0-2	1-1	5-1	1-0	0-4
22-Nov	Coventry C. v Aston Villa (Sky)	0-1	0-1	0-3	1-2	1-2	1-2
23-Nov	*Champions' League 2nd Group Phase – Matchday 7*						
24-Nov	*Champions' League 2nd Group Phase – Matchday 7*						
25-Nov	*UEFA Cup 3rd Round, 1st Leg*						
27-Nov	Arsenal v Derby Co.	–	–	–	2-2	1-0	1-0
27-Nov	Coventry C. v Leicester C.	–	4-2	–	0-0	0-2	1-1
27-Nov	Everton v Aston Villa	0-1	2-2	1-0	0-1	1-4	0-0
27-Nov	Leeds U. v Southampton	0-0	0-0	1-0	0-0	0-1	3-0
27-Nov	Middlesbrough v Wimbledon	–	–	1-2	0-0	–	3-1
27-Nov	Newcastle U. v Tottenham H.	0-1	3-3	1-1	7-1	1-0	1-1
27-Nov	Sheffield W. v Manchester U.	2-3	1-0	0-0	1-1	2-0	3-1
27-Nov	Watford v Sunderland	–	–	–	–	–	–
27-Nov	West Ham U. v Liverpool	1-2	3-0	0-0	1-2	2-1	2-1
28-Nov	Chelsea v Bradford C. (Sky)	–	–	–	–	–	–
04-Dec	Aston Villa v Newcastle U.	0-2	0-2	1-1	2-2	0-1	1-0
04-Dec	Bradford C. v Middlesbrough	–	–	–	–	–	–
04-Dec	Derby Co. v Leeds U.	–	–	–	3-3	0-5	2-2
04-Dec	Leicester C. v Arsenal (Sky)	–	2-1	–	0-2	3-3	1-1
04-Dec	Manchester U. v Everton	1-0	2-0	2-0	2-2	2-0	3-1
04-Dec	Southampton v Coventry C.	1-0	0-0	1-0	2-2	1-2	2-1
04-Dec	Sunderland v Chelsea	–	–	–	3-0	–	–
04-Dec	Wimbledon v Watford	–	–	–	–	–	–
05-Dec	Tottenham H. v West Ham U. (Sky)	1-4	3-1	0-1	1-0	1-0	1-2
06-Dec	Liverpool v Sheffield W. (Sky)	2-0	4-1	1-0	0-1	2-1	2-0
07-Dec	*Champions' League 2nd Group Phase – Matchday 8*						
08-Dec	*Champions' League 2nd Group Phase – Matchday 8*						
09-Dec	*UEFA Cup 3rd Round, 2nd Leg*						
11-Dec	*FA Cup 3rd Round*						
18-Dec	Arsenal v Wimbledon	1-1	0-0	1-3	0-1	5-0	5-1
18-Dec	Aston Villa v Sheffield W.	2-2	1-1	3-2	0-1	2-2	2-1
18-Dec	Bradford C. v Newcastle U.	–	–	–	–	–	–
18-Dec	Chelsea v Leeds U.	1-1	0-3	4-1	0-0	0-0	1-0

Date	*Match/Event*	*93-94*	*94-95*	*95-96*	*96-97*	*97-98*	*98-99*
18-Dec	Leicester C. v Derby Co.	–	–	–	4-2	1-2	1-2
18-Dec	Liverpool v Coventry C.	1-0	2-3	0-0	1-2	1-0	2-0
18-Dec	Middlesbrough v Tottenham H.	–	–	0-1	0-3	–	0-0
18-Dec	Sunderland v Southampton	–	–	–	0-1	–	–
18-Dec	Watford v Everton	–	–	–	–	–	–
18-Dec	West Ham U. v Manchester U.	2-2	1-1	0-1	2-2	1-1	0-0
26-Dec	Coventry C. v Arsenal (Sky)	1-0	0-1	0-0	1-1	2-2	0-1
26-Dec	Derby Co. v Aston Villa	–	–	–	2-1	0-1	2-1
26-Dec	Everton v Sunderland	–	–	–	1-3	–	–
26-Dec	Leeds U. v Leicester C.	–	2-1	–	3-0	0-1	0-1
26-Dec	Manchester U. v Bradford C.	–	–	–	–	–	–
26-Dec	Newcastle U. v Liverpool	3-0	1-1	2-1	1-1	1-2	1-4
26-Dec	Sheffield W. v Middlesbrough	–	–	0-1	3-1		3-1
26-Dec	Southampton v Chelsea	3-1	0-1	2-3	0-0	1-0	0-2
26-Dec	Tottenham H. v Watford	–	–	–	–	–	–
26-Dec	Wimbledon v West Ham U.	1-2	1-0	0-1	1-1	1-2	0-0
28-Dec	Arsenal v Leeds U.	2-1	1-3	2-1	3-0	2-1	3-1
28-Dec	Aston Villa v Tottenham H.	1-0	1-0	2-1	1-1	4-1	3-2
28-Dec	Bradford C. v Everton	–	–	–	–	–	–
28-Dec	Leicester C. v Newcastle U.	–	1-3	–	2-0	0-0	2-0
28-Dec	Liverpool v Wimbledon	1-1	3-0	2-2	1-1	2-0	3-0
28-Dec	Middlesbrough v Coventry C.	–	–	2-1	4-0	–	2-0
28-Dec	Sunderland v Manchester U. (Sky)	–	–	–	2-1	–	–
28-Dec	Watford v Southampton	–	–	–	–	–	–
28-Dec	West Ham U. v Derby Co.	–	–	–	1-1	0-0	5-1
29-Dec	Chelsea v Sheffield W. (Sky)	1-1	1-1	0-0	2-2	1-0	1-1
03-Jan	Coventry C. v Chelsea	1-1	2-2	1-0	3-1	3-2	2-1
03-Jan	Derby Co. v Watford	–	–	–	–	–	–
03-Jan	Everton v Leicester C.	–	1-1	–	1-1	1-1	0-0
03-Jan	Leeds U. v Aston Villa	2-0	1-0	2-0	0-0	1-1	0-0
03-Jan	Manchester U. v Middlesbrough	–	–	2-0	3-3		2-3
03-Jan	Newcastle U. v West Ham U.	2-0	2-0	3-0	1-1	0-1	0-3
03-Jan	Sheffield W. v Arsenal	0-1	3-1	1-0	0-0	2-0	1-0
03-Jan	Southampton v Bradford C.	–	–	–	–	–	–
03-Jan	Tottenham H. v Liverpool	3-3	0-0	1-3	0-2	3-3	2-1
03-Jan	Wimbledon v Sunderland	–	–	–	1-0	–	–
04-Jan	*FA Cup 4th Round*						
05-Jan	*FIFA World Club Championship – Brazil: Rio de Janeiro and Sao Paulo* *Finishes 15 January*						
15-Jan	Arsenal v Sunderland	–	–	–	2-0	–	–
15-Jan	Chelsea v Leicester C.	–	4-0	–	2-1	1-0	2-2
15-Jan	Coventry C. v Wimbledon	1-2	1-1	3-3	1-1	0-0	2-1

Date	*Match/Event*	*93-94*	*94-95*	*95-96*	*96-97*	*97-98*	*98-99*
15-Jan	Everton v Tottenham H.	0-1	0-0	1-1	1-0	0-2	0-1
15-Jan	Leeds U. v Manchester U.	0-2	2-1	3-1	0-4	1-0	1-1
15-Jan	Middlesbrough v Derby Co.	–	–	–	6-1	–	1-1
15-Jan	Newcastle U. v Southampton	1-2	5-1	1-0	0-1	2-1	4-0
15-Jan	Sheffield W. v Bradford C.	–	–	–	–	–	–
15-Jan	Watford v Liverpool	–	–	–	–	–	–
15-Jan	West Ham U. v Aston Villa	0-0	1-0	1-4	0-2	2-1	0-0
22-Jan	Aston Villa v Chelsea	1-0	3-0	0-1	0-2	0-2	0-3
22-Jan	Bradford C. v Watford	–	–	–	–	–	–
22-Jan	Derby Co. v Coventry C.	–	–	–	2-1	3-1	0-0
22-Jan	Leicester C. v West Ham U.	–	1-2	–	0-1	2-1	0-0
22-Jan	Liverpool v Middlesbrough	–	–	1-0	5-1		3-1
22-Jan	Manchester U. v Arsenal	1-0	3-0	1-0	1-0	0-1	1-1
22-Jan	Southampton v Everton	0-2	2-0	2-2	2-2	2-1	2-0
22-Jan	Sunderland v Leeds U.	–	–	–	0-1	–	–
22-Jan	Tottenham H. v Sheffield W.	1-3	3-1	1-0	1-1	3-2	0-3
22-Jan	Wimbledon v Newcastle U.	4-2	3-2	3-3	1-1	0-0	1-1
29-Jan	*FA Cup 5th Round*						
05-Feb	Aston Villa v Watford	–	–	–	–	–	–
05-Feb	Bradford C. v Arsenal	–	–	–	–	–	–
05-Feb	Derby Co. v Sheffield W.	–	–	–	2-2	3-0	1-0
05-Feb	Leicester C. v Middlesbrough	–	–	–	1-3		0-1
05-Feb	Liverpool v Leeds U.	2-0	0-1	5-0	4-0	3-1	1-3
05-Feb	Manchester U. v Coventry C.	0-0	2-0	1-0	3-1	3-0	2-0
05-Feb	Southampton v West Ham U.	0-2	1-1	0-0	2-0	3-0	1-0
05-Feb	Sunderland v Newcastle U.	–	–	–	1-2	–	–
05-Feb	Tottenham H. v Chelsea	1-1	0-0	1-1	1-2	1-6	2-2
05-Feb	Wimbledon v Everton	1-1	2-1	2-3	4-0	0-0	1-2
12-Feb	*FA Cup 6th Round*						
12-Feb	Arsenal v Liverpool	1-0	0-1	0-0	1-2	0-1	0-0
12-Feb	Chelsea v Wimbledon	2-0	1-1	1-2	2-4	1-1	3-0
12-Feb	Coventry C. v Sunderland	–	–	–	2-2	–	–
12-Feb	Everton v Derby Co.	–	–	–	1-0	1-2	0-0
12-Feb	Leeds U. v Tottenham H.	2-0	1-1	1-3	0-0	1-0	2-0
12-Feb	Middlesbrough v Aston Villa	–	–	0-2	3-2	–	0-0
12-Feb	Newcastle U. v Manchester U.	1-1	1-1	0-1	5-0	0-1	1-2
12-Feb	Sheffield W. v Southampton	2-0	1-1	2-2	1-1	1-0	0-0
12-Feb	Watford v Leicester C.	–	–	–	–	–	–
12-Feb	West Ham U. v Bradford C.	–	–	–	–	–	–
26-Feb	Arsenal v Southampton	1-0	1-1	4-2	3-1	3-0	1-1
26-Feb	Bradford C. v Aston Villa	–	–	–	–	–	–
26-Feb	Chelsea v Watford	–	–	–	–	–	–
26-Feb	Coventry C. v Tottenham H.	1-0	0-4	2-3	1-2	4-0	1-1

Date	*Match/Event*	*93-94*	*94-95*	*95-96*	*96-97*	*97-98*	*98-99*
26-Feb	Liverpool v Leicester C.	–	2-0	–	1-1	1-2	0-1
26-Feb	Middlesbrough v Leeds U.	–	–	1-1	0-0	–	0-0
26-Feb	Sheffield W. v Newcastle U.	0-1	0-0	0-2	1-1	2-1	1-1
26-Feb	Sunderland v Derby Co.	–	–	–	2-0	–	–
26-Feb	West Ham U. v Everton	0-1	2-2	2-1	2-2	2-2	2-1
26-Feb	Wimbledon v Manchester U.	1-0	0-1	2-4	0-3	2-5	1-1
29-Feb	*Champions' League 2nd Group Phase – Matchday 9*						
01-Mar	*Champions' League 2nd Group Phase – Matchday 9*						
02-Mar	*UEFA Cup 4th Round, 1st Leg*						
04-Mar	Aston Villa v Arsenal	1-2	0-4	1-1	2-2	1-0	3-2
04-Mar	Derby Co. v Wimbledon	–	–	–	0-2	1-1	0-0
04-Mar	Everton v Sheffield W.	0-2	1-4	2-2	2-0	1-3	1-2
04-Mar	Leeds U. v Coventry C.	1-0	3-0	3-1	1-3	3-3	2-0
04-Mar	Leicester C. v Sunderland	–	–	–	1-1	–	–
04-Mar	Manchester U. v Liverpool	1-0	2-0	2-2	1-0	1-1	2-0
04-Mar	Newcastle U. v Chelsea	0-0	4-2	2-0	3-1	3-1	0-1
04-Mar	Southampton v Middlesbrough	–	–	2-1	4-0		3-3
04-Mar	Tottenham H. v Bradford C.	–	–	–	–	–	–
04-Mar	Watford v West Ham U.	–	–	–	–	–	–
07-Mar	*Champions' League 2nd Group Phase – Matchday 10*						
08-Mar	*Champions' League 2nd Group Phase – Matchday 10*						
09-Mar	*UEFA Cup 4th Round, 2nd Leg*						
11-Mar	Aston Villa v Coventry C.	0-0	0-0	4-1	2-1	3-0	1-4
11-Mar	Bradford C. v Leeds U.	–	–	–	–	–	–
11-Mar	Chelsea v Everton	4-2	0-1	0-0	2-2	2-0	3-1
11-Mar	Liverpool v Sunderland	–	–	–	0-0	–	–
11-Mar	Manchester U. v Derby Co.	–	–	–	2-3	2-0	1-0
11-Mar	Middlesbrough v Arsenal	–	–	2-3	0-2	–	1-6
11-Mar	Newcastle U. v Watford	–	–	–	–	–	–
11-Mar	Sheffield W. v West Ham U.	5-0	1-0	0-1	0-0	1-1	0-1
11-Mar	Tottenham H. v Southampton	3-0	1-2	1-0	3-1	1-1	3-0
11-Mar	Wimbledon v Leicester C.	–	2-1	–	1-3	2-1	0-1
14-Mar	*Champions' League 2nd Group Phase – Matchday 11*						
15-Mar	*Champions' League 2nd Group Phase – Matchday 11*						
16-Mar	*UEFA Cup Quarter-Finals, 1st Leg*						
18-Mar	Arsenal v Tottenham H.	1-1	1-1	0-0	3-1	0-0	0-0
18-Mar	Coventry C. v Bradford C.	–	–	–	–	–	–
18-Mar	Derby Co. v Liverpool	–	–	–	0-1	1-0	3-2
18-Mar	Everton v Newcastle U.	0-2	2-0	1-3	2-0	0-0	1-0
18-Mar	Leeds U. v Wimbledon	4-0	3-1	1-1	1-0	1-1	2-2
18-Mar	Leicester C. v Manchester U.	–	0-4	–	2-2	0-0	2-6
18-Mar	Southampton v Aston Villa	4-1	2-1	0-1	0-1	1-2	1-4

Date	*Match/Event*	*93-94*	*94-95*	*95-96*	*96-97*	*97-98*	*98-99*
18-Mar	Sunderland v Middlesbrough	–	–	–	2-2	–	–
18-Mar	Watford v Sheffield W.	–	–	–	–	–	–
18-Mar	West Ham U. v Chelsea	1-0	1-2	1-3	3-2	2-1	1-1
21-Mar	*Champions' League 2nd Group Phase – Matchday 12*						
22-Mar	*Champions' League 2nd Group Phase – Matchday 12*						
23-Mar	*UEFA Cup Quarter-Finals, 2nd Leg*						
25-Mar	Arsenal v Coventry C.	0-3	2-1	1-1	0-0	2-0	2-0
25-Mar	Aston Villa v Derby	–	–	–	2-0	2-1	1-0
25-Mar	Bradford C. v Manchester U.	–	–	–	–	–	–
25-Mar	Chelsea v Southampton	2-0	0-2	3-0	1-0	4-2	1-0
25-Mar	Leicester C. v Leeds	–	1-3	–	1-0	1-0	1-2
25-Mar	Liverpool v Newcastle U.	0-2	2-0	4-3	4-3	1-0	4-2
25-Mar	Middlesbrough v Sheffield W.	–	–	3-1	4-2	–	4-0
25-Mar	Sunderland v Everton	–	–	–	2-0	–	–
25-Mar	Watford v Tottenham	–	–	–	–	–	–
25-Mar	West Ham U. v Wimbledon	0-2	3-0	1-1	0-2	3-1	3-4
01-Apr	Coventry C. v Liverpool	1-0	1-1	1-0	0-1	1-1	2-1
01-Apr	Derby Co. v Leicester C.	–	–	–	2-0	0-4	2-0
01-Apr	Everton v Watford	–	–	–	–	–	–
01-Apr	Leeds U. v Chelsea	4-1	2-3	1-0	2-0	3-1	0-0
01-Apr	Manchester U. v West Ham U.	3-0	1-0	2-1	2-0	2-1	4-1
01-Apr	Newcastle U. v Bradford C.	–	–	–	–	–	–
01-Apr	Sheffield W. v Aston Villa	0-0	1-2	2-0	2-1	1-3	0-1
01-Apr	Southampton v Sunderland	–	–	–	3-0	–	–
01-Apr	Tottenham H. v Middlesbrough	–	–	1-1	1-0		0-3
01-Apr	Wimbledon v Arsenal	0-3	1-3	0-3	2-2	0-1	1-0
04-Apr	*Champions' League Quarter-Finals, 1st Leg*						
05-Apr	*Champions' League Quarter-Finals, 1st Leg*						
06-Apr	*UEFA Cup Semi-Finals, 1st Leg*						
08-Apr	Arsenal v Sheffield W.	1-0	0-0	4-2	4-1	1-0	3-0
08-Apr	Aston Villa v Leeds U.	1-0	0-0	3-0	2-0	1-0	1-2
08-Apr	Bradford C. v Southampton	–	–	–	–	–	–
08-Apr	Chelsea v Coventry C.	1-2	2-2	2-2	2-0	3-1	2-1
08-Apr	Leicester C. v Everton	–	2-2	–	1-2	0-1	2-0
08-Apr	Liverpool v Tottenham H.	1-2	1-1	0-0	2-1	4-0	3-2
08-Apr	Middlesbrough v Manchester U.	–	–	0-3	2-2	–	0-1
08-Apr	Sunderland v Wimbledon	–	–	–	1-3	–	–
08-Apr	Watford v Derby Co.	–	–	–	–	–	–
08-Apr	West Ham U. v Newcastle U.	2-4	1-3	2-0	0-0	0-1	2-0
09-Apr	*FA Cup Semi-Finals*						
15-Apr	Coventry C. v Middlesbrough	–	–	0-0	3-0		1-2
15-Apr	Derby Co. v West Ham U.	–	–	–	1-0	2-0	0-2

Date	*Match/Event*	*93-94*	*94-95*	*95-96*	*96-97*	*97-98*	*98-99*
15-Apr	Everton v Bradford C.	–	–	–	–	–	–
15-Apr	Leeds U. v Arsenal	2-1	1-0	0-3	0-0	1-1	1-0
15-Apr	Manchester U. v Sunderland	–	–	–	5-0	–	–
15-Apr	Newcastle U. v Leicester C.	–	3-1	–	4-3	3-3	1-0
15-Apr	Sheffield W. v Chelsea	3-1	1-1	0-0	0-2	1-4	0-0
15-Apr	Southampton v Watford	–	–	–	–	–	–
15-Apr	Tottenham H. v Aston Villa	1-1	3-4	0-1	1-0	3-2	1-0
15-Apr	Wimbledon v Liverpool	1-1	0-0	1-0	2-1	1-1	1-0
18-Apr	*Champions' League Quarter-Finals, 2nd Leg*						
19-Apr	*Champions' League Quarter-Finals, 2nd Leg*						
20-Apr	*UEFA Cup Semi-Finals, 2nd Leg*						
22-Apr	Aston Villa v Leicester C.	–	4-4	–	1-3	1-1	1-1
22-Apr	Bradford C. v Derby Co.	–	–	–	–	–	–
22-Apr	Chelsea v Middlesbrough	–	–	5-0	1-0		2-0
22-Apr	Everton v Liverpool	2-0	2-0	1-1	1-1	2-0	0-0
22-Apr	Newcastle U. v Leeds U.	1-1	1-2	2-1	3-0	1-1	0-3
22-Apr	Sheffield W. v Sunderland	–	–	–	2-1	–	–
22-Apr	Southampton v Manchester U.	1-3	2-2	3-1	6-3	1-0	0-3
22-Apr	Tottenham H. v Wimbledon	1-1	1-2	3-1	1-0	0-0	0-0
22-Apr	Watford v Arsenal	–	–	–	–	–	–
22-Apr	West Ham U. v Coventry C.	3-2	0-1	3-2	1-1	1-0	2-0
24-Apr	Arsenal v West Ham U.	0-2	0-1	1-0	2-0	4-0	1-0
24-Apr	Coventry C. v Everton	2-1	0-0	2-1	0-0	0-0	3-0
24-Apr	Derby Co. v Southampton	–	–	–	1-1	4-0	0-0
24-Apr	Leeds U. v Watford	–	–	–	–	–	–
24-Apr	Leicester C. v Tottenham H.	–	3-1	–	1-1	3-0	2-1
24-Apr	Liverpool v Aston Villa	2-1	3-2	3-0	3-0	3-0	0-1
24-Apr	Manchester U. v Chelsea	0-1	0-0	1-1	1-2	2-2	1-1
24-Apr	Middlesbrough v Newcastle U.	–	–	1-2	1-1	–	2-2
24-Apr	Sunderland v Bradford C.	–	–	–	–	–	–
24-Apr	Wimbledon v Sheffield W.	2-1	0-1	2-2	4-2	1-1	2-1
29-Apr	Aston Villa v Sunderland	–	–	–	1-0	–	–
29-Apr	Bradford C. v Wimbledon	–	–	–	–	–	–
29-Apr	Chelsea v Liverpool	1-0	0-0	2-2	1-0	4-1	2-1
29-Apr	Everton v Arsenal	1-1	1-1	0-2	0-2	2-2	0-2
29-Apr	Newcastle U. v Coventry C.	4-0	4-0	3-0	4-0	0-0	4-1
29-Apr	Sheffield W. v Leeds U.	3-3	1-1	6-2	2-2	1-3	0-2
29-Apr	Southampton v Leicester C.	–	2-2	–	2-2	2-1	2-1
29-Apr	Tottenham H. v Derby	–	–	–	1-1	1-0	1-1
29-Apr	Watford v Manchester U.	–	–	–	–	–	–
29-Apr	West Ham U. v Middlesbrough	–	–	2-0	0-0		4-0
02-May	*Champions' League Semi-Finals, 1st Leg*						
03-May	*Champions' League Semi-Finals, 1st Leg*						

Date	*Match/Event*	*93-94*	*94-95*	*95-96*	*96-97*	*97-98*	*98-99*
06-May	Arsenal v Chelsea	1-0	3-1	1-1	3-3	2-0	1-0
06-May	Coventry C. v Sheffield W.	1-1	2-0	0-1	0-0	1-0	1-0
06-May	Derby Co. v Newcastle U.	–	–	–	0-1	1-0	3-4
06-May	Leeds U. v Everton	3-0	1-0	2-2	1-0	0-0	1-0
06-May	Leicester C. v Bradford C.	–	–	–	–	–	–
06-May	Liverpool v Southampton	4-2	3-1	1-1	2-1	2-3	7-1
06-May	Manchester U. v Tottenham H.	2-1	0-0	1-0	2-0	2-0	2-1
06-May	Middlesbrough v Watford	–	–	–	–	–	–
06-May	Sunderland v West Ham U.	–	–	–	0-0	–	–
06-May	Wimbledon v Aston Villa	2-2	4-3	3-3	0-2	2-1	0-0
09-May	*Champions' League Semi-Finals, 2nd Leg*						
10-May	*Champions' League Semi-Finals, 2nd Leg*						
14-May	Aston Villa v Manchester U.	1-2	1-2	3-1	0-0	0-2	1-1
14-May	Bradford C. v Liverpool	–	–	–	–	–	–
14-May	Chelsea v Derby Co.	–	–	–	3-1	4-0	2-1
14-May	Everton v Middlesbrough	–	–	4-0	1-2		5-0
14-May	Newcastle U. v Arsenal	2-0	1-0	2-0	1-2	0-1	1-1
14-May	Sheffield W. v Leicester C.	–	1-0	–	2-1	1-0	0-1
14-May	Southampton v Wimbledon	1-0	2-3	0-0	0-0	0-1	3-1
14-May	Tottenham H. v Sunderland	–	–	–	2-0	–	–
14-May	Watford v Coventry C.	–	–	–	–	–	–
14-May	West Ham U. v Leeds U.	0-1	0-0	1-2	0-2	3-0	1-5
17-May	*UEFA Cup Final*						
20-May	*FA Cup Final*						
24-May	*Champions' League Final*						
29-May	*Football League 1st Division Play-off Final*						